EWALD'S

HISTORY OF ISRAEL.

VOL. III.

THE
HISTORY OF ISRAEL.

BY

HEINRICH EWALD,

Professor of the University of Göttingen.

TRANSLATED FROM THE GERMAN.

EDITED BY

J. ESTLIN CARPENTER, M.A.

'*The Old Testament will still be a New Testament to him who comes with a fresh desire of information*' ....FULLER.

VOL. III.

The Rise and Splendour of the Hebrew Monarchy.

Eugene, Oregon

Wipf and Stock Publishers
199 W 8th Ave, Suite 3
Eugene, OR 97401

The History of Israel, Volume 3
The Rise and Splendour of the Hebrew Monarchy
By Ewald, Heinrich
ISBN: 1-59244-883-6
Publication date 9/27/2004
Previously published by Longmans, Green, and Co., 1871

EDITOR'S PREFACE.

THE TWO VOLUMES of the History of Israel now offered to the public represent the third volume of the German edition, which appeared likely to prove somewhat cumbrous if reproduced in English without division.

The Editor has endeavoured to carry on the translation as far as possible in the spirit of his predecessor. As in the previous volumes, the ordinary orthography of proper names has been preserved, with the exception of the name Jehovah, in which case the form Jahveh has been employed as the equivalent of the Hebrew JHVH. The notation of chapters and verses is that adopted in the printed Hebrew Bibles; where it differs from that of our Authorised Version ('A.V.'), the English numbers are inserted in brackets.

With some hesitation the Editor has also followed the example of his predecessor in excluding from the text and notes all allusions to contemporary German politics. These references are exceedingly rare and very short, and, though highly characteristic of Professor Ewald's thought and style, they could have little intrinsic interest for the English reader, and throw no light upon the history itself.

To each volume an Analytical Table of Contents has been prefixed, and an Index added. The latter will be found to contain references to the principal passages of the Old Testament writings which are made the subject of literary or exegetical comment.

The Editor desires to express his great obligations to those friends who have kindly assisted him by placing passages of translation (amounting to nearly half the present issue) at his disposal, and permitting him to make such changes as seemed necessary to secure some approximate unity of manner. Only those, perhaps, who are acquainted with the intricacies of Professor Ewald's style, will appreciate the difficulties of this task. The section on the 'progress of science, poetry, and literature' under Solomon (vol. iii. pp. 274–286) has been contributed by Dr. Nicholson of Penrith.

The Editor also gladly avails himself of this opportunity to render his most grateful acknowledgments to Russell Martineau, Esq., M.A., whose counsel and aid have been rendered the more valuable by the readiness with which they have invariably been given. To him is due, in particular, the verification of numerous references which were inaccessible to the Editor.

Of the imperfections of this translation, prepared under the pressure of other labours, the Editor is only too conscious; but if it shall at all convey to any reader the historian's vivid realisation of the truths committed to the kingdom of Israel to develope, his grasp of the principles of Hebrew polity, and his deep insight into, and sympathy with, the prophetic spirit,—faults of workmanship may perhaps be overlooked in the interest and importance of the work.

LEEDS: *September* 1871.

CONTENTS

OF

THE THIRD VOLUME.

BOOK III.

THE BASILEO-THEOCRACY.

	PAGE
INTRODUCTION	1
1. Need of an undivided human Authority	2
2. Peculiar Modifications of Monarchy by the side of the Theocracy	4
3. Diminution of the Violence inherent in Jahveism	8
4. The three Eras of Monarchy in Israel	12
SECTION I. FOUNDATION OF THE MONARCHY; THE PERIOD OF SAUL AND DAVID	15
A. SAUL AND HIS HOUSE	15
I. SAUL'S ELECTION AS KING	15
1. His first Interview with Samuel	18
2. The three Signs	20
3. Mizpeh and Gilgal	23
II. SAUL'S PROPHETIC REJECTION	29
1. The War of Michmash	29
2. The Amalekite Campaign	36
3. The Breach between Saul and Samuel	40
III. THE FALL OF SAUL AND HIS HOUSE	48
1. Saul's Struggles after a higher Life	48
2. Death of Saul: Accession of Ishbosheth	51
3. Length of Saul's Reign	52
B. DAVID	54
HIS RELATION TO HIS AGE	54
I. THE EARLY HISTORY OF DAVID	67
1. His Introduction to Saul	67
2. Saul's Jealousy of him	73
3. David and Jonathan	78
4. His Flight to Gath	81
II. COMMENCEMENT OF DAVID'S INDEPENDENT RULE	84
1. As Freebooter on the Confines of Judah	84
1) Life in the Wilderness	86
2) His Magnanimity towards Saul	94
3) Nabal and Abigail	97

CONTENTS OF

SECTION I. FOUNDATION OF THE MONARCHY; THE PERIOD OF SAUL AND DAVID—*continued.*

	PAGE
2. As Philistine Vassal at Ziklag	99
1) His settlement at Ziklag	101
2) His Dismissal by Achish: Pursuit of the Amalekites	103
3) Battle of Mount Gilboa: Death of Saul	106
3. As King of Judah	109
1) Relations with Saul's House: Abner reconquers Israel from the Philistines	109
2) War between Israel and Judah	113
3) Fall of Abner: Murder of Ishbosheth	115
III. DAVID AS KING OF ISRAEL	120
1. The Internal Organisation of the Kingdom	121
1) Conquest and Fortification of Jerusalem	123
2) Removal of the Ark to Jerusalem	125
3) Treatment of Saul's Descendants	135
2. David's Wars against the Heathen	137
1) His Military Organisation	139
2) Survey of his Wars	146
a.) With the Philistines and Amalekites	146
b.) With the Moabites	149
c.) With the Arameans, Ammonites, and Edomites	150
3) The Census	160
3. David's Temptations	163
1) His Polygamy	165
2) Consequences of his Intrigue with Bath-sheba	165
3) Conspiracy of Absalom	170
4) Rebellion of Absalom	178
5) Restoration of David and Revolt of Sheba	189
4. Close of David's Career	195
1) His Prophetic Spirit	195
2) General Results	199
a.) Outward Stability and Power of Israel	199
b.) Inward Unity secured by the Basileo-Theocracy	199
c.) Spiritual Effect of the Monarchy on the Nation	201
d.) Personal Foundation of the Messianic Hopes	202

SECTION II. THE SPLENDOUR OF THE MONARCHY; THE AGE OF SOLOMON 204

I. THE BEGINNING OF SOLOMON'S REIGN	208
1. His Policy on his Accession	208
1) Attempt of Adonijah to seize the Throne	209
2) Treatment of Abiathar, Joab, and Shimei	212
2. Attempts of foreign Nations to throw off the Supremacy of Israel	216
1) Revolt of Edom under Hadad	217
2) Subjugation of Rezon, King of Damascus	218
3) Rising of Gezer and Hamath	218
3. The Two Paths open to Solomon	221

SECTION II. THE SPLENDOUR OF THE MONARCHY; THE AGE OF SOLOMON—*continued.*

	PAGE
II. THE ORGANISATION AND GREATNESS OF SOLOMON'S GOVERNMENT	224
1. The Sacred and Royal Buildings	226
1) The Temple	226
a.) David's Preparations	226
b.) Forced Service of the Canaanites	229
c.) Site of the Temple	230
d.) Preliminary Works	231
e.) The Sacred House	235
f.) The Furniture of the Sanctuary	241
g.) The Sacred Grove	245
h.) Dedication of the Temple	245
i.) Reorganisation of the Levites	247
2) The Palace	248
3) Solomon's other Works	251
a.) The Water-supply of Jerusalem	252
b.) His Gardens	256
c.) His Towers on Lebanon	257
2. Measures for the Security and Prosperity of the Realm	257
1) Fortifications and Armaments	258
2) Development of Commerce	260
a.) By Land	261
b.) By Sea	262
c.) The Royal Revenues	264
3. Administration and Manners of the Monarchy under Solomon and his Successors	266
1) His Ministers	266
2) Introduction of Foreign Manners	271
4. Progress in Science, Poetry, and Literature	274
III. THE RESULTS OF SOLOMON'S REIGN	286
1. His Royal Pomp and Royal Debts	291
2. His Position towards Religion and the Priesthood	296
3. His Relation to Prophetism	299
4. The New Importance of Jerusalem	305
5. The Disruption of the Kingdom of David; the Beginning of its Decline	308
IV. LATER REPRESENTATIONS OF SOLOMON	315
INDEX	321

Errata.

Page 124 line 11, *for* Kedron *read* Kidron.
   140 *note* 2, *for* Kerî *read* Qerî.
   172 *note* 1, *for* Kerî *read* Qerî.
   180 line 12, *for* Kedron *read* Kidron.
   215 line 11, *for* Kedron *read* Kidron.
   241 *note* 1, *for* יסור *read* יסוּר.
   244 lines 4, 14, *for* cauldrons *read* caldrons.
   256 *note* 1, *for* Dragon Well *read* Serpent's Pool.
   321 col. 2, line 31, for *ibid* read *ibid.*

NOTE.

THE EDITOR is glad to refer the readers of these volumes to Mr. J. Frederick Smith's translation of Ewald's 'Introductory Hebrew Grammar.'[1] This work, though not the same as the 'Ausführliches Lehrbuch' cited throughout the 'History,' will nevertheless be found to contain many illustrations of the grammatical principles so freely applied to the elucidation and emendation of the text in the notes to these volumes: and the admirable indexes appended to it will much facilitate its use in connexion with the independent study of the original authorities. Moreover, it adds fresh testimony from this country to the value of the profound scholarship of the author, and enables English readers to verify for themselves still more satisfactorily that estimate of the importance of Ewald's labours on the Old Testament which has prompted the present undertaking.

[1] Published by Asher & Co.

HISTORY OF ISRAEL.

BOOK III.

THE BASILEO-THEOCRACY.

INTRODUCTION.

HAPPY the nation to which a virtuous youth has imparted such intrinsic strength and courage as may enable it to seize the favourable moment, and obey the Divine signal for adding to all its former blessings yet one other, now become indispensable for its continued and honourable existence! Many a nation, it may be, catches sight in dim vision of some such unattained blessing, which looks like a pure gift of heaven on the very eve of bestowal, while by some of its members it is longed for even with devouring passion: but while it is busied with gazing and yearning, the harvest time passes away; and it strives in vain, in the wintry days that follow, to gain a blessing which it was too great a toil to gather in when ripe. But a nation which is not deterred by the difficulty of the task from carrying out a reform clearly recognised as necessary—carrying it out, not merely experimentally, but with full renunciation of opposing prejudices, and with willing submission to all the sacrifices needed for its accomplishment—such a nation, without losing any substantial advantage belonging to its past life, will triumph over all complications, and rise to new strength, able to cope with the highest problems of human existence. For nations cannot die, like individuals, from mere exhaustion of their powers, after a calculable term of years. Being capable only of moral decay, a nation may, on the contrary (if the higher religion, once perfected within it, retains healthful vitality), be thereby preserved to pass through an indefinite succession of such new developments, may participate in every gift of heaven and earth, and may continue to exist, till its final doom is spoken by the voice of Him who created it.

This crisis of transformation was successfully reached by Israel, before the perfected religion appeared in its midst, but while it was striving after it, and was already blessed in that strenuous and healthful endeavour. This enabled it not only to overcome the most obvious dangers of imminent destruction, but to attain in a comparatively short time an extraordinary stage of higher development; putting forth blossoms whose fruit, long after very different powers were at work to sap the existence of the community, helped to preserve and augment the good already won, and ripening into the most glorious maturity of which that soil was capable within the entire period of the unfolding of this history.

1. What was then wanting, and had now become indispensable, was an undivided and firmly established human authority, within the already existing community of God. The various disasters of the last centuries had no doubt contributed, with ever-increasing force, to make them conscious of this necessity; now at length the right moment had arrived to prepare the people for this innovation. But it was yet to be seen whether the nation would willingly and permanently undertake the new burdens and duties requisite for the actual establishment of human sovereignty, or would merely set up an experimental monarchy, expecting to benefit by its protection, but ready to abandon it again to decay, if it either made new demands on its supporters, or did not immediately fulfil all that was hoped from it; and this could only be proved by the actual trial of the new institution. There is a most powerful charm, however, in the feeling of greater independence and freedom of movement in a land subject to no stern rule, especially when this feeling has also the support of deep-rooted habit, and can always appeal to a public law with a standing of centuries, which cannot be abrogated, but at the very utmost supplemented. And although very possibly one single class or portion of the country may give in its adhesion to the new law, and find its advantage in so doing, yet the question remains, Will all ranks and all districts, even those from whom the change may seem, at first, to take more than it gives, at once stand unanimously by the new constitution, and resist all temptation to abandon it, whatever dangers may threaten?

And if thus the mass of the nation is inclined, or at any rate offers no stubborn resistance, to the new constitution, it still remains doubtful whether the higher powers by whom the previous constitution was formed and defended, will be able to accommodate themselves to the new without sweeping away the best fruits of the old; and further, whether these powers, without whose active cooperation no permanent change can be successfully effected, will acquiesce, of their own free will, in the necessity of reform, and be ready to conduct it to a prosperous issue, or at least to secure to it an unimpeded course. Now, it is true, these higher powers were then (as they are virtually always), those abstract truths which had already been so powerfully exhibited—those truths on which, at the commencement of the history of Israel, the community had been formed and the Theocracy founded; which were to animate all members of the community, and be defended by all. But as such superhuman truths rarely have sufficient vital power over the multitude, and at this period in Israel no longer retained the full vitality which they had in the time of Moses and of Joshua, their influence was now, for the most part, confined to the members of the classes specially intrusted with their charge; less, however, to the priestly order, already somewhat degenerate, than to the members, few or many as might be, of the newly aspiring class of Prophets. Now, however high we may suppose this prophetic class to have then stood in nobleness of spirit, and willingness to resign all the external advantages accruing to it from the existing state of things, it might still hesitate to assist in setting up a strict and permanent human sovereignty, with its possible dangers and errors, by the side of the previous constitution; since that aspired to the infinite ideal of a pure Theocracy, and realised it as far as it went. For it might easily appear as if precisely what was greatest and most characteristic in Israel as God's people, its pride and its distinction among the nations, would thus be lost. Nor was this a mere illusion. Actual and imminent dangers really threatened the supremacy and free action of the ancient religion, if a human sovereignty should be established which should from the beginning deliberately and distinctly exclude the religion of Jahveh from its borders.[1] From the inmost sanctuary of the existing religion a spirit stubbornly bent on holding exclusively to the old institutions, might break forth into violent opposition to the new power which it was proposed to establish for the sake of uniting all under a firmer rule. Or,

---

[1] What is said with regard to this point, 1 Sam. viii. 4–22, x. 18 sq., xii. 7–20 (although, as will be shown hereafter, first expressed in this manner by the later historians of the kings), exactly hits the important truth of the actual state of things. Comp. ii. p. 145 sqq.

tolerating the latter for a time as a mere experiment, this spirit might afterwards rise against it in exasperation at every offence, real or imaginary, and seek to restore the former state of things. And thus from this very influential quarter, religious prejudices might present a difficulty greater than any on the other side.

And even should it be possible at last to overcome all such hindrances from without, a still greater obstacle had to be encountered in the new institution itself, which it was now attempted to introduce as an acknowledged necessity. For no such monarchy as had previously existed in the ancient world could possibly grow up here, at least, not on the legal basis of the ancient religion and constitution; because this religion had sprung into vigorous life in great part out of opposition to all which then passed for human monarchy, and therefore could not recognise such monarchy without utterly denying and renouncing its own existence. In this case, therefore, the problem was, in what manner and to what extent an agreement could be effected between a monarchy which should possess sufficient strength for all salutary action, and the higher religion which forbade the exercise of human caprice. And as this new power was to have the decision in all external matters, it was necessary that all this should be distinctly thought out, and on both sides energetically contested, at the very beginning of its erection and development, if any successful cooperation was to be effected between it and the earlier authorities of the nation and the community. Any unsuccessful attempt on either side, unless most fully retracted, might very soon destroy all.

2. Such were the difficulties which might oppose the introduction of a change now indispensable, and thereby render impossible the entire reformation of the existing constitution. And if some only of these difficulties were fully conquered for a considerable period, the happy effect could not but be great, and an entirely new turn must have been given to the whole history of the people of Jahveh. True, its form of government could no longer remain so simple as before. To the Theocracy was now added the Monarchy, not to subvert or gradually supersede it, but to fulfil the wants of the age by its side. Hence, as the Monarchy was not intended to call in question the foundation of the Theocracy, but rather to stand and work on the same basis with it, it was bound to leave untouched the necessary living instruments through which the Theocracy then acted, especially the Prophets. There was consequently formed what we may call a mixed constitution and sovereignty; and the pure Theocracy became a Basileo-Theocracy. But the formation of this sort of mixed rule was the very best thing possible at that time. For generally, in every form of community, *that* will be the best constitution, by which no power whose free action might be beneficial to the whole is hampered or excluded; in which, rather, all possible powers of good, though at times really or seemingly opposed, cooperate for good, the one-sidedness of each being corrected by the other, and the best result being thus attained. Now insofar as the previous Theocracy excluded temporal royalty, an all but indispensable element, it inevitably acquired in course of time a certain stiffness and one-sidedness, and became less competent to fulfil its own mission; as the preceding history has shown. Thus the entrance of monarchy soon surprises us by the great increase of variety, movement, and vigour which it produces; and while the two strongest powers of the state, by their combination, alternately hostile and friendly, kindle a new life in the higher departments, such a fresh energy soon so far penetrates the lower also, that Israel in a short time makes up for the delays of centuries. As in the merely human dominion (the State) nothing but mutual cooperation between king and people can draw forth all the good which it is capable of producing; so even a purely divine dominion (a Church), if it is to exist on earth, cannot develop itself freely without a like reciprocal action of the human and the divine king. For as the king of a temporal state ought to desire only the good of his people, while yet it is only by a mutual understanding between his people and himself that he can carry out this object, secure against possible obstacles and misapprehensions: so in what we call the divine dominion, though there is no other moving power than pure divine truth, desiring communication with the human sphere and to draw men to itself, yet that this may be effectually accomplished, the human element must be able to stand up vigorous and independent before the divine, if it is at length to be entirely pervaded by the latter, and to resemble it.

At this point we understand plainly how different were the demands made by this community on their king from those of any other among the nations of antiquity. To maintain all the best powers and influences of the kingdom in unity and subordination, not crippling their salutary action, yet permitting to none any absolute, i.e. counter-regal exercise of authority, lies in the very essence of royal power as such. Should it at first fail to take in the full scope and necessity of its activity, it will soon in the course of its development become conscious of its proper function. The king of Israel was also necessarily to be endowed with true royal authority to judge, command, and compel throughout the whole kingdom; in token of which, like heathen princes, he received the staff (sceptre), and was crowned. If similar distinctions had been already borne by other rulers in Israel,[1] they all assumed in him a higher significance, proportioned to his higher dignity. But since he furthermore received the unction[2] (hitherto confined to the High-Priest), from the hands of the High-Priest himself, or some prophet more influential still, the symbols of all high offices previously existing in the community are centred in him, and the whole power of state and people culminates in him alone. More important, however, than all these external symbols, is the fact that, simply as the 'Chosen of Jahveh,'[3] or the 'Anointed of Jahveh,' he has an inviolable sanctity and majesty, such as no other personage of the community possesses. In the community of the true God, sanctity has a meaning more sublime and strict than anywhere else in the ancient world; its lofty splendour now becomes the king's defence and shield, his majesty and pride. Thus the crime of treason against Majesty, which in the old pure Theocracy was possible against Jahveh only,[4] becomes at once capable of extension to him also. He becomes the only mortal who can be crowned with a sanctity which has hitherto been regarded as pertaining exclusively to the Immortal.[5]

But now in this community, face to face with the human king stands the Theocracy; a something still higher, and inviolable; with all its long-standing sacred laws and arrangements, and still continuously revealing itself through prophets and their words, valid as a Divine command. Thus command confronts command; and though sometimes these two distinct powers may easily understand each other, and remain in peace side by side, at others they may chafe violently against each other. If then the royal power would attain its own proper completeness, without subverting the intrinsic truth of the Theocracy, it must not content itself with a position equal, still less subordinate, to the prophetic, and least of all must it attempt

---

[1] See the *Alterthümer*, p. 342, 376.
[2] See more fully in the *Alterthümer*, p. 319, 123.
[3] As even Saul is designated in ordinary discourse, 2 Sam. xxi. 6; cf. 1 Sam. x. 24. David himself, according to 1 Sam. xvi. 8-13, has no higher title belonging to that period.
[4] Vol. ii. p. 161.
[5] Hence the very peculiar form in which the idea of this crime is expressed, 'to blaspheme God and the king;' where we see plainly that the original stricter conception had been only expanded: 1 Kings xxi. 10, 13; cf. my *Alterthümer*, p. 252 sq.

simply to annihilate it; but must appropriate to itself whatever in the prophetic power is true and necessary. The discord between the two rules is then composed, and the true human king of such a state is found. And human monarchy once established within the Theocracy implied strictly the expectation of one who would fulfil all the conditions of this monarchy, and become its ideal man, and the true King (or Messiah) of the community. We know with sufficient certainty that every king of Israel, immediately upon his accession, was pledged to the existing fundamental laws of the kingdom; in token of which he was required, when the crown was placed upon his head, to lay above it a written copy of the law, and with these sacred symbols to show himself to the people, to be anointed.[1] Thus he was not to be a king ruling arbitrarily, as in heathen kingdoms, where at most a few nobles, the populace, or an imperfect oracular system limited his power. Here, if he desired to be really king, it could only be through his entering more fully than anyone else into the mind and spirit of Jahveh, and becoming through Him the proper human ruler in the midst of the Theocracy. If he enters fully into that mind and spirit, he reaches the highest perfection of which human nature is capable; a weak being like man becomes, through the powerful operation of Divine grace, himself the strongest and worthiest instrument for Divine purposes.[2] And even if this true and infinite mission was not at once clearly recognised, and was then misunderstood or but imperfectly realised by many; nay, if even the visible monarchy in Israel passed away without achieving it; yet it could not fail, when the right time came, to be understood and striven after with all possible force. If all previous kings had failed to fulfil what was hoped from them, the advent of the true king (Messiah) could not but be constantly looked forward to, when once the basis of this hope was recognised. Of such incalculable influence, even upon the remotest times, was the present crisis; and so certain is it, that the government of Israel, having had from the period of its institution under

---

[1] If we knew this only from the words of the Deuteronomist, Deut. vii. 18–20, it might seem doubtful with regard to earlier times; but the description in 2 Kings xi. 12 (2 Chron. xxiii. 11), so much more graphic, though merely brief and incidental, admits of no dispute. That no mention is made in Solomon's case, in the account 1 Kings i. 38 sq., of either the law or the crown, proves at most only that his successors were the first to be so inducted; but we see from this account that they were anointed, like the High-Priest, with oil taken from the Tabernacle, i.e. the Sanctuary. Respecting the custom of laying a written document on the head, comp. my observations on Job xxxi. 36.

[2] This, which is the best that can be said respecting the monarchy of the true community, is expressed in the passage 1 Sam. xv. 17.

Moses, a wholly different object from that of other kingdoms, could never again deviate, in any great crisis of its history, from its true and lofty aim.

3. We perceive accordingly, that this great crisis of the history, as soon as its immediate aim is attained, presses on at once to a new development of a still loftier character. Although the first or Mosaic epoch had indelibly fixed a truth capable of infinite development, which was to be the soul of the entire history of Israel, it could at first obtain general acceptance only under a most rigid external form, which by its very rigidity at length brought about the freer form which we have now to consider, in this second great era of the history. But the nation in this era, as soon as its immediate temporal and visible object is attained, is found to have a further aim; and the attainment of this end involves a still greater crisis, through which the nation must pass before it can reach that ultimate goal, which it has now for the first time divined in the distant future—the Messianic Era. We here approach, therefore, the grand central point, and the strongest motive power of the whole history; where its threads combine as in one firm knot, where the grand connexion of its greater or lesser crisis is the most plainly discernible; and where, in fact, the loftiest spiritual effort and the most unwearied exertions reach their highest possible climax.

For, unquestionably, if monarchy in Israel did not now attain its highest end and become the ideal of all human monarchy, and if, during its course, men learnt more and more distinctly to hope for that ideal only in a future kingdom, the ultimate cause of this must be sought in a want still unsupplied in the ancient religion itself. By its reconciliation with human monarchy, that religion had, at this very moment, filled up the first defect which[1] had marked it from the commencement of its temporal existence. Now just when this was corrected, the institution of the monarchy at once revealed the second defect which[2] had also adhered to it from the beginning—that of violence. Every religion based upon oracles as the immediate Divine word and command, involves an element of violence,—grasping, compelling, ruling by mere force. This was especially true of Jahveism, as proceeding from the purest and highest prophetic power, and still deriving thence its continual growth and progress; and the prophetic function had been hitherto the only arbitrarily commanding and irresponsible autocracy in this community. But monarchy

---

[1] According to ii. p. 115 sq., 150 sq.   [2] According to ii. p. 52, 113 sqq., 421 sq.

tends no less to absolutism, though from a distinct cause and in a different way; viz. as being in itself the highest earthly force for maintaining national unity and strength. With this aim, it must necessarily seek to keep all the other forces and powers of the nation, that of prophecy included, united in subordination to the national aim. Since therefore, violence still clung to the very life of the ancient religion, which in its turn repudiated it on principle in relation to the state,[1] and, by demanding that all should be equal before Jahveh and serve Him alone, condemned all human self-will and one-sided violence, this exposed monarchy in Israel to its most dangerous temptation. In view of prophetic violence, it ought to keep clear of everything of the sort, although itself the highest temporal authority, armed with full powers of coercion and punishment; what then shall be its guiding star, and how shall it hold its own? Here was the field for inevitable, severe, and obstinate conflicts with the prophetic power; which had not only been the original creative agency in this community, but also, on this long-settled basis of true religion, had a strong, inextinguishable feeling, that human force, come from whom it might, even from the king himself, was irreconcilably antagonistic to Jahveism, and could never be sanctioned. This, then, first enables us to perceive why monarchy in Israel attained its true object with such extraordinary difficulty, and what were its severest temptations and dangers, sufferings and pains. But the fact that the defect of the ancient religion showed itself here in its most essential and sensitive point, rendered it possible, at the same time, to make the most correct estimate of its nature, and the most profound conjectures as to the best means of its removal.

The advance of this great epoch of the history, as compared with the preceding, is shown also in this—that the violence inherent in Jahveism from the very beginning, and pervading in manifold ways every movement and ramification of the national life, is in this second stage in one important point considerably diminished. As in the first period the great legal freedom of the people, being still without any limitation from human authority, degenerated more and more into license, self-will, and separation of individuals, cities, and tribes, the better spirit of the whole true community could often only maintain itself by the most violent expedients. The severe chastisement, and even the destruction, of recusant cities and tribes was of

---

[1] See for instance 1 Sam. ii. 9 xvi. 7.

very common occurrence.[1] The spirit and will of Javeh Himself appeared most fully to sanction it; and for the most part it was only after violent and stringent measures against powerful individuals, that any long period of quiet and respect was restored for the community at large. Now, in proportion as the monarchy advances to a higher and purer standard, this species of violence disappears; sweeter repose and for longer periods revisits Israel, and single cases of internal dissension, insubordination, and revolt, become less formidable. The whole visible penal authority being now centred in the king alone, encompassed by a constant majesty and dread, is coextensive with the whole community; and this is, in fact, the main cause of the greater peace and prosperity of the times which followed. And, since the offences and excesses of individuals now no longer appear directed immediately against the will of the mysterious Invisible, but rather against that of the king, a milder spirit became possible in judgment and punishment; even the rigid law of which he is the living guardian, may, through him, be made more humane. To him belong all authority and all punishment; but in this way certainly the ancient tendency to violence becomes his own greatest temptation; and in him, as the most arbitrary temporal power which Jahveism or any other government could produce or endure, it has now to be distinctly shown whether such a power should now rule in Israel, and what fruits it would bear.

Violence, it is true, is the dismal shadow which monarchy everywhere throws, and by which its own course is so often hindered and perplexed. But in actual history, the result depends upon the special object towards which its full energy is directed, or with which it comes into hopeless collision. For even the highest power in the state, being human, neither can nor ought to escape supervision and scrutiny from other beneficent powers. If it should attempt to do so, monarchy makes its own arbitrary will and violence its law and life, becomes the very opposite of what it should be, and thereby brings about its own destruction sooner and in ways more perilous to the general weal. Thus every good and necessary power may become a means of such supervision, and act as a check upon the dangerous encroachments of royalty: be that power knowledge, or the church, or the people, organising itself as a consultative body; or be it a foreign or a domestic power. Christian monarchy,

---

[1] See the numerous examples, ii. p. 353 sq., 377 sq., 387 sq., 394 sq.

which can now look back clearly to the perfect King and Lord, should by this time have learnt in every nominally Christian land, to fear no correct examination or scrutiny on the part of any such power. Knowledge, however, as will afterwards appear, first became an important power in Israel in the course of that tranquil development which the monarchy brought with it; and a Christian church was, from the time of Moses, only in the mere dawn of its existence. It is true that estates of the realm, i.e. the people assembled in an organised body to consult and decide respecting all the most important concerns and laws of the land, existed in Israel from very early times,[1] and were not to be in any way superseded by the monarchy, but on the contrary, continued throughout the whole period of royalty in Israel;[2] and how the public voice then resounded in that national assembly, is sufficiently shown by the many striking imitations preserved in poetic language.[3] But these estates (so far as we can yet discover) always maintained their simplest form, as representatives of the people, qualified only by birth or office, or *Elders*.[4] As unchangeable powers, they might easily occupy a dangerous position towards the government, and they were therefore assembled as rarely as possible. During the period when the monarchy was rising in all its first strength, they spontaneously withdrew into the background; and probably met of their own accord only at the commencement of every reign, to treat with the new king, and to ratify his accession. It is not till towards the end of the whole period of the monarchy, that they seem, from reasons hereafter to be mentioned, to have enjoyed, with the general national life, a freer development. Far more independent and matured was the Prophetic power, which confronted the monarchy in Israel from the very beginning with a purity and strength unknown in any other ancient state. That power on which the very foundations of the national existence had been based, was now fully capable of comprehending within itself all true spiritual knowledge and force. The very rise

---

[1] See my *Alterthümer*, p. 282 sq.
[2] See 1 Sam. x. 17 sqq.; xi. 14 sqq.; 2 Sam. ii. 4; v. 1-3; 1 Kings xii. 1 sqq.; 2 Kings xi. 13; xxiii. 1 sqq.; Jer. xxxiv. 8-10; such words also of Isaiah as iii. 14, cf. verse 2, are explicable only if 'the Elders of Israel' were responsible, conjointly with the king, and in some respects more than he, for the welfare of the kingdom.
[3] Ps. l. for instance, or Ps. lxxxii., alludes very distinctly to the customs and speeches of the great national assembly; to which the poets have been indebted for their first idea.
[4] There is no proof whatever that even a portion of the members were chosen each time by the people for one single assembly; though, in the absence of more particular information respecting separate periods in these five centuries, we must form our judgments with some reserve.

of this monarchy would have been impossible without most devoted cooperation from the prophetic power, yet, after its establishment, the latter would by no means think of sinking its own pretensions. The action and counter-action of these two powers could not fail from the very beginning to be most strenuous and critical; and as even in early times [1] the prophetic power was in danger of falling into violence, attack and repulse must be here the strongest. It was only when one of them was able simply to stem the excesses of the other, without itself lapsing into violence, that its influence could be salutary; and the realisation of the highest welfare and blessing of that age was only possible when both understood and helped each other towards that higher Ideal, which was equally above them both. But it is certainly in the very essence of monarchy to aim at supremacy over every rival power in the state. It might gain an easy triumph over Prophecy, because that power could offer so little material resistance, and was itself also exposed to the danger of lapsing into violence. And in proportion as the monarchy here yields to this temptation, it must lose its pure heart and its best force in the very flower of its strength and prosperity; if only because no adequate counterbalancing power now remained to exercise perpetual supervision over it, and unchecked absolutism might become its abiding law; irreconcilably opposed as it would be to the deepest instincts of this community, of this people of God.[2]

4. This suggests, however, in general terms, the peculiar development of the history of the kingdom of Israel. For under the absolute necessity of monarchy, with which the previous division concluded, there now remains, at the beginning of this new era this one question only—how the difficulties, before mentioned as likely to prevent its establishment and development altogether, could be overcome, either entirely, or as far as the fundamental principles of the ancient religion permitted.

A general survey now shows that such difficulties certainly ex-

---

[1] According to vol. ii. p. 114 sq.

[2] This makes it clear upon what points special stress should be laid in a general history of the monarchy in Israel. But this is precisely what is wanting in the *History of the Hebrew Monarchy from the Administration of Samuel to the Babylonish Captivity*, London, 1847; although the anonymous author of this work, which is somewhat too condensed, shows a most praiseworthy independence of spirit, only too rare at present in England. But this liberal spirit should not ignore real historic greatness and estimate the affairs of Israel as of less importance than they really were. K. A. Mengel's *Staats- und Religionsgeschichte der Königreiche Israel und Juda*, Berlin, 1853, is characterised by a low tone. Comp. the *Jahrbücher der Biblischen Wissenschaft*, v. p. 289 sqq.

isted, and were only to be overcome by severe struggles; but that, thanks to the unimpaired energy still latent in the community, these struggles were not only to a great extent successful, but of comparatively short duration. The history of Saul and David occupies this first act of the new great era of Israel's history. We then see under Solomon, as the ripe fruit of these successful struggles, the rapid rise of the greatest splendour which this era, or, in external magnificence, the whole history of Israel, could produce, in this the very centre of its glory. But in the clear daylight of these times of greatest prosperity, all those deep deficiencies become apparent, which even under the new organisation remained irremediable, chiefly because the perfection of true religion was yet wanting. And these defects, interfering in unchecked force with the lofty machine of matured temporal monarchy, worked its destruction steadily and surely, though retarded awhile by its inalienable wealth of spiritual treasures. This concludes the third and last act of this era, the history of the two kingdoms from the division of the kingdom of David to the destruction of both. That these three periods are very unequal in length, the first comprehending more than sixty years, and the second not much beyond forty, cannot be set against the obvious truth of facts. The entire development of these (approximately) five centuries divides itself plainly into these three stages, neither more nor less, each of which is of just the same importance as the others. They are the three periods of the auspicious commencement, the glorious maturity, and the slow decay, of Monarchy in Israel.

It is self-evident from this, that the whole history of human monarchy in Israel turns upon points entirely different from those on which the destinies of the other kingdoms of the ancient world depended. These latter considerations were indeed by no means unimportant for the kingdom of Israel also. No monarchy and no dynasty can last long which fails to satisfy even the subordinate conditions of its existence, and is unable to protect the unity and power of the people, to agree with the hereditary or elected representatives of the people (the Deputies) about laws and principles of government, to appreciate or promote all good work and useful labour in every craft or profession, to avail itself advantageously of all real light and knowledge, whether new or old, and to exercise an impartial rule over all interests, classes, and religions in the realm. And on all this depended in many respects the fortunes of the numerous kings of Israel also, as will appear hereafter. But on the monarchy in Israel there devolved in addition other quite different duties and labours. What the monarchy should be in the community of the true God, and before His very face—this was the question from the pressure of which it could never escape, the point which touched even those who would willingly have ignored it. And though not one of these kings might become the perfect king and man actually demanded by the deepest purposes and aspirations of Jahveism, and at last longed for with ever-growing fervour, there yet arose upon this soil kings in whom many forms of royal and manly excellence were exemplified, and whose like would be vainly sought among other nations in those early times. There only, in all antiquity, was the true ideal of monarchy persistently aimed at. The visible kingdom might at last perish; but its monarchy could only be destroyed with the kingdom itself, by foreign hands.

In proportion as the whole history of Israel gradually rises at this stage to that culminating point at which its eternal significance for all ages is for the first time fully determined, and even far distant regions of its past receive fresh glory, the amount of documentary and other evidence belonging to it is much greater; so that we are able to recognise most of its more important events with far greater completeness than in the previous period. Yet even here there are still many intervals of considerable obscurity to us; nay, even many names of men at one time doubtless illustrious, to which we are unable to assign places in the entire course of the history, by decades, or even centuries.[1]

[1] At what time, e.g. did Hanan son of Igdaliah live, whom Jeremiah, xxxv. 4, honours with that highest of all titles, *man of God?* One of the chambers of the Temple was named after his sons, i.e. disciples, and was probably built by them or was the place where he habitually taught. He was thus evidently at one time a great prophet in Jerusalem, like Joel, and perhaps flourished as early, or even earlier; yet we now know nothing farther respecting him.

SECTION I.

FOUNDATION OF THE MONARCHY; THE PERIOD OF SAUL AND DAVID.

A. SAUL AND HIS HOUSE.

Of the history of this royal house we certainly know more from extant authorities, than we do with regard to many others after the time of Solomon; yet we must not disguise from ourselves, that, much as has been preserved, this is still but little, compared with the importance of this period of the history, which does not derive its significance from its duration. We possess adequate knowledge of the final issue of this history; from its mid-career, also, many points start forth in bright distinctness to our view; but its beginning is still shrouded, as far as the sources in question go, in that mysterious obscurity which envelops the origin of all events which take the world by surprise, especially those of such immense importance as the first establishment of true, and therefore divinely consecrated monarchy in a primeval people.

I. SAUL'S ELECTION AS KING.

The Bible, even in direct historic narrative, often affords us types of eternal truths; stripping off by degrees the gross material covering of actual events, and retaining only their ever-living religious significance, which it brings vividly before us embodied in some form of corresponding beauty. Thus does it treat even that portion of the history of Israel which, in itself, as well as to succeeding ages, is one of the most important. What is human sovereignty in general—and what in the community of Jahveh in particular? What is its origin and development? What principles and conditions are the basis of the pledge of its divine necessity and sanction, and therefore of its undisturbed existence, as respects even the special individual, and the special dynasty, summoned at a particular time and among a particular people to bear its honours and its burdens? Such questions are easily and simply answered by recalling the rise of that king who was the first to be invested with the full glory of true royalty; and in whose history, precisely because he was the first, all such questions must actually have presented themselves most vividly, before any clear and permanent solution of them could be arrived at.

However well qualified a man may be by birth, as well as in body and soul, i.e. by nature, to govern and so to acquire supreme honour and power among men, yet these external advantages, though needful as preliminary conditions, are not always attended by that Divine predestination and consecration, as the second of the two indispensable conditions without the union of which the germ of true monarchy can nowhere be developed. In this, as in so many smaller matters, the Divine possibility and opportunity must come to meet the human; and if in this most exalted of human relations both possibilities coincide, Divine grace and predestination come in their full might to aid frail human nature in this highest of all tasks; bestowing on him the Divine power and consecration of spirit needful to enable him to perform that function with the elementary qualifications for which nature has already endowed him. No one, with whatever other advantages, can become a true king, whose heart has not previously been at some time touched and stirred by some benign ray of heavenly light.

We have here, however, nothing but the two fundamental conditions without whose coincidence no result in this direction is possible, and as the presence of these intrinsic possibilities is nowhere necessarily followed by their immediate realisation, so it does not always happen that everyone immediately becomes king, in whom these two fundamental conditions are united. Yet since the dignity of a man so qualified is already a fact, recognised in heaven, and cannot therefore remain wholly inoperative, before he attains it outwardly he encounters various signs and traces of the power working secretly within him. Not that they are brought forward, however, by any will or purpose of his own: rather they take him by surprise: yet they arise in the very necessity of things, and bring him at the same time joy and strength by their more distinct intimation of his destiny. The belief in omens was indeed universal in antiquity, especially when such important matters were involved as the election of a king and changes of government; and the perversions to which such a belief is liable are clear enough to us in these modern days. But it remains unquestionable, that upon ground already prepared, preliminary sparks of flame may be, as it were, involuntarily kindled by the first movement of that same spiritual power which afterwards breaks suddenly forth, and wraps all things in its blaze; and that the truly predestined ruler, even before he becomes such outwardly, must receive at the fitting time divine intimations and impulses towards the career which lies before him.[1]

And when, in accordance with these principles, and with these auspicious signs which thus joyfully anticipate futurity, at the appointed time he actually becomes king over the people, he does not yet gain much by this mere external recognition. Nothing but true royal action for the welfare of the state, alike bravely undertaken and firmly carried out at the right moment, can win for him that real deference, that joyful, voluntary cooperation in state purposes, from all his subjects, without which his sovereignty must ever remain most feeble and equivocal.

Supposing him, however, to have at last attained everything that he can desire, to stand already on the steps of the temple of immortal fame! yet in this dizzy elevation it is all the more necessary for him never to forget the lowly origin from which he sprung. Thus must he constantly bear in mind, that above him there abides another king—the Eternal; and that only in as far as he works together with God, and consequently with all spiritual truth, can any earthly monarch be a king after the heart of the King of kings. In this community especially, the community of Jahveh, of which he is but a member like everyone else, he must never forget that from the beginning a boundary has been traced, an inviolable law fixed for him, to transgress which would be self-annihilation. This truth is alike the last and the first, and is consequently supreme and most decisive, within the whole range of our perceptions on this matter; a truth which, though breathed only in a whisper, and shrouded in mysterious darkness, perpetually supplies its own proof.

These four truths, then, exhaust the entire subject. By them, the first especially, must every king be measured; and should he be found wanting, if only in the last, his kingly career must be accounted a failure.

It is the prophetic narrator (as he may be briefly characterised) of the Histories of the Kings, who enfolds Saul's life in the closely-woven net of these higher, or, in other words, prophetic truths; obviously because it was those very truths which its history appeared to him to convey for the instruction of all succeeding ages.[2] What portions of the narrative which now, through the vitality of these truths, coheres as a living whole, he

---

[1] Just as, in reference to a position which still better exhibits the elevation of human power of government, dreams announce to the boy Joseph his future greatness: i. p. 419.

[2] Taking the fall of Saul as the fifth act, we have here again a complete drama; as in ii. p. 407.

may have found already existing in earlier unconnected accounts, we are unable, in the absence of older sources, precisely to determine. It is at all events clear that through the graceful drapery in which all the more definite portions of the narrative are closely wrapped by these truths, we may still discern many fragments of pure tradition; and that this narrator was the first to fling over the whole such a radiantly transparent veil. The earthly, human element is still perfectly appreciable under the thin disguise; nay, even the traces of that popular wit which must early have mingled abundantly in this king's history with its alternations of the lofty and the low, are but little effaced; but it is only through the breath of higher prophetic truth that the whole is vivified and transfigured into a form of beauty. It is evidently owing to this prophetic transfiguration that Samuel, in his relation to human kings, appears merely as the organ of the divine spirit. The cognisance and regulation of all that concerns Saul, which in this representation is attributed to Samuel, is in fact typical of the operation of the divine spirit in its complete independence upon the human sovereign; it predetermines, it strengthens, and it sympathises, but it also warns, and it discloses glimpses of an inviolable Ideal. Samuel serves, therefore, in this narrative as the easiest representation, so to speak, of the actual operation and design of the divine spirit with regard to the human sovereign. It by no means follows that in what is thus attributed to Samuel, there is not very much that is based upon actual recollection; but the peculiar mode and colouring of the extant representation is derived, in the first place, from that higher conception of the whole. We must now turn our attention to the details.

1. Saul, a man still in the prime of youthful strength and beauty,—nay, excelling in beauty all of his age, taller by the head and shoulders than all the people, and besides as brave in battle as any, is the son of a freeborn Benjamite of some note, by name Kish.[1] In respect of birth as well as of person and character, he is adequately qualified for sovereignty; for at that time all the freeborn of good family were accounted noble

---

[1] For the genealogy of Saul see 1 Sam. ix. 1; xiv. 50 sq. If in 1 Chron. ix. 35-38, the name of the city Gibeon (ii. p. 251) is interchanged with Gibeah, and the name of the father of Kish, יעיאל with אביאל, 1 Sam. ix. 1; xiv. 51, this grandfather of Saul must have borne the title of honour, 'father of Gibeah,' and have been famous as the father of ten distinguished sons. Among these ten were Kish and Ner; and the last is mentioned in 1 Sam. xiv. 50 sq., very emphatically, as Saul's uncle. It is therefore perhaps only by some later misconception that in the account given, 1 Chron. viii. 33; ix. 39, of Saul's genealogy, Ner appears at the head as his grandfather; otherwise we must suppose the branch Ner to have been omitted in the earliest sources.

in Israel, while all the privileges which the judges or their sons, for example, enjoyed, were strictly personal, not derived from any privileged hereditary rank. His father dwells in Gibeah, a city of the tribe of Benjamin, where his son afterwards, even as king, continues to reside (see below); just as almost every judge had chosen his birthplace as his permanent abode.[1]

But though qualified for sovereignty, he does not seek it; for no exalted position, acquired by selfish devices, or grasped by mere human ambition, can ever prove a real blessing. It is therefore finely conceived,[2] that Saul, sent forth by his father to seek the strayed asses, after long unavailing search[3] comes on the third day, almost against his will, to Samuel who was before but little known to him. His object is to enquire of him respecting the asses, and he is destined to receive, instead of his lost property, a kingdom from him. For the prophet, whose purpose is at this time to erect a monarchy in Israel, has already selected him, before he is himself aware of it. The true spirit of Jahveh, full of compassion, has already on the preceding day whispered to Samuel, that for the deliverance of Jahveh's people sorely pressed by powerful foes, most of all by the Philistines, a Benjamite must be anointed king. Thus when Saul comes before Samuel, bashfully pursuing his humble quest, in apparent unconsciousness of the power slumbering within him of aspiring and attaining to the highest place, the great Seer receives him in a way quite differently from all that he could have hoped for or feared. At the moment of their meeting the Seer has come forth from his house, on the way[4] to the solitary sacred height of Ramah, the city of his residence,[5] where he sacrifices on the altar to

---

[1] Comp. vol. ii. p. 362.
[2] 1 Sam. ix. 1-14; cf. verse 20.
[3] The direction of his three days' search (verse 20) is given according to 'lands,' in 1 Sam. ix. 4 sq. Most of the names here mentioned are certainly obscure to us; if, however, Saul's birthplace, according to Is. x. 29; Josh. xviii. 28; and Josephus, Bell. Jud. v. 2. 1, was only about a league and a half north of Jerusalem (somewhat south of Ramah), and Samuel's Ramathaim, or as abbreviated, Ramah (according to vol. ii. p. 421 sq.) the present Ram-allah, lay further northeast of it; Saul probably proceeded at first westward over the mountain, then still further westward to the present Sârîs or Sârûs (Wilson's Lands, ii. p. 266; Lynch's Narrative, p. 453), if this corresponds to the district Shalisha; and finally westward to the Sha'albim mentioned vol. ii. p. 330, if the שְׁעָלִים, 1 Sam. ix. 4, is an abbreviation of this; hereupon he turned eastward again into Benjamin's territory, and finally northward to the land of Zuph, where Samuel resided. The way back, x. 2-5, was shorter because more direct. Besides this, some MSS. of the LXX., according to Holmes, do actually read Σαρισά. If it were known more definitely where שַׁעֲרַיִם (1 Sam. xvii. 52) was situated, it might perhaps prove to be identical with שְׁעָלִים. And Shalisha is probably identical with Baal-Shalisha, 2 Kings iv. 42; cf. the Onomast. of the Fathers under Beth-Shalisha.

[4] As Ramah, Samuel's city, was certainly not large, 'in the middle of the city,' verse 14, is not very different from 'in the middle of the gate,' verse 18.

[5] Vol. ii. p. 421 sq.

Jahveh, or is wont to partake of a sacred sacrificial repast with some of his closest friends. He at once desires to take Saul also with him, telling him beforehand how unimportant was the immediate object of his enquiries, and that the matter was already settled; but that for him and his whole house was reserved a very different and far better destiny in Israel. And although, in his unassuming simplicity, he would fain waive the honour which is obscurely hinted (so little does he yet know his better self),—the holy man, more discerning, takes him with him to the sacrificial meal which is already prepared; nay, assigns him the place of honour among the thirty guests before invited,[1] while he is served with a portion of the sacrificial meat, put by as it were specially for him; for in like manner a portion other and higher than that of ordinary men has been long reserved for him by heaven.[2] And when by thus partaking of the Seer's meal, nay, of his sacrificial feast, he has taken the first step towards participating in his mind and spirit, the Seer, on their return to the city in the evening, appoints to him, with equal respect, the roof as his sleeping-place.[3] Early on the following morning, he assigns him honourable escort, but at their solitary parting cannot refrain from saying and doing all that is to be said and done. Solemnly anointing him, and kissing him in token of homage, he predicts distinctly and minutely three signs which he will encounter on his return home; but he lets drop at the very end a mysterious warning, that when he shall be elevated in accordance with these divine auguries to his rightful sovereignty, and shall be able in the plenitude of kingly power to accomplish all his desires, from one thing he should nevertheless refrain![4]

2. Ah, who would not feel within him a new heart, and be transformed into a new being, if, when already fitted by nature for a loftier dignity, he is at the same time thus animated and uplifted by the grace and glory of the divine spirit! God, proceeds the narrative, gave to Saul another heart, and he at once begins to encounter the three appointed signs.

---

[1] The resemblance to Gen. xliii. 34, arises more from the nature of the subject, not from one passage being an imitation of the other.

[2] In verse 24 for לֵאמֹר הָעָם קָרָאתִי, we should read, partly following the LXX. כִּי מִשָּׁאָר חָעָם קְרֻאֵת, 'in token that thou wast invited before the rest of the people;' cf. verse 22; or still nearer to the LXX. קְרִיאָת 'that thou art separated from the rest of the people.'

[3] As also in 2 Kings iv. 10, such a retired apartment on the roof is mentioned as the place of honour. In verse 25 sq. we should read with the LXX. וַיִּרְבְּדוּ לְשָׁאוּל, &c.

[4] 1 Sam. ix. 15–x. 8; with x. 7 comp. 2 Sam. iii. 21. Much is related also among other nations of the σημεῖα μοναρχίας as in Ael. xii. Var. Hist. 46.

These three signs are obviously selected and arranged with exquisite skill. Each of them meets the future king (as the Seer had already predicted) at a sacred spot; this is as little accidental as the belief, so often expressed in the Psalms, that help comes from the holy place; and the central district, the land of Benjamin and Ephraim, through which Saul's course now lay, was peculiarly rich in such sacred localities.[1] There is also in the signs themselves a regular progression, so that the astonishment and effect produced should grow greater and greater. First of all, near the sepulchre of Rachel,[2] he is met by two men in great haste,[3] bringing the joyful intelligence that the asses are found, and that his father is anxious not about them but about his son. Thus happily vanishes the burden of cares belonging to his former humble life, because more important interests are henceforth to be the object of his anxious consideration! Proceeding further, he is met near the Terebinth of Tabor[4] by three men journeying to the great Sanctuary at Bethel, one bearing three kids, the second three loaves, the third a skin of wine, constituting together all the materials for sacrifice. These gifts are indeed designed for the sanctuary; yet, as if suddenly prompted by some unseen power, they offer the unknown wanderer, with friendly salutation, two of the three loaves of first fruits.[5] Thus the actual, though yet unrecognised king, can accept this unexpected gift as an act of homage, just as to the infant Jesus the three Wise Men from the East brought offerings. The fact that

---

[1] Vol. i. p. 304 sq.

[2] The origin of this is explained in Jacob's history, Gen. xxxv. 16-20; xlviii. 7, and there can be no doubt that in both passages the same place of primæval sanctity is intended. In 1 Sam. x. 2 it is added that it lies 'on the border of Benjamin;' unfortunately it is not explained of which side this border is to be understood, for the *in meridie* of the Vulgate for בְּצַלְצַח is certainly only conjecture. Now if that monument somewhat to the north of Bethlehem, which has been shown since the Middle Ages under this name, and has been described with such manifold exactness in modern times, were here intended, the whole of Saul's journey would be unintelligible. But here as well as in Genesis, we may very well understand the northern boundary of Benjamin, as it might begin somewhat south-east of Ram-allah.

[3] צָלְצַח, taken as the name of a place, does not suit the context; its meaning is rather, according to the LXX., something like 'hastening;' 'leaping.' Comp. لَطَ, صَلْتَ, סלד.

[4] תבור is certainly only a dialectic variation from *Deborah*; comp. i. p. 294. But in Gen. xxxv. 8 אֵלוֹן is pointed as אַלּוֹן, 'oak.' This place was situated, according to Judg. iv. 5, north of Ramah, just where Saul might have to pass; and if according to Gen. xxxv. 8 (cf. 16-20) it appears to lie farther north than the sepulchre of Rachel, it is to be remembered that Gen. xxxv. 1-8 is derived from the Book of Covenants, but 9-21 from the Book of Origins.

[5] After לחם some such word as בִּכּוּרִים seems, according to the LXX., to have dropped out. Such a description of the loaves as first-fruits, i.e. sacrificial bread, suits very well with the context; and it is by no means clear how it could make its way into the text of the LXX. without warrant.

this startling prelude to all gifts which should in future be made to the king, was taken from sacrificial loaves, is an intimation that the king should henceforward receive some portion of those products of the soil which had hitherto been appropriated exclusively to the sanctuary. Finally, on approaching his native city, likewise a holy place,[1] he is met by a number of prophets, coming from the altar on the hill where sacrifice had just been offered, plunged in prophetic raptures amid the loud music of various instruments. He is himself so carried away by their enthusiasm, that, to the amazement of all his former acquaintances, he flings himself with them into the prophetic ecstasy.[2] And so the entire spiritual transformation which had begun within him at his parting from Samuel, is now manifested openly and before the eyes of the world; and if he who was before but a simple citizen is now become the equal of prophets in spiritual strength and greatness, why should not his spirit be worthy also of royalty? (Cf. p. 6 sq.)[3]

And yet, though many involuntary signs seem to combine to proclaim the hitherto unproclaimed king, and his homeward journey becomes a path of flowers, he himself in his modesty is so far from feeling himself in the eyes of the people also really a king, that on his return home he does not disclose even to the dearest of his questioning relatives[4] anything of what Samuel had said to him respecting the kingdom. So diffident is he still in himself, having withal good ground for not speaking out as yet too boastfully; since he still lacks the public consecration, i.e. the recognition in solemn national

---

[1] We certainly do not know on what the historic sanctity of this place was founded; but its having a בָּמָה, i.e. a separate place of sacrifice, and being here distinctly named גִּבְעַת אֱלֹהִים, 'Gibeah of God,' is sufficient proof of its being a holy place. This is also presupposed in 2 Sam. xxi. 6, 9, although it is scarcely the same place where, according to Josh. xxiv. 33, the aged High-Priest Phinehas lived (ii. p. 313). After the time of Saul, who evidently enlarged it and made it a royal residence, it is generally called, to distinguish it from so many towns of the same name in other tribes, *Gibeah of Saul*; and was, according to Jos. *Bell. Jud.*, v. 2. 1, a league distant on the direct road northwards from Jerusalem. On the other hand, *Gibeah of Benjamin*, according to 1 Sam. xiii. 15 sq., is probably the present Geba, south of Michmash, and only a little north-east of the one just named. This was undoubtedly the one which, according to ii. p. 352, was in early times much the larger and more renowned. Besides, the names *Geba* and *Gibeah* are often interchanged.

[2] To understand this more fully, comp. ii. p. 425 sq.

[3] In verse 12 read אָבִיהוּ, according to the LXX., for אֲבִיהֶם; and then, following the *Cod. Alex.*, הֲלוֹא קִישׁ, 'is it (his father) not Kish?' should be inserted; the astonished people must first convince themselves that he is really Saul and the son of Kish. In verse 13 הַגִּבְעָה should be read, following the LXX., for הבמה.

[4] This דּוֹד is probably introduced here as making these enquiries, because his son Abner afterwards plays the most important part in Saul's reign; for, according to xiv. 50 sq., Ner must in all probability be intended as the uncle.

assembly, without which every inward or outward consecration remains incomplete.[1]

3. Samuel indeed does all that farther lies in his power to promote the great cause. He calls a national assembly at Mizpeh, where he has before summoned similar meetings.[2] Here Saul is proclaimed king; the sacred lot, it is stated, fell among all the tribes of Israel upon Benjamin; among the families of this tribe, on that of Matri;[3] and in this family, on Saul the son of Kish. If we consider the general use in those ages of the sacred lot,[4] we shall find that, taking the whole account in this connexion, it exhibits nothing but the great truth, that for the full and auspicious acknowledgment of Saul as king, his mysterious interview with the Seer did not alone suffice; publicly, in solemn national assembly, must the spirit of Jahveh choose him out, and mark him as Jahveh's man. That is the real sign of the truly great prophet, and bears not the slightest resemblance to the proceedings of the great Seer's later imitators in the kingdom of the Ten Tribes; as will be farther explained in the course of its history. And even then (the narrative very characteristically proceeds), when by the Divine voice he is publicly acknowledged as king, Saul hid himself in shy reserve behind the baggage heaps of the assembled people, overpowered by his sense of the momentous consequences which must result from his inauguration—so little does a good man force himself into office, still less into this highest of all offices. A second divine announcement was consequently required to discover his hiding-place, and draw him forth. But when, after being thus brought out almost against his will, he is not only presented to the impatient people as the chosen of Jahveh, but visibly justifies that choice by his towering height, the whole assembly is satisfied, and unanimously proclaims him king. And now, for the first time, the new constitution is legally announced, and registered in written archives; while the new king, surrounded by a band of devoted followers, whom a divine enthusiasm for him had at that moment seized, proceeds to his own home.[5]

---

[1] 1 Sam. x. 9–16.

[2] vii. 5, 16; comp. ii. pp. 362, 413. This city, pronounced by the Hellenists Μασσηφά מַצְפָה, must from the time of Samuel have attained such sanctity, that the remembrance of it was preserved even in the period of the Maccabees. The pronunciation מִצְפָה might refer to the Skopos; but מַצְפָה would be quite a different word. The place itself probably lay to the west of Jerusalem.

[3] Unless מַטְרִי is a corruption from בִּכְרִי; comp. the [passages given in i. p. 368 respecting the genealogy of Benjamin.

[4] See my *Alterthümer*, p. 338 sqq.

[5] 1 Sam. x. 17, 20–26; respecting verse 18 sq., which must have been interpolated by a later editor, see below. Instead of

24   FOUNDATION OF THE MONARCHY.

Yet what avail such solemnities, discourses, promises and hopes, if followed by no corresponding result, no abiding impression, no confirmation, no great deed bravely undertaken in divine trust? if even the object most urgently necessary is not carried out as soon as possible with that same joyous courage which the festal days may be supposed to have kindled? Evil-disposed people (the account proceeds) doubted contemptuously whether this king would help them, and brought him no tribute. A month, however, had scarcely elapsed,[1] when the Ammonite king Nahash invaded the northern frontier of the kingdom. His first step was to lay siege to the city of Jabesh-Gilead.[2] The citizens, sorely pressed by him, and threatened with penalties most shamefully severe unless they immediately surrender unconditionally, send to their brethren on the other side Jordan for speedy succour within a week. The people, on hearing of it, weep, but give no help. An ordinary king would not have allowed so distant a danger, on the frontier of the country and beyond the river, to startle him from his repose. But as soon as the tidings reach Saul, who has peacefully resumed his private occupations, as he is following the plough, that higher spirit, whose stirring presence he had already once experienced, seizes him instantaneously with power before undreamt of. In fearful wrath, he turns the yoke of oxen he was at that moment driving, into the terrible war-signal; hews them in pieces and sends them to all the tribes throughout the entire nation,[3] which he thus rouses to action as prompt as his own. He immediately musters the army in Bezek on the Jordan,[4] sends back thence the messengers of the threatened city with comforting promises, and on the following morning with his troops admirably disposed he surprises the besiegers, and swiftly achieves before the heat of the day the most complete victory. In all this activity and triumph in his capacity of king, he was not without the cooperation of Samuel.

Thus then have his people learnt really to know their king. In the first outburst of delight at the happy result achieved

---

[1] הֶחֱיָל, verse 26, we ought with the LXX. to read בְּנֵי הַחַיִל; cf. ix. 1.

[1] For כְּמַחֲרִישׁ, verse 27, we ought, according to the LXX. and Jos. *Ant.* vi. 5. 1, to read כְּמֵחֹדֶשׁ; since it is obvious, from the entire context, that here least of all could the specification of time be omitted.

[2] Vol. ii. p. 337.

[3] Respecting this custom see ii. p. 340 *note.*

[4] A city on the Upper Jordan, ii. p. 284 *note.* The LXX. make a singular addition בַּבָּמָה, which may probably signify some sacred height close to the city, as in ix. 12. Jos. *Ant.* vi. 5. 3, makes this into Baάδ without any mention of Bezek. The numbers of the combatants in v. 8 are also most unnecessarily raised, in the LXX. and Josephus, to 600,000 (700,000) men from Israel and 70,000 from Judah,

by the establishment of royal authority, they would fain punish with death the cavillers who had previously doubted whether Samuel's choice had fallen in Saul upon a competent sovereign; but he, as true king, has too much discretion to allow any private revenge to mar such a day of divine triumph. But that which seemed wanting, and in the case of many weak men had indeed been wanting, not entirely without ground, was now at the right moment retrieved. At Samuel's own desire, the community assembles in Gilgal,[1] there with solemn sacrifices to ratify anew, because more numerously and unanimously than the first time, the act of royalty in Saul's favour;[2] and great (it is said in conclusion) was the universal joy.[3]

Not till now, according to this narrator, was the great event, the successful establishment of the monarchy in Israel, completed: but now it is completed indeed; and it needs nothing more to show how perfectly all this followed in harmonious sequence, connected by the one fundamental thought, without redundance or deficiency.

But the last narrator but one, who[4] remodelled in the seventh century the earlier works of the history of the kings, found much to introduce just here, in this important section, derived partly from a somewhat later narrator,[5] and to a still larger extent from his own notions. An event of such infinite significance as the legal establishment of monarchy in Israel affords, indeed, material sufficient to require the labour of several writers to do it justice; and however satisfactorily the representation of the earlier narrator may exhibit, by Saul's example, the essential character of genuine monarchy in its origin, there is no denying that it stops altogether with contemplating the short history of the monarchy from this, the nearest, point of view, and that it is this alone which gives it its especial beauty. But little consideration is paid to the fact that this monarchy has its origin in a community so entirely peculiar as Israel, and consequently under conditions quite different from those in any other nation. Here, then, was left an important gap to be supplied by later writers; and we now see the deficiency supplemented by more recent narrators. A free and comprehensive survey is generally easier to writers

---

[1] P. 29.
[2] As we sometimes meet with, in the Middle Ages, in the case of German kings and emperors; see a similar case 1 Chron. xxix. 22; comp. xxiii. 1. A still more exact parallel is to be found, according to Plutarch's *Numa*, ch. vii., cf. ch. iii. in the distinction between the *designatio* of the ancient kings and their *electio per suffragia*.
[3] 1 Sam. x. 27–xi. 15.
[4] Vol. i. p. 157 sqq.
[5] Vol. i. p. 151 sq.

removed by the lapse of time from the events they describe, and the relation of the monarchy in Israel to the eternal truths and principles of the community could only be made clear through its own prolonged development. It is natural, then, that we should find these narrators forming their conception of this special history of the origin of the monarchy chiefly from a wide retrospective view of the entire history of Israel as the community of Jahveh, and describing it in the light reflected thence upon it. And it is quite in keeping with this freer treatment, that the Deuteronomic admonitions thence resulting are, in the graphic account of the last narrator but one, put immediately into the mouth of Samuel, who was fully recognised as the great prophet of Jahveh. The main truth which was here to be supplied, concerns the relation of the Theocracy to the Monarchy. Had the former truly realised in every age its original destiny, the Divine King, obeyed in all things by all members of the community, would have made the human sovereign superfluous. What was Israel's especial pride, as well as a fundamental law of its foundation and constitution, its redemption and government by the Invisible alone, seems to perish by the innovation; and if human monarchy be once established, how easily may it be perverted into pure despotism, and bring upon a nation the severest oppression, instead of the expected blessing! It is obvious that, at this period, the different sides of this great subject had long undergone the severest scrutiny; that monarchy in Israel had already unfolded itself fully, even on its dark side; and that, on looking back to the first foundation of the community, the wide contrast between the condition of the nation under its later kings and its original state under Moses was observed with pain. We shall, on the other hand, perceive with increasing clearness in the course of this history that, during the first period of the monarchy, in the joy of its final attainment, its great advantages were much more fully recognised; and that the question then was less as to the existence of a human monarchy, than as to who should be invested with it. It is entirely in this spirit that the earlier narrator describes its foundation. The view here introduced by the later narrator, though not without substantial ground, belongs to a later and far maturer age. And yet, again, it is impossible for such a narrator to regard the human monarchy as wholly rejected by Jahveh; if only because he knew how long it had endured, and how often besides, as under David, its existence had been the greatest blessing to the people; but it was further involved in the higher conception of the true God, that by no human change could He be changed, so long as the community did not prove faithless to the deepest meaning of His words—those divine words which, after all, comprehend so much besides the kind and mode of government. The additional matter interpolated by the last narrator but one in the words of the earlier account assumes, accordingly, the following form:—

The people alone originate the demand for the king, because the sons of Samuel are bad judges.[1] Now although this last circumstance may rest upon a tradition[2] that is perfectly true, yet this view of the appointment of the first king with the primary purpose simply of judging[3] is entirely at variance with that taken by the previous narrator, who everywhere represents the deliverance of the people from their foreign enemies as the immediate object of Saul.[4] Whether any external motives were admitted by the earlier narrator as influencing Samuel's determination to appoint a king, is uncertain; as a long passage of the earlier document has dropped out before chapter ix. But this narrator regards Samuel as so entirely an instrument of the divine spirit, and he looks on the monarchy as such an unmixed good, that he could not well represent any external considerations as determining him to the choice. The demand of the people is, however, ill received by Samuel, who prays to Jahveh for a decision, but is admonished by Him to yield to their desire,[5] even though it really sprang from a reprehensible perversity. But he represents to the people,[6] in a warning speech, all the burdensome services which the king would claim from them as his due, and how they would hereafter vainly wish to be freed from this yoke; yet as they, notwithstanding, will not relinquish their demand, he promises, with the sanction of Jahveh, to choose

[1] 1 Sam. viii. 1–5.
[2] Vol. ii. p. 429.
[3] As is expressly stated, viii. 5, 6; not until verse 20 is the king's going forth to battle alluded to, and then it is mentioned after his judging, as if supplementary and less important. The reference of the same later narrator to the Ammonite campaign, xii. 12, as the immediate cause, is no doubt suggested by the preceding narrative, ch. xi., and does not, as we see by verse 2, invalidate the other reasons.
[4] 1 Sam. ix. 16, 17; also x. 1, following the fuller reading of the LXX. The whole account in ch. xi. also belongs to this. Yet the expression Samuel 'judged Israel *all the days of his life*' (vii. 15), is not to be taken too literally (cf. the similar instances, vii. 13; 1 Kings v. 5 [iv. 25]; besides xi. 25); for this notion of judging had already become very indefinite.
[5] 1 Sam. viii. 6–9.
[6] It would be a sad mistake to identify this so-called 'king's right' of vv. 11–17 with the 'state-right' intended by the earlier narrator, x. 25, and to deduce from the former words the special force of the latter, which certainly did not comprehend anything nearly so objectionable. The king's right evidently rested in later times entirely on usage, and was never a written code. But unfortunately the confusion between these two has done much harm, even in Christian states,

for them a king.¹ In like manner, at the national assembly at Mizpeh, he touches again, though briefly, on the ingratitude of the people to Jahveh, but nevertheless, in compliance with their will, proceeds to the election.² At Gilgal, however, where all the proceedings of the election are finally concluded, he enters with the people into solemn consideration, point by point, of this most critical change.³ First he pronounces his own farewell address, laying down with the most dignified composure the office he has hitherto filled. Only a Samuel could thus quit office, proudly challenging all to convict him of one single injustice in his past career, and by the act of resignation gaining, not losing greatness.⁴ No longer Judge and Ruler, but simple Prophet, he is able now to discourse with the greater freedom of the monarchy about to be introduced; and he seizes the moment to cast a more distant glance into all the past and future of the community. That the recent conduct of the nation had displayed ingratitude towards Jahveh, its true king, could not be denied; and only by more faithful service of Jahveh in future on the part alike of king and people, can the ruin they have deserved be averted.⁵ A sign from heaven itself in answer to the prophet's prayer—a sudden thunder-storm in harvest time—testifies to Jahveh's wrath, and to the reality of His threatened vengeance.⁶ But when the people, in real terror, entreat the prophet's intercession, he addresses them in words of comfort; for even the new constitution is not incompatible with the fundamental moral principles of the community, though its abuse will involve both king and people in a common ruin.⁷ Such is, in fact, the expression, towards the end of the Monarchy and Theocracy, after the more intelligible revelation of their truths by the actual course of events, of the loftiest sentiment possible within the limits of the Old Testament concerning this infinitely important crisis.

---

[1] 1 Sam. viii. 10–22.

[2] The entire style and colouring of the verses, x. 18, 19, betray a later hand; as, however, their omission from the present context would leave a hiatus, though but a slight one, in the account of the older narrator, we must presume that the compiler has here left out some words of the original record.

[3] 1 Sam. xii.

[4] 1 Sam. xii. 1–5.

[5] 1 Sam. xii. 6–15.

[6] vv. 16-18. The sign is here described precisely as might be expected after the model of the great prophets of the ninth and eighth centuries. But the powerful influence exercised by the writings of these prophets upon the general representation of the narrator may be traced besides in the entire colouring and manner of the prophetic discourses. There is much, also, that reminds us of the accounts of Moses in the early history, as if Samuel were regarded as the Moses of his time; cf. for instance, viii. 21 sq. with Ex. xix. 8. On a close examination it is very obvious that, in these few interpolated passages, the whole style of composition differs widely from that of the earlier narrator.

[7] vv. 18–25.

II. Saul's Prophetic Rejection.

1. ' Now thou art free ' (this, according to the earlier narrator, was the gist of Samuel's fourth and last address to Saul, at his mysterious prophetic consecration, p. 20), ' as king chosen and approved of God, filled also with His spirit, to do whatsoever thine hand shall find (i.e. as circumstances shall lead thee); but if thou go down *before me* into Gilgal, I will come unto thee, to offer sacrifices of every sort; seven days shalt thou tarry, till I come unto thee, and show thee what thou shalt do.'[1] The essential meaning of this is, in fact, as we have already seen, no other than this : that even to the royal supremacy in the state there is a limit not to be overstepped which is fixed, and must ever remain fixed; that even above the most rightful, divinely-inspired king, in the plenitude of his power, there is ever an inviolable something on which, however sorely tried, in evil days and apparent danger, he must not lay his hand. It may be that this general truth is here set forth in somewhat fantastic and trivial guise; yet it is only in the collision of historic contrasts, and particular questions often of seemingly little moment, that the highest general truth can be brought to the test, and even attain its proper development. At that period, we must accordingly affirm, it was just on the external co-ordination of those inwardly antagonistic tendencies, that the stability and progress of this eternal truth depended; and so, many things which now appear insignificant to us, may then have been of the deepest import and have involved the most serious consequences.

Gilgal, on the south-western bank of the Jordan, was evidently at that time one of the most sacred places in Israel, and the true centre of the whole people. Even in earlier ages[2] it possessed a similar importance, which at the time in question was no doubt all the greater, because on the west the Philistine power extended so far in, that the centre of gravity of the kingdom was necessarily pushed back to the banks of the Jordan. There was the place of assembly for the people on national questions of common interest; and thence, after solemn sacrifice, did they march forth in arms to battle. It was therefore in the very nature of things, that the relative position of the two independent powers existing within the state should be brought under discussion and receive a complete expression, or at any rate be placed on some permanent basis, at this particular spot.

---

[1] 1 Sam. x. 7 sq.   [2] Vol. ii. p. 244 sqq.

Now at the time when, according to this narrator, such a crisis was impending, Saul had already reigned two years;[1] he had become better acquainted with his position, and had already learnt by experience the best course to be pursued in military affairs. With the view, therefore, of carrying on operations against the superior force of the Philistines more effectively than was possible by the mere plundering excursions of numerous but untrained levies, he formed a select, well-trained band of 3,000 practised soldiers (as the first beginning of a standing army, raised from the nation itself). He himself took the command of two thousand at Michmash[2] and at Bethel to the north-west; the remaining thousand were stationed under Jonathan at Gibeah, and the rest of the people were dismissed to their homes, for the peaceful cultivation of the land. But after these judicious arrangements on the king's part, the young prince, Jonathan, impelled by his daring spirit, and by shame at the continued indignities which his country had to endure from the Philistines, slays the officer placed by the Philistines in Gibeah, doubtless for the collection of tribute remaining due after former levies.[3] No farther details remain of the origin of this particular quarrel. Jonathan, however, appears throughout as the perfect type of a warrior according to the requirements of his age: he is everywhere the first in courage, in activity, and speed; slender also, and of well-made figure. This personal beauty and swiftness of foot in attack or retreat gained for him among the troops the name of 'The Gazelle':[4] in all this, as in his uprightness and fidelity, he showed himself the right worthy son of a king. But as it was easy to foresee what a tumult would inevitably arise among the Philistines when this feat of Jonathan's should become known, Saul followed up the announcement of this occurrence, and

---

[1] It can only be by some kind of confusion that the words 1 Sam. xiii. 1, are wanting in the LXX., as they certainly belong to the original context; cf. more on this point hereafter. Besides this, something has certainly dropped out of the older document between chapters xi. and xiii., as, in xiii. 2, Jonathan appears without any previous intimation.

[2] This city, now re-discovered as Mukhmâs, is always spoken of as lying farther to the east; and, according to the reading of the LXX. ver. 5, comp. xiv. 23, 31, its position is fixed south-east of Bethaven. On the other hand, the Beth-horon of the LXX. lies, according to Robinson, due east of Michmash.

[3] נְצִיב (wholly different from נְצִיב, a *pillar*) can have no other meaning than the one here assigned to it, as is clear on comparing the passages 1 Sam. x. 5— where we should read נְצִיב—and xiii. 3 sq. with 2 Sam. viii. 6, 14; 1 Kings iv. 19 (cf. verse 7), as well as from the incident itself as here described. This led the LXX. to regard it as a proper name Ναοίβ, 1 Sam. xiii. 3 sq., but they mistook its meaning in x. 5.

[4] That is to say, of the larger species. The first line of the song, 2 Sam. i. 19, can only be explained on the supposition that Jonathan bore this designation in the army at all events, and was clearly enough indicated by it.

SAUL AND HIS HOUSE.

of the threatened danger from the Philistines, by summoning the whole people to assemble in military array at Gilgal. And most vehement indeed is the wrath excited among the Philistines against Israel. Thirty thousand of them in chariots, and six thousand horse,[1] with large numbers of other troops besides, gather themselves together in a strong camp near Michmash, and thence overrun the territory of Israel; so that many Israelites (as formerly under Gideon)[2] hide themselves in caves and in holes, in rocks, in clefts,[3] and in pits; while some flee for refuge beyond the Jordan to the lands of Gad and Gilead.

Meanwhile, all the Israelites in any way capable of bearing arms, gather, full of terror, under Saul's standard at Gilgal. Yet, though the king deems it fully time to march against the enemy, and during the delay those assembled around him are beginning to disperse, he waits seven days till Samuel shall arrive to consecrate by sacrifices the advance of the troops. At length, overcome by impatience, on the seventh day he himself offers the burnt-offering. The ceremony, however, is scarcely over, when on the very same day[4] Samuel punctually arrives; and all the king's cordial greetings and anxious excuses are fruitless, after he has neglected that mysterious warning, and transgressed the only prohibition laid upon him by the higher voice. That what he dreaded in his impatience would not have happened, had he not neglected the divine voice, is known by that same voice which had before so expressly warned him; and Samuel is now obliged to reveal to him, that he has, by his folly, wantonly forfeited the permanence of his kingdom before Jahveh, and that already Jahveh has selected another man after His own heart as prince over His people. And, as if the beginning of his punishment followed at his heels for all to see, Saul, who had hoped by himself offering sacrifice to keep the people together about him, finds himself, on his parting from Samuel, at once deserted by almost all his followers; only about six hundred men being eager enough for battle[5]

---

[1] Unless by some early error these two numbers have been here transposed, as in other passages the number of those fighting in chariots is always inferior to that of the cavalry (2 Sam. x. 18; 1 Kings x. 26; 2 Chron. xii. 3); or, as is still more likely, the number of chariots has been exaggerated. Similarly, the number of chariots is given as 7,000 in 1 Chron. xix. 18; but only as 700 in 2 Sam. x. 18; while Josephus, *Ant.* vi. 6. 1, has as many as 300,000 foot-soldiers, 30,000 chariots, and 60,000 cavalry.

[2] Vol. ii. p. 336.

[3] צרחים LXX. βόθροι should, in my opinion, be compared with ܣܠܥܐ, *rock*; the context shows that it has no analogy in meaning with צְרִיחַ, Judg. ix. 46–49; which is rather to be compared with برج, and the Syriac ܚܣܢܐ, *fortress*. Perhaps חוֹרִים should be read for חוחים.

[4] This must necessarily be taken as the true sense of the narrative.

[5] 1 Sam. xiii. 1–15; verse 15, now greatly mutilated in the Hebrew, has for-

to follow him and his thousand trained warriors to Gibeah. Samuel, on the other hand, after so solemn a declaration, cannot but separate himself for ever from this king, since his prophetic heart and eye are already turned towards another.

Thus, according to the view of this narrator, the happy connexion, hardly even then securely established, is disturbed after two or three years. The union between the two independent powers which augured so many blessings to the people, and was already beginning to fulfil its promise, is again broken up; and broken on that very side which, as the superior in wisdom, had originally anticipated and effected it. But the more trivial the occasion of this breach may appear to us, the more certainly are we able to discern that the isolated case which is here related received its true significance from a long series of connected events, the meaning of which was not obscure. The ruler who out of mere impatience precipitately grasps at that from which he should have withheld his hand, wantonly throws away his true power and his best influence; just as Saul, thinking the seventh day already elapsed, and in consequence prematurely doing what had been forbidden him, had cause on that same seventh day, through Samuel's arrival, bitterly to repent his impatient and unlawful deed. This is the meaning of the last of those four trials of the true king, which is just the one in which Saul failed, and the account of it is distinguished by the same thoughtfulness which marks, with all their brevity, the representations of the first three. Whatever be the particular tradition on which this account is based (for without some such foundation it would not have arisen), it has manifestly only retained, with a sort of vivid reflection, the general impression of that characteristic temperament through which Saul threw away his power. And as if this narrator himself felt that this general aspect of Saul's character as king, with its tragical importance for him, should be more fully exhibited in other instances, he immediately proceeds to relate, from the oldest source, an occurrence which, although taken from the lower side of life, and introducing us farther into the complicated movements of the age, still shows Saul in essentially the same light, injuring by his impatience both himself and his cause.

At that time—proceeds the narrative—the relations of Israel to the Philistines were the most ignominious possible. The Philistines had now added to their conquests the strong camp

---

tunately been preserved quite entire in the LXX.; the words εἰς ἀπάντησιν suggest לַקְרָב 'to battle,' in agreement alike with the context and with 2 Sam. xvii. 11.

SAUL AND HIS HOUSE.

at Michmash,[1] and sent forth thence three bands of soldiers, which in three directions swept plundering through the country;[2] one northwards towards Ophrah, another westwards towards Beth-horon, the third south-east towards the valley of Zeboim. In addition to this, they had for a long time past allowed no smiths to dwell in the land,[3] to prevent the Hebrews from procuring even the most indispensable weapons, swords and spears, so that all the Israelites had to go down into the Philistine territory, when necessary to have their agricultural implements sharpened.[4] Accordingly, in the war which had now broken out,[5] many of the Israelites about Saul and Jonathan had neither swords nor spears; even for these two generals themselves, including of course their immediate servants and armour-bearers, sufficient weapons could with difficulty be found.[6]

Now when during this shameful state of things the advanced guard of the Philistines had pushed forward even beyond the camp at Michmash,[7] Jonathan was impelled by a mixture of youthful impatience and higher courage, accompanied only by his armour-bearer and without his father's knowledge, to advance against it. Two sharp jutting rocks, the extreme points of longer mountain-chains, Seneh running south and Bozez north, separated him from the enemy's position; but neither this, nor the sight of their large numbers could hinder him who, like Israel in the old days under Moses, hopes for victory from Jahveh, thinking 'there is no restraint to Jahveh to give victory with many or with few.' In this mind he finds his comrade in arms also willing to follow him everywhere, as a friend his friend.[8] Yet before actually beginning the work, he

---

[1] P. 30.

[2] המחשית 1 Sam. xili. 17, xiv. 15, is exactly the الغير the freebooter, who goes out only to ravage and plunder, who makes *Algáren* (plundering excursions of cavalry), as they say in Mohammedan and Spanish countries; and thus forms the exact contrast to הַמֻּצָּב the fixed encampment.

[3] Vol. ii. p. 428.

[4] In verse 20, for the last מחרשתו it would be better to read חֲרִיצוֹ and in like manner, in verse 21, חָרִיץ for הַצִּיב, as we see partly from the LXX. (who, however, in each instance, mistook the meaning), and in part from 2 Sam. xii. 31; and if, in ver. 21, we further read לפצירה the sense will be: 'they went to sharpen each one his spade, his ploughshare, his axe, and his threshing-flail; so that with difficulty, i.e. scarcely, was there an edge to their spades, ploughshares, forks, and axes, and pointed threshing-flails.'

[5] It appears from the LXX., that in verse 22, מכמש is wanting after מלחמת: This particular campaign was certainly long called 'the war of Michmash,' on account of the stationary camp there.

[6] 1 Sam. xiii. 16-22.

[7] Verse 23, for מַעֲבַר read מְעָבֵר.

[8] He replies, 'Do all to which thy heart moves thee; I will be with thee, my heart is as thy heart.' We see from the LXX., that the reply, xiv. 7, must be thus amplified; the בְ should be taken from בלבבך and נְטֵה read in place of נְטֵה.

VOL. III. D

longs for a heavenly sign; he will approach the enemy openly and address them; and if they in audacity call out to him to 'come up, they have a word to speak with him,' he will then take this challenge of theirs as a call from Jahveh to advance boldly against them with divine confidence of victory.¹ On the actual occurrence of this sign, he clambers on hands and feet up the precipice, followed by his armour-bearer. The enemy, astonished at such daring, stare at him paralysed; but no sooner is he within reach of them than he strikes them down, while his companion behind him despatches those whom he has disabled.² At the very beginning he thus strikes down twenty men at once, 'as if a yoke of land were in course of being ploughed,' which must beware of offering opposition to the sharp ploughshare in the middle of its work.³ This causes a panic in the camp as in the field, among the soldiers of the garrison as well as among the roving bands of plunderers; the earth resounds with a clamour as if a god had terrified them. When Saul's watchmen on the lofty tower in Gibeah perceive this commotion in the enemy's camp, and on Saul's enquiries Jonathan and his armour-bearer are missed, the king at first wishes to consult the high-priestly oracle as to what should be done; but he is obliged by the terrific increase of the tumult every moment to intermit it, and he rushes forth with his troops into the mêlée.⁴ The slaughter and uproar became then still greater; even the Hebrews who had been forced into service as militia in and around the camp of the Philistines,⁵ took sides with Saul and Jonathan;⁶ the Hebrews also who, in fear of the Philistines, had hidden themselves in holes and corners of the earth,⁷ came forth at the first report of their flight, to join in the pursuit; and great was the victory over an enemy whose strength had been doubtless previously diminished by the despatch of bands for plunder.⁸

---

¹ This gives a very instructive example of how such signs were regarded in actual life, how they were sought and accepted; cf. ii. p. 127, sq.

² xiv. 13, is to be read, according to the LXX., וַיִּפְּנוּ־נָיו אֹתָם as the context shows.

³ 1 Sam. xiii. 23–xiv. 14. מַעֲנָה is here the ploughing itself; and the phrase (misunderstood, however, by the LXX.) thus affords an exceedingly fine and picturesque image; indeed, the descriptions of this narrator overflow throughout with creative insight.

⁴ Verse 16, according to verse 19, and partly, also, according to the LXX., should be thus restored: הֶהָמוֹן בַּמַּחֲנֶה וַיֵּלֶךְ הָלֹם.

Similarly, in verse 18, partly after the LXX., אֵפוֹד should twice be inserted before אֲרוֹן; we should also read וּבְנִי for וּבְנֵי, and farther on, in verse 20, וַיַּעַל for וַיִּזְעַק.

⁵ Vol. ii. p. 428.

⁶ In verse 21, אֲשֶׁר is wanting after הָעִבְרִים, as we see also by the LXX. לִהְיוֹת is used as an infinitive for the description of a surprising fact. Cf. Lehrb. § 351c.

⁷ P. 31.

⁸ 1 Sam. xiv. 15–23.

After the host of the Philistines, in their flight westward, had already pushed through Beth-aven, and about 10,000 men had assembled around Saul, the battle now rolling over Mount Ephraim from city to city,[1] Saul, seeing how the people thronged together and impeded the pursuit, broke forth with an oath, forbidding any man, under pain of death, to take food before the evening, and before complete vengeance was taken on the king's enemies. Accordingly no one ate anything; even when they came to a place where a large surface of ground was covered with wild honey,[2] no one dared, however exhausted, to stretch out his hand to it, for fear of the king's oath. But Jonathan, who had heard nothing of the oath, refreshed himself with a little honey taken on the end of his staff, which he had dipped, as he hastened by, into a honeycomb; and when informed of the condition of the people, broke out into just complaints against his father's want of foresight, which prevented his exhausted men from properly following up their victory. And in fact, when, continuing their pursuit of the enemy without even the refreshment of that wild honey, they arrived at Ajalon in the tribe of Dan, the over-exhausted people seized so greedily on some of the cattle which had been taken as spoil, that Saul could with difficulty restrain them from devouring the flesh with the blood, contrary to law, by hastily setting up a great stone as an altar, on which, in accordance with sacred usage, the cattle should be slaughtered for sacrifice. But when the king, with the ready assent of the people, proposes to sally forth again that very night, still further to chastise the foe, the priest requires that the oracle should be consulted; and as this does not give a favourable answer, the king, seized with misgiving, loudly proclaims before the assembled chiefs that

---

[1] Whatever of these words is wanting in verse 23, must be supplied from the LXX., as properly belonging here. On the other hand, the words of the LXX., verse 24—'and Saul fell into a great error'—awkwardly forestall the course of the narrative; whereas we should here rather be informed what was the exciting cause of the king's oath; and we ought therefore probably to read וַיִּרְא שָׁאוּל אֶת־אִישׁ יִשְׂרָאֵל נִגָּשׁ.

[2] The words, verse 25, of which even the LXX. had lost the correct reading, may possibly be restored by reading בְּאֶרֶץ for בָּאוּ; *the whole land was excavated by wild honey*, or full of holes of wild honey. For יַעַר is undoubtedly wild honey, as we see from *Cant.* v. 1,

while דְּבַשׁ in its primitive meaning is sweetness only, and therefore like دِبْس, may easily be applied to artificial honey also. In יַעַר with this meaning, as we see from ܣܘܓ݁ܠ (which itself interchanges with the מרץ מלץ explained in Job vi. 25), the *j* is softened from *n* or *m*, see my *Lehrb.*, § 51e, 52a; thus וְעָרָה, verse 27, is properly discriminated from it as it is used verse 25 sq.; according to my *Lehrb.* § 176a. And جَحْل, *bee*, whose letters belong to the same phonetic series, is of the same origin, and seems to be spoken for جَحْل, as μέλισσα is derived from μέλι.

there must be some transgression clinging to the people, and that were Jonathan himself the transgressor, he would not spare his life. And so, feeling inwardly bound by his oath, and holding purity before God dearer than his own or his son's life, he presses for decision by means of the sacred lot,[1] amid the ominous silence of the horror-stricken people; and when it falls upon his son, is actually ready to deliver him up to the punishment which even he may not escape. And he is at last hindered only by the determined opposition of the people, who see God's real will with more impartial vision, from sacrificing to God him through whom God had given such deliverance to the people, and thus committing a still more frightful deed than Jephthah[2] once actually carried into execution. Still the people must ransom Jonathan by the death of another in his stead;[3] and under these distressing circumstances, a vigorous pursuit of the victory was not to be thought of.[4] So little capable is Saul, with all his other excellences, of maintaining a lofty circumspection, discretion, and calmness. This may be easily gathered from the present narrative; and if this had become clear already in his far more important connexion with Samuel, it now appears that, after his separation from the latter, the king has gained nothing by the presence of the priest Ahijah[5] and his oracle in his camp.

2. But while the occasion [of the separation of the two powers in the state, as described by this earlier narrator, is certainly only one particular conception of the decisive crisis in the life of Samuel, we further gather from it that we have before us, in chapter xv., another special conception and description of the same great change. This passage was not, it is true, first written by the Deuteronomic editor of the History of the Kings;[6] its whole character indicates that it originated in that period when the prophetic conception and presentation of the older history reached just its highest flight, about the time of the third prophetic narrator of the Primitive History;[7] it is thus of greater antiquity than the Deuteronomic redaction, and more recent than the older work, yet, nevertheless, not by the second principal narrator. But the Deuteronomic editor of the older work has certainly inserted this passage here from another work intentionally, because it

---

[1] xiv. 41, for תָּמִים read תָּמִים, and supply the rest from the LXX.

[2] Vol. ii. p. 394.

[3] Such is certainly the meaning of this passage. A similar interposition of the people, but without any such substitution is related in Liv. viii. 35.

[4] 1 Sam. xiv. 23-46.
[5] 1 Sam. xiv. 3, 37.
[6] Vol. i. p. 157 sq.
[7] Vol. i. p. 106 sq.

depicts the great moment of the history with the utmost vividness, and, if possible, with still loftier and purer truth.

Saul's victorious campaign against Israel's ancient enemy, the people of Amalek,[1] was at least briefly mentioned in the second older work, and raised into prominence as one of the greatest and most meritorious deeds of this first king.[2] It must also, besides this, have been described in an older work, after some detailed tradition; since even the present narrator of chapter xv. has interwoven so many fragments of such a tradition into the midst of his otherwise strictly prophetic representation. One trait of such a primitive tradition is certainly to be found in the narrative which here attracts attention by its very peculiar antique language,[3] viz., that Saul, contrary to the ancient custom of war,[4] spared much of the richer spoil of this campaign, and especially the captive king himself. That this unsanctioned innovation did not pass without protest from the defenders of the old code of the Theocracy, needs not to be said; indeed, there is no difficulty in supposing that it was at this time opposed by Samuel himself, as what is here [5] related of his part in subsequent events bears the clearest traces of antique phraseology and primitive tradition. But the passage before us passes from this isolated tradition to a high prophetic conception of the decisive moment when the two powers of the state separate for ever; and in the lines, so much more sharply drawn, with which the counter-position of Theocracy and Monarchy is indicated, as well as in the most decidedly strong colouring of the prophet's speech against the king, we seem to see the opposition between the two powers carried out to its utmost height and intensity, as it appeared in the kingdom of the Ten Tribes. The narrative by itself stands accordingly as follows:—

Samuel, by special Divine commission, commands Saul, as the king anointed by Jahveh through him, to undertake the sacred war against Amalek; which involved the destruction of all the spoil as a matter of course.

Saul accordingly collects all the forces and musters at Telaim,[6] on the southern frontier, where the army, pushing far southward, assembles to the number of 200,000 foot and

---

[1] Vol. i. p. 259.
[2] 1 Sam. xiv. 48.
[3] 1 Sam. xiv. 9.
[4] Vol. ii. p. 154 sq.
[5] Ibid. verse 32.
[6] This place seems the same as טֶלֶם, Josh. xv. 24. The LXX, indeed, instead of this, read *Gilgal*, as if the advance had commenced from this sacred spot; but the actual muster would more naturally take place on the southern frontier, as the troops from Judah would hardly move at first so far north as Gilgal,

10,000 men of Judah.¹ He advances safely as far as the capital of the enemy, and having placed part of the army in ambush in a valley, is ready for the assault; but he first of all summons the Kenites from the midst of the enemy to join him, that he may spare them.² The plans of the brave leader are perfectly successful; the enemy are beaten throughout the length and breadth of their land, from Havilah in the east to Shur in the west, on the Egyptian frontier; but much of the most valuable part of the spoil, with king Agag himself, is spared by the king. In particular, the best herds and the stores of provisions are not destroyed, the flourishing vineyards not laid waste.³ The victorious king, accordingly, returns with rich booty and with king Agag, whose life he has spared, to the city of Carmel in southern Judah, where he commences the erection of a trophy of victory; then, after a short rest, he returns northeast towards Gilgal, and in this consecrated centre of the kingdom offers in sacrifice the first-fruits of the spoil.⁴ Samuel is then surprised in a dream by the announcement of Jahveh, that Saul can be no longer looked upon as the king who is worthy to stand before God. As a type of the true Prophet, he is at first himself terrified at these evil tidings, and wrestles in prayer the whole night through to be set free from the duty thus implicitly imposed upon him. But it is in vain. When he meets Saul, and the latter, receiving him with due honour, professes to have fulfilled Jahveh's commission, the distant lowing of the herds which had been saved from the general destruction betrays to the quick ear of the prophet what must have happened. Saul cannot deny it; and when Samuel goes on to demand how he, who must know himself to be as a mere man so insignificant, and yet had been exalted so high by Jahveh,⁵ could out of mere greed of booty have so transgressed Jahveh's express command, it is in vain that the king seeks to excuse himself, on the ground that he had been compelled to offer the sacrifices at the people's request.⁶ Then,

---

¹ The LXX. raise the numbers to 400,000, and 30,000 respectively. In the words which follow, Saul's plans for the battle and their execution are given only fragmentarily from the earlier source, so that it is not surprising that later readers found special difficulty in understanding the וַיָּרֶב in verse 5. We must therefore assume that an ambush had been previously laid, as in Judg. xx. 33 sq.

² Vol. ii. p. 44 sqq.

³ xv. 9. From the context and construction, מַשְׁמַנִּים is to be read, following the LXX., for מִשְׁנִים—comp. Neh. viii. 10; and again, כָּרִים for כָּרְמִים; since the destruction of the vineyards may certainly be reckoned in the total destruction of the most valuable property of a nation; Is. xvi. 7-9. In Saul's speech, verse 15, an enumeration of all details, beyond the flocks and herds, is not to be expected.

⁴ 1 Sam. xv. 1-12; to this effect is the Hebrew text, verse 12, to be restored from the LXX.: cf. vv. 15 and 21.

⁵ P. 6 sq.

⁶ 1 Sam. xv. 10-21.

as in a sudden storm of exalted feeling, the prophet pours forth the winged words which will not be repressed :

> Hath Jahveh pleasure in burnt-offerings and sacrifices
> As in obedience to the voice of Jahveh?
> Behold, obedience is better than sacrifice,
> And to follow than the fat of rams!
> For disobedience is the sin of heathenism,
> Disbelief is idols and devils;
> Because thou hast rejected the word of Jahveh,
> He hath rejected thee also as His king.[1]

Earnestly indeed does Saul entreat forgiveness, professing that he had only acted so from fear of the people, nay, when Samuel declares himself unable to accept this (certainly idle) excuse, he seizes the skirt of the prophet's robe with such despairing energy that it is rent. But even this unexpected chance becomes—as Samuel, carried away by the exaltation of the moment, hastens to add—a confirmatory sign that even so is his kingdom torn from him, and given by Jahveh to one more worthy; and only to maintain the honour of the reigning king before the Elders and the people, does Samuel turn back in apparent peace with the self-abasing Saul.[2] But first of all Samuel will himself execute on the Amalekite king, Agag, the judgment which Saul—as if kings, for the very honour of their craft, must spare each other—had omitted to inflict. Waiting in the holy place to hew him down with his own hand as a sacrifice, he calls out to him:

> 'As thy sword hath made women childless,
> So shall thy mother be made still more [3] childless.'

And how acceptable to the altar this sacrifice really proved in atonement for the many misdeeds of his people, was shown by the advance of the Amalekite king towards him, not, as might have been feared, and as Saul probably had feared, unwilling and struggling, but rather, as if suddenly transformed by a loftier impulse, with delight and joy, exclaiming, 'Surely the bitterness of death is past.'[4]

---

[1] It is, indeed, a sin to follow heathen customs, to serve idols (און), and devils (properly house-gods, private gods); but it cannot be more sinful than rebellion against the higher eternal truth: resisting this in unbelief is really equivalent to heathenism. Thus clearly is one of the highest prophetic ideas anticipated here. After ממלך —verse 23—לו is probably wanting, some such word being here almost necessary to the sense, however appropriate the admirable brevity of these verses may be in other passages. The LXX. supply still more.

[2] 1 Sam. xv. 22–31.

[3] *Still more*, because in losing her son she loses also the king of her people, and her loss is thus greater than that of any other bereaved mother in the nation.

[4] Vv. 32–34. It is well known that the ancients accounted it an evil omen if the victim resisted when led to the altar, or was snatched away from it (vol. i. pp. 330, 332). And this very portion of the narrative seems to be of great antiquity. The description of Cassandra's death in the *Agamemnon* of Æschylus, l. 1245, sqq. is very similar.

3. It is then incontestable, that each of these two higher representations only raises into prominence one special feature of the great crisis in Saul's life as king, and connects with it the embodiment of the whole truth, which was too profound to be grasped at once. The relative position of such powers as the prophetic and the monarchical belongs altogether to the depths rather than to the surface of life, and their alliance or hostility does not rest on single and apparently casual incidents of history; the solitary instance which is noted and was perhaps the most frequently retold, is only a special expression of a permanent state of feeling between the two powers, which had long before acquired its strength in secret.

But all this only confirms the decisive fact which emerges from all these manifold conceptions, and is at the same time recognised plainly enough by its consequences throughout the whole subsequent development of the history. The two powers of the state, which had at first begun by harmoniously cooperating for the suppression of the deep-rooted corruption of the age and the establishment of that prosperity which the nation so much needed, now fell into lasting disunion. The same power which, as the older, had recognised the need of the younger, and had striven zealously to raise it to an equal elevation, seems now, without very important grounds, to be the one to separate. The same man who, nobly willing to sacrifice his own power, had brought about this happy change, appears inexplicably to shatter the very vessel which he himself had chosen.

But a deeper investigation of the whole connexion between the development of centuries and all the great historical truths, proves most conclusively how necessary, how inevitable even, as a consequence of his unique greatness, was the action of this prophet, who in our modern times has been a riddle to many superficial readers. For we must above everything beware of importing into the age of the commencement of monarchy in Israel, the idea of royal authority fully developed, with its independent grasp and control over everything in the kingdom, as we see it prevailing, certainly to our great advantage, in our own states. To conceive such an idea, at least in the clearness with which we are now generally able to apprehend it, and consequently under the necessary limitations with which, at any rate in the best states of our day, it is both understood and applied, was not so easy and natural for that primitive age. The early history of true monarchy in Israel shows us that its origin had nothing to do with the external grandeur of a state, but sprang out of the deepest needs of a particular age for the true welfare of the people; and at the same time it makes it clear that a power which arises out of such necessities, under the pressure of special times and circumstances, finds at first only a limited sphere of activity, and has as much as it can do to perform even those duties with tolerable efficiency. But it is equally characteristic of it not to remain long confined within such narrow bounds; and it may early feel the impulse to aspire beyond the limits immediately imposed on it, for the full development of its absolute power in every direction. But as long as it fails to satisfy the immediate purpose of its existence, and yet on the other hand aims at subduing beneath its authority what it is still incapable of comprehending, it will lose even that footing which it has at first successfully obtained.

The earliest narrative, as we have seen above, represents Saul to have been chosen not so much for the common business of a judge, i.e. for the purpose of giving decisions between citizens according to the existing law, or, in default of precedent, according to his own best judgment; still less with reference to religion, as if he were authorised arbitrarily to determine its rites and institutions; but to secure unity and strength for the state. It is to enable him to make the nation powerful and honoured abroad, united and well-ordered at home, and to maintain it so, that he is invested with authority, such as had been given before to no one in that community; and that not temporarily, but for ever. Whatever sacrifices of former rights and liberties may be necessary for this end, the people must and will now endure; and Samuel was not the man to concede royal authority by halves. If, then, the whole nation desires to obtain through a king the blessings of greater union at home and power abroad, it must grant him all means needful for the purpose, must indeed, so far as necessity requires, place all its powers at his disposal; and with this royal authority Saul is, in fact, invested from the beginning. He alone possesses supreme civil and military power, and has the right of calling out the levies; for permanent purposes, however, of war or administration, or for his own service, he can take any subject he pleases to be his servant in a higher or lower capacity.[1] His demands, therefore, on his subjects for personal services could not help being larger and more varied, in proportion to the absence of arrangement or custom for the payment of con-

---

[1] The further details given on this subject in 1 Sam. viii. 11–17, are only the later one-sided development and distortion of the proper ancient prerogative of the king. See p. 27; comp. 1 Sam. xiv. 52.

tributions in kind or taxes in money. And as he is best able to estimate the services which any individuals of especial merit or ability may render or have it in their power to render to the common weal, he has also the right of releasing individuals from the ordinary services of subjects, and in so far constituting them freeholders; and this high distinction would easily come to be looked upon as hereditary, like royalty, in the whole family, and as forming an intermediate stage between the king and a simple subject.[1] All these essential attributes of royal prerogative are accordingly possessed and freely exercised by Saul.

And at the beginning, he knows very well what is the main purpose for which he has become king; and working in this direction, he soon finds his authority among the people strengthened. The judicial office accordingly remains at first very much what it previously was; Samuel, it is expressly recorded,[2] judged the people all the days of his life; and the institutions of religion continue what their historic development had made them. Samuel is still, as before the change, the revered prophet; the usual functions of the priests sustain no interruption. That the increase of the king's power at home should keep pace with his victories abroad, and thus attain, by quiet unobtrusive steps, the full extent belonging to it, followed as a matter of course. We do not read that Samuel was dissatisfied because the people turned to the king as an ultimate appeal; even the fact that he offered sacrifices in the name of the whole people, and thus assumed what was earlier the High-Priest's office, is not by any means—at least, according to the narrative in ch. xv.—a subject of reproach from the Prophet; while the offering of those sacrifices which Samuel, according to the earlier narrator,[3] had reserved to himself under special circumstances, and in Gilgal alone, need by no means imply that in the writer's conception the king had in general no right of sacrifice. Had Saul, therefore, understood the art of allowing the royal power to unfold itself with the quiet progress of time, he would unquestionably, at a period in every way favourable to the growth of this indispensable authority, have gained the same high degree of it which we afterwards see his great successor David attain, so much to the welfare at once of himself and his people.

---

[1] חָפְשִׁי is used in this sense in 1 Sam. xvii. 25; on the other hand, חֹר or חוֹר is more often simply *noble, noble-born*; and is more a term of later use. An example of this *freedom* in other oriental states may be found in the *Journal Asiatique*, 1857, i. p. 404.

[2] 1 Sam. vii. 15. The names of Saul and Samuel are actually used together in a command to the people, xi. 7.

[3] 1 Sam. x. 8; xiii. 8–12.

But Saul is not quite the man for this. His virtues are indeed undeniably great; and it is quite probable that among his contemporaries of his own age there might be none so well fitted as he for the royal dignity. Those qualities which must have been most essential and most imperatively demanded of him as king in that age—warlike courage and skill, indomitable energy to push his conquests in all directions, a sense of honour ever vigilant for the welfare of his people against their many and powerful foes, zeal and perseverance in carrying out his plans;—that he possessed all these in a high degree, is clear from every trace of his life which we can anywhere discover. That he was in all points the ablest in war, and so often brought back from it rich booty to the women who celebrated his victories, is indeed almost the only, but it is also the just praise bestowed by David in his lament on the newly-fallen hero;[1] and this no doubt only echoed the general judgment of his contemporaries. We cannot now, it is true, follow his wars in much detail, since it is only of those with the Philistines and the Amalekites, that we find any particulars recorded. According to the brief summary of his royal achievements given by an earlier narrator,[2] he had to fight, immediately on assuming the sovereignty, with all the neighbouring nations in turn; with the Moabites, Ammonites, or Idumæans on the east, with the kings of Zobah on the north-east,[3] with the Philistines on the west, and the Amalekites on the south. It would seem as if all these neighbouring tribes had bestirred themselves the more boldly during his reign, from the well-founded foreboding which they might naturally feel, that if once the new monarchy became strong in Israel, their own power must come to an end. But that he was generally victorious, follows from the brief words which this narrator appends to the enumeration of the nations with whom he fought; 'wherever he turned, he conquered.'

We must guard against under-estimating the glory of a

---

[1] 2 Sam. i. 21-24.

[2] 1 Sam. xiv. 47 sq., where for ירשׁיע (which seems to have been introduced into the text through the later strongly unfavourable opinion of Saul, like the points above the letters, Gen. xxxiii. 4), יושׁיע should be read. In the important passage 1 Sam. xiv. 47 sq. the LXX. mention besides a Βαιθαιώρ; if for this we read Βαιθασώρ, we get the ancient Canaanite name חצור, only that the one intended here would not be that in Judges iv. 2, but in Jer. xlix. 28. In this case the passage would then contain a noteworthy allusion to an ancient kingdom. Comp. also the suggestion in ii. p. 325 respecting the results of Saul's great wars. He has received most honour from the Arabs, through Islamism; Mohammed himself (Sur. ii. 247-257) having coupled him, under the similarly-formed name Tâlût (cf. also Tâghût) with G'âlût, i.e. Goliath as his true antagonist.

[3] See below, under David.

hero whose history is thrown into the shade by the stronger light of his greater successor, and yet under whom a real heroic school of great warriors must evidently have arisen. And even if the Philistines, at that time [1] so exceedingly strong, were never permanently subdued by him, and towards the end of his reign, when everything in the kingdom was sinking lower and lower, pushed their advantage with renewed violence—on the other hand, his victory over the Amalekites was all the more decisive, inasmuch as, for a long period, they almost disappear from history. What lasting aid he had rendered to the inhabitants of Jabesh [2] was shown even after his death, when grateful citizens came thence over the Jordan to bear in secret from the field of battle the disfigured corpses of himself and of his sons, and give them honourable burial among themselves.[3] The efficiency of the protection he had afforded, up to the very time of his death, at any rate to the country beyond the Jordan, is evident from the fact that his son and successor fixed the seat of his government there for some years. Besides this, a noble zeal for the maintenance of the customs of the ancient religion animates his soul; and although he is not himself consecrated (Nazirite) or a prophet, but according to the well-known narratives is only visited for a moment by the breath of prophecy,[4] he is yet evidently at first possessed not a little by that powerful impulse of strict religion and daring enthusiasm for the cause of Jahveh,[5] which is the characteristic life and greatness of this period. With what zeal, even while eagerly engaged in pursuing a foe, he checks a transgression against the laws of religion, such as eating flesh with the blood, we have already seen;[6] and the stern expulsion of all kinds of sorcerers from the land,[7] as well as the numerous altars with their proper sacrifices which he built to Jahveh,[8] shows how he employed the leisure he could snatch from war in restoring with a strong hand, even in the interior of the country, the purity of the ancient religion. Nor are traits of truly royal magnanimity wanting, especially at the beginning of his reign.[9] And how faithfully he adhered during his whole reign, even after he had won important victories and had assuredly tasted at times the seduc-

---

[1] According to vol. ii. p. 428.
[2] P. 24.
[3] 1 Sam. xxxi. 11–13; cf. 1 Sam. xxi. 12 [11].
[4] Vol. ii. p. 425.
[5] Vol. ii. p. 391 sq.
[6] P. 35.
[7] 1 Sam. xxviii. 3, 9, an account evidently authentic.

[8] This follows from the short intimation in 1 Sam. xiv. 35, that the altar there referred to was *the first* which he built; the narrator was then going on to explain the origin of the others; how much of his work must, according to this, have been lost!
[9] 1 Sam. xi. 12 sq.

tive repose of peace, to the simplicity and modesty of his primitive domestic habits, is evident from the circumstance that he had only one wife and one concubine.¹ And how readily, despite occasional faults, the people acknowledged his merits in the main, and what affection he was able to inspire towards himself and his house, is very plainly shown by the fact, that we find no trace of a rising against him, or of any general discontent; and it needed the confirmed folly of his son and successor to drive the tribes of Israel as a body to desert his dynasty. We must beware of undervaluing, on account of the gloomy events which obscure his later history, the greatness of a hero who was the first to win honour and dignity for the monarchy in Israel, and whose virtues were far greater than those of so many later kings who, in the shadow of a firmly established throne, had a softer, often only too soft, a seat. That infinite charm which the name 'Anointed of Jahveh' carried with it for centuries, and the effect of which was the most marvellous at first, was first spread by him; nay, he won for himself besides, from the people's lips, in the brightest period of his reign, the still higher title, 'Chosen of Jahveh.'² The truest testimony to this opinion of his time respecting him, is given by his own great rival and younger contemporary, David; who, even when pursued by him, cherishes the most scrupulous reverence for the 'Anointed of Jahveh.' Nor could a more beautiful expression be given to the way in which two really great spirits, who are each pursuing a different course, may still, under the constraining influence of Divine truth, meet in freer moments as friends, than in the story of the involuntary compulsion by which Saul is forced, out of magnanimity, to acknowledge the still higher magnanimity of his enemy David.³

But with all these kingly virtues, there is gradually developed in him a peculiar bent of mind, quite capable of neutralising a great part of their most valuable effects. An extreme impetuosity in following up an enterprise easily fostered in eager natures by an age of strong excitement and immoderate practice of vows, marks his behaviour at the battle of Michmash;⁴ and in the same way that this impetuosity then led to the inconsiderate imposition of a vow upon the people, and to other lamentable consequences, it was not uncommon for the first king of Israel to be betrayed under pressure of circumstances into similar acts of thoughtlessness. But the bitter

---

[1] 1 Sam. xiv. 49; 2 Sam. iii. 7; xxi. 8-12.   [3] 1 Sam. xxvi. 25; see below.
[2] P. 6.   [4] P. 33 sqq.

fruits of such precipitation easily excite in a man who is conscious at the bottom of his original good intentions, that jealous suspicion the poison-breath of which is nowhere so near and at the same time so deadly to the sufferer and all his surroundings as in that elevated rank, where it can always ally itself with the greatest outward power, and can thus easily carry out its sinister suggestions. And it is indisputable that Saul, to be able to act as king at all, had to overcome difficulties and remove obstacles about which none of his successors needed to trouble himself nearly as much. It was only human nature that in proportion to the resistance his good intentions might encounter, he should sink the deeper into the snare of an ever-growing suspicion of everything around him. And further, in a community like that of Israel, where, even for the most elevated in the nation, there remained always standing clear before them something higher still, an inviolable sanctity and blessed life,—in such a community, it cannot be denied, it was all the more easy for the king to fall into an uncomfortable and depressed condition, did he not continually approach more and more closely to that higher life, and ever strive the more bravely in right faith and deed to cleave the dark cloud which seemed to part him from it. But the growing subjection of the great hero of God's people to this human passion and gloom, without being able to free himself again from its power, presents itself as the momentous crisis of his life, where human excuse and Divine blame meet side by side. We cannot now trace the first germ and growth of Saul's passion; in the tradition respecting him, it appears almost at once in full violence. The evil spirit which, according to the tradition, perpetually troubled him, is nothing but this royal jealousy, ever reappearing in stronger and more deadly guise; sometimes indeed appeased for a while, but constantly returning in fresh strength, and as constantly finding new material to work upon. Before it vanish at last all consistent action, all wise and moderate rule. If it impels him to-day from whatsoever motive (were it only to display his royal supremacy) to spare more of the booty than is permitted by sacred usage,[1] it urges him to-morrow to deal more unsparingly than custom sanctioned with the Gibeonites,[2] or even to destroy an entire priestly city for a mere suspicion.[3] And from this influence all men have to suffer alike, friend and foe, servant and son, priest and prophet. But how in David he drives away not only his bravest but his most faithful subject, will be shown farther on.

---

[1] P. 38. [2] 2 Sam. xxi. 1-6 ; see more below. [3] 1 Sam. xxii. 9-23.

In this, then, lies the true reason of the breach between Samuel and Saul. For that Saul by no means despised the prophetic voice as such, or desired to make himself quite independent of it, is self-evident from the whole history of the age. No king of that period would or could have done so. Saul, according to the earlier narrator, as soon as Samuel has departed from him, asks counsel of a high-priest;[1] according to a later narrator, he even craves for consolation from Samuel after his death.[2] But no true prophet could suffer the king, a mere shuttlecock of passion, to violate the inviolable; and Samuel was the last person to do so. And so, if Samuel had before been great as Judge, Prophet, and Founder of the Monarchy, he now displayed still nobler qualities by his action at this crisis contrary to the whole bent of his life. As soon as this tendency became unmistakably manifest in Saul, he turned away from him with the same decision with which he had before raised him up; like a father regardless of his own beloved child reared up to manhood with care and hope, when the ruin of others is involved. For had he spared this his spiritual child, when to spare him would have been contrary to the fundamental law of the Theocracy itself, the worst possible precedent would have been afforded for future ages by this first king. But he had not founded the monarchy that the Theocracy might become a kingdom of human caprice and self-will. The very motive, therefore, which induced him, in spite of all considerations, to found the new institution as a necessity, must have equally induced him to exert all his power to shield it, when once founded, from any perversion during the first period of its development.

The only weapon which he employs for this purpose is separation from Saul, in the impossibility of cooperating with him for the true objects of his life. There is no evidence that he ever employed worse instruments against him, as will be seen still more clearly hereafter. In doing this, however, he only did what he was bound to do; and it was in fact without his own will that this action became his weapon. Even in his separation from the king he is still great enough, and has important work enough to do. He retires to Ramah, his native city and his old prophetic seat, there to devote himself only more exclusively to the training of younger prophets and citizens, and to lay the true spiritual foundations of national welfare the more indestructibly for the future.[3] And as he

---

[1] P. 35 sq.
[2] 1 Sam. xxviii. 3-25; see below.
[3] 1 Sam. xix. 19-24; comp. xiii. 15 (LXX.); xv. 34; xxv. 1; xxviii. 3.

can thus work quietly and gradually, yet in the end irresistibly, upon king and people, he thus gains a second and really more dangerous, though wholly inoffensive, weapon.

But should anyone suggest, that if this was to be the end of it, Samuel would have done better not to choose in the beginning an instrument which would have to be rejected, he would be trying in his acuteness to be wiser than history and the Bible itself. The Bible does not hesitate to relate that the Spirit of God through Samuel chose and rejected Saul. It thus leaves proper scope to human freedom, since the rejection does not occur without actual guilt on Saul's part; yet it intimates besides that above both choice and rejection stands something Higher than the great prophet himself. For to suppose that Samuel would have chosen Saul had he foreseen his aberration as it really occurred, would be to make him out what he was not, a bad man; and that (as some moderns have conceitedly presumed) he purposely selected the king out of Benjamin, then the weakest tribe of Israel, in order that he might more easily control him, is nothing but a miserable conjecture, which only shows what would have been the conduct of the persons who have hit upon this silly idea, if they had been called upon to act under the same circumstances as Samuel. It is enough to note that the tribe of Benjamin[1] was the most warlike of all; that Saul's native city Gibeah was at no great distance from Samuel's residence; and that this Gibeah was a holy place, the dwelling-place of prophets, where a heroic youth might easily catch some similar inspiration of higher life;[2] and especially that, as we have seen, the tribe of Ephraim, or, failing that, the closely allied tribe of Benjamin, possessed from the earliest times a claim to the dignity of a leading tribe, and therefore also to royalty, which it was the duty of Samuel not to overlook.

III. THE FALL OF SAUL AND HIS HOUSE.

1. We have seen that Saul, the royal hero of his time, could not but injure himself and his kingdom more and more, by the jealous suspicion growing and spreading in his mind like a creeper winding round the healthy stem. The stages of the development of this evil and its manifestation towards others can no longer be traced in detail or with chronological precision. The extant narratives content themselves with indicating their progress by one single example, which the magnitude of its

[1] Vol. ii. p. 281. [2] P. 22.

subsequent consequences certainly renders the more important and striking, that of David; yet this is better reserved for the life of the younger hero himself.

No mention, however, is made of any display of this jealousy towards Samuel, even after his separation; moreover, from the facts of the case we have every reason to suppose, that Saul never ventured to turn his rage against the hoary Prophet, who had once elevated him to the royal dignity, and who now stood aloof from him in silence. For a hero like Saul is great even in his fall, and is more easily guilty of some inconsistency in action, than wholly forgetful of the cause to which he owes his first elevation from humble rank, and his brightest memories of better years. The silence of Samuel's separation Saul carefully maintains on his part; the two great powers of the state, which could only work for the general welfare when united in friendship by the higher truth, are separated by an over-ruling power, but do not attack each other with such weapons as the wily popes of the Middle Ages sedulously employed to weaken and annihilate our best emperors.

But since Saul, although king, can never forget his origin, this silent withdrawal of the great Prophet, when it is once seen to be a decided and irrevocable step, may well be enough to touch him in the most tender point. He thought perhaps for a time that on the proud eminence of royalty he should be able to do without the timely warnings and restraining influence of the Divine voice within, and he acted at least as if he really thought so. But now that he has reached the moment for dispensing in reality with that which he fancied himself able to dispense with, it becomes for the first time evident how little it is possible for him to do so; and he sinks back deeper and deeper into an abyss of perplexity and weakness. He has not the strength to raise himself again in the right way and without any surrender of kingly dignity to that sunny height which he had in other days so nearly approached, and whose warmth had once animated even him for the better life. Nor, again, is he so degenerate as really to destroy that prophetic elevation, even if in some rash moment he had wished to do so. Once (so runs the beautiful and only too true narrative) he was informed that the dreaded David was in the school built near Ramah,[1] and he despatched messengers thither to take him.

---

[1] 1 Sam. xix. 19–24 by the second narrator. For נוית which occurs six times between xix. 18 and xx. 1, the Keri reads every time נָיוֹת as if it meant נָאוֹת *dwellings*; but this usual meaning is here entirely unsuitable, and it is much better to treat נָוִית as a word of quite different formation in the sing.; it would then be

No sooner, however, did they behold the circle of prophets at that moment engaged under their teacher Samuel in their sacred exercises, than they felt themselves seized by the same spirit, and joined the circle in similar exercises. The same thing befell fresh messengers, a second, nay, a third time. Then Saul, enraged, rushed himself to Ramah, enquired at the well by the threshing-floor on the adjoining hill where the (newly-built) school was; but on the very way thither, as he looked down from the hill upon the school, and heard the loud-pealing songs issuing from it, he was seized by the Divine spirit, and when he at last reached the spot, sank into the same condition of enthusiasm still more deeply than all the messengers whom he had previously despatched.[1]

It was thus out of the hero's power to abandon in his inmost heart what he had in earlier times acknowledged as his better self. But he was still too weak to raise himself to it once more in full activity, and thus that better aim, which he despised even while he still felt it a necessity to him in his heart of hearts, and ever yearned after it, at any rate, in secret and darkness, was avenged on him, inasmuch as he really did once more turn towards it, but not till too late, in the last agonising moments of his life. This is the true end of his destiny, the supreme tragic suffering beneath which the great hero of his time succumbs. And it is from the point of view of the fulfilment of this higher truth, that the last moments of Saul's life are conceived by that narrator who had also portrayed with the most vivid colouring the decisive moment of his life as king, the separation of the two powers of the state.[2] It is possible and credible that, long after Samuel's death, his shade was the subject of the spectral illusions practised by necromancers; who artfully imitated the whole language and manner of the great Prophet for those who were desirous of hearing his voice once more. From the earliest ages such black arts had their home in Egypt, the native land of necrolatry, and were thence transferred to Canaan; and the majority of enquirers would certainly wish to hear from among the dead those who in life had given the best oracles. Accordingly, when Saul—so it is related[3]—in the greatest alarm, before the battle

---

much the same as *school*, properly *studium*, just as ذ٠ indicates the special direction of mental power upon something; and is study anything else? The purport of the whole narrative shows that the school was not situated in Ramah itself. In verse 22 we should read, according to the LXX., הַגֹּרֶן for הַגָּדוֹל and שְׂפִי for שְׂכוּ, or at any rate, the latter is to be interpreted as 'view,' i.e. height.

[1] A very similar event is related in the life of Buddha. See the *Journal of the American Oriental Soc.*, iii. p. 63 sq.
[2] 1 Sam. xv.; p. 36 sqq.
[3] 1 Sam. xxviii. 3–25.

in which he was to fall, had tried in vain by dreams,[1] by priestly oracles and prophets to hear the voice of Jahveh, the very man who in earlier and better days had banished all magicians,[2] was conducted in disguise to a well-known sorceress in Endor; he hushes her dread of discovery, and requires her to conjure up Samuel. But the instant she beholds the shadow of the mighty dead ascending, she starts up with a scream of terror, for she sees him arise no longer calm and mild, but with gestures of fearful menace, such as he could only show towards a deadly enemy, i.e. towards Saul. The woman thus perceives that Saul is her questioner, and asks why he has deceived her by his disguise. But he is satisfied as soon as he knows that Samuel is really there, and kneels down in homage, yet only to receive from the angry spirit of the dead the blame he deserves, and the mournful announcement of the approach of his last doom; so that, instead of finding comfort, he sinks in an agony of terror to the ground, and can scarcely be encouraged to rise up, and, after some needful refreshment, go on his way.[3]

2. But deeply as the hero has fallen from the elevation at which he started, yet the bright side of his history reappears at the end in his death, a death worthy of his virtues. He falls by no traitor or domestic foes; he still fights bravely in the hardest battle of his life against the Philistines; but, ever accustomed to victory, he will not survive the defeat already but too plain; and so he falls, to receive immediately from his own great rival the rightful praise of his virtues, and in his immortal song to live for ever among men as his better self.[4]

The fall of the founder of a new kingdom and dynasty, if affairs are out of order at the time of his death, is apt to entail the ruin of his whole house. It is, therefore, the mark of an unusual attachment on the part of the peoples to their first king, that all the tribes except Judah, even under the most unfavourable circumstances, raised his only surviving son, Ishbosheth, to power, although, so far as appears, before he

---

[1] I.e., through sleeping in a sacred place (cf. i. 329); it is remarkable that this also should be done with reference to Jahveh. See an instance in Athenæus' *Deip.* xiii. 68.

[2] By this addition, vv. 3, 9, Saul's act is condemned beforehand by the narrator as running counter to the religion of Jahveh; but it is equally certain that the narrator means that what Saul heard was really the angry spirit-voice of Samuel, and not mere deceptive words from the witch. He thus condemns this mode of seeking an oracle as impious, but does not deny that the dead, or at least, a spirit like Samuel's, could speak after death. On R. Tanchûm's explanation, see the remarks in the *Tüb. Theol. Jahrbb.* 1845, p. 574.

[3] In modern times Saul has been often made the subject of a tragedy. The account of the first narrator, as I have remarked in the new edition of the first vol. of the *Dichter des Alten Bundes*, is probably derived from a drama.

[4] 2 Sam. i. 19-27.

assumed the sovereignty, he had not gained any particular distinction. And had he, at least as king, shown himself worthier of his father, he would probably never, or at any rate far less readily, have sunk before David's rising might. But his own folly brought him in a few years to the ground; and with him the house of Saul, of which only a few miserable off-shoots could have been left, fell for ever from the throne. But all this, being so closely connected with the history of David, will be better explained further on.

3. And finally, the duration of the whole reign of Saul is not without influence on the view taken of the fall of his house. On this subject we find no information in the present Books of Samuel; but it cannot be doubted that it was supplied in the work of the older narrator;[1] it can, then, only have been lost in the later re-casting of this work on the part of the Deuteronomic narrator, at a period when no great importance was any longer attached to such chronological specifications in this portion of the history. Recent scholars, taking their stand on Acts xiii. 21, have very generally assumed forty years as the duration of Saul's reign; without reflecting what serious contradictions would thence arise. For[2] Saul had only reigned two years when he organised the picked bands of warriors, and placed his son Jonathan over one of them. He must, consequently, at the beginning of his reign have had a son already about twenty years old; and indeed it was naturally to be expected that no very young man would have been chosen for the first king of Israel, when the country was involved in the most serious difficulties. If, then, Saul when he became king was already in the prime of manhood, and had a son twenty years old, he would, according to this assumption of a forty years' reign, have fallen in a grey old age, and Jonathan on the verge of it, in the battle which carried them both off; and who will accept such a result, in the face of the surviving particulars of the history? But, in fact, the origin of this number forty has been already explained;[3] and so far has certainly its proper meaning. Jose-

---

[1] Without observing that this narrator fixes other periods even for the history before Saul, it is sufficient to point out that he allows much smaller periods in the history of Saul; in x. 27, according to the LXX., cf. above, p. 24, and xiii. 1, he gives two dates about Saul at the same time. In the latter passage the number of years of Saul's age on his accession must have fallen out after בן; perhaps in the redaction of the work, at all events, at a very early date, since even the LXX. omitted the verse as untranslatable. As we see from the Hexapla, an old Greek reader had here supplied the number thirty, certainly only by his own conjecture, and it will probably remain impossible for us to fill up this hiatus. How absurdly Eusebius attempts to explain this corrupt passage, is best read in his own words, *Chr. Arm.*, i. p. 170. The explanations of the Rabbis are equally ridiculous: see Tanchûm *in loc.*

[2] According to p. 30.

[3] Vol. ii. p. 369 sq.

phus, however, by no means asserts absolutely that he reigned forty years; but that he reigned eighteen years until Samuel's death, and thus contemporaneously with him, and twenty-two after his death; but instead of the number twenty-two, there is found as a different reading the number two; and we have every reason to consider this reading the more correct.[1] We thus obtain a period of twenty years for Saul's reign, which corresponds to all the other remaining indications; and that Samuel died only about two years before the end of Saul's own life, is the purport of all the accounts of his relation to David and Saul. Even in the present work the mention of his death is pushed so far forward,[2] that he is evidently assumed by this authority to have died but a short time before the death of Saul and the reign of David. Whence Josephus derived these dates, we are indeed no longer able to specify particularly; but they are so little exposed to contradictions, that one feels inclined to assume that they were obtained from earlier sources.

If Saul's reign, accordingly, lasted only about twenty years, a better explanation is afforded why his kingdom was still so far from being firmly established, and why his house could easily lose the sovereignty after his death. And indeed, the increasing entanglement of such a hero, in many ways so worthy of royalty, in the snares of a growing jealousy, is, humanly speaking, easier to understand, if he had already attained the prime of life when first raised to a dignity so novel to himself and in Israel so entirely strange. For if, even for one born a prince, without having been early trained (like David) by the severe discipline of life to kingly thoughts, it is often difficult to keep free from jealousy, and in pure trust in God to trust also the best among men, how much more so for him who only attains in ripe manhood a dignity of which neither he nor his nation has had any experience! Such considerations do not, it is true, diminish Saul's guilt; but it is for us to recognise how difficult it is to maintain moral greatness, when even such a hero fell from the purest elevation of life into ever deeper degradation.

---

[1] Because only twenty years are assigned to him (*Ant.* x. 8. 4). That Saul reigned at the same time as Samuel, and that the latter died two years before him, is asserted also by Clem. Alex. *Strom.* i. 21; to Samuel he assigns twenty-seven, to Saul twenty years; but twenty-seven is obviously a mistake for thirty-seven or thirty-eight. Eupolemus, in Eus. *Præp. Ev.* ix. 30, ascribes twenty-one years to Saul; and in the Chronicle, Eusebius puts forty years for both together; while G. Syncellus wrongly assigns to Samuel twenty, and to Saul forty years. Cf. ii. p. 371 sq.

[2] 1 Sam. xxv. 1; xxviii. 3; cf. particularly with xxvii. 7, and the further explanations given below. That Samuel died about two years before Saul may be deduced with certainty from these passages.

B. DAVID.[1]

HIS RELATION TO HIS AGE.

Now come the sunny days of David's rule,—the great period in which the people whose history we are tracing, reached with a marvellously rapid development the highest pitch of power and glory attainable on the basis of their existing dominion and religion. And now for the first time we fully comprehend the healthy influence of Samuel's whole course of action—not only of his gentleness in developing the mixed form of monarchy, but also of his severity against its perversion. Yet what now came to the surface was really the result of all the recent aspiration of the national mind, which, as we have seen, had long been directed upwards, and by which Samuel himself was affected. The higher religion, or in other words the Theocracy, when, though scarcely yet established on earth, it appeared to be losing an assured position for its free development, rescued itself by a spasmodic movement from the threatening danger; the nation manned itself against its enemies, first by the prowess of single heroes of action, and then in ever-widening circles, as if destined to become only a military school. The spirit of religion turned inwards to its own depths with greater earnestness and energy, thence to direct itself more decisively upon external events through prophecy, which was now waking up to greater strength and purity. Thus the great alteration of the fundamental constitution which could no longer be delayed without great damage —the admission of the human alongside of the divine monarchy —was already irrevocably introduced through noble self-denial and self-sacrifice. On the appearance of a king, therefore, who fully carried out the immediate object of this institution, unity at home and security abroad, the point was undoubtedly

---

[1] The ancient mode of writing the name דוד (which saved a letter) still predominates in the O. T., and does not pass into דויד except in writers belonging to the kingdom of the Ten Tribes (Cant. Hos. iii. 5) or to the people (Amos. vi. 5), and in those of later date generally (first in Zech. xii. 7, 8; xiii. 1; Ez. xxxiv. 23; cf., however, verse 24). Since, however, the vowels *u* and *i*, where they come close together, easily pass into one another (according to my *Lehrbuch*, § 42c) we find tolerably early the dialectic form Δαέτ داود, in Armenian always ꜹꭺꭼꝸ and also with *t* at the end; the spelling داوود can only denote *Dâûd*.

reached towards which the whole age had long been toiling, insofar as that point had been the simple attainment of worldly advantages, such as the complete subjugation of the heathen nations within the country and on its borders. But beyond this a special debt is due to Samuel's lofty spirit, in that the attainment of this point was accompanied not only by these material advantages, but also, in conformity with the higher religion, by new spiritual power and the opening of a hundred blossoms of a higher intellectual life; for it was Samuel who, although he himself died some time before David's reign, really shaped the character of this period, and its glory was the result of his splendid efforts.

A debt is due to his severity, especially the severity to Saul which we have noticed above; for without this discipline the monarchy would have remained much as we first beheld it, losing sight of its true goal through jealousy and caprice, with no real cohesion and elevation, without even suspecting the infinite nature of its final destiny. For the great lesson taught by the first stage of the history of the whole of this period is, that the monarchy could not, without injury to itself, separate from the Theocracy, and (though as yet it was too weak clearly to grasp this point) from its purest instruments—the prophets. Let it turn to the Theocracy, then, in a closer and more friendly spirit, look into its face with braver confidence, and reconcile itself with it as far as possible. But this can only be done by entering into its truths, and by a living participation in them. The greater, then, and the more independent the participation of the monarchy in the truths of the Theocracy, the better for the community at large.

But a still greater debt is due to Samuel's gentleness; which enabled him, up to the last year of his life, to work unwearied as a teacher of youth, and to tame the wild spirit by the peaceful arts of the Muses. Thus did the two opposites of severity and gentleness work together in Samuel, flowing from one source and directed towards one lofty object; for the higher religion, whose severity he enforced, yet fosters the utmost gentleness of heart and delights in all the peaceful arts of the Muses: and in the same way these two fundamental principles, though they seem at first sight to be irreconcilable, are found working together towards one object in the growing efforts of the next age to reach the highest point of national elevation, and their union constitutes the true greatness of this era. It frequently happens that at such periods of national elevation the rudiments of all the arts have long existed among the people; and if at the same time a fresh impulse in that direction is vividly excited and a purer religion prescribes moderation in all things and forbids the one-sided pursuit of external power as the highest object, then the reaction of their newly acquired external power on their internal capabilities will easily succeed in bringing these germs to an earlier maturity. In Israel, Samuel was the chief instrument in exciting this impulse at the happy moment; and his unbending maintenance of the severity of the true religion preserved his people from the danger of the one-sided pursuit of military power, even in the intoxication of the most dazzling victories over other nations. And so a period of national glory now dawned on Israel which reminds us far more of the first fair days of Greece after the Persian wars, than of the time when the Romans meditated the conquest of the world; although, if we think of the power of the royal authority and national unity as now established, we might sooner have expected a Roman universal empire as its result than a field of Grecian emulation in the arts of peace.

David most happily combined all the qualifications for becoming the true support of the extraordinary efforts of this period; and he thus succeeded in winning not only a name unequalled in glory by any other king of Israel, but also a halo of kingly fame as ruler of the community of the true God, unattainable by a king of any other nation of antiquity. To this most important result, no doubt, the very period in which he was placed largely contributed, both by supporting and urging him on, and also, on the other hand, by tempering and restraining him; and since, all the while, the noblest powers of the age were employed in the genuine eradication of old defects and the establishment of a better order of things, the zeal of the individual was already inflamed by that of the community. But it was not the age alone which made David what history proves him to have been: we must also recognise in him the glorious originality of a creative spiritual power, such as rarely shows itself in any people; and we have the greater confidence in crediting him with it, in proportion to the certainty with which we still recognise the most vivid utterances of his lofty spirit in his songs.

Besides this we have, no doubt, the additional advantage of possessing, in historical works, richer and more varied recollections of his life and times than of any earlier, and I might almost add, any later period. The Davidic age, with those that lie immediately round it, towers by its special glory like a giant mountain above a wide tract of more level periods. It was, moreover, soon afterwards recognised by the nation itself as a period of unique glory in the fortunes of the monarchy; and its memory has therefore been preserved in the historic narrative with the most exuberant fulness and detail. We are searching amid the confusion of the twilight regions of a remote antiquity, when at this point a strong light, shining far and wide, suddenly bursts upon our view! All is now in full movement and almost in its original life, while round the chief hero a crowd of other figures are woven into the mighty drama, and even these are illumined by the bright rays of his sun; nay, even what would be insignificant elsewhere, acquires importance here from the conspicuous eminence of Israel's greatest king. Such is the impression left upon us by the extant fragments of these narratives, although some indications of the later spiritualising and generalising method of handling the history, are discernible even here. And yet, precious as these sources of history are which now flow for the first time in a full stream, they are even surpassed in value by the personal outpourings which their great hero has left behind him in his songs. In these we see his innermost spirit unveiled, and are enabled thereby to compare his outward actions with the most secret workings of his soul. And although no competent judge can at the present day attribute to him the whole or even half the Psalter in a gross historic sense, yet we may all the more certainly ascribe to him such songs and fragments in the Psalter and the second book of Samuel as prove themselves afresh, after closer and closer examination, to owe their origin to none but him; and of these a sufficient number are still extant to enable us to recognise the true spiritual glory as well as the artistic power of this hero.[1]

If we proceed to put together, in its most general features,

---

[1] It is unnecessary to repeat here what is brought forward in my *Dichter des Alten Bundes*, vols. i. and ii. (especially in the 2nd edition of 1840), and is still further supported in a new edition of these volumes. On the other hand, we have no independent accounts of David from outside the Bible, for the information given by Eupolemus (apud Euseb. *Præp. Ev.* ix. 30), wherever it steps beyond the Biblical accounts, consists almost entirely of the transposition of certain events from Solomon's life to that of David. On Nicholas of Damascus (apud Joseph. *Ant.* vii. 5. 2) see below. Even what Islam has to tell us of him (e.g. *Sura* xxi. 78 sq.; Jalâl-eldîn, *History of Jerusalem*, translated by Reynolds, London, 1836, p. 287 sq.) is derived from very late sources. Samuel Chandler's *Life of David* is valuable, as containing a diligent collection of much analogous matter from classical sources, but in all other respects it is a very unsatisfactory work, for simple good-will can be of but little use in a case like this. We have now, therefore, all the more reason for referring to Dean Stanley's very full article on David in W. Smith's *Dictionary of the Bible*, vol. i.

the whole picture of David which results from all these historical testimonies, we find the very foundations of his character to be laid in a peculiarly firm and unshaken trust in Jahveh and the brightest and most spiritual views of the creation and government of the world, together with a constant, tender, sensitive awe of the Holy One in Israel, a simple pure striving never to be untrue to Him, and the strongest efforts to return to Him all the more loyally after errors and transgressions. He is no prophet, it is true, and assumes no priestly character; but no layman of his day could live in the higher religion with more honest sympathy or more joyous devotion than did he. His mouth continually overflows with heartfelt praise of Jahveh, and his actions are ever redolent of the nobility inspired by a real and living fear of Him (for the errors by which he is carried away stand out prominently just because of their rarity); and thus by the lofty elevation of the thoughts that crowd upon him, he often involuntarily becomes a prophet;[1] and at the end of his long career he feels himself in a state of divine illumination and foresight which no prophet could well experience in greater strength.[2] And so again his life, as he corrects its special errors, shows a constant growth in holiness, which could be looked for only in a priestly life; so that, even in his own times, a prophet applies to him the lofty title of priest-king—a king, that is, who was as holy in the sight of God as any born or consecrated priest.[3] Thus, in the clear day-light of Israel's ancient history, David furnishes the most brilliant example of the noble elevation of character produced by the old religion, when still in its simple and unbroken strength, in one who surrendered himself unreservedly to its influence; and of the extent to which one thoroughly imbued with its spirit might become, in his turn, a light and a stimulus to others. Moreover, the progress which the old religion had recently made in depth and refinement is shown by nothing more clearly than by the comparison of the songs of Deborah,[4] breathing so strongly of war and wild revenge, with those of David, still indeed animated by a thoroughly warlike spirit, but at the same time powerfully touching the deepest sources of all moral strength, and revealing a rich fulness of originality in their interpretation of nature.

Again, while the moral refinement just alluded to, which

---

[1] As Ps. xxxii. 8; iv. 4–6 [3–5].
[2] In the 'last words' of David, 2 Sam. xxiii. 1–7.
[3] Ps. cx.; compare below.
[4] Vol. ii. p. 377 sq.

is everywhere displayed in the songs and actions of David, points to a peculiarly high morality and gentleness of disposition, such as might proceed at that time from the newly awakened prophecy in Israel, we further see him taking part in the arts which may have been cultivated in the prophetic schools then in existence. This interlacing of noble deeds and noble language, impressing themselves upon morals and art, cannot be a matter of chance, either with David or with Samuel's prophetic schools,—as the nature of the case would prove to us, even if no closer historical traces, such as we shall soon observe, led us to the same conclusion. The mighty influence of this newly-wakened spirit of prophecy seized even Saul; but he was only for a single moment, as it were, caught up by it as by a power which, although it overmastered him, yet always remained a mystery to him, and never became a part of himself. In David, on the other hand, the spirit of prophecy meets a kindred spirit, not only closely related to itself and of fully as lofty origin, but even working with a creative originality in the same field; and thus it causes his inborn artistic glory to blaze forth all the sooner. At this early period, then, David, as the poet of Song, stands at a height which was never afterwards surpassed in Hebrew poetry. It is true that some of his songs, which have come down to us as mere sketches, exhibit the thoughts but little worked out, and still retain about them something of the stiffness and heaviness of antiquity;[1] but most of them show, side by side with a vigorous fulness and creative truth of thought (which is not wanting in the earlier songs, as Ex. xv., Judg. v.), an easy flexibility and softly moving flow of style which dates its existence as a characteristic of Hebrew poetry from this point. Thus the loftiest power of thought is accompanied by the most exquisite form of expression, and the whole of the most ancient poetry or Lyric of the nation is perfected in David; especially as, even when a powerful king, he did not disdain to encourage at his court the composition and vocal execution of songs, even up to his extreme old age.[2] On this account poetry subsequently passed from songs to fresh branches of the art; and such songs as were composed after David's time only show an advance on the point which he had reached in isolated directions. Poetry, moreover, was by no means

---

[1] As 2 Sam. iii. 23 sq.; xxiii. 1–7; the former a short lament over one who had deserved well, but yet had not merited so artistic an elegy as that over Saul and Jonathan, 2 Sam. i.; the latter the 'last song' of the hoary poet, aiming at prophetic brevity rather than running into poetic fulness.
[2] 2 Sam. xix. 36 [35].

so restricted in the hands of David as in its manifestations in later times, and especially among us; for he appears to have been not less celebrated as a player of musical accompaniments to songs. This we infer, not only from the narratives which tell us how he alone understood the art of soothing Saul's evil spirit with the harp, but also from the fact that we afterwards find the cultivation of music so widely spread and so completely naturalised in Israel, that in the time of Amos, some two hundred years after David, it was even pushed to excess in the temple and palace, and laid itself open to reproof on the charge of affecting vain display and imitation of David.[1] And as music and song excite a dance of sound and thought, and at their origin were certainly connected closely with actual dancing, we see David, on one solemn occasion, even when a mighty king in Jerusalem, perform various dances before all the people, although by this conduct he brought down upon himself the contempt of his royal-born wife Michal,[2] so powerfully did this third art of the Muses also strive for expression in him. And not only do all the arts press forward in him with creative power, and a sort of irrepressible force, from the beginning to the close of his career, but his entire conduct in life too, with hardly an interruption, appears to be urged on by a divine harmony, so to speak, of the powers of every other art of refined life. We see, for example, not only from his life, but from an explicit statement,[3] that he had few rivals in eloquence.

The possession of these two qualifications seems to mark a man out as destined to a distinguished position as a prophet or musician; but in David's case a third characteristic, capable of producing a far greater result, is added to them, and even more than for any other vocation he is born, as it were, to rule mankind. For this destiny he is qualified, in the first place, by a sinewy frame, which seems, from its concentrated strength and indefatigable energy to have been made for war,[4] a point which was still of great importance in those times; in the next place, by the inexhaustible strength and firmness of his trust in God, and his lofty courage in the presence of every danger; by his remarkable power of fascinating everyone with his gracious and gentle demeanour; by his wise circumspection in human affairs

---

[1] Amos vi. 5; comp. v. 24; viii. 3, 10.
[2] 2 Sam. vi. 14–22. In verse 14 the longer account uses two verbs which are found nowhere else to describe the dance, while in verse 16, for the sake of brevity, only one is used; this points unmistakably to two different modes of dancing whose characteristics were afterwards so little known that in 1 Chr. xv. 29 two verbs in quite ordinary use have been substituted.
[3] 1 Sam. xvi. 18.
[4] Observe how David himself, in his great hymn of victory, exalts these personal advantages, rendering thanks for them to Jahveh. Ps. xviii. 33–35 [32–34].

and his reverential conscientiousness in those that are divine; and by the wonderful power to which all this led, of always surrendering himself at the right moment to the divine guidance, without loss of personal dignity and elevation. Royalty was inborn in him; and even the severest struggles and dangers of his early youth, when once overcome, could only serve to strengthen and confirm in him his innate majesty. As to warlike prowess, he stood as a warrior and conqueror on a level with any hero-king of the age; but in how much was he superior to the ordinary royal hero! Now, since his youth fell in a period in which the true king was more sought for than found, his inborn aptitude for governing a great and united nation might well come so prominently into the foreground as to render subordinate his no less innate capacity for the fine arts. He possessed, too, as already shown, enough self-denial and genuine devotion to prevent his ever permanently forgetting the reality of the Theocracy, even when he had become a powerful king and was jealously guarding his own prerogative; and so there appeared in him the most perfect king for Jahveh's community whom that age was capable of producing.

Finally, if that king be truly great to whom his contemporaries spontaneously offer the full measure of admiration and love, and who rules over them with a strong hand, whilst appearing not to rule over them at all; viewed in this light also, there could not have been a greater king than David. Israel, though fascinated by the regal form of government, was not yet quite accustomed to its forcible restraints, and set no great value on the existing monarchy as an external institution. Still, the deep enthusiasm which David kindled in all who came in contact with him in his youth, sustained itself without abatement up to his extreme old age.[1] Although he was feared for the penetration before which nothing could remain concealed,[2] yet his ordinances were approved of far less from slavish fear than from the perception that he always hit upon the right measure.[3] Nay, even the faults in which he was from time to time overtaken, were unable permanently to alienate from him the spontaneous love of the whole people; for he had enough self-denial and strength of character to recover himself at once and completely. To such a king, with such a people—as yet uncorrupted, and absolutely devoted to him—what was not possible?

[1] Comp. 1 Sam. xviii. 3, 16 with 2 Sam. xxi. 17.
[2] 2 Sam. xviii. 13.
[3] 2 Sam. iii. 36. The enmity of certain Benjamites, relations of Saul, and the revolt of Absalom, can neither of them go far towards disproving this assertion.

We certainly must not allow these considerations to blind us to the faults which attached to his character,—faults which are unhesitatingly ascribed to him in the earlier writings, though no longer alluded to in the Chronicles. Amongst these, however, we should hardly reckon what appears to us his excessive harshness in punishing the conquered enemies of his nation, and offenders belonging to the people itself, for by all indications David was not of a cruel disposition, even when king, and only carried punishment as far as tradition and usage demanded. In the course of the preceding centuries, when Israel had to fight to the death for its existence as Jahveh's people, the times had become more and more warlike, and Israel's entanglements with other nations more and more complex; and among the significant peculiarities of this age, is the rapid popularity gained by the new appellation of the true God, 'Jahveh of Armies' [A.V. the 'Lord of Hosts'] in which the whole warlike spirit of the times, seizing on the higher religion itself, finds its most concise expression.[1] It is but natural, then, that the convulsive rising of Israel against her foes, which first realised its object under David, should still have been capable of perversion into excessive harshness against these foreign nations; and yet we shall see farther on that even this harshness brought its own punishment in subsequent times. Again, there is nothing in itself culpable in the great craftiness which we unquestionably find in David, and in which the great ruler is second to no Odysseus;[2] for in times like these, of pressure from so many

---

[1] Comp. i. p. 133, *note* 2. There is no intimation of the origin of this name in the Old Testament; but we may clearly see from Ps. xxiv. 10, that in David's time it was still full of living power, for it appears there as the most impressive and lofty title of Jahveh. As the form in which it now occurs is obviously much abbreviated, it is very difficult for us to fix its original meaning. This much, however, is clear—that the purely celestial meaning 'God of the armies of heaven,' i.e. 'the stars,' although indicated in the later passage, Isaiah xl. 26, is not in keeping with the warlike age which evidently gave rise to it. Again, it would be too tame to understand simply the 'army of Israel' which the Book of Origins calls the 'army of Jahveh,' Ex. vii. 4, xii. 41; comp. 1 Sam. xvii. 45 and vv. 26, 36. The name has evidently a loftier meaning. The most probable supposition then seems to be that the name arose on some occasion when the army of Israel turned the enemy to flight in a great battle, as though they had been mightily strengthened by the army of Jahveh itself coming down from heaven. Isaiah xxxi. 4 alludes to this meaning of the name, and ancient images such as Judges v. 20 lead to the same conclusion. According to this, the name described Jahveh as coming with all His heavenly armies to the assistance of the armies of Israel; and when the military spirit of the nation died away, it might easily be applied to God simply as marshalling the celestial army or stars. We find an analogous name which may even have arisen on a similar occasion in the Pallas φοβεσιστράτη, Aristoph. *Knights*, v. 1173, or the Ζεὺς στράτιος of the Carians and other peoples of Asia Minor (comp. Appian, *Mithridates*, c. 70, Ælian, *Nat. Hist.* xii. 30); but the special conceptions of Jahveh among His people give quite another signification to the Israelite title.

[2] Comp. 1 Sam. xxi. 14 [13] sq.; xxiii. 22; xxvii. 8–12.

quarters, even the most straightforward man could hardly push through without it. But what was so disastrous in its effects in David's case, as it must always be, was the habit of telling lies under pressure of circumstances,—the offspring of the necessities of those ages. It is true that this special form of craftiness might easily be developed, when a people like Israel, of such a peculiar genius and such strong spiritual aspirations, had yet so many unfavourable surroundings to contend against and so much pressure on every side to fear; and at an early period it seems to have been widely spread among the ancient people in conjunction with artifice and dissimulation, and not to have been regarded as altogether dishonourable, for its practice is ascribed with little disguise even to those lofty exemplars of the nation, the Patriarchs.[1] But for all that, the darkest passages in David's otherwise bright history—the massacre of the priests of Nob by order of Saul, and the gloomy fate of Uriah with all its connected guilt—are brought about through no other cause than this; nor is there any point of view from which we see so clearly the immense deficiencies of even so great an Old Testament hero as David.

Yet since this was rather the fault of the past character of the nation than of the individual man, it does not touch the fact that the general spiritual elevation of the age found its natural leader, at last, in the person of David. Raised by it, he raised and glorified it in return, and standing at the crowning point of the history of the nation, he concentrates in himself all its brilliance, and becomes the one man of greatest renown in the whole course of its existence. Indeed everything appears singularly perfect at this point; and it is an essential feature of the glory of the age and its leader, that while other founders of fresh dynasties, who rise from the bosom of the people to royalty, usually make their entry in the midst of conspiracy, treachery, and ambitious strife, David, on the other hand, rises to power simply by his own loftiness of character and almost against his will, though in obedience to a higher necessity, and, far from destroying or banishing the surviving members of the earlier dynasty, makes special provision for their maintenance. But we can only understand how this was possible, by studying the early history of David before the fall of the house of Saul had made him king of all the tribes: before proceeding further, therefore, we must bring up this previous history to the point which we have now reached.

A sufficiently clear knowledge of David's early history, both

[1] Gen. xii. 11–13; xx. 2; xxvi. 7.

before and after it connects itself with the general history of Israel, may be gained from an abundance of detached traits of a genuinely historical character. But when the attempt was first made to take a more complete survey of the king's life, and to trace it as far back as possible, it could not be expected that the connexion of its earliest events should still be clear; for long before his life became interwoven with the main history of the monarchy, he had already passed through the most complicated and varied fortunes, the full historical bearings of which could not at the time have seemed to anyone important enough to merit close observation and record.[1] The consequence is, that though the earlier narrator was still in possession of a mass of very clear and circumstantial accounts of the events of David's early life, yet even he looks at them from a special and elevated point of view, in accordance with which he endeavours so to mould them into a whole as to lay a solid and worthy foundation for what follows. After the close of David's career, no one who took a clear view of it would fail to observe the destiny to which the powers working in his history —considered as purely divine—called him from the very first. And thus the scattered reminiscences of his earliest youth acquired an inner unity of spirit and an outward connexion with each other, from this one idea which ran through them all, viz., that David instead of Saul, was destined by God to become the true human king in Jahveh's kingdom; that in accordance with this destiny, he had received his higher calling and consecration from the first, and that his star, therefore, shone out with ever-increasing power, while that of Saul as steadily declined. It is a necessary result of this that, as soon as David appears upon the scene, the history of Saul loses all importance except as the antitype to that of David, and inasfar as the two (like the fundamental antagonisms of a drama) can be brought into the closest connexion with each other. At the same time it is very instructive to observe in respect to this that the earlier narrator avails himself of this lofty point of view and the contrast it involved, only to reanimate the very earliest history of David up to his compulsory flight from Saul, and even there, it is only at the culminating point that he represents everything as brought about by pure divine truth; whereas the later narrators go far beyond him in both particulars, and introduce greater freedom into their representations.

[1] The particulars recounted by the later Jews of the lives of David and his father are arbitrary inventions.

At this point, then, we must examine next the lofty representation which serves as prelude to the whole history. With respect to the monarchy in Israel, Samuel was already[1] regarded by the earlier narrator as the pure vehicle of divine truth—nay, rather as the outward form which this truth necessarily assumed. In view of it, David is the only true king after Saul is rejected, and, therefore, even before he is outwardly consecrated, he must have obtained that true divine consecration on which the other necessarily rests. And so the narrator tells us at this point, how Samuel, after the divine rejection of Saul, impelled by the Spirit, anointed the youthful David, and with words of lofty prophecy strengthened him for all the difficulties which would beset his future course; just as, in the case of Saul, he had allowed the higher consecration and the divine anointing to anticipate the outward form which, indeed, is in vain without the presence of the other.[2] This event supplies to this narrator the proper connexion for the whole human history of David; for since he represents the Spirit of God as flowing upon the king elect[3] with the divine anointing and encouragement, it follows that this Spirit in coming to David must have left Saul, so that the latter, tortured by an evil spirit, cannot help longing after and searching for the former: this is the link which was wanting for the representation of a historical connexion between the two kings; the one recognised but declining and false, the other unrecognised as yet, but rising and true. Thus, then, the whole of this lofty picture depends on the equally lofty truth, that in the real kingdom of God a true king is never wanting; but, even though nowhere present in outward form, he always exists already in inward spirit, by divine vocation that is, ready to step forward at the right moment and assume his outward dignity.

The later narrator, however, to whom we owe the second version of Saul's rejection,[4] has substituted, at this point, for the older narrative of David's anointing (which was probably shorter in its contents) another,[5] in which the special position

---

[1] According to p. 18.
[2] P. 19 sq.
[3] This follows from 1 Sam. xvi. 13, compared with x. 6, 10. The representation is essentially the same as in the New Testament, where the Spirit of God comes upon everyone on whom the Apostles have laid their hands.
[4] P. 36 sqq.
[5] That there must here have been an account from the hand of the earlier narrator of the consecration of David by Samuel, is clear from his incidental allusion to it as early as 1 Sam. xiii. 14, and his reference back to it in xxv. 30. Besides, the representation of the departure of God's Spirit from Saul, xvi. 14, sqq. (which unquestionably comes from this narrator), is quite incomprehensible unless something of the sort had preceded it. But the truth is, that the colouring of the older narrator still shines through in

of David as the youngest of eight brothers by the same father, is brought into prominence and endowed with a high significance. When Samuel (so it is related) grieved long and almost too deeply over the divine rejection of Saul which was now unalterable, Jahveh commands him to shake off, at length, his excessive sorrow, and betake himself to Bethlehem to the house of Jesse, amongst whose sons one was to be chosen king. On his expressing a fear that Saul might kill him for it, if it came to his ears, Jahveh bade him take with him a calf as an offering, and during the sacrifice obey the inspiration from above. Thither he goes accordingly, no little to the surprise of the inhabitants of Bethlehem, prepares the sacrifice in Jesse's house, and has his sons summoned to be present at it. But when he sees the first-born and thinks assuredly Jahveh has destined him to be His anointed, Jahveh teaches him the contrary; for men are not esteemed in God's sight for outward size and strength. It is the same with the six next brothers, but the youngest, who is in the field as a shepherd, must be sent for, as the sacrificial feast cannot begin without him, and as he approaches—a lad with ruddy skin and hair, beautiful eyes, and a fine figure—the voice of Jahveh impels Samuel to anoint him as the chosen one of God, and from that moment the divine Spirit is upon him.[1]

If we understand by this narrative that David was openly anointed king with his own knowledge and that of his kinsfolk, it is difficult to conceive how either he or they could all remain so totally unconcerned, and how he could visit Saul's court with a clear conscience. But according to the true significance of the narrative, although Samuel anoints him with his spirit, and knows what this means in the sight of God (the result, moreover, showing itself at once in the influence of the Holy Spirit), yet, as far as outward appearances go, he simply chooses him as his closest companion and friend in the sacrifice[2] without publishing aloud that the anointing has any further significance; but if, as the history develops itself, the truth is divined by one or two others, such as Jonathan[3] and Abigail,[4] that is all the better. The advent of higher life which prefaces the whole history is thus at the beginning but loosely attached to what follows; for the sequel, though developing itself quite in accordance with the introduction, yet implies that neither the young hero himself nor anyone else knew all from the beginning, so as to be compromised by it. The

---

xvi. 8; only the representation in xv. 35–xvi. 7 is entirely from the later hand, as appears from the use of מָאַס, מֶלֶךְ, and the whole manner and style.

[1] 1 Sam. xv. 35–xvi. 13.
[2] Comp. 1 Sam. ix. 22; see above, p. 20.
[3] xx. 13; xxiii. 17.
[4] 1 Sam. xxv. 30.

development of the subsequent history advances, accordingly, even if we set aside this previous revelation of the divine destiny of the great hero, quite intelligibly in itself.[1] It seems undeniable, even from a more strictly historical point of view, that Samuel had a most powerful influence over David (as the extant records of an early narrator know of at least one visit of David to Samuel at the time of his flight from Saul),[2] and also that, long before he was king over all Israel, David received prophetic intimations of his future greatness;[3] but it is quite as clear, that the narrative of the anointing of David by Samuel simply forms a lofty introduction to the whole history, and can be rightly estimated only in the light of the pure divine truth which it embodies, and the lesson involved in it, which is drawn out clearly by the whole history.

I. The Early History of David.

David's early history up to the commencement of his independent action, may be very happily divided into four parts, in accordance with the obvious progress of the subject-matter indicated by the hand of the earlier narrator.

1. At the furthest point to which we can trace back David's early history, the reminiscences of him tell us of the two characteristics by which, in general, he was so specially distinguished —his love of the arts and his undaunted courage in the midst of the wildest strife; for though these two characteristics appear to contradict each other, and are seldom found united in the same man, yet in him they were both manifested together and in the highest degree, from the very first. While yet a boy, he exercised himself in both amid the secluded scenes of his home; and early in his life, his occupation as a shepherd brought them both into play. The pastoral art of flute-playing, glorified among the heathen in the young Apollo and Krishna, is perhaps the earliest kind of music to which not women but men, and a whole class of men rather than individuals, devoted themselves;[4] but David—this same shepherd boy who exercises his youth in

---

[1] Just as, in the Book of Job, the progress of the human history would be quite intelligible in itself, even without the Divine introduction. This resemblance becomes all the more striking if we suppose these lofty narratives to owe their earliest origin to a previously existing drama; and it has already been noticed incidentally, p. 51 *note*, that this supposition by no means lies beyond all bounds of possibility.

[2] 1 Sam. xix. 18–xx. 1.

[3] Comp. 2 Sam. iii. 18; v. 2; prophets such as Gad were with him from an early period; 1 Sam. xxii. 5.

[4] The שָׁרְקוֹת עֲדָרִים in Deborah's song, Judges v. 16, where it is clearly enough described; nor can it be doubted that the Greek σύριγξ is connected with this שׁרק, just as so many of the oldest arts with their associated words passed over to the Greeks from the Semites.

these arts—must also wrestle with the lion. When a lion comes with a bear, and carries off a lamb from the flock, he runs after him, strikes him, and snatches the plunder from his jaws; and when the lion turns upon him with redoubled fury, he seizes him by the throat, smites and slays him together with the bear.[1] The marvellous two-fold power of the future hero is here foreshadowed in its wild as well as its gentle phase.

The older narrator, however, does not begin David's history from its human point of view till his public appearance before Saul, and only glances back on his earlier life from that point. But, even in the very description of the way in which he came to Saul's court, this narrator shows us the alternation of his two wonderful characteristics, making him come before Saul's notice and as it were become his complement both by the one and the other. Such is the point which this narrator assigns as the beginning of all David's earthly history.

When an evil spirit from Jahveh (so runs the narrative) had fallen upon Saul, his servants, with his own sanction, sought for a harper to scare it away with his music in the moments of its rage. Then a skilful player is found—a youth of equal strength and skill in fight, eloquent in speech, beautiful in person, and full of the spirit of Jahveh—it is David of Bethlehem; and since his father cannot withhold him from the king's service, he sends him to the court. Here he soon finds such grace and favour with Saul, that the latter begs him of his father for his constant companion; and so the object of his appointment is fully accomplished.[2]

But it is not always the time to listen at court to the soft strains of the lyre, submitting one's soul to be soothed by all the arts of the Muses. The Philistines have ventured upon another inroad into the country; and this time they have advanced a great distance in a southerly direction, and have taken up a firm position on the slope of a mountain, Ephes-Dammim, between Shochoh and Azekah[3] in Western Judah. Israel, under the leadership of Saul, encamps over against them on the slope of a second mountain, at a place called the

---

[1] 1 Sam. xvii. 34–36, where the וְאֵת חַדּוֹב is to be taken in accordance with § 339a. compared with § 277d. p. 684 of my Lehrb.

[2] 1 Sam. xvi. 14–23. The whole tone of the colouring and thought of this passage shows it to proceed from the earlier narrator, who had already incidentally noticed, xiv. 52, that Saul possessed and exercised the right of summoning into his service any warlike or otherwise capable man; moreover, the assertion in xiv. 52 points at the same time to the further account of the Philistine wars which now follows, xvii. 1 sqq.

[3] That Azekah lay west of Shochoh follows from the whole description, xvii. 1. Robinson, ii. p. 422, thinks he has found Shochoh in *Suwaikheh*, south of Jarmûth.

INTRODUCTION TO SAUL.

valley of the Terebinth; and between the two camps lies a deep narrow valley, which seems destined as a field on which the warriors of either side may exercise their valour. And now from the Philistine camp there advances a champion, Goliath of Gath, six cubits and a span high, with a bronze helm, a coat of mail weighing 5,000 pounds of bronze, bronze greaves, a bronze javelin hanging from his shoulders, and a spear with a shaft like a weaver's beam and a head weighing 600 pounds of iron.[1] His shield-bearer advances before him, and he scornfully challenges to single combat any one of Israel's warriors, but no one appears to contend with him. Forty days long, to the horror of the terrified people, he makes himself heard morning and evening without receiving an answer, until David (who has accompanied Saul to the war) offers himself for the combat, unable any longer to hear Israel and her God mocked so contemptuously. So he goes forth, slays him in the combat, and thus not only removes the reproach from Israel, but at once leads on the people to a great victory. And this was how he first gained the love of Jonathan the king's warlike son, who (probably) had been prevented by the king and the people from undertaking this combat himself; and so close a friendship is now knit between the two that, as a token of it, they exchange their garments and their arms.[2] Moreover, Saul employs him further in military commissions, and places him in a position of authority where he manages everything entrusted to him so discreetly as to earn the esteem of Saul and his surrounding servants as well as that of the whole people.[3]

It is beyond doubt, on the one hand, that it must have been some such extraordinary feat of arms which first brought David into Saul's notice, as a hero of whose warlike capacity he ought to avail himself; and as to the sequel, we know from the histories of many ancient nations that in those times a whole war might turn on a single combat undertaken with due formalities

---

[1] It is remarkable that no mention or description of the sword is found here; other indications, however, show us that it must have played an important part in the account of the earlier narrator; cf. xvii. 45; xxi. 10 [xxi. 9]; xxii. 10. It also follows from this, that we no longer possess the original representation of this affair by the earlier narrator, and that this description of the enormous weapons comes from no earlier hand than that of a third and later author. Comp. Plutarch's *Demetrius*, ch. xxi. for what was considered the maximum in such matters by the Greeks. These pounds are of course far smaller than ours.

[2] Like the Homeric heroes, *Il.* vi. 230-236.

[3] We assume that even the earlier narrator mentioned the single combat between David and Goliath: the passages xviii. 6, xix. 5, xxi. 10 [xxi. 9], leave us no doubt on this point; besides, the words which describe the final result of the achievement, xviii. 1, 3-5, to judge from their colouring are from the earlier narrator; again, the description of the camp, xvii. 1-3, comp. xiv. 4 sq., betrays the hand of the same author. Possibly the whole verse, xvii. 45, is also from him.

by the heroes of the two armies.¹ But, on the other hand, it is equally evident from many clear traces that this first warlike feat of David—the greatest hero of that heroic time, soon gained a specially lofty significance as the type of all the greatness of the age; and so, being told and retold with infinite frequency and delight, gradually assumed a form of ever-increasing circumstantiality and expansion.

We have already said that only a few fragments of the earlier narrator's description are left to us, and it is not improbable that even in them the name of the Philistine giant may have been introduced from another source; for we know from one of the earliest accounts² that Goliath of Gath—the giant 'whose spear-shaft was like a weaver's beam'—was really slain by a certain Elhanan the son of Jair of Bethlehem; and indeed, according to the same authority, this event did not take place until David had already become king. Since we cannot doubt that the giant so described is the same whose name is now introduced in David's early history, we must suppose that his name was transferred to the Philistine whom David slew (who is, moreover, generally called simply 'the Philistine,') when his proper name had been lost. This would be all the more likely to happen, because Elhanan, like David, was a native of Bethlehem.

The second narrator, again, brought the first great warlike feat of David into a somewhat different connexion, in representing this amazing feat as the only means by which David became known to Saul. According to him, David is sent by his aged father from Bethlehem to the army, with provisions, and a present for the captain under whom his three elder brothers are serving in the camp, to ask after their health and bring back to the old father some token to show that they are still alive. On his arrival, under these circumstances, at the camp, David hears the taunting words of Goliath; and learns that whosoever will venture to undertake the combat, will be rewarded by the king, if victorious, with great riches, his own daughter in marriage, and the elevation

---

¹ Vol. ii. p. 339.

² 2 Sam. xxi. 19 and 21 is really the ancient model of the greatly elaborated representation in 1 Sam. xvii.; cf. vol. i. p. 136 sq. on the whole passage. According to 1 Chron. xx. 5, we should read יָעִיר for יָעִי and strike out the following אָרְגִים. The alteration in the Chronicles of the word בֵּית, which follows next, into אֵת, may have happened in the first instance through a simple mistake of the copyist, but when the words were taken to mean 'he slew Lahmi' as though Lahmi were the giant's name, it would certainly be very natural to make the further change of reading אֲחִי for the succeeding אֵת, making the meaning 'Goliath's brother,' as though this Lahmi had not been Goliath but simply his brother. There would then be no mention in this passage of the fall of Goliath; but it is perfectly clear that the text, as it now stands, is corrupt.

of his house to noble rank.¹ On this he advances, trusting in the true God and in the strength which had proved victorious when matched against a lion in the open field, and conquers the giant. When the combat begins, he is so little known in the army that Saul cannot even learn his parentage from his general Abner, but the victory gives him such a glorious introduction to the king, to whom he brings Goliath's head, and to the other chiefs of the army, that Saul will not suffer him to leave him. The unexpected but surprisingly majestic manner in which the heroic young stranger suddenly becomes known, and the unlooked-for way in which Saul himself comes to know him, are essentially characteristic of the event, according to this representation, and bring it to an appropriate close.²

There was still one other point left for more detailed description; for when David was once considered as a shepherd boy, the disproportion between the weapons of a simple stripling such as he, quite inexperienced in war,³ and a giant like Goliath might be brought into greater prominence. Accordingly we are told that when David has made known to Saul his fixed determination to accept Goliath's challenge, the king, by way of precaution, gives up to him his own massive armour; but David, after trying in vain to move freely when thus encased, lays it aside again and takes nothing but his shepherd's staff and wallet, together with his sling and five smooth pebbles from the watercourse (putting four of these in his wallet as a reserve); and thus equipped, draws near to the giant, who is at first so enraged by the ridiculous preparations of the slightly-built and unarmed lad, that he can hardly persuade himself to enter upon the contest! The earliest source of this most free manipulation and description of the event is a third narrator, while one still later fused together the representations of all his predecessors into the very minute account which we now read.⁴ The pursuit of the flying

---

¹ P. 42.

² We may perceive from this what passages in the narrative of ch. xvii. can be considered as original to this narrator; xvii. 55–58, xviii. 2, especially, are from his hand without alteration. Fl. Josephus has done well, therefore, in dropping this trait from his otherwise very servile reproduction.

³ On the other hand. according to the earlier narrator xvi. 18, David was already known as a practised young warrior before he came to Saul.

⁴ 1 Sam. xvii. 1–xviii. 5. It is consequently only here and there that we can still recognise the words and descriptions peculiar to the first and second narrators. For example, בֵּית הַלַּחְמִי, xvii. 58; cf. xvi. 1,

points to the second; the almost synonymous אֶפְרָתִי, xvii. 12, cf. i. 1, to the first; רָאִי or מַרְאֶה, xvi. 12, xvii. 42, to the former; and תֹּאַר, xvi. 18, to the latter. But since the different fragments of the older narrators, collected here by the latest hand, have nevertheless not been completely amalgamated, and so have remained clearly contradictory to each other when carefully compared, even ancient readers may have preferred to leave out the passages xvii. 12–31, xvii. 55–xviii. 5. At least, there is no other probable explanation of their omission from most of the MSS. of the LXX. Cf. further R. Tanchûm's conjecture that there has been a great deal of transposition in this passage.

enemy (which seems to be described in part by the earlier and in part by the later narrator) was carried on with great slaughter along the way from Shaaraim [1] as far as Gath and Ekron. On returning, Israel plunders the camp of the Philistines, whilst David brings Goliath's head to Jerusalem (it is clear that he did not do this till afterwards, when he was king), and deposits the weapons of which he has stripped him in his own tent.[2]

And yet, through all the manifold varieties of form which may have been assumed in the following centuries by this first great warlike exploit of David, it preserved its own peculiar importance, and all the many narrators whose traces we can detect, are united in the feeling of its high significance. Even supposing these stories of successful prowess against Philistine giants had been told and applauded a hundred times in Israel, in no other spirit than that in which the Romans boasted of similar achievements against Gallic giants, or the Greeks of Odysseus' victory over Polyphemus, the feeling would still have been an honourable one, and would have sprung from a higher spiritual aspiration. For as the hero of inferior stature but of nervous arm, unshaken courage and superior skill, fights and conquers the terrible but uncouth and awkward giant, just so, in all essentials, do the nations who, though smaller, are yet spiritually active and artistically cultivated, contend against those which are stronger but less refined. In the victory of a David over a Goliath, the whole nation—unfortunate sometimes but never despondent—rejoices in its spiritual superiority over its mightier foes, who are certain, for all that, to be conquered again at last. And so these combats are the foreshadowing of future victories still greater and more extensive, the symbols of the first successful efforts of a general spirit of lofty aspiration; and the idea we have seen manifested in Samson's life [3] finds its embodiment again in David. But neither the heathen nor even Sampson himself can rival the special glory, so prominent in David's case, and consonant with his whole nature, of a courage supported by the higher religion; and this peculiar elevation transforms this human strife into a public contest between two religions. The Philistine curses the

---

[1] This town in the tribe of Judah may well be supposed, from the connexion in which it appears with Shochoh and Azekah, Josh. xv. 53 sq., to have lain due west of these cities, so that the pursuit towards Philistia must have passed by it; see also p. 19 and Seetzen's *Reisen*, ii. p. 393. Even the LXX. had already lost the meaning of the words.

[2] On the other hand, the older narrator must have told us how David presented Goliath's sword to the High-Priest and afterwards found it in his possession, xxi. 10 [xxi. 9], xxii. 10. This also shows us that much of the earlier narrator's account must have been lost.

[3] Vol. ii. p. 402 sq.

apparently defenceless stripling by his invisible God, whilst David, though not unskilled in war, trusts more than in anything else in the name of Jahveh of Armies, the God of Israel's battle array,[1] and it is He who gives him courage and victory. And thus the two-fold greatness of David and his whole age already steps into the foreground—the courage that is bold without rashness, which is inspired by the newly wakened energy of the higher religion, and vindicates for itself a victorious freedom from even the strongest and most threatening of its foes.

2. Thus has David come into contact with Saul, and indeed become forthwith almost necessary to him in peace and war, so that it now rests with Saul to avail himself of the service of this most gifted of his subjects. But when the army of Israel is returning home from the campaign in which David's exploits had no doubt been the most prominent, and the women, in celebration of the feast of victory, sing in their simplicity:—

Saul has struck his thousands down,
but David his ten thousands![2]

the king is overtaken by his dreadful curse, and becomes jealous of David also; and though the latter affords him not the slightest grounds for his fears, the thought already rises within him that the hero of the panegyric now only lacks the kingdom! It is in these times of repose that the sting of envy works itself deeper and deeper into his soul through these ungoverned thoughts, until, even while David is once more playing quietly at his side to chase away his evil humour, the frenzy of the evil spirit comes over him in a totally new form, with such irresistible power, that he seizes the spear which stands as a sceptre at his side, and hurls it against the wall by which David sits, intending to transfix him;[3] the singer draws back his head from the blow, but he seizes the spear again, and it is only the rapid execution of a second retreat that protects the innocent man from his furious outburst of rage.[4] Thus wonderfully

---

[1] 1 Sam. xvii. 43, 45.

[2] The great importance which is attached to this verse, wherever it occurs, cf. xxi. 12 [11], xxix. 5, proves that the earlier narrator, who at this point appears again quite by himself and henceforth is predominant alone, really took it from an old national song; besides, it is by no means in the manner of this narrator to insert verses unless he has taken them from the old tradition or some other historical source. Cf., however, the remarks below.

[3] Just as a Syrian queen Cleopatra shot down her own son from jealousy, as Appian distinctly states, *Syr.* ch. lxix.; cf. Liv. *Epit.* lx.; Justin, xxxix. 1. It is known, however, that the sceptre of kings and princes was originally nothing but a staff, which reached down to the feet like a shepherd's, Gen. xlix. 10 (Æschylus, *Ag.* 195), and so, especially in war, served as a spear also (Ps. cx. 2).

[4] 1 Sam. xviii. 6–11. It follows, however, from the very different tone of the description in xix. 10, that on this occasion, and also in xx. 33, the matter went no further than a simple cast of the spear.

rescued from this wild frenzy, the youthful David only excites Saul's secret dread the more; and after the failure of his open attempt which would be the more easily excused by those who surrounded the afflicted king, in consideration of his well-known madness, he seeks for some crafty means of crushing the youth, or rather the dreaded Divine Power within him.

Under his special command he places a small troop of 1,000 men with which to conduct independent operations against the enemy, hoping that the incessant warfare in which he will thus become engaged will soon prove fatal to him; but the propitious presence of Jahveh's spirit is not withdrawn from David, and he not only remains uninjured through all these conflicts, but, as he develops his powers on a more independent footing at the head of his little troop, he wins the love of the whole people in a yet higher degree.[1]

In order to spur him on yet further to wild feats of war and excite him more powerfully to the most extravagant adventures, the king determines to raise him to a position of yet greater honour and distinction, and is ready to make him his own son-in-law upon condition that he will pursue the holy wars against the national foe with still greater eagerness. But at the same he will only give him Merab, his elder daughter, who is already married to another, Adriel of Meholah, and must therefore be taken away from him.[2] David at first declines, saying, 'Who am I and who are my kindred,[3] my father's family in Israel, that I should be made the king's son-in-law!' yet, for all that, he has to conform himself to the king's gracious will. But as the marriage is about to take place, Michal, Saul's second daughter, who is yet free, declares her love for David; and though the attitude which Saul assumes for a time with respect to David's suit, threatens increased difficulty in gaining his consent to this second request, yet he has at the same time determined in his own mind to take the fullest advantage of this turn of affairs also, for his own purposes. He therefore secretly instructs his courtiers to drop a hint to David that he need not place any heavy sum

---

[1] 1 Sam. xviii. 12–16.

[2] This is no more extraordinary than that Michal should afterwards be taken back again, by David's command, from the man to whom she had been given in marriage by her father, clearly against her own will, after David's flight, 1 Sam. xxv. 44; 2 Sam. iii. 14–16. On such loose treatment of marriage relations see my *Alterthümer*, p. 223 sqq. In the passage 2 Sam. xxi. 8, a simple copyist's error may have crept in at an early period, as is noticed below.

[3] חַי, 1 Sam. xviii. 18, must be an ancient idiom equivalent to 'my relations,' as is clear from what follows. It will therefore mean the same as the equally antiquated form elsewhere חַיָּה *fem. sg.* Ps. lxviii. 11 [10]. See my *Lehrbuch*, § 179c.

of purchase-money for the girl in her royal father's hands, but by presenting him with a hundred foreskins of Philistines he may make him friendly to his cause. Since the interval before the marriage with the elder daughter is not yet passed, David actually marches out at once with his little retinue,[1] slays 200 Philistines, and causes their foreskins to be presented to Saul.[2] And so, without attaining his object of seeing him destroyed by the dangers of war, Saul is compelled to give David the fair young Michal, and has to bear the additional vexation of seeing him loved by Michal as well as by the whole people. This causes his hatred and dread of him to rise higher and higher;[3] and yet for the sake of outward appearances it was desirable that the king should now confer some post of honour on his son-in-law. At any rate, he can no longer remain an armour-bearer or esquire as he was before, and accordingly he appears at this time if not earlier (for the authorities on this point have not been fully preserved to us) to have obtained the second place in the court as commander of the king's body-guard, next to Abner, who had long[4] occupied the post of commander-in-chief, which was the highest dignity in Saul's court. That David actually held this appointment appears yet more certainly from scattered indications.[5]

During the campaigns of the next few years, David continues to be successful in his attacks against the Philistines, and his name becomes dearer and dearer to the whole people, and Saul, therefore, can no longer refrain from calling (quite openly) on all his courtiers and his son Jonathan to take the first op-

---

[1] 'He and his men,' xviii. 27, i.e. with his two or three squires, as Joab had ten armour-bearers, 2 Sam. xviii. 15; the fact that at that time of the year there was no war, and that 1,000 men would have had no difficult task against 100 or 200, makes it all the more certain that the 1,000 men over whom he was captain are not meant. Samson's exploit, vol. ii. p. 405, is here much more to the point.

[2] Fl. Josephus makes 600 *heads* of them throughout. According to Rougé in the *Rev. Archéol.* 1867, p. 42 sq., this was an Egyptian custom, and must, therefore, have been borrowed thence by Israel.

[3] xviii. 17-29; since everything is thus seen to hang very well together from xviii. 6 onward, and to show the hand of the earlier narrator throughout, the numerous omissions in the Vatican MS. of the LXX. must be purely arbitrary.

[4] Not from the first, for in the war of Michmash (p. 33) it is not he, but in default of such an officer, Jonathan, who appears still to occupy the post he afterwards filled.

[5] That David held the second office at court, next to Abner, follows from 1 Sam. xx. 24-27, and from xxii. 14 we learn that this was the post of captain of the body-guard. In this latter passage סָר LXX. ἄρχων = שַׂר, *prince*, must be read for סָר (compare also 1 Kings xx. 39), and אֶל must be regarded as confused with עַל: *prince*, i.e. captain, *over thy obedience*, i.e. thy body-guard, who always surround the king, obedient to every sign, as with us an *orderly* is a soldier specially assigned to the officer. This is the meaning of מִשְׁמַעַת, as appears also from 2 Sam. xxiii. 23 (1 Chron. xi. 25); 1 Kings iv. 6, LXX. (see below); cf. 2 Sam. viii. 18; xx. 23. Something the same is expressed by the phrase 'keeper of the king's head (life),' 1 Sam. xxviii. 2; and according to the old account in 1 Chron. xii. 29 Saul's body- or house-guard consisted of a considerable number of Benjamites.

portunity of destroying him. It is at this juncture that the first proof is furnished of the true nature of a friendship which must ever be regarded, even now and among Christians, as the eternal type of such a friendship, the parallel of which would be sought in vain among all the Homeric heroes. True friendship is something far purer and more divine than sexual love, since it excludes, when genuine, even that sensuous element which is found in the other; as David himself, in his elegy on Jonathan, exclaims with truest feeling, as he looks back on all their intercourse which is now closed, 'More wonderful was thy love to me than the love of woman.'[1] Nothing can establish a true bond between two friends and produce pure friendship except a loftier necessity which stands above them both, and which both alike burn to satisfy with ever-increasing fulness—the necessity, namely, of finding and loving in others, if possible in a yet higher degree, the purely divine power already felt within, and thus mutually living under its influence. Anything else which calls itself friendship is unworthy of the name, and is rather an empty hypocrisy, by means of which one of the two merely seeks his own advantage, to compass which he is ready, if need be, even to deceive and betray his friend. It is in an age, therefore, which is possessed, above all things, by a pure aspiration to obtain noble gifts, that the blessing of such a genuine friendship will also most readily be [2] realised; and so the period in Israel's history with which we are now concerned furnishes, among so many other glorious spectacles, that of a friendship which shines for all ages as an eternal type. If we find in David, who occupies a lower rank, a more original, strong, and productive love of divine things, expressing itself in a corresponding grandeur and nobleness of action, yet in Jonathan, whose position is loftier, we recognise a love of the same thing, no less pure than David's, though at first rather owing its own warmth to the glow of his friend's; and, accordingly, the fruit of this friendship also, as will be shown in the sequel of this history, is as glorious and rich in blessings as is possible.

In the present instance Jonathan can neither betray David (as is self-evident) although it is his father's direct command, nor act to the prejudice of his father, which would be the result of his simply advising David to flee and thus depriving his father of the firmest support of his kingdom. He therefore advised David to conceal himself on the following day in a

---

[1] 2 Sam. i. 26.
[2] Resting on a 'Covenant of Jahveh,' 1 Sam. xx. 8.   i.e. a sacred oath between the two friends,

corner of a certain field to which he purposed accompanying his father. He would then converse about him with his father and let him hear the tidings, so that, if his father were really resolute in such a very evil purpose towards him, he might at once flee from the open field. On the next day, then, he represents to his father, in the open field, all David's virtues and the great services he had already rendered to him, adjuring him at the same time not to shed innocent blood. Saul cannot withstand the truth of these representations, and takes a solemn oath to make no attempt to injure him; and then Jonathan brings his friend once more before him, and David performs the duties of his office in Saul's court exactly as before.[1]

But no sooner does David return from a fresh campaign against the Philistines in which he has once more gained important victories, than jealousy and envy again take possession of the king; and one evening, as David is playing by his side, he attempts in another fit of rage to transfix him with his spear. This time too, David fortunately avoids the blow, but he cannot now be blamed for leaving Saul's dwelling at last, and retiring to his own which was probably situated in the lower town. But when Saul even sends messengers to his house to ask whether he is there, his own wife, Saul's daughter Michal, advises him to seek safety in the country at a distance, and devises means of facilitating his escape. Their house being at first simply watched, with the view of preventing David's escape by night and having him removed next morning under a suitable guard, she lets him secretly down by night through a window, takes the image of their house-god, in shape like a man, throws a sheet over it, and lays it in his bed with a fly-net over its head, so as to prevent the image from being recognised, at any rate at a first glance, and to make it appear as if her husband himself had covered his face with a fly-net.[2] On the following morning, therefore, when a sufficient guard actually arrives to take him prisoner, she gives out that he is ill in bed; and when Saul sends again to fetch him up to him, bed and all, she cannot, indeed, dissemble any further, and alleges in her terror that she was really compelled to let him escape, for he threatened to kill her if she refused; but meanwhile the

---

[1] 1 Sam. xviii. 30–xix. 7.
[2] This seems to be the easiest way of understanding the בְּבִיר עִזִּים; it is well known that in hot countries people often cover their faces in bed with fly nets, and equally so that goats' hair is much used there for curtains, cloaks, and tents; cf. طَبْلَب, Layard's *Nineveh*, i. p. 57; Lynch's *Narrative*, pp. 206–8; it was thus the costly κωνωπεῖον with which the sleeping Holophernes protected his head from flies, and which Judith threw over his stolen head: Judith x. 21; xiii. 9, 15; xvi. 19.

fugitive has had time enough to withdraw to a distance, and Saul perceives that his project is foiled.[1]

3. Now that he has barely escaped from the king with his life by flight, what is he to do? The majority of Christians of the present day would think that all the patience of a subject, especially of one whose position was already so high, would be exhausted, and that nothing would remain except to leave so ungrateful a country and try his fortune in foreign lands, or, still better, to levy war against the king and seek revenge. Not so David, who seems to have composed the eleventh Psalm just at this crisis. He certainly cannot remain any longer in the kingdom without finding some protector to take his part in case of need against the king; so he goes at once, according to the second narrator,[2] to Samuel at Ramah, and tells him how he has been treated by Saul, and is taken by him to the School of the Prophets which is situated near the town. Here he remains, and since he is a hero no less distinguished in the peaceful arts of music than in war, he takes his share in the exercises of the place, and, while thus employed, easily forgets all his troubles. But as soon as Saul hears of this, he cannot rest till he has forced David to flee from even this peaceful retreat.[3]

According to the first narrator, there is now nothing left for him to turn to in the whole land, except what he may possibly get by the friendship of Jonathan, which has already stood one test; for perhaps (it must seem to him) he may once more succeed in softening Saul's wrath by means of Jonathan, as he had done before. To him, therefore, he betakes himself, as to a protector bound to him by ties of hospitality and friendship, and asks him in all sincerity wherein he has failed in duty so as to deserve death at Saul's hand. Jonathan seeks to reassure his friend by representing to him that if his father's designs were indeed so evil, he would not have concealed the fact from himself; but David justly replies that he has omitted to do so only for the sake of sparing him pain, that he knows only too well that but one step divides him from death, and that consequently he is now anxious to obtain, by his help, a sure token of Saul's

---

[1] 1 Sam. xix. 8–17.
[2] It is true that the narrative in xix. 18–xx. 1 is closely woven into this connexion by the last author, but it is not likely that David should flee back to Jonathan once more from Samuel at Gibeah; and as the representation is a different one from that of the first narrator, x. 10–12, we must here recognise the hand of the second narrator. The somewhat drier and shorter representation of this second narrator, who does not stand far below the first either in time or historic capacity, has left other traces scattered through cc. xxi.–xxiii.; and the last author seems in this place to have adopted from him the name Ahimelech for Ahijah; ii. p. 415.
[3] 1 Sam. xix. 18–xx. 1; cf. p. 50.

real disposition towards him. In order to concert some plan for doing so, the two friends retire from the town to the open country, and Jonathan, earnestly reflecting on what may happen, takes an oath to his friend, that, during the next two days as soon as he has gained any certain knowledge of Saul's disposition, whether it augurs well or ill for him, he will report it faithfully to him. If it augurs ill, David must think of his own safety, and, as Saul's true successor, begin his own rule under as happy auspices as once were Saul's; but by the great love with which he loves him as himself, he hopes that when once David has taken triumphant possession of the kingdom, he will treat him with Godlike mercy if he is himself still living, and will never withdraw his favour from his house, even should he himself be dead. Whenever God shall destroy from off the earth all David's enemies, may the house of Jonathan still rest in peace by the house of David, but as for the real enemies of David, may God chastise them![1] With these and similar words, in this hour so full of forebodings, does the noble prince adjure the friend he loves so deeply; while the balance trembles over everything which, to vulgar sight, concerns not him but David alone, but which he, as a true friend, only takes the more deeply to heart on that account. As to the sign which it was their purpose to concert, Jonathan agrees, by David's desire, to observe whether Saul misses him during the next two days at a celebration of the feast of the New Moon, when the king was wont to assemble the chief officers of the court at his table; for he might conjecture that David was with Jonathan, and so expect that when Jonathan came to court he would be accompanied by his friend. Meanwhile David himself is to hide in the open country by a desolate heap of stones in the place where he had once before[2] concealed himself under similar circumstances; Jonathan is then to come into the neighbourhood of it and discharge three arrows towards it as if he were making that his mark; in reality, however, he is either to overshoot it or to let his arrows fall short of it;[3] then, as his attendant runs to-

---

[1] וְלֹא, the first and second time in verse 14 and the second time in verse 15, must be understood according to § 358*b*. of my *Lehrb.*, and then partially following the LXX., who still had on the whole a better text here, we must read וְאִם אֱמוּת for וְלֹא א׳, and in verse 16 וְלֹא וַיִּכְרֹת for יִבּוֹן בֵּית. In the same way in verse 19 we must read תֵּרֵד for תִּפָּקֵד. Cf., moreover, 2 Sam. ix. 3.

[2] Namely, when the spear had been cast at David, xix. 1-7; a sort of filial reverence here induces Jonathan to call that day simply 'the day of the affair,' to avoid having to give to that affair its right name.

[3] Vv. 36-38 furnish some additional proof that this is the meaning of verse 20 sq.; thus the expression לִשְׁלֹחַ לִי לְמַטָּרָה, verse 20, means 'leaving *it* (the heap of stones indicated) as my mark,' not using it as a mark, but shooting either this side

wards the mark, if he cries to him 'The arrows lie nearer this way,' David is to come forth confidently, for that is the token of a possible reconciliation with Saul, but if he cries to him 'They lie further on,' then David is to go whithersoever God may send him.[1]

In accordance with this arrangement, David hides in the field; but Saul, at the feast of the new moon, takes his accustomed seat of honour at the table, with his back against the wall opposite the door, Jonathan takes the seat opposite him,[2] Abner that on one side, while on the other side the seat of David, who is the fourth person for whom the table has been prepared, remains empty; but Saul is not surprised at his absence, for he supposes that it is perhaps accidentally caused by some bodily uncleanness.[3] On the second day of the feast, however, he asks Jonathan why 'the son of Jesse' is not in his place this day also; Jonathan answers, according to their private arrangement, that he has asked leave from him to go to Bethlehem where his kinsmen are observing the celebration of their family sacrifice, at which David's eldest brother has specially desired his presence. Upon this, Saul bursts into a fit of rage and hurls the bitterest reproaches against Jonathan;[4] he knows well enough that his own first-born has entered into a league with David, although his own prospect of accession to the throne, and even his life, can never be safe while David is alive: he must bring him to his presence at once, that he may be put to death; and Jonathan can scarcely get out another word on David's behalf, before he sees his father poising his spear to transfix him. In great agitation he leaves the table, tasting nothing the whole day through the depth of his grief for the undisguised rejection of David by Saul. The next morning he goes into the country to the rendezvous agreed upon with David; and the arrows, shot beyond the appointed mark, inform his anxious friend soon enough that the disaster

---

of it or that, just as להעברו, verse 36, 'shooting beyond it (the heap of stones);' see my *Lehrb.*, § 280*d*. We must follow the LXX. in reading הָאָרְגָּב, *heap of stones*, for הָאֶבֶן, verse 19, or at any rate for הנגב, verse 41, for אבן might have much the same force; and for הָאָצֶל, verse 19, read הָאָזֵל, 'the solitary or desert;' comp. عزل.

[1] 1 Sam. xx. 1–29.
[2] In verse 25 we must follow the LXX. in reading וַיְקַדֵּם for ויקם.

[3] According to my *Alterthümer*, p. 177 sq.
[4] Instead of the words בן נעות המרדות, which give no sure meaning, we should read, following the most probable reading of the LXX. and Vulgate, בֶּן־נַעֲרוֹת הַמִּרְדּוֹף, 'thou son of the girl of following,' i.e. the lowest girl, who runs after the man. The whole connexion places it beyond doubt that some such strong expression of contempt is intended here, and the following ערות אמך says essentially the same thing.

is inevitable. When he has sent his attendant back to the town with his weapons, David creeps forth, his soul full of the deepest emotion, and the two friends weep long together; but David more than Jonathan, who does not forget the possible danger in which they were at that moment standing, and urges his friend to speedy flight, reminding him, however, at parting, of the promise to which their mutual vow has bound them for all future time.[1]

This is the culminating point in the mutual relations of the two friends who furnish the eternal type of the perfection of noble friendship; and, moreover, in these last hours before their separation, all the threads of their destinies, henceforth so widely different, are secretly woven together. It is also at this point, consequently, that the clearest anticipation of the whole subsequent history already shines through. As Jonathan here foresees, David afterwards obtains the kingdom; and in accordance with his oath to his friend, he afterwards, when a powerful king, always spares the descendants of Jonathan, in grateful remembrance of his dearly loved friend, and never loses an opportunity of showing them kindness. If it is evident at this point, that the style of the language in the entreaty and covenant of Jonathan has been intentionally selected in such a manner as, at a later point, to place the perfect correspondence of the actual sequel in a yet more striking light, and to lead the way up to it beforehand, we yet may well believe that when, in after-years, David drew to his court the posterity of Jonathan, he often told them himself of these last events before their separation (with which no one but the two friends could be acquainted), and that our present narrative springs ultimately from this source.

4. David is thus compelled at last to avoid the king for ever; the most loyal and innocent of subjects to flee from the land, before the prince who might have had in him the firmest, nay almost the most necessary support of his kingdom; and should he ever venture to appear in the presence or within the reach of his father-in-law, instant death awaits him. But it never comes into his thoughts to enter upon hostilities, on this account, against Saul, 'the Anointed of Jahveh,' to levy war against him, or even to support his enemies; he has too much genuine reverence for God and His commandments, which clearly forbid a man to engage in even the smallest undertaking against his own people, how much more against the community of God, and their lawful leader upon earth! It is

[1] 1 Sam. xx. 24-xxi. 1 [xx. 24-42].

true that the result is to entangle him still more closely than before in an impenetrable network of the most dangerous situations and the most extreme privations, and that his fortunes upon earth seem to sink hopelessly lower and lower. But in reality his inward strength is thoroughly tempered for the first time under the heavy pressure of these sufferings; and when his perplexities have reached their very extremity, he finds himself at last, against his will, at the head of an independent community, and learns to rule on a small scale and under difficulties, so as to be able to do so on a large scale with the greater ease. Thus, then, this very period of his deepest sufferings becomes the decisive turning-point of his whole history, at which it enters upon its true upward course, thence to rise ever higher and higher; while his real destiny, viz., to rule, is now for the first time not only foreshadowed but already begun, though only on the smallest scale; and the clearest proof that this actually is his destiny is found in the fact that he begins to work it out without consciously exerting himself to do so.

David is now forced to flee from the whole district under Saul's dominion, and has therefore secretly escaped without provisions or weapons from Gibeah. There he is seized with the longing, before he leaves the country altogether, to see once more the venerable priest at Nob from whom in earlier times he had often drawn spiritual strength, to question his oracle as to the dark future of his life, and if possible receive a cheering response from it;[1] perhaps, too, to satisfy some of his most pressing bodily necessities there, for in time of need relief of every kind was sought at the sanctuary with equal readiness. So he repairs to Nob, a sacerdotal city situated somewhat to the south of Gibeah and the north of Jerusalem, to the priest Ahimelech,[2] with the further request that he will furnish him as well as he can with provisions and weapons; and unhappily he deems it necessary to avail himself of a fictitious pretext to allay the priest's surprise at his arrival unaccompanied and without arms. The priest replies that he has, at the time, nothing but consecrated bread, no common bread being at hand; and that, in order to eat that without offence,

---

[1] The subsequent description, 1 Sam. xxii. 9-15, of the further results of this deed, to which David was urged by his necessities, first shows us clearly that it must all be understood as represented in the text above.

[2] See, concerning him, vol. ii. p. 415.

In Mark ii. 26 he is confused with his son Abiathar or Ebiathar, and in other late writings the two names are not seldom confounded: see below. On the other hand, A*b*imelech, 1 Chron. xviii. 16 (see below), and LXX Ps. lii. 2, is simply a transcriber's error.

FLIGHT OF DAVID.

David's attendants (whom he pretends to have left behind him at a certain place whilst executing a secret commission of the king's) must none of them have touched a woman on the previous night. When David has removed this scruple,¹ the priest supplies him with some holy bread from the altar; but can think of no arms to give him except Goliath's wonderful sword, which David had before presented to the sanctuary and which was still hanging there on a nail, carefully wrapped up in a cloth, and also covered with the priest's oracular robe, which was hanging on the same nail. Thus provided, David departed; but the proceeding, harmless enough in itself, had been witnessed by a person who afterwards maliciously distorted it—Doeg the Edomite, who seems to have gone over to Saul during his wars with Edom,² and whom Saul had made chief overseer of his flocks. He had adopted the Jahveh-religion, and may have been then staying at the sanctuary in performance of some vow.³

To get beyond the boundaries, David now betakes himself to Achish⁴ the Philistine king of Gath, for he certainly lived in perpetual feud with Saul; so that a fugitive from the latter might expect the safest refuge with him. His reception by him is in fact favourable; but by some means or other (perhaps, according to the original meaning of the tradition, it was Goliath's sword that betrayed him) the courtiers discover that he is no other than the renowned David himself, and inform the king of the fact. Since there is now good reason for David to be afraid that the king may be tempted by this discovery to make him a prisoner for life,⁵ or even to execute him in revenge for his having formerly conquered so many Philistines, he can think of no other means, in his perplexity, of disarming the king's suspicion, than by openly feigning madness, beating with his fists upon the city gates as if they were kettle-drums,⁶

---

¹ He says, verse 6 [5]: 'Women have not been accessible to us since the day before yesterday; when I left home the bodies of the young men were pure, although it was on ordinary business (no religious service on which we were sent out); how much more will they be pure in body to-day!' So must we connect and understand the words contrary to the accent, only we must read יְקֻדַּשׁ for יִקְדַּשׁ, as indeed the LXX did. Since the question is one of bodily purity or impurity, כְּלִי can only mean the vessel of the man himself, i.e. his body, in which sense σκεῦος also may be used.

² P. 43.

³ 1 Sam. xxi. 2-10 [1-9].

⁴ The LXX always spell this name Ἀγχοῦς, probably because it was still a well-known Philistine name at that time.

⁵ The superscription to Ps. lvi., whose author surely found this history still in a somewhat fuller form, assumes that David was at that time actually taken prisoner. That the Philistine king had determined to hand him over to Saul when occasion served, is rendered unlikely by the good faith which then characterised that nation.

⁶ תָּנָה, verse 14 [13], must be equivalent to תָּפָה from תָּף, according to my *Lehrb.*, § 121a: perhaps the prison was near these city gates.

letting his spittle run over his beard, and similar devices. By this conduct the king became at last convinced that he was really imbecile, harmless, therefore, but also useless to him; and irritated by the sight of such foolery, he ordered him to be expelled from the city.[1]

II. Commencement of David's Independent Rule.

1. *As Freebooter on the Confines of Judah.*

It has now become clear that David's life is not safe even among the enemies of Israel, unless he will unite with them against his own people; and this his fear of God will not permit him to do. In this extremity he might certainly have found refuge in other kingdoms, that of Moab for instance, but the result would have been the same or perhaps even worse. Just at this time, however, he must have heard that a number of persons, indignant at the persecution to which he had been subjected, or otherwise disaffected towards Saul, were already awaiting him in Judah as their leader, ready to assemble under his standard. He determines, therefore, to become, for the time being, a second Jephthah,[2] and to take refuge again in the territory of his native tribe Judah, but with no intention of levying war against Saul. Accordingly he betakes himself to a cave in the barren district of Judah east of the range of mountains which cuts through the territory of this tribe from north to south,—a cavernous district with which his early life had no doubt made him thoroughly familiar. On the report of his arrival in the country, not only did all his kinsfolk from the neighbouring Bethlehem come to see and perhaps to support him, but a number of other fugitives and malcontents soon collected spontaneously round him. Some of these, it is true, were simply pressed by 'the difficulty of finding a living,' or were pursued 'for debt' by creditors; but the situation of the kingdom, which was becoming more and more melancholy

---

[1] 1 Sam. xxi. 11–16 [10–15]: compare similar examples of this stratagem in the story of Ulysses as well as amongst the Arabs (*Hamâsa*, p. 322, 21); also *Journ. As.* 1844, ii. p. 181. According to the Shâhnâmeh, Kai-Khosrev (like another David) fights, while still almost a child, with lions and so on, and afterwards has to feign idiocy in the face of mortal peril. The fact that David afterwards entered into friendly relations with the same king, 1 Sam. xxvii.–xxix., gives no ground for suspicion against the historical character of this narrative, for several years had intervened and David stood in quite another position at the head of 600 men and as Saul's reputed rival. It is certainly possible that the Achish who appears afterwards was a successor of this one; indeed this first king is called Abimelech rather than Achish in Ps. xxxiv. 1, unless the author of the superscription of this Psalm simply had this name floating in his mind from Gen. xx. 2 sqq.; xxi. 22, 32; xxvi. 8 sqq.

[2] Vol. ii. p. 392 sqq.

under Saul, filled others with 'bitterness' or sorrow of heart, and drove them to a leader from whom they might hope better things for the future.[1] David did not send these men away, so that he soon saw himself surrounded by about 400 men who acknowledged him as their commander (or 'prince'); but he was certainly not urged to this course by any idea of levying war against Saul with his men, but rather by his native instinct of commanding and ruling others, especially in their time of need and in war. He must easily have foreseen that, when commanding a company such as this, he might, without injuring the king, be of the very greatest use to the people; he might protect the southern frontiers of the kingdom from the plundering incursions of the surrounding tribes, and so play into the hands of the king himself, though not in the way he would most have desired. The actual course of events soon realised some of these expectations.

Such is the general knowledge respecting this period of David's life which we are able to attain with certainty; but it is more difficult for us to recognise the connexion and sequence of the separate events which must have then taken place and of which no doubt there were far more than are now recorded. During the whole of this period, the reserve of David's army remained in constant occupation of the territory of eastern Judah, from the cave of Adullam (lying somewhat south of Bethlehem[2]) to the north, down to Maon (still well known by its modern site), to the south; a tract of land of considerable mileage both in length and breadth, in some parts mountainous, wooded and cavernous, in others stretching far into desolate wastes, and admirably suited by its whole conformation to shelter fugitives and small armies. From this position, the little army could easily command the surrounding districts far to the south, or, by climbing the mountain ridge to the west, could push through to the Shephélah or great plain of Judah, to oppose the Philistines who were always making incursions there. But within this circle, as we learn from many indications, the little army must often have changed its quarters, as convenience or its varied necessities or the cry of the oppressed demanded. Never long in any city, especially a fortified one, where it might be besieged

---

[1] 1 Sam. xxii. 2.
[2] Robinson's opinion (*Bib. Res.* ii. p. 175) that this cave lay west of the mountain-ridge in Judah, seems to us to be in opposition to the whole history of these years of David's life; nor can it derive any support from Josh. xv. 35, since the Adullam described in this passage as lying in the plain of Judah was not a cave at all but a city; comp. 2 Macc. xii. 38. So long, therefore, as nothing more certain is known, we may adhere to the tradition that it is identical with the present *Wâdi Kdhureitûn*, south of Bethlehem; cf., however, *Jahrb. der Bib. Wiss.* iii. p. 193 and Saulcy's *Voyages*, ii. p. 95 sq.

and captured,[1] drawing itself off on the approach of every danger to the steep heights easy of defence, it encamped upon the mountain top or in the shelter of the wood, upon the hillside or in the wilderness, just as chance directed.[2] Besides the connected narrative, we still possess a catalogue, which is evidently derived from very ancient sources, of towns of Judah, to the Elders of which David became known at this time by his acts of service and neighbourly conduct, and the friendly remembrance of which he desired also to retain afterwards at Ziklag;[3] the number of these towns is considerable. Further, this freebooting life must have lasted several years: but not even this section supplies us with any dates; and, moreover, the representation of the earlier narrator has not come down to us without many gaps. All that we can know for certain of the separate events in the course of this period may be related as follows:—

1) The cave of Adullam whither David first betook himself, soon became the resort of so many fugitives who sought his protection, that he occupied the nearest mountain height with the four hundred men or so, who acknowledged him as their leader, and there entrenched himself;[4] and since he could not but fear that as soon as Saul came to hear of these proceedings he would seek to revenge himself, at all events on his parents who dwelt at Bethlehem, even if not at once on himself, he escorted them beyond the Dead Sea, to a fortress in the land of Moab, and commended them to the good faith of the king

---

[1] This is the meaning of the words in 1 Sam. xxiii. 14, 19.

[2] Comp. 1 Sam. xxiii. 7.

[3] In the passage 1 Sam. xxx. 26–31, where the earlier narrator keeps very close to the most ancient authorities. The cities are: 1. בֵּית צוּר (which we must read instead of בֵּית אֵל after the LXX), known from the history of the Maccabees; 2. Ramoth in the south; 3. Jattir; 4. Aroer, Robinson, ii. p. 199 sqq., Ritter's *Erdkunde*, xiv. p. 123 sq.; 5. Ἀμμάδι, according to the LXX, perhaps the עֵין גֶדִי mentioned 1 Sam. xxiv. 1; 6. שִׂפְמוֹת no further known as yet, but like an ancient Canaanitish name, 1 Chron. xxvii. 27, Num. xxxiv. 10 sq.; 7. Eshtemoa, now identified as Samûa; 8. LXX *Gath*, probably an abbreviation of מוֹרֶשֶׁת גַּת, Micah i. 14; 9. LXX Κιμάθ, perhaps identical with קִינָה, Josh. xv. 22; 10. LXX Σαφέκ, perhaps a corruption of אָפֵק, Josh. xv. 53; 11. LXX Θημάθ, uncertain, unless identical with רוּמָה, Josh. xv. 52; 12. *Carmel*, which must be read for בְּרַכֶל, see above p. 38; 13. The cities of the Jerahmeelites, 1 Chron. ii. 25 sq., 42, and of the Kenites; 14. Hormah, vol. ii. p. 190, omitted by the LXX; 15. LXX Ἰεριμούθ Josh. xv. 35; 16. בּוֹר עָשָׁן, cf. Josh. xv. 42; 17. עָתָךְ, or rather עֶתֶר, Josh. xv. 42, xix. 7, this and the preceding are omitted by the LXX; 18. LXX, Beersheba; 19. LXX, Νομβέ, but not identical with Beit-Nûbah or Nobe in Jerome, *Epitaph. Paulæ*, p. 673, *Epist.* lxxxvi.; 20. Hebron. The LXX have here on the whole a better text.

[4] The connexion of the words in xxii. 1–5, obliges us to suppose that David repaired thither; so that a statement to that effect must have fallen out after verse 2. But we may conjecture that the omission here is of a far graver character from the sudden mention of the prophet Gad, verse 5, whose arrival must necessarily have been further described after verse 2.

there, 'until he should see what God would do with him.' Since he desired to place his parents in safety in a foreign land beyond the reach of Saul, and since he could no longer trust the Philistines after his latest experience,[1] Moab was his nearest resort; and this consideration gained weight from the old clan relations which subsisted between Moab and Judah, and especially (according to the book of Ruth) with the house of David.[2]

This state of affairs seems to have lasted a considerable time; and we are still more definitely informed, by a very ancient authority,[3] that when David had gained a firm footing on this mountain height, mighty men from every tribe of Israel streamed to join him, considering that the times offered no better alternative than to put themselves under his command. From the tribe of Gad beyond the Jordan, there came (to follow this account) eleven heroes of renown, whose names are enumerated, fully versed in the art of war, equipped with shield and spear, like lions in aspect, and yet coursing over the mountains with the swift foot of the gazelle;[4] the feeblest of them equal to a hundred and the mightiest to a thousand men.[5] On one occasion (perhaps at the very time of their secession to David) they passed in spring time over the flooded banks of the Jordan, swollen high by heavy falls of rain and melted snow, and, moreover, put to flight their pursuers, who had rallied from east and west in the plain of the Jordan. David's troop was further increased by men of Benjamin and Judah, and though their names are now omitted from the Chronicles, the following circumstance is narrated of them. As they approached, David advanced ceremoniously to meet them, and addressed them, declaring that 'if they had come in a friendly spirit to help him, he would have one heart and one soul with them; but if they had come to betray him, when some future occasion served, to his enemies, although he had done no wrong, then he called on the God of their fathers for revenge upon them!' Upon this, their leader Amasai,[6] suddenly

---

[1] P. 83 sq.

[2] 1 Sam. xxii. 1–4. The recurrence of a similar proceeding in the times of the Maccabees is worthy of note.

[3] 1 Chron. xii. 8–18; cf. vol. i. p. 137.

[4] We are forcibly reminded of similar images undoubtedly derived from that period: 2 Sam. i. 23; ii. 18; Ps. xviii. 33–40 [32–39].

[5] These words of verse 14, on the other hand, have quite the tone of an addition from the hand of the Chronicler himself.

[6] This עָמָשַׂי appears to be identical with the עֲמָשָׂא who plays so prominent a part in the war of Absalom, cf. infra; at least, this last was of the tribe of Judah and at the same time a nephew of David, 2 Sam. xvii. 25, 1 Chron. ii. 16 sq.; his mother Abigail, however (according to 2 Sam. xvii. 25), and her sister Zeruiah, Joab's mother, were certainly not the daughters of David's father Jesse, but only of his mother by a former husband of the name of Nahash. Amasa's father was an Ishmaelite, strictly speaking therefore a foreigner, of the name of Ithra, 2

seized with a genuine inspiration, cried out; 'Thine are we, David, and with thee, thou son of Jesse; peace, peace unto thee, and peace to thy helpers, for thy God helpeth thee!' So he received them in friendship and appointed them officers. These words of unwonted precaution on David's part seem to indicate that he had already witnessed, to his own detriment, shameful instances of the deceit and treachery of deserters such as these, especially from the tribe of Benjamin. Indeed, we have every reason to suppose that until the death of Saul there were plenty of people in Israel who sought openly and secretly, at his instigation, to injure David. The example of the Ziphites will be noticed in detail below; and it was perhaps at this very time that the Benjamite Cush (of whose treachery David, who was thereby brought into extreme danger, complains so bitterly in the beautiful seventh Psalm) played his part; for the style of the song alluded to marks it out as belonging to the time when David was already the independent commander of an army.

On another occasion three of the greatest heroes came to David while he was occupying this mountain fastness, where he, too, like Saul, was the object of attack from the Philistines. Although their head-quarters were in the valley of Rephaim south-west of Jerusalem, they had pushed forward an advanced guard (or post) further south to Bethlehem. David descended from his mountain hold to take part in the engagement against them, but in the toil of battle he felt so exhausted, that he longed above all things for a draught of clear water from the well at the gate of Bethlehem. When the three heard this, they started of their own accord, burst into the camp of the Philistines at the gate of Bethlehem, drew the water, and brought it to David; but he would not drink it, but poured it as a thank-offering to God upon the ground, and said, 'God forbid that I should do this! shall I drink the blood of the men that went in jeopardy of their lives?'[1]

The second oldest narrator, from whose hand alone we have anything like a connected history of David during this period, has certainly already begun to pay less attention to such isolated events and individual traits; but he indicates the gradual increase of David's band by the fact of his henceforth estima-

---

Sam. xxii. 25, or Jether, 1 Kings ii. 5, 32, 1 Chron. ii. 17, which is apparently nothing but a shorter form of the same. Cf. vol. ii. p. 25, *note* 7.

[1] From the very ancient source, 2 Sam. xxiii. 13–17, where קְצִיר, verse 13, must be corrected in accordance with 1 Chron. xi. 15–19. Similar stories are sometimes told of later generals, as of Alexander for instance; but here we have a primitive type, the historical character of which is beyond dispute. This picture is presented in great detail and with some peculiarities in 4 Macc. iii. 6–16.

ting the army that accompanied him no longer at 400, but at about 600 men;[1] an important number, of which we shall have more to say below. But the band of David's followers already included a prophet also, of the name of Gad, doubtless the same who still appears at his side in Jerusalem, when his age is more advanced;[2] this would make him about contemporary with David, and hence the conjecture forces itself upon us that the two had already contracted a close intimacy in earlier times in Samuel's Prophetic School, and that it was this which induced Gad to follow him into the desert regions. The character of the times of which we are speaking made it no small good fortune to have at one's side a prophet, and in his person a kind of oracle, especially for so small an army devoid of other supports; and we soon have evidence of the loftier encouragement and guidance which he afforded. The prophet requires in the name of Jahveh (no further particulars are given), that the army should leave the mountain height and descend deeper into the land (of Judah); so David marches to a forest which lay in the heart of the country.[3] Subsequently news arrives that the Philistines are besieging the city of Keilah,[4] situated in the low land, west of the mountain ridge, and are plundering the threshing-floors all over the surrounding plain, which the harvest time had just filled with corn. David consults the oracle of this prophet, and is encouraged to make an expedition to drive away the marauding Philistines, and relieve the sorely-pressed city. At first the army does not share in the lofty courage aroused by this response in their leader. It feels that even its present position is not free from anxiety and danger; how much less can it venture to engage the well-ordered ranks of the Philistines in battle! But since the oracle, on a second consultation, gives the most positive assurance of a defeat of the Philistines, David breaks up his camp and leads the army thither, drives away their herds from the Philistines, defeats them in a great battle, and relieves the city, in which he then establishes himself and his army.[5]

---

[1] 1 Sam. xxiii. 13; cf. xxii. 2.

[2] 2 Sam. xxiv. 11; on the other hand, he seems to have been already dead at the time of Solomon's accession to the throne; the other great prophet of David's time, Nathan, was probably therefore younger, and to judge at least from the indication in 1 Kings iv. 5, of priestly descent.

[3] 'The forest of Hareth,' xxii. 5, is not otherwise known, nor is the πόλις Σαρίκ of the LXX any clearer to us; perhaps, however, חֹרֶשׁ should be read for חרת

according to xxiii. 15, 18 sq. Joseph. Antiq. vi. 12. 4 reads Σαρίς, but Wilson (Lands, ii. p. 266) is wrong in joining this with the Sârûs noticed p. 19.

[4] Since it lay, according to Josh. xv. 44, between the cities of Nezib and Mareshah, and these, according to Robinson's Bib. Res. ii. p. 404 sq., 422 sq., lay east and south of Eleutheropolis, the position of this city may be defined with tolerable accuracy.

[5] 1 Sam. xxii. 5; xxiii. 1–5.

Meanwhile, as this last event was taking place, a black deed of royal jealousy was already accomplished at Saul's court without the knowledge of David, which could not but bear bitter fruit for Saul, and was also not without influence on David's further history. When Saul had received trustworthy information that David and his followers had established themselves in the almost inaccessible regions of the south, he held a solemn reception in an open place on the height of his capital Gibeah, sitting under a venerable tamarisk tree,[1] where those who sought his judicial decision might appear before him. Here, surrounded by the magnates of his kingdom, chiefly drawn from amongst the Benjamites, he alludes with bitter vexation to the affair of David: 'No doubt the son of Jesse would load all of them too with honourable gifts and offices, since they had all conspired against him; not one of them would communicate the truth to him, while his first-born had already made a league with David; not one would share his deep grief in that his son had raised up his own subject now to lie in wait against him!' Upon this, Doeg the Edomite,[2] steps forth from the ring of officers round the royal seat[3] to relate how he has seen the High-priest Ahimelech at Nob give David an oracle, provision for the journey, and the sword of Goliath, whereupon the king has this priest and the other male members of his whole house brought at once from Nob to Gibeah, and accuses them of high-treason. Ahimelech answered, with perfect justice, that he had known nothing of David except that, as son-in-law of the king and commander of the royal body-guard,[4] he was more trusted and honoured at the royal court than anyone else; that as to the oracle, he had always before communicated it to him when he desired it; that the king must not ascribe to him and to his house a crime of which he could never have had the smallest knowledge. Saul, however, entangled in the unreasoning delusion that this priest must have joined in conspiracy with David, resolves without further delay to put him and all his relatives to death,—nay, when the body-guard hesitate to carry out this order, through reverence for their priestly rank, Doeg himself, at Saul's behest, executes all the innocent men, to the number of eighty-five,[5] and then, in addition,

---

[1] Like the earliest Teutonic kings.
[2] P. 83.
[3] His office, which gave him the right of being present here and of volunteering to speak, is described in xxii. 9, having been designated somewhat more generally in xxi. 8 [7]; but in this last passage we must read פָּרְדִּי, according to the LXX, instead of עַבְדִי; he was overseer of the king's mules, or as we should say, the king's chief equerry.
[4] P. 75.
[5] The LXX adopt, in preference, the number of 305, Fl. Josephus 385.

slaughters every living thing in the sacerdotal city of Nob, women and children, men and beasts. The narrative needed not to intimate further how much Saul lost in public estimation by this act![1]

Only one single son of this priest, Abiathar by name, found means of escaping this massacre. As a matter of course he betook himself as soon as possible to David, who received him with all the deeper emotion because he now remembered to have seen the Edomite Doeg with his father Ahimelech at the time,—not without a foreboding that he would betray the whole affair to Saul. He might regard himself, therefore, as the ultimate cause of so great a calamity to a noble sacerdotal house. For although no one could well have suspected beforehand that Saul would lay his hand on even one single priest for having afforded to an innocent refugee spiritual consolation and bodily sustenance, yet a man of such tender feelings as David would rightly take it deeply to heart that he had, even indirectly, been the cause of such great misery; and so he now desired at least to hold sacred, as a costly pledge entrusted to him, the one member of the sacerdotal house who had been rescued, and to protect his life as though it were his own. And, at the same time, this fugitive was already a priest whose rank empowered him to give oracular responses, and he brought with him the sacred apparatus of his oracle; so that David had gained in him a friend, whose priestly oracle, according to the popular ideas of the age, would rank far higher than the purely prophetic oracle of Gad. From this time forward, therefore, we find that he plays no unimportant part in David's history. An example of this occurs immediately. David already occupied the conquered Keilah at the time of Abiathar's escape to him,[2] and when Saul heard that he had established himself in that 'city of gates and bars,' he made preparations for war, and proclaimed a general levy, so as to capture him and all his army in the city. On hearing of this, David resorted to this priestly oracle, rather than to that of Gad, with the double

---

[1] 1 Sam. xxii. 6–19.

[2] This is the evident meaning of the words in xxiii. 6; and since we have no reason to doubt, on any other grounds, that this is the chronological connexion of the events, we must suppose that the oracle mentioned in xxiii. 2-4 was not that of this priest but that of Gad mentioned in xxii. 5. But the most distinct indication of this fact which the narrator gives is really found in another passage, xxiii. 9 sq.; cf. xxx. 7 sq., where he describes the manner in which the priestly oracle was consulted and its responses were given as quite different from that of the preceding oracle, xxiii. 2-4. No doubt even earlier readers already confused all this, and therefore altered the reading of verse 6 as is seen in the LXX; but it is not until then that the inexplicable difficulty arises how the representation could lose all its order and principle of arrangement.

question of whether Saul would descend upon Keilah, and whether its inhabitants would at once deliver up himself and his men, if Saul should appear with his army. The oracle answers both questions in the affirmative; and so David, with his force of about 600 men, retires from the city to his earlier hiding-places in such good time that Saul, when the news reaches him, abandons his campaign.[1]

We cannot expect to find, however, that Saul at the same time lost his passionate rage, burning for David's destruction; and in fact we see, from many significant traces, that he endeavoured repeatedly to get David into his power. The earlier narrators indicate these long-continued hostilities in but few words,[2] yet in the history of those sad, bewildered efforts which were ever brought to nought by a divine destiny, two special events are prominent.

On one occasion, as David lay in the depth of a wood within the wilderness of Ziph[3] south-east of Hebron, he was thrown into the utmost terror by the approach of Saul. We are not further informed of the special circumstances, but no doubt the great anxiety of the hero was sufficiently justified. Just at this moment, Jonathan, as though led by God, made his way to David in the thickets of the forest, and consoled him as if with words and promises from God Himself: so far from falling into Saul's power, he should one day rule as king of Israel, and, as for himself, his only wish was to be next to him in the kingdom, and so to be the first of his subjects; thus had he spoken even to Saul, and never would he tire of striving to influence his father to the same purport. On these assurances the two renewed their covenant of friendship, and in this mood they parted.[4] Now there certainly can be no mistake that with this free impulse of the purest and most self-sacrificing love the earlier narrator designedly—already referring, that is to say, to the whole sequel of the history—closes his account of the connexion between the two heroes: this is the last time that either sees the other, and it is this which forms the crowning

---

[1] 1 Sam. xxii. 20-23; xxiii. 6-13.
[2] 1 Sam. xxiii. 14.
[3] On the situation of Ziph see Robinson, ii. p. 191 sqq.
[4] This is the meaning of the narrative xxiii. 15-18, which we cannot understand rightly as long as we preserve in verse 15 the reading וַיַּרְא which was followed indeed even by the LXX; for we do not see how the fact that David *saw* the danger is connected with Jonathan's arrival. But since in other respects verse 15 is certainly connected with verses 16-18, and we have no grounds for supposing the text to be mutilated here, we must read וַיִּרָא, the only word which fits the sequel of the whole narrative. But then a statement of what it was that finally hindered Saul from taking David captive on that occasion, seems to have fallen out after verse 18.

point of this sacred friendship. There is no difficulty, however, in believing that on some occasion, when his friend was in danger, Jonathan really did seek him out, penetrating even to his desert abode.

On another occasion,[1] some of the rude inhabitants of the wilderness of Ziph itself went to Saul to offer him their services in capturing David; and the king, highly commending their zeal towards himself, urges them at the same time to ascertain exactly in which of the many haunts of the crafty fugitive he is actually to be found, so that, be it in what corner of Judah it may, with the assistance of their information and guidance, he may succeed in capturing him.[2] They accordingly advanced before Saul to the desert of Ziph. David had already drawn off further south, to the yet more barren desert of Maon; but since his resting-place was betrayed to Saul, who, as he heard, was engaged in an expedition against him, he dropped down from the steep mountain on which his army had encamped,[3] and for fear of being surrounded and starved out, remained on the uncultivated plain, ready for a further retreat as soon as it should become necessary. But Saul, thoroughly apprised of all his movements by spies, anticipated him; and now there was nothing between the two armies except the hill which David had abandoned, and whilst he, on one side of it, made repeated preparations for adroitly effecting his escape from the king with the greatest rapidity, Saul with his men sought so to surround him on all sides as to leave no possible outlet for escape. David and all his army were now in the utmost danger of being taken prisoners, when Saul was called off by a special messenger to check the Philistines who had penetrated far into the country, apparently northwards, and were everywhere victorious.[4] Never before had David and his army been in such extreme danger; no wonder, then, that the very rock where his fate had finally come to such a wonderful crisis, long bore the name of Destiny-rock![5]

---

[1] 1 Sam. xxiii. 19–28.

[2] הָכִין, verse 22, is 'to make sure,' as appears from נָכוֹן, verse 23, 'the certain, trustworthy.'

[3] יָרַד הַסֶּלַע, verse 25, is 'to descend the rock,' down from it, therefore, as we might express it more definitely; but as early as the LXX we find the false reading εἰς τὴν πέτραν, which does not at all suit the context of the narrative.

[4] It is possible, and even probable, that it was Saul's expedition against David which incited the Philistines to make an expedition themselves, and as this was unexpected, it was not at the usual time of the year; but there is nothing to prove that David had called them to his assistance.

[5] Since the meaning elsewhere assigned to הַמַּחְלְקוֹת, verse 28 (the word in question), is not suitable here (for if so, we should have to understand 'rock of the divisions of the army,' i.e. rock of the army, which would not be sufficiently sig-

David himself now withdrew further eastwards to the mountain heights of En-gedi on the shore of the Dead Sea; but in spite of this, when Saul, at the close of the campaign against the Philistines, heard of his movements, he took the field again with 3,000 chosen warriors to seek David and his men on the 'rock ledges of the chamois.' We have no further information from the same earlier narrator as to the means by which this second enterprise, prompted by the king's implacable hatred, was frustrated; but we can scarcely suppose that David would fail to perceive (as this narrator states that he did clearly) the impossibility of maintaining himself any longer in these desert regions of Judah, or indeed in any part whatever of Saul's dominions. Such then, according to the representation of the earlier narrator, is the close of the whole of this period of David's life.[1]

2) At the conclusion, however, of the mutual relations of David and Saul, the later narrators have interwoven in the narrative a lofty conception, which could not easily have been brought into striking prominence at any other point. Generosity towards his foes was a part of David's very being, so that if accident had thrown his adversary into his power, he would not seize the opportunity for gratifying his revenge, but would rather dismiss him with honour. Indeed, David himself indicates as much, quite briefly and incidentally but clearly enough, in the poem Psalm vii. 5 [vii. 4]. Again, even if he had had a favourable opportunity of inflicting a deep injury on Saul himself, the pure conception of 'God's Anointed' which filled his soul, would have been enough in itself to restrain him from doing him any bodily harm. And at this point, no doubt, the earlier narrator also, whose fragments are defective here, gave some account of how David had delivered Saul when he had run too far into danger; for without the supposition of some such original narrative, even the representations which we have are inexplicable. Moreover, we may easily perceive that even in the more popular tradition this story of David's generosity was almost as great a favourite

nificant), there seems to be nothing left but to understand it, like the simple חֲלָק, of a decree of fate. Since the name is certainly quite historical, we need not be surprised at its peculiar formation.

[1] It clearly follows from xxvii. 1 sq., that the connexion of the whole history in the earlier narrator's mind was such as is indicated above (for on the other hand, after the close of the present narratives in xxiv. and xxvi., David would have had no reason whatever for fleeing from the country through fear of Saul); and also from xxiv. 1-4 [xxiii. 29-xxiv. 3], we certainly still have the words of the earlier narrator, both because of their general tone and because the mention of the 'sheepfolds by the way' sounds as historical as, in its present connexion, unintelligible and superfluous.

as that other tale of his youthful combat with Goliath; and accordingly was told as often and finally assumed as many different forms. How Jahveh's true servant must reverence 'Jahveh's Anointed,' how he must seek his good even at the cost of his own, but hold it the greatest sin so much as to lay a hand upon him,—all this could now be brought vividly to mind from the history of him who afterwards furnished the type of such an Anointed one himself, but who could hardly have thus embodied the idea, had he not previously borne it with him in his own soul, and never sinned against it in his life. But while David behaves in the noblest manner to the 'Anointed of Jahveh' from a true conception of his real function, the deeper meaning which increasingly penetrates these representations is not quite complete until even Saul, as if moved by David's matchless generosity, is himself conceived as treating his supposed enemy in a manner worthy of the true 'Anointed of Jahveh.' He is represented not only as having had to thank David for the preservation of his own life at the very time when he was seeking his, but also as having been seized at the moment by a true and irresistible feeling of David's exalted greatness, so that he acknowledged to him himself that the future sway over Israel was his due, and upon that entered into a league of friendship with him. This was, in fact, the origin of the loftiest representations of pure truths which are conceivable in this direction; for he alone is the true hero who, like David, forces involuntary recognition and friendship, even from his bitterest foe; and he is an 'Anointed of God' through whom, as through Saul, according to this representation, the lightning flash of pure truth, dispelling all the shades of darkness, unexpectedly darts at the right moment, even though a darker night has already clouded his brow. But according to the earlier narrator, it was only at a former time that Saul was still capable of these sudden moments of illumination with respect to David;[1] moreover, the earlier narrator certainly confines to Jonathan the anticipation and sanction of David's future rule on the part of the House of Saul itself, together with the artistic foreshadowing which it contains of the whole subsequent course of events; whereas the later representation prefers to extend all this to Saul. But it is equally clear that this is simply a further expansion of the original narrative, in which the ideal conception at last becomes quite predominant.

Two narratives of this description are contained in the

[1] P. 75 sqq.

present book, both alike flowing into that style of representation in which the simple act sinks into insignificance before the grandeur of the sentiments which it illustrated, yet each bearing in its style of composition traces of a special narrator. Just in the same way, we had before to distinguish between three narrators of the history of Goliath,[1] to which the present story bears an analogy throughout. The two accounts agree in representing the opportunity afforded to David of taking vengeance upon Saul, as a deep sleep into which the king had fallen in a cave[2] during his campaign against David; we need not doubt, therefore, that this was a trait in the original narrative;[3] but the account in 1 Sam. xxiv. (which proceeds from the earlier of these two narrators) connects the event with David's abode at En-gedi, while the other, 1 Sam. xxvi. (which holds more closely to many words of the older narrator, and by all indications is due to a yet later hand), lays the scene in the wilderness of Ziph at the hill of Hachilah situated in that district.[4] Both represent David as urged by his men to seize the opportunity of revenging himself upon Saul; but it is only the latest narrative ch. xxvi. which mentions Abishai,[5] the brother of Joab, as accompanying David when he approached the king, and Abner as laying himself fairly open to the taunts of David by his careless watch over Saul. According to each account, David takes from the sleeping king that which may serve as a sign of his having been at his side, so as to be able to show it to him when he wakes with indignant yet affectionate expostulation; but according to ch. xxiv. he cuts off the border of his royal garment, and then, somewhat alarmed himself by the over-boldness of the deed,[6] checks the eagerness of his people by strictly forbidding any

---

[1] P. 70 sqq.

[2] In 1 Sam. xxvi. 4 the LXX at any rate still read אֶל נְכוֹן קְעִילָה, instead of אֶל־נָכוֹן, but we ought rather to read אֶל־נֶכֶר מְעָרָה, 'in the cleft of a cave,' or even נֶכֶר, unless נָכַר means the same.

[3] In 1 Sam. xxiv. 4 [3], הָסֵךְ אֶת־רַגְלָיו is commonly taken as signifying 'to obey the necessities of nature,' but this by no means suits the narrative, since one cannot (for many reasons which it is hardly worth while to enumerate) conceive how David and his friends could have done what they did on any such occasion as that; besides, in Judges iii. 24, the above interpretation does not allow for as much time as is there described as elapsing. Now if the expression properly means to cover his feet, i.e. to squat down, it perhaps might bear the usual interpretation, but might just as well signify the sleep of simple fatigue in the middle of the day without covering.

[4] 1 Sam. xxvi. i–3, according to xxiii. 19.

[5] The description of Abishai, xxvi. 6, seems to have been taken from an earlier passage 2 Sam. xxiii. 18. Ahimelech (LXX Ἀβιμέλεχ) the Hittite, who is mentioned here together with Abishai, but represented as inferior in valour, does not appear anywhere else in the extant records, but no doubt the narrator found him already mentioned by some earlier authority.

[6] Cf. 2 Sam. xxiv. 10, whence this expression, 1 Sam. xxiv. 6 [5], is no doubt borrowed.

DAVID AND NABAL.

attack upon Saul; while according to ch. xxvi. he takes away his spear and the cruse of water.[1] The conclusion is much the same in both narratives. The later form, ch. xxvi., which is fullest throughout, makes David's admonition to the king especially prominent: 'if it is Jahveh who (by an evil spirit) has incited him to persecute the guiltless, let Him smell an offering, i.e. let Him have a sufficient sin-offering brought to Him; but if it is men who have thus misled the king, he prays that they may be accursed, for they have forced him to leave the holy land and (in strange countries) to serve strange gods, whilst his one only wish is that his lot should not be cast far from the holy place (the temple).' Through these words we seem to hear the sound of the bitter complaint of the numbers who were driven into banishment at the beginning of the great national dispersion about the seventh century, by unjust kings like Manasseh.

3) Apart from the relation in which David stood to Saul, the earlier narrator has left us a very graphic picture of other aspects of his life in these desolate regions. It is contained in a very detailed narrative which only hinges, it is true, on one single occurrence;[2] but it is an occurrence which assumes a greater importance from its consequences. For some reason, of which we no longer know the particulars, David and all his men descended after the death of Samuel (towards the close, that is,[3] of the whole of this period of David's life) from the eastern cliffs by En-gedi to the south-eastern desert by the city of Paran,[4] where he heard that a great rural festival was being held in the neighbourhood. There was a very rich Calebite[5] who lived at Maon, and sent his herds which were of unusual size to pasture on Mount Carmel, which lay somewhat

---

[1] A very ancient usage explains why the cruse of water is here brought into such special prominence. According to this custom, some high dignitary always had in keeping a costly ewer for the king's necessary ablutions, and it was specially his duty to take it with him and present it to the king during campaigns or other journeys; so that its disappearance would involve almost as great disgrace to the king as the loss of his sceptre. I have shown long ago in reference to Ps. lx. 9 [8], that this custom still existed in the age of David. Besides, there are many other instances of similar stories, in which the future conqueror and founder of a new dynasty is represented as having received at first some symbol of royalty from his predecessor, by accident as it were, or in sport. Thus Alexander at first takes the royal divining cup from Dârâ as if in sport; a story which, even in the Shâhnâmeh, no longer appears in its original light; and in nothing was the belief in omens so strong as in the high affairs of state.

[2] 1 Sam. xxv.

[3] P. 52 sq.

[4] It appears from the LXX Vat. that there must have been a various reading מָעוֹן here, since the wilderness of Paran, well-known in Mosaic history, ii. p. 189, appeared to lie too far south to be the one here intended; no doubt, however, this Paran was the same, and lay further south than the far better known Maon.

[5] Vol. ii. p. 284 sq.

more to the north; and it was he who was celebrating the
annual shearers' feast on his estate on the hills. Now, since
the inhabitants of these southern regions received little or no
protection in person or property from Saul (as we have already
seen[1] in the case of the city of Keilah), they would have been
constantly exposed to the rapacity of the tribes of the desert
south of Judah, had not David and his flying troop undertaken
to protect them. It was not, therefore, at all unreasonable in
David to wish to receive a small share of the superfluities of
the feast for the immediate necessities of his people. He
certainly did not at that time exact stated contributions from
any of these districts; but without a certain participation in
the abundance of the inhabitants whom he took under his
protection, he and his army could not have subsisted; as must
always be the case under similar circumstances. Accordingly
he sends ten of his followers to congratulate the rich Calebite,
and intimate to him their master's modest request. But un-
luckily they had to do with a churlish fellow, who easily allowed
himself to be hurried by his thoughtlessness into acts of violence, and so seemed actually to be what his name signified,
Nabal, i.e. fool. In accordance with his character he turns
away the deputation, and adds some insulting expressions
about David, the low-born traitor who rebelled against his
rightful lord! On the return of his messengers, David determines to be revenged for the slight thus openly put upon him,
and leaving the rest behind to guard the baggage, marches off
at the head of two-thirds of his whole force, which amounted to
600 men, with drawn swords, to surprise and destroy everything
the following night. Fortunately, however, the discreet and
beautiful Abigail, Nabal's wife, receives timely notice of all
that has happened, from one of the servants who was acquainted
with every circumstance, and had therefore good reason for his
evil forebodings; and towards evening, when Nabal surrenders
himself to the most careless revelry, she hurriedly collects,
without his knowledge, a suitable present of all kinds of provisions,[2] sends it forward, packed on asses, to meet the advancing force, and then follows after it in person. Hardly
has she reached the slope (the 'covert') of the hill, when she
comes upon David descending from the southern hill right

---

[1] P. 89.

[2] How simple these provisions were at that time may be seen from the enumeration of them in verse 18: 200 loaves, 2 skins of wine, 5 dressed sheep, 500 small measures of peeled barley, 100 similar measures of raisins, and 200 of dried figs. After חמש it seems that מאות has fallen out, for a *seah* of grain, according to Gen. xviii. 6, did not contain much more than enough for a couple of men, and even an *ephah*, which is substituted by the LXX, would still be too small. Cf. also 1 Sam. xxx. 11 sq.; 1 Chron. xii. 40.

opposite her. She beseeches him to accept her present; and her representations, while offered with the utmost humility, are such as must appeal most powerfully to a good man's heart: 'surely now he is withheld by God himself from coming to shed blood and to take vengeance with his own hand; since he fights the battles of Jahveh,[1] and has done no evil, assuredly God will one day establish his house in prosperity; and when God gives him his long-appointed rule over Israel, he will have no thought of blood spilt and vengeance taken to turn to bitter reproaches in his heart.' David, on his part, accepts the present with joyful thanks to God for having restrained him in time from a further advance, and then turns back. On her return home, Abigail finds her husband spending the night in a drunken revel, and is unable to tell him anything that has passed; when she does tell him of it the next morning, the affair, now doubly vexatious to him, drives him into such a brutal rage, that he falls into a fit on the spot, and dies ten days after from a stroke of apoplexy; no wonder that a divine retribution was discerned in his death!

No doubt the narrator was all the more ready to give such a detailed account of these events, because the close of the whole of this section of David's life seemed a convenient place in which to introduce a survey of his domestic life at that time. When the time of mourning had passed, David sought the hand of the rich and apparently childless widow Abigail, and obtained her consent. Before this[2] he had already taken to wife Ahinoam, who came from the little town of Jezreel[3] not far from this neighbourhood, but we are unacquainted with the circumstances of the marriage. He was all the more justified in contracting these marriages from the fact that Saul had meanwhile taken away Michal from him, no doubt designedly, and given her in marriage to another husband, whom he desired to attach to the fortunes of his house.[4]

2. *As Philistine Vassal at Ziklag.*

When David at last came to the conclusion,[5] that it was not safe, either for himself or his men, to remain any longer in the territory of Israel at all, his thoughts reverted to the same Philistine king Achish of Gath, in whose court[6] he had found an

---

[1] Vol. i. p. 67.
[2] The position of the words 1 Sam. xxv. 43, xxvii. 3, xxx. 5, 2 Sam. ii. 2, shows that this had happened earlier.
[3] According to Josh. xv. 55 sq.
[4] 1 Sam. xxv. 39-44.
[5] P. 94.
[6] P. 83 sq.

asylum on his first flight from Saul several years before; but now, as the independent and tried chieftain of a band of 600 warriors, he could assume a very different position towards him from that in which he stood on the former occasion. No doubt king Achish, on his part, had by this time long been aware of his previous mistakes about his extraordinary visitor; and the more bitterly he repented of them the more readily would he now feel inclined to harbour the distinguished leader of a considerable warlike troop, who had been subjected to such open and severe persecution by Saul. One commander and prince, in truth, is ready to work with another, if only for the sake of their common 'craft;'[1] but happily for the good cause, and (as will be seen in the sequel) for David himself, there yet remained certain individuals at the Philistine court, who looked upon him with other eyes than those of the king.

All that David, indeed, could reasonably expect was to secure protection and sustenance for himself and his followers, in return for certain stated services which he promised to render to the king. These were, firstly, a stated share of the booty taken in his independent expeditions,[2] which it was thus tacitly assumed would generally be directed against Saul's subjects; and secondly, service in the Philistine army itself whenever the king should demand it.[3] In this way he entered at once as an independent chieftain (like an Italian Condottiere of the Middle Ages) into the king's service; and the worst of the matter was, that he thereby became liable to be compelled to fight against Saul and Israel, from which, nevertheless, all his feelings in the first instance so violently recoiled. And yet it would not be his fault if ever he found himself fighting under a foreign standard at last, against the man who had persecuted him with such groundless and unremitting rage; moreover, he was possessed of enough wiliness and skill to turn his independent position rather to the advantage than the injury of his own people; and at least he might cherish in his inmost heart the hope that if the worst should come to the worst, and he should be compelled to fight in the ranks of the Philistines against Israel, no grievous results might follow, and if absolutely necessary, he might run the risk. He could not as yet maintain himself anywhere as a perfectly independent prince; and consequently he could not have sought protection for himself and his men in any quarter whatever without expecting to be em-

---

[1] I use this expression here because the late king of Prussia used it in Hanover when crown-prince in 1839.

[2] This follows from 1 Sam. xxvii. 9, when the words are rightly understood.

[3] This results from 1 Sam. xxviii. 1 sq.

DAVID AT ZIKLAG.

ployed on some occasion against Saul. The knot is disentangled speedily and satisfactorily enough, but far less by the hero's human skill than by the over-ruling of a higher destiny.

1) Soon after he had passed over to the Philistines, David himself certainly made an important step towards securing greater independence. At first he established himself according to agreement in the capital city of Gath, and was therefore in the immediate neighbourhood of the king; but he was not accompanied by the 600 warriors alone, but by a complete little tribe, for almost every one of these warriors had a wife and children.[1] This might furnish him at once with an excuse for begging the king, whose entire confidence he acquired immediately, to make him the grant of a country town in his territory, in which he and his people might live. The king granted to him for this purpose the city of Ziklag, of which he thus became feudal lord, thereby laying the foundation of a family estate (demesne); so that in later times, on the division of the Davidic kingdom, this city was considered to pertain to David's house and therefore to the territory of Judah.[2] Amongst other nations, too, it has not seldom happened that a chieftain such as David then was, has been thus made proprietor of a small territory, which has possibly become the foundation of a kingdom of constantly increasing independence and extent. As a matter of fact, David in this city laid the foundation of all his kingdom. Here he could already rule with greater freedom and independence, collect fugitives and deserters around him in larger and larger numbers, send or receive embassies like a prince,[3] and as a ruler over soldiers and over peaceable citizens rehearse, on a small scale, those arts by which he afterwards acquired and maintained his great kingdom.[4] Moreover, being a genuine poet and lover of art, he took advantage of all his opportunities in this direction also, and exercised himself as a musician, in the Gittite, i.e. the Philistine style, which he afterwards transferred from there to Judah and Jerusalem.[5]

---

[1] As follows from 1 Sam. xxvii. 3; cf. 2 Sam. ii. 3.

[2] 1 Sam. xxvii. 6. See more on this point below, under Rehoboam. The site of this place has not yet been ascertained by any modern traveller. It originally belonged to the tribe of Simeon, Josh. xix. 5, but was also, according to ii. p. 287 sq., reckoned as Judah's, Josh. xv. 31. That it lay very far to the south, follows alike from the narrative of David's life and from the situation of the other places which belonged to its district, Josh. xv. 30 sqq., xix. 4. sq., the nearest of all being the Hormah mentioned ii. p. 190. The conjecture of some recent writers that it is identical with el-Sukkarîyeh (i.e. 'the sugary'), south-west of Beit-Jibrîn, is quite groundless. We might think with more reason, since צִיק would signify *strait*, of the present el-Lukiyeh.

[3] Cf. 1 Sam. xxx. 26-31.

[4] 1 Sam. xxvii. 1-6.

[5] That this is the most correct view

We still possess a very ancient and accurate notice[1] of the illustrious heroes who gathered round David at Ziklag, as soon as he had established himself there as a feudal lord. There were Benjamites, and some even of Saul's own kindred, who could hardly have gone over to David except from great dissatisfaction with the turn which things had taken under Saul; men like all the Benjamites,[2] equally able to use the right or the left hand in slinging and shooting: again, there were several from Judah,[3] all of them mentioned by name, except that the Chronicler has here, as in so many other places, greatly curtailed the enumeration of names which he found in the ancient documents. But since the earlier narrator still continues as before[4] to speak of David's army as composed of only 600 men,[5] we see clearly that this is to be taken merely as a round and constant number; and we shall take occasion hereafter to investigate further how this use of the number arose.

We have already observed that it was at this time a necessity for David and his men to make warlike expeditions from Ziklag, which were, at best, nothing but forays hither and thither in search of rich booty. But whenever he went on these raids, he invariably marched against the Geshurites[6] and Amalekites, who were the Aborigines of these countries, and spread partly to the north, but chiefly to the south of the territory of the Philistine king, as far as Egypt, leading for the most part a nomadic life. He seized their herds of camels and their garments, and then brought the covenanted portion of the booty to king Achish at Gath; but (we are told) whenever he was questioned by him about the direction of his expeditions, he always pretended that he had fallen upon the south of Judah, especially upon the Jerahmeelite and Kenite settlers.[7] On the same principle he put to death all his prisoners, for fear the king should learn, through his share in this portion of the booty, where he had really been and what he had been doing. By this means, it is true, he succeeded in keeping the king favour-

---

appears from Ps. viii. 1 [title]. See the remarks made on this subject in my *Dichter des Alten Bundes*, vol. i.

[1] 1 Chron. xii. 1-7; cf. vol. i. p. 136 sq., and above, p. 86 sqq.

[2] Vol. ii. p. 382.

[3] We are guided to Judah by the places, Gederah, 1 Chron. xii. 4, which, according to Josh. xv. 36, was not very far distant from Ziklag, and Gedor, ver. 7; cf. Josh. xv. 5, 8: the Korhites, ver. 6, can hardly have been members of the well-known Levite family; but, according to 1 Chron. ii. 43, they too were of the tribe of Judah. The derivation of the family name חרופי, or Keri, חריפי, ver. 5, is uncertain.

[4] P. 89.

[5] 1 Sam. xxx. 9-24; just as xxiii. 13, xxv. 13, xxvii. 2.

[6] Or Gazerites, according to ii. p. 328 sqq.

[7] It is clear that his reason for making special mention of these peoples was simply that they led, for the most part, a nomadic life, just as we know for certain (ii. p. 286) the Kenites did.

ably disposed towards himself, and yet sparing his beloved country; but at the same time we cannot help regretting that it was only by dissembling and untrue pretences of this kind that he found the means of extricating himself from so embarrassing a situation, and satisfying those whose friendship it seemed indispensable to him to retain.[1]

2) When about a year and four months, however, had thus elapsed,[2] a general Philistine war was kindled against Saul. As a Philistine vassal, David was obliged to take a part in it, and then began the great struggle in which his feudal duty came into collision with his patriotic feeling. When king Achish informed him that he was to take the field against Israel with him, he could not refuse to comply; but he only answered, 'the king should soon know what he would do;' and since the latter only took this really very ambiguous answer in a favourable sense, he rewarded his vassal's willingness by promising to appoint him captain of his body-guard, i.e.[3] to make him the foremost man in the kingdom, next to the commander-in-chief.[4]

The scene of the general war of all the Philistine princes against Israel, which was now to begin, was laid this time in the more northern territory of Israel; and while, according to the earlier narrator, the camp of Israel was pitched at Ain, in the territory of Jezreel, i.e. in the southern portion of that division of the country which subsequently received the name of Galilee, that of the Philistines was pitched more to the west, at Aphek, or according to the other narrator, at Shunem.[5] The central province in which Gibeah, the seat of Saul's government, lay, seems from this, to have been either strongly occupied by the Philistines at this time, or so far devasted as to enable them to push the war into the extremely fertile territory to the north, in the hope of soon reducing the whole of Israel under their yoke; for, had they not been by this time tolerably secure in the southern and central districts, the ease

---

[1] 1 Sam. xxvii. 7-12.
[2] This period is fixed by 1 Sam. xxvii. 7, and xxix. 3; only that in the last instance the more vivid language gives a vaguer tone to the definition of the time 'this year or these years.'
[3] P. 75.
[4] 1 Sam. xxviii. 1 sq.
[5] The most recent investigations, including those of Robinson, point to the conclusion that *Shunem*, xxviii. 4, is identical with the present Sôlam; and in that case *Aphek*, xxix. 1, probably answers to 'Afûleh, which lies somewhere to the west; at any rate, Aphek is as yet undiscovered if this be not its site. If so, Ain, xxix. 1, can hardly be an abbreviation of En-dor, xxviii. 7, since the two places would be separated by the whole of the lesser Hermon; it is, therefore, far preferable to follow Robinson, *Bibl. Res. in Pal.* iii. p. 167 sq., in regarding it as an abbreviation of the present Ain Jâlûd, since this is situated on Mount Gilboa: 1 Sam. xxviii. 4, xxxi. 1 sqq., 2 Sam. i. 21.

with which their own kingdom might be attacked from those quarters would have made them afraid of transferring the seat of war so far north. Thus David and his army had a considerable distance to traverse from Ziklag to the camp, and was obliged to employ several days in the journey. He and Achish brought up the rear of the great Philistine army, which marched with its hundreds and thousands in battle array. The other princes, however, conceived a suspicion that the Hebrews might prove faithless at the decisive moment of the battle, and perhaps the dreaded David might wish to make his peace with his old master Saul, at the expense of Philistines' heads. This is, in fact, only the same suspicion which had induced Achish to persecute David, and at last compelled him to take to flight several years before.[1] Achish himself was at this time as far as possible from entertaining any such suspicions, and endeavoured on the other hand to overcome those of his confederate princes, by commending his vassal's long-tried fidelity; but in spite of this, he found himself compelled by them to request David, in all friendliness, to return to Ziklag, and he, after making, in his turn, the most earnest protestations and assurances of his fidelity, complied. Thus, before the last decisive moment drew nigh, he was released unexpectedly from his painful dilemma. What he would really have done had he been obliged to remain, the ambiguity of his former answer still leaves uncertain; but when we remember the consummate skill with which he had always managed to avoid injuring his own people, or contending against them up to that time, we cannot help believing that he entertained no idea, even then, of preferring the good of the Philistines to that of his own nation.[2]

But there was yet another circumstance which made this leave of absence most opportune for David.[3] Ziklag was more than two days' journey distant from the place where he and his men had been dismissed by Achish, and when he reached it again on the third day he found it in a most frightful condition. A strong band of Amalekites (encouraged, it would seem, by the news that the bravest Philistine and Israelite troops had moved northwards) had issued from the southern wilderness in a successful raid against the adjacent towns of Philistia and Judah, and on the last day had approached Ziklag, having heard, no doubt, of the departure of the terrible David. Here they had not only seized, as a matter of course, the property of the original inhabitants, who offered but a feeble resistance, but had also borne off, amongst other booty, all the

[1] P. 83 sq.   [2] 1 Sam. xxix.   [3] 1 Sam. xxx

wives and children of David and his men as prisoners, and had set fire to the city.¹ No sooner had the soldiers who returned from the war under Achish, recovered from the first cruel shock, than they gave way to the most violent indignation against David as their leader: they even threatened to stone him; nor can it be denied that it was really thoughtless in him to leave the city to the feeble defence of its original inhabitants alone, after having given such gross provocation to the Amalekites by his former plundering incursions. But (as the narrator expressly states in this case) he quickly regained his composure from Jahveh, his God, enquired of the priest-oracle whether a pursuit of the enemy would be advisable, and, on receiving an answer in the affirmative, gave chase at once with all his 600 men. When they come to the brook Besor,² only 400 men pass over it, the rest remaining behind from excessive fatigue; but David does not allow this to prevent his continuing an eager pursuit. On the road they find an Egyptian slave of one of the Amalekites, deserted by his master on the march to Ziklag three days before, because he was sick. This man was with great difficulty brought back to life, and served as a guide to the enemies' camp, which they reached that evening. Here they find the Amalekites scattered about the country in complete disorder and carelessness, carousing and making holiday. David accordingly falls upon them the next morning and smites them till evening with such effect, that only 400 of the common soldiers escape on camels; he captures from them not only the women and children from Ziklag (all of whom they had fortunately kept alive, in hopes of a high ransom), but also the whole of their immense spoil, laden with which he returns. When they reach the brook Besor the victors are unwilling to cede any portion of the booty to the 200 men who had remained behind there, but at last they allow themselves to be persuaded to do so by the eloquence of David, which pointed to a higher justice;³

---

¹ But for the mention of this last circumstance, one would almost have suspected that they had been called in by the original inhabitants, to whom they were related; at any rate, they must have been kept well informed by them, or they would not have known how to hit upon the right moment so exactly.

² Its position has not yet been rediscovered any more than that of Ziklag itself, although certain recent geographers have been beforehand in setting it down in their maps. The whole context shows that some such words as וַיַּעַבְרוּ אַרְבַּע

מֵאוֹת אִישׁ must have fallen out before וְהַנּוֹתָרִים, verse 9; their authenticity is by no means disproved by their absence even as early as the LXX.

³ This has reference (1) to God, who had given them this unexpected victory, so that man could not boast of his own merit in obtaining these possessions, verse 23 (where אֶת־אֲשֶׁר must be taken as an exclamation, according to my *Lehrb.* § 329a, *think of what* . . .); and (2) to man, since, even humanly speaking, they could not demand that this wish of theirs should be humoured, verse 24.

so thenceforth, it became a fixed custom in Israel to assign an equal portion of the booty to those who had been in action and those who had stayed behind to guard the baggage.[1] David had never before captured so large an amount of spoil, and he did not neglect to send rich portions of it as presents to all the friendly Elders of the cities of Judah with whom he had come into contact at an earlier period.[2] In this way the disaster actually resulted in a real gain; and at no other time could friendly relations towards the Elders of Judah have involved consequences of greater importance.

3) For while all this was happening in the southern districts of the country, in the north the great drama so closely connected with these events was being played out; and the catastrophe which could not have furnished a more gloomy presage for Israel's immediate future, necessarily recalled David from his present position. In the battle of Jezreel the victorious Philistines pressed forward to the south-east from the plain in which they had been at first stationed, up to Mount Gilboa. Here Saul and his faithful followers made a desperate resistance, but so many of their bravest fell, that the Philistines not only plundered the camp of Israel in the full tide of victory, but even gained possession of the whole territory as far as the Jordan, and so reached the utmost limit of their desires. Hard pressed by the Philistines, there fell in the slaughter of that same battle, not only Saul's three sons Jonathan, Abinadab, and Melchi-shua, but also Saul himself; but as might easily happen on so miserable an ending of the campaign, slightly varying reports as to the details of his death were soon in circulation. According to one account[3] he was so hotly beset[4] by certain archers, that, covered as he was with wounds already, and seeing no possibility of escape, he entreated his armour-bearer to run him through, for fear his enemies should do so with insults and mockery; and when he shrank in terror from the act, Saul threw himself upon his own sword, upon which the armour-bearer in despair followed his example and died with him. According to the other account[5] the son of an Amalekite serf

---

[1] I have already noticed in my *Alterthümer*, p. 348 sq., with regard to a corresponding regulation of the Book of Origins, the importance of this simple and ancient testimony to the rise of this custom.

[2] P. 86.

[3] 1 Sam. xxxi.: to judge by all indications it comes from the second narrator.

[4] The context shows that וַיָּחֶל, or instead of it וַיָּחָל, is most correctly taken as coming from חָלַל, 'to be wounded, to suffer,' Ps. cix. 22, and so far the LXX give correctly ἐτραυματίσθη, only what follows cannot safely be rendered by εἰς τὰ ὑποχόνδρια.

[5] 2 Sam. i. 1–16, by the earlier narrator. It is contrary to the intention of the narrative to suppose that the Amalekite simply pretended that he had slain the king,

came accidentally upon Saul on Mount Gilboa, as, hotly pursued by chariots and horses, he sank down and rested his head for weariness on the spear[1] he still held in his hand. Looking anxiously behind him the king saw this man, and urged him to kill him outright, for though he still breathed, convulsions had seized his frame. Thinking that the king could never recover from this collapse, the Amalekite obeyed his orders, took the crown from his head and the golden bracelet from his right arm and brought them with all speed to David, together with the fatal news. Both accounts are evidently ancient, but one represents the faithful armour-bearer, the other a rough and careless fellow, not even of the Hebrew race, as being at the side of the falling hero when he expired; as though these two accounts were the respective representations of those who dwell on the good or on the evil of Saul's career.

In the rent clothes of a mourner, this same Amalekite (the earlier narrator tells us), on the third day after David's return to Ziklag, brought him this news of Saul and Jonathan, and of his own deed, no doubt expecting some high reward. But David broke with his men into the deepest lamentations over the death of these two and so many other heroes, and over the disaster thus entailed upon the whole people. On the morrow the Amalekite was executed as one who had sacrilegiously laid his hand on Jahveh's Anointed. So little pleasure had David in the fall of his implacable foe, and so earnest was his desire that all, without distinction, should reverence even in its decline the glory of true monarchy! But in fact, even the claims of rigid justice would not have allowed him to act otherwise than he did, for the falling king might possibly have still had long to live. And the deep sorrow for Saul, and yet more for Jonathan, which he cherished in his heart, his readiness to recognise true worth, even in a foe, the incomparable tenderness of his love for Jonathan,—all this shines forth in his elegy over the two heroes with unspeakable pathos, and yet with such truth and simplicity, that David could have given posterity no surer pledge of the loyalty and uprightness of his own heart. And as such an elegy comprises in condensed and noble language all the praise which can be given to the dead, David took special care that it should be learnt by heart by the younger Israelites, for instance, in the army, in order that it might be preserved

---

and he could not have thought that such a pretence would have been a higher recommendation than the crown and bracelet which he brought to David.

[1] Saul's spear, which this narrator brings into such prominence everywhere, has its office to perform for him even here.

for ever, and that the latest ages might sing the praises of the two heroes.¹

But what further steps was David to take at this great crisis? Jonathan, between whom and himself a noble rivalry in self-renunciation might now have arisen, had fallen; Ish-bosheth,² it is true, another of Saul's sons, was still living, and was old enough to enter at once upon the government, but since hereditary succession to the crown was not as yet legally established, David could in no way be considered as owing allegiance to his person; and indeed, even if he had acknowledged him as king, it would not have done much good, since the whole of Saul's kingdom (as we shall see presently) was at that time in the last stage of disintegration, and all the central and northern territory west of the Jordan was in the hands of the Philistines. The thought of declaring against Saul's house and at the same time struggling for dominion over all Israel, could certainly never enter so noble a heart as David's; but in earlier years he had already maintained himself in the territory of his own tribe of Judah as a protecting chief, and had bound many of its cities in ties of gratitude to himself. He might well therefore, consider it a duty to defend it (since none appeared better able to do so), against the incursions of the Philistines and other foes, who waxed bold through recent events. The further consequences he would leave to God.

We know, moreover, from a very ancient source³ that immediately after Saul's great disaster, while David still maintained himself at Ziklag, a large number of the most valiant warriors came over to him from independent districts, and looked for his leadership to save Israel; seven captains of thousands of the tribe of Manasseh are mentioned by name, and all such chiefs no doubt brought with them the greater part of their men. And besides these, from day to day fresh warriors came to help him or to seek their fortune with him, 'so that his camp waxed great, like to a camp of God.'

And so he could no longer stay inactive here, or simply remain in his former relation to Achish. He consulted the

---

¹ 2 Sam. i. 17-27; cf. the *Dichter des Alten Bundes*, vol. 1, and above, i. p. 17, note 1.

² The four sons of Saul are most distinctly named in 1 Chron. viii. 33, ix. 39, according to which Jonathan is the eldest, Ish-bosheth the youngest; but the latter is there called Esh-baal, according to vol. ii. p. 380, *note* 2. The LXX and Fl. Josephus have 'Ιεβοσθέ, but surely this is a transcriber's error for 'Ισβ. The names enumerated by the second narrator, 1 Sam. xxxi. 2, correspond to this list; but in that of the earlier narrator, 1 Sam. xiv. 49, Abinadab is wanting, and יִשְׁוִי must be another form of the name Ish-bosheth, unless it is a copyist's mistake; the LXX read יִשְׁוִי.

³ 1 Chron. xii. 19-22.

oracle (says the earlier narrator) whether he should go to a city of Judah, and was answered in the affirmative. To which? he asked again, and in reply was directed to Hebron, the ancient city of Judah. Thither he accordingly marched, and his people with their households settled down in the little towns round about the capital. Nothing surely could be more pleasing to the Elders of the whole tribe, in the altered position of affairs; so they assembled at Hebron and anointed him king of Judah.[1]

3. *As King of Judah.*

David reigned over Judah seven years and six months at Hebron; and meanwhile Ish-bosheth, Saul's son, reigned over all the rest of Israel for two years. At a first glance, the utter want of harmony between the two numbers is puzzling, for David certainly became the ruler of all Israel immediately after the death of the rival king,[2] without any interval of five and a half years. It is quite true that we know very little of this period of David's life altogether, but yet if we put together, as vividly as we can, the various indications which remain, we gain the following results.

1) After Saul's death, it was only in Judah that David could maintain a government at all, for the consequences of the great Philistine victory were so disastrous, that at first a new kingdom of Israel could hardly be established anywhere else. The Philistines, who must have already conquered the central territory, were now in possession of that to the north also, while the inhabitants of the cities of the great plain of Jezreel and of the western bank of the Jordan, fled, we are very distinctly informed, across the river.[3] Every indication leads to the belief that the Philistines never crossed the Jordan; but there had been, from of old,[4] such a want of firm organic unity among the Transjordanic cities, that they could not afford any firm support to a government. Had Saul's immediate successor, indeed, been a man of distinguished qualities, he might have found it easier to establish a fresh kingdom on the ruins of his father's; but Ish-bosheth, as far as we know anything about him, had no strength of character. If there had been no unwillingness to

---

[1] 2 Sam. ii. 1–4.
[2] But the earlier narrator more strictly regards Ish-bosheth as the real and David as the rival king. This is clear from his mentioning Ish-bosheth, 2 Sam. ii. 10 sq., before David and giving his age at his accession to the throne, whereas it is not till David becomes king of all Israel that he gives his age too at the time of his accession. 2 Sam. v. 4 sq.
[3] 1 Sam. xxxi. 7. Just as, in Joshua's day, the Canaanites once fled before Israel.
[4] Vol. ii. p. 344.

depart from the strict succession, many a hero might, no doubt, have been found, more or less closely related to Saul, of greater capacity than this his only legal heir; but although no distinct law for the regulation of the succession to the throne appears to have been at that time in existence, yet it was a perfectly healthy popular instinct which directed that it should in every respect follow the ancient law of all family succession. This is, in fact, the only means of securing the proper peace and quietness of succession, and the people themselves should consider it their duty to supplement and remove the deficiencies of even an inefficient successor to the throne.

Under these circumstances, as soon as David had established himself at Hebron as the acknowledged king of Judah, the immediate prospect opened before him of being requested at once by all the tribes, to become their protector and ruler; and if such a request had been made, he certainly would not have declined to take at once the step which he actually took seven years later. A fact which is worthy of note on other grounds, offers one proof at least that David himself felt the possibility of such a result, and took a sufficiently comprehensive view of the various relations in which he was placed. As they were stripping and spoiling the bodies on the battle-field after their victory, the Philistines found amongst others the bodies of Saul and his sons. They severed Saul's head from his body, stripped off his arms, had their victory proclaimed in the temples of the idols and the market-places all over their country, and then laid up Saul's arms in the principal temple of Astarte, and his skull in the temple of Dagon; they fixed his trunk, however, together with the bodies of his sons, by way of insulting the Hebrews who dwelt beyond Jordan, high up on the wall[1] of the city of Beth-shan (afterwards Scythopolis), situated on the Jordan to the east of Gilboa. But the citizens of Jabesh beyond the Jordan,[2] who had once been rescued by Saul,[3] moved to indignation by the spectacle and by such treatment of the body of the king whom they held in revered and grateful memory, journeyed a whole night through, removed all the bodies and buried them with honours under the tamarisk, i.e. their place of public meeting. As soon as the news of this act of respect reached David at Hebron, he courteously send a formal em-

---

[1] So the second narrator; the older, however, according to 2 Sam. xxi. 12, with greater precision, named the market-place by the gate.

[2] The situation of the town in the Wâdi, which now bears a similar name, was closely investigated by Robinson on his second journey, but was not discovered with exactitude; see his *Bib. Res. in Pal.* iii. 319 sq.

[3] P. 24.

bassy to them, to thank them, with many hearty good wishes, for the love they had manifested for the king, to exhort them to continued steadfastness, and to inform them that he had himself been anointed king by the tribe of Judah.[1] No mention is here made of any son of Saul's as their present king, and had the lords of Jabesh desired to enter into further negotiations with David, he would no doubt have willingly granted their request that he should become their protector, and in consequence their ruler. But if this were not their wish, the anxiety he had shown concerning the honour of the fallen king and his energetic friends, must in itself have redounded to his credit everywhere.

It now became evident, however, that the ground was not sufficiently prepared for David's extended activity. No doubt his military talent had been universally acknowledged for a long time, but his recent connexion with the Philistines might give offence to many; and when we consider that he was left at peace by these Philistines as long as he reigned at Hebron, but had to sustain the severest contests with them the moment he became king of all Israel, it seems only too probable, in spite of the silence of our authorities, that he paid tribute to them, and owed to this circumstance the tranquillity of his early rule. Besides this, there were still a great number[2] who had genuine scruples against revolting from the house of Saul, which they regarded as lawfully established; and finally, there may well have been others who sought the restoration of Saul's kingdom in the hope of thus laying the foundation of their own future prosperity. A number of Benjamites must, from the nature of the case, have formed the bulk of this last party, although, even in Saul's life-time, many of them had gone over to David.[3] One Benjamite in particular, namely Abner, whose history comes into the foreground during these years, made once more the most daring efforts for the house of Saul. This Abner, was, as we have seen,[4] a son of Ner, the brother of Saul's father, and appears (not indeed in the first great war carried on by Saul with the Philistines,[5] but on every subsequent occasion) as commander-in-chief, that is, as the first man in Saul's kingdom, and the representative of the king. The escape of a man so brave and distinguished from the slaughter which accom-

---

[1] 1 Sam. xxxi. 8-13, 2 Sam. ii. 4-7. In 1 Sam. xxxi. 10, after בֵּית עַשְׁתָּרוֹת should be inserted (according to 1 Chron. x. 10) the words וְאֶת־גֻּלְגָּלְתּוֹ בֵית דָּגוֹן cf. 1 Sam. v. 2, although they had already dropped out of the text of the LXX. Otherwise, the text of the Chronicles is, it must be confessed, generally less near the original.

[2] P. 51.   [3] Pp. 90, 102.
[4] Pp. 18, 22.   [5] P. 30.

panied Saul's defeat, was a piece of good fortune amid all the misfortunes of the house of Saul, which might easily have enabled it to regain all its former power. In virtue both of his office and of his kinship, Abner was called upon to take under his special protection his nephew Ish-bosheth, Saul's only surviving son; and he fulfilled the utmost claims of duty which could be made on him in this double capacity. But the whole kingdom lay in ruins at the time, and hardly a single city west of the Jordan either could or would acknowledge the rule of the house of Saul; while even on the east, though single cities like Jabesh were willing to submit to such a king as Ish-bosheth, yet the country as a whole was hardly prepared to do so. Under these circumstances the only course, which for the present lay open to the valiant Abner, was to attempt the gradual reorganisation and reconquest of the territories which were either thoroughly disintegrated, or subdued and occupied by the Philistines; and to accomplish this it seemed advisable to leave David in quiet so long as he confined himself to Judah. The extreme difficulty of the problem which Abner had to face, and the great honour which he gained by his ultimate success in solving it, may be readily understood. His first step appears to have been to reunite under his protection the country of the east, and thence to consolidate his forces for the accomplishment of his further designs. This is the necessary inference from a consideration of all the circumstances, and it is confirmed by the fact that the seat of Ish-bosheth's government was not, like that of his father, at Gibeah, or in Benjamin at all, but beyond the Jordan at Mahanaim, a city, it would seem, of ancient greatness and sanctity, which was certainly of high importance at that period,¹ and still retained its sanctity in far later times.² A further indication of the same fact is contained in the way in which the districts finally ruled over by Ish-bosheth are enumerated: 'Abner' (says the earlier narrator) 'took Ish-bosheth, brought him across to Mahanaim, and made him king over Gilead, the land of Geshur, Jezreel, Ephraim, Benjamin, and all Israel (except Judah).'³ In this list of the districts west

---

¹ David also takes up his abode at this place when compelled to flee across the Jordan, 2 Sam. xvii. 24 sqq., 1 Kings ii. 8. Ruins have now been discovered at a place called *Mahneh*, in about the same latitude as Scythopolis, but far east of the Jordan; but if the Jabbok is to be identified with the Greek Hieromax (vol. ii. p. 295), then the ancient Mahanaim, according to Gen. xxxii. 2 [xxxii. 1], must have been situated north of this place.

² This follows from Cant. vii. 1 [vi. 13]; cf. Gen. xxxii. 2 sq. [xxxii. 1 sq.].

³ 2 Sam. ii. 8 sq. For אשורי, the LXX read תשורי or תשירי; there is more probability in favour of the reading of other ancient translators, גשורי, for according to ii. 302, this place appears elsewhere as a country lying far to the north-east, the capital of which, גְּשׁוּר at that time had a king of its own: 2 Sam. iii. 3, xiii. 37, xiv. 23; cf. xv. 8, from

of the Jordan, the order in which Abner reconquered the districts occupied by the Philistines, may at the same time be indicated. Whilst Abner was making these efforts, some five years must necessarily have elapsed, nor could Ish-bosheth have been solemnly anointed as king of Israel until after the expiration of this period; for it would be no such easy task to compel the Philistines to relinquish the conquests in which they had already firmly established themselves.

2) But now that Abner had accomplished this great project, consistency of purpose would urge him to make the attempt to unite Judah once more to the kingdom of the house of Saul. It was, however, to be anticipated that David would not voluntarily abdicate, after having already governed for five years. The consequence was, that the mutual taunts of the soldiers on either side provoked a war between the two houses, which evidently occupied the greater part of the two years of Ish-bosheth's reign. Abner and his troops, just victorious over the Philistines and proud of their maintenance of the king's cause, obviously began the quarrel with David's men; and though we cannot give any detailed account of the way in which the latter had spent the five preceding years, they had no doubt been exercised in wars against the southern and western peoples (except the Philistines),[1] and were consequently not only penetrated by David's spirit of lofty cheerfulness and confidence, but also strengthened in all the arts of war by constant practice. A company of extraordinarily valiant and courageous warriors must by that time have been formed around David, —the kernel of that army of heroes with which he subsequently laid the foundations of an imperial power; and even Abner seems hardly to have had a just appreciation of this phenomenon—unknown to Israel since the days of Joshua—when, trusting to the numerical superiority of his own troops, he sought to engage those of David, inferior to his own in nothing but numbers. In particular, David's army reckoned among its officers Joab his general, Abishai, and Asahel, the three heroic sons of David's sister, who, on this account, were commonly called not after their father, but after their illustrious mother Zeruiah.[2]

Abner (says the earlier narrator,[3] whose account becomes predominant again, for the most part, from this point) proceeded

---

which it appears that the inhabitants of this little country were Arameans. Jezreel appears as a name for the vale of Galilee in Josh. xvii. 16 as well.

[1] P. 111.
[2] 1 Chron. ii. 16.
[3] 2 Sam. ii. 12–iii. 1.

with Ish-bosheth's subjects in battle array to Gibeon, in the tribe of Benjamin;[1] there, however, he was met by Joab, who had lost no time in advancing with David's men, and the two armies encamped over against each other at the pool near the city. Here Abner proposed, half in sport and half in earnest, by way of entertaining the two armies, a contest of champions; and on Joab's giving his assent, twelve warriors of Benjamin stepped forth from the side of Ish-bosheth as if they were the representatives of all the tribes of Israel, and they were confronted by twelve of David's adherents. These champions entered upon the contest armed with swords, but the crafty Benjamites, renowned of old[2] for using the left and right hand with equal effect in war, instead of engaging in straightforward sword-play, each seized his opponent's head with the left hand, and at the same moment plunged his sword into his side with the right:[3] the men of Judah however, with equal craft and activity, dealt in like manner with their opponents, so that they all fell together, and the spot was known ever after as 'the field of the malignant.'[4] But this only kindled a general battle, in which Abner's men sustained heavy loss. Amongst David's heroes, special distinction was won by Joab's youngest brother, Asahel. Swift of foot 'as a gazelle on the mountains,' he had selected as his opponent no less a person than Abner himself, whom he pursued without swerving. Abner, who knew him, turned round at last and begged him to seek out some private soldier and strip him of his armour; but Asahel would not desist, so once more Abner begged him to leave off. He shrank from striking Asahel to the ground, out of simple consideration for his brother Joab, into whose face he could never look again after such a deed; but he would not turn back, and so Abner struck him in the belly and right through the back with the butt end of his spear which was simply pointed, so that he fell down dead. This misfortune at first restrained the pursuit of the flying Israelites, since everyone who came to the spot halted at the sight of the dead body. Joab and Abishai, it is true, continued to pursue Abner, and all the more hotly,[5] although the sun had already set; but the Benjamites, on their side, perceiving the great danger of their leader, took

[1] Vol. ii. p. 251.
[2] Vol. ii. p. 282.
[3] In verse 16, after אִישׁ the little word יָדוֹ has dropped out; the LXX still had it.
[4] הַצָּרִים, as the LXX (τῶν ἐπιβούλων) still read instead of הַצֻּרִים; if we were to spell this הַצָּרִים, 'field of the opponents,' no indication of the peculiar nature of the conflict would be conveyed by so ordinary a name. The above representation merely explains somewhat more in detail what is implied in the few words which are employed.
[5] The minute description of the point up to which they came, verse 24, still remains obscure, since Robinson, *Bibl. Res. in Pal.*

hurried possession of the hill and closed round Abner in a compact circle. On this he cried out to Joab no longer to pursue his brethren so relentlessly, and to reflect how bitterly it might all end; and Joab gave way, but declared that the pursuit would have lasted till break of day had not Abner thus spoken. The two armies then parted. Abner's troops, after sustaining a loss of three hundred and sixty men, returned to Mahanaim on that very night; while Joab's men, who had lost twenty, including Asahel, buried Asahel that same night on their way back, in his family sepulchre at Bethlehem, and reached Hebron early in the morning.

This battle is no doubt described thus minutely on account of Asahel's death and its subsequent results; but in this opening scene of the two years' war, we discern at once the reason why, as it went on, David's army always remained victorious, and his power rose higher and higher. Together with his external successes, his family connexions likewise became more extensive, a method of aggrandisement not unfamiliar at the present day to princes of those countries; for sometimes he sought by marriage to gain the support of some powerful house which he thus bound over to his interests, and sometimes these houses themselves endeavoured to secure his friendship by a matrimonial alliance. Thus during those seven or eight years at Hebron, his six wives presented him with six sons, amongst whom was Absalom whose mother was a daughter of the king of Geshur.[1]

3) But, after all, the hand which was stretched forth to effect the immediate ruin of Ish-bosheth, who was not an ill-meaning but a weak and timid man,[2] was no other than his own. While the war was still going on, Abner had married Saul's concubine Rizpah. Ish-bosheth interpreted this act as an indication that he was aiming at the throne, in which he was, no doubt, justified by the court custom of the country and the time, since such a proceeding was frequently regarded as the symbolic occupation of the inner house (the harem) of a preceding king;[3] but, on the other hand, there was no necessity at all to put this meaning on Abner's act, since he gave no further evidence of cherishing designs upon the supreme

---

i. p. 456, *note* 10, though he speaks of the water-springs by Gibeon, makes no more particular reference to our passage. The description of the route pursued beyond Jordan, verse 29 (*through the whole of Bithron*), is also unintelligible to us as yet; the Bithron appears to have been a long valley or mountain ridge.

[1] P. 112, *note* 3. 2 Sam. iii. 2–5; cf. 1 Chron. iii. 1–3.

[2] 2 Sam. iii. 6–v. 3; cf., with special reference to Ish-bosheth's character, iv. 11.

[3] Cf. 2 Sam. xvi. 21, xx. 3, 1 Kings ii. 13–25; the same custom was in force at the Egyptian court (see the history of Armais, according to Manetho in Joseph. *Contr. Ap.* i. 15), and at the Persian court, Herod. iii. 68, and is even yet in force amongst the Tartars; cf. Riculf in Laurent's *Peregrinatores quatuor*, p. 116.

power; whereas, had he done so, he would undoubtedly have given other indications of his plans, since it would have been easy for him, as the most powerful man in the kingdom, to supplant the king openly. Ish-bosheth, however, became suspicious, and took Abner to task for what he had done; upon which the latter, vehemently incensed,[1] reproached him with ingratitude, and swore that he would allow the crown to fall to David, to whom the oracle had long ago promised dominion over the whole of Israel. It is plain that this was but the chance spark falling upon dry ground which had long been ready for it. The feeling that David was the only man worthy to rule over the whole of Israel, and that it would be better to lay aside the present civil strife, must have already penetrated the masses of the people a long time since, and even secretly entered the mind of Abner himself; so that nothing but an accidental occasion was needed to give the thought a definite shape and an open vent. Ish-bosheth, in fact, terrified by the anger of his powerful subject, is silent on the whole matter; but Abner on the spot sends messengers to open negotiations with David, who on his part is willing to be reconciled with him for this purpose, but only on condition of his securing the surrender of his first wife, Saul's daughter Michal. No doubt it was of great importance to David, on every account, to maintain this matrimonial connexion with the house of Saul as long as possible, in order to preserve the sort of claim to the succession which his alliance gave him, and he had a right to require, under these totally different circumstances, the surrender of his wife Michal, who had been unjustly taken away from him;[2] but an additional motive which urged him to demand her restoration, was the prudential desire of possessing in her a pledge against possible treachery on Abner's side. Since Abner now supported the demand which David made, Ish-bosheth gave orders to have Michal taken away from her present husband Phaltiel, although it caused him the deepest pain to be compelled to relinquish her.[3] But Abner, after he had

---

[1] The cry of rage, verse 8, 'am I a dog's head of Judah,' gives a glimpse of the sort of expression occasionally indulged in at the court of Mahanaim to describe what was utterly contemptible.

[2] P. 99.

[3] He followed her (we are told) weeping to Bahurim, where Abner ordered him to turn back. This little town (which Josephus, *Ant*. vii. 9. 7, appears indeed to have known as existing in his time, but the site of which he does not describe with any more exactness) lay, according to 2 Sam. xvi. 5, on the direct road from Jerusalem to the north; and at that time, therefore, it must have been situated on the boundaries of the tribe of Benjamin on the way to Hebron. This explains the reason why Abner ordered Phaltiel to stop there. The place is still mentioned in Anton. Mart. *Itiner*. p. 89, Tobler, and in Burchard, vii. 57 sq., in Laurent's *Peregrinatores quatuor*, p. 62.

infused into the Elders of all the tribes, at last even of Benjamin, sentiments favourable to David, or rather after he had met half way with his eloquence the favourable sentiments which most of them already entertained, proceeded himself with a guard of twenty men to David at Hebron, where he was honourably received by him, and discussed with him the conditions under which the union of the whole kingdom was to be effected. Finally he was dismissed, promising to return at the head of all the Elders of Israel; and though we are not informed what was to become of Ish-bosheth, no doubt his honourable retirement was stipulated for. It is probable that Abner had intentionally chosen a time for this negotiation when he knew that Joab and the army were absent on a raid; but he had hardly left Hebron before Joab returned from the opposite direction. On hearing of what had happened, Joab uttered the most violent reproaches against David for allowing a man so open to suspicion as Abner to depart in peace, and sent after him, without David's knowledge, to beg him to come back to a secret conference with himself. When Abner returned, however, Joab, with the assistance of his brother Abishai, craftily hurried him into the dark recess of the city gateway, and there ran him through, in revenge, as he might declare, for the death of his brother Asahel at Gibeon.[1]

The violent emotion which David exhibited at this event, when in his boiling rage he uttered the bitterest imprecations on Joab,[2] his orders for a general mourning over the death of the princely hero, his own participation in the funeral ceremony, with the short but deep-toned elegy[3] composed on the occasion, which caused the tears of all present to flow yet more abundantly, his refusal of food during the whole day,—all this was no doubt perfectly sincere on his part, and did not fail to produce the most favourable impression upon everyone else, who might otherwise perhaps have suspected him of having had some understanding with Joab. It was one of those moments in which a king, even with the best intentions and the greatest

---

[1] In verse 30 we must follow the LXX in reading אָרְבִי, instead of הרגו. The murder might, however, pass for blood vengeance, in so far as it was no doubt considered dishonourable among the ancient Israelites (as it was among the ancient Germans, according to *Saxo Gramaticus*) for a man in the prime of manly strength like Abner to strike down a stripling like Asahel. This had made Abner shrink from the very first from striking him down, on account of Joab.

[2] These curses, however, are not made to apply to Joab himself so much as to his posterity; who are to be afflicted with all kinds of leprosy, and to be lame, assassinated, starved! verse 28 sq. Here the narrator ties one of the last knots which the further development of the history is to unloose (cf. i. p. 142 sqq.); cf. 1 Kings ii. 28 sqq., where indeed the beginning of the fulfilment of the curse is related.

[3] See the *Dichter des Alten Bundes*, vol. i.

power, must feel, to his own heavy cost, the weakness of everything human, and the limits of human supremacy; for how much must even he permit to go unpunished, which he would never tolerate, were he not, even as king, subject to the inherent weakness of all human institutions. 'To-day,' he cried at last, 'is a great prince fallen in Israel! Truly now I live in palaces [1] and am anointed king, and yet are these sons of Zeruiah beyond my reach; may God repay to the evil doer what he deserves!' Thus must he leave Joab's punishment, albeit with heavy heart, to God, since he could not well spare him, and his black deed might really have found an excuse in the ancient right of the blood-avenger. No doubt Joab had found an additional motive to it in secret jealousy, since he suspected, or perhaps had already heard, that Abner was to receive the highest office in David's kingdom; at any rate, this is a probable inference from his similar conduct towards Amasa.[2]

The news of Abner's death deprived the weak Ish-bosheth of all courage, and threw the whole of the northern kingdom of Israel into consternation. It was felt that with Abner had fallen the only support of the scarce re-established monarchy. At the same time the movement in this kingdom in David's favour had already become too strong to be put to rest by Abner's death, and since it was now deprived of proper guidance, it degenerated (as would easily happen) into mere violence. Two of Ish-bosheth's officers, themselves also Benjamites, Baanah and Rechab of Beeroth,[3] who cherished a special animosity against the house of Saul on account of an old blood-feud, shortly after this, one day effected their entrance into the house of Ish-bosheth at noon. The female door-keeper had fallen asleep while cleaning some wheat,[4] so they slipped into the chamber where the king lay sleeping on a couch, cut off his head, and hurriedly pursuing their journey through the whole night, brought it to David at Hebron, thinking that they should be doing him a favour in ridding him of his enemy.

---

[1] This or something similar is the meaning of רַךְ in this connexion; cf. Isai. xlvii. 1, Deut. xxviii. 54–56.

[2] 2 Sam. xx.

[3] The words inserted at 2 Sam. iv. 2 sq., 'Beeroth also was reckoned to Benjamin, but the Beerothites fled to the neighbouring (Neh. xi. 33) town of Gittaim, and were refugees there until this day,' must clearly be intended to stand in close connexion with the narrative itself, or else they would not have been inserted. Now the connexion shows that they are meant to explain how it was that these two, although Beerothites and therefore Benjamites, could do such a thing, from which it follows that they no longer dwelt in Beeroth at that time; the probable cause of this flight and also of their crime will be explained below.

[4] In iv. 6, we must read after the LXX וְהִנֵּה אֲשֶׁר עַל תּוֹךְ הַבַּיִת סֹקֶלֶת חִטִּים, נִפְלָט, &c., if וְרֶכָב, then וּתָנָם וַתִּישָׁן may mean 'to slip in.'

But David swears by Him 'who has delivered his soul out of all distress,' that he is still less able to forgive them than he had been to pardon Saul's murderer, and orders them to be executed, and, with their hands and feet cut off, hung up as a warning at the pool by the city.[1]

There now remained no direct representative of the house of Saul except Jonathan's son Meribosheth;[2] and he had been lame since he was five years old, when his nurse let him fall from her arms, in her wild flight on receiving the terrible news of the death of Saul and Jonathan. There was nothing left, therefore, but for the Elders of all the tribes to present themselves at Hebron, and offer the kingdom to that 'fellow-countryman who had ever led them to victory, even before Saul's death, and to whom, by divine destiny, the rule over all Israel had long been due.' There was a great festival in Israel, when these Elders of all the tribes, together with their numerous and well-armed followers, met at the national assembly at Hebron and remained there three days, liberally supplied with necessaries collected from the whole country.[3] They returned home after having established and confirmed the laws of the new kingdom with David, who was at this time about thirty-seven years old.

---

[1] Some think that they have rediscovered the locality of the pool, as well as that of the well *has-Sira*, from which Abner (iii. 26) returned to Hebron. Wilson's *Lands of the Bible*, i. p. 368 sq. 385.

[2] 2 Sam. iv. 4, ix., xvi. 1, xix. 25 sq. [xix. 24 sq.], according to the LXX Μεμφι-βοσθέ. The name was in use amongst other members of the house of Saul, 2 Sam. xxi. 8. On the name itself cf. ii. p. 380, *note*.

[3] It is thus circumstantially described 1 Chron. xii. 23–40, undoubtedly from very ancient sources, although the Chronicler here and there adds a few words in his own style.

III. DAVID AS KING OF ISRAEL.

Seldom indeed has a king reached sovereign power in an important state in the manner in which David attained it! He was not called to be a ruler by hereditary right, and yet he constantly rose in power without entering into any conspiracy or practising any other hostile arts against the reigning dynasty; he was not summoned by a majority of votes to the throne of an avowedly elective monarchy (though no doubt the hereditary descent of the crown was less clearly defined than it is now), and yet he was finally acknowledged, spontaneously and with enthusiastic love, by the whole people, as the only man worthy of being called to be their ruler; he was not thrown to the surface by the accident of a sudden revolution, and so possibly a mere child of fortune, immature and essentially incompetent; but in the fulness of time, and at the right moment, in perfect vigour of body and mind, he grasped the supremacy which was offered him, after having passed through every outward stage of power and honour, and every inward test of heavy trial and varied strife. But though he was the most worthy of gaining this prize and by far the greatest man of his time, yet both the real facts of the case and his own consciousness combined to warn him that he had only reached this lofty position by his reverence for the Holiness which had, once for all, been embodied in the community of Israel, while Saul, on the other hand, had fallen through despising it; and so he was clearly urged by these striking examples, above all things to seek true welfare hereafter even on the 'throne of Israel' in nothing but a faithful clinging to the 'rock of Israel' and his 'shining light,'[1] and thus he might expect a more and more glorious development of the new period of his kingly career. For certainly his accession to the throne could not fail to be the beginning of fresh labours and struggles, even if of a different kind. The disintegrated and shattered kingdom must be reorganised, a firmer basis of monarchical rule must be laid down, many an ancient error must be atoned for, and many a grievous deficiency made up; and, since the neighbouring peoples would not look quietly upon so independent and mighty an upheaving of the

---

[1] To use David's own expressions, Ps. xviii. 29-31 [xviii. 28-30].

INTERNAL ORGANISATION OF THE KINGDOM.

nation, further and constantly extending wars were unavoidable; but all the toils and problems might prove the steps to power and glory which lay in the path at the feet of the new monarch. But now that, true to that Holiness, he had reached, by wise and persevering effort, the furthest point of the power and glory which lay right before him—a point of dizzy height to which no member of the nation had ever climbed before—the first question which had to be decided was, whether at this height he would still suffer himself, as king, to be led by the same spirit of Jahveh that had raised him so far, or whether, in the power of unprecedented greatness, he would banish that spirit from him in proud self-reliance. The way in which he stood this keenest test, a test which could only be applied to him, determined the issue of his life, and his abiding significance for the history of the future.

It is to be regretted that the accounts of these thirty-three years of David's life have come down to us, for reasons already explained,[1] arranged according to the subject-matter, rather than the sequence of the events to which they refer, so that our existing authorities do not put us in a position to present a connected chronology of the period, and we are compelled, in consequence, to adapt our survey to the various subjects in turn. Nevertheless it appears, on closer investigation, that the chief direction of David's deeds and fortunes must have been greatly modified as time went on.

1. *The Internal Organisation of the Kingdom.*

The first important undertaking of the new king was, doubtless, the conquest of Jerusalem,[2] which the Jebusites, who had occupied it for centuries,[3] still held. The city is known to have been called Jebus[4] by the Canaanites; and since this name may signify a *dry* mountain, so that, changing the name but preserving the signification, it might also be called Zion,[5] we may draw the conclusion, confirmed by all the circumstances,

---

[1] Vol. i. p. 147 sq.
[2] 2 Sam. v. 6–12; cf. 1 Chron. xi. 4–9, xiv. 1 sq.
[3] Vol. ii. p. 284.
[4] Judg. xix. 10 sq., and because the Canaanite inhabitants called themselves after it, vol. i. p. 234. Concerning the Jebusites of Cyprus see the *Acta App. Apocrr.* ed. Tischendorf, p. 72 sq.
[5] Formed like חֶבְרוֹן, and a number of similar ancient names of cities in the country, cf. צִיָּה; hence the Syrians (and following them the Arabs) write more intelligibly in their language ܨܶܗܝܽܘܢ.

A corresponding صهيون lies between Hamath and Laodicea in northern Syria, but its history is still obscure (see Bahâ-eldîn's *Life of Saladin*, p. 82, and Kemâl-eldîn, p. 125, 15. *Journ. As.* 1855, i. p. 57, 61. Matthew of Edessa, p. 22 [384]).

that the erection of the whole city began from the broad dry mountain to the south, which easily formed a strong citadel, whence the rest of the city gradually spread farther and farther to the north and east. There are many indications that even the name Jerusalem[1] did not spring from Israel, but was more probably the ancient name, and came down from the primitive occupants, since this mountain was no doubt inhabited from the earliest ages in consequence of its convenient situation.[2]

Its situation almost in the middle of the country, and its great strength as a fortress, rendered an organised government of the whole of Israel hardly possible as long as any such hostile city midway between the northern and southern tribes remained independent. But the inhabitants, still proudly confident in the strength of their position and the freedom of centuries, answered David, when first he summoned them to surrender, with the scornful words, 'thou shalt not come in here, but the blind and the lame will chase thee away,' as though it would not even be necessary to bring warriors or sound men against him, but the lame and the blind of the city would suffice to drive him away.[3] But giving a different turn to these words, David cried out to his own warriors:

> Whoso shall conquer the Jebusite,
> Let him hurl down from the cliff
> The lame and the blind together,
> Hated of David's soul,[4]

---

[1] It has always appeared to me probable that this name is a contraction, as stated in the *Kritische Grammatik*, p. 332, of יְרוּשׁ שָׁלֵם, just like מְרִיבְשֶׁת, vol. ii. p. 380 *note*; according to this it would mean *Salem's inheritance* or *habitation*, or if the first word is not a proper name, *peaceful city*. The abbreviated form שָׁלֵם, does not occur in prose (vol. i. pp. 307, 328), and in poetry only in Ps. lxxvi. 3 [2]; but when the Hellenists had discovered a ίερο- in the sound of the first part of this as of so many other geographical names in Palestine, they might easily believe the original name of the city to have been *Solyma* only, and they often call it so in prose; nay, they next connected even the Solymites of Homer with Jerusalem (which Bochart refuted); Jos. *Bell. Jud.* vi. 10; *Ant.* vii, 3. 2; Tac. *Hist.* v. 2.

[2] We might therefore regard as historical Manetho's mention of Jerusalem as early as the time of the Hyksos and Moses (vol. ii. pp. 77–82), were it not for the simultaneous mention of the temple, which shows us that in this passage Manetho is transplanting into the primitive age the names and ideas of later times. On much later narratives see Chwolson's *Ssabier*, ii. pp. 389 sq. 542, 679 sq. In very late times it became a common trick to heap the greatest possible number of names upon the city of ancient sanctity; see some odd examples of this in Jalâleldîn's *History of Jerusalem* (transl. by Reynolds, Lond. 1836), p. 4.

[3] Images which the prophets of the later Jerusalem apply to the Israelites themselves, Isai. xxxiii. 23 sq.

[4] This is the probable sense of a verse which, if thus explained, need not be regarded as a mere fragment without any complete sense. We have, then, only to read וְיַגַּע in the Hiphil, making this word a part of the apodosis, *Lehrbuch*, § 347a. צִנּוֹר is elsewhere, when it refers to water, a cataract; but this Greek word itself originally means nothing but a falling

and took the city by storm. On this success we may well believe that the inhabitants really met the fate with which they are here threatened; that is to say, that their warriors, at all events, were hurled over the precipice from the conquered rocks,[1] or in some other way destroyed. This metrical saying of David's was never forgotten, and it may well have been the origin of the proverb, when Jerusalem became a holy place, that no blind or lame man should enter the temple.

1) In this conquered city David now resolved to fix the seat of his government. The conquest had made it *his* city above any other in the country, thus far; besides, it was situated in the tribe of Benjamin, not Judah, where it would certainly have been distasteful to the other tribes to see him establish himself, and yet it was not far from his native tribe; moreover, he may have thought it of some importance to fix his permanent abode in the ancient leading tribe of Benjamin-Joseph;[2] and lastly, some influence on his choice was doubtless exercised by the fact, that from its position it was easily capable of being strongly fortified. What glory this conquest conferred on David, and how constantly his power increased ever after it, is still shown by the short extant narrative. He himself perceived (we are told) that Jahveh had destined him to be king over Israel, and had raised up his kingdom for the sake of his people Israel.[3] Success, therefore, enabled his consciousness of royalty to rise higher and higher; and if once this consciousness be quickened in the true direction, as it was with David, what good fortune may attend the efforts and achievements which may flow from it!

As far as we can now judge, the city was made up, even at that time, of two great divisions. The long broad ridge which stretches to the south (known also as the upper-city[4]), was then the only real fortress, and it was to this that the ancient name of Zion originally belonged;[5] while over against it spread a

---

down (hence even a trap-door); and so the Hebrew word also may mean the precipitous descent of a rock. What the Chronicler substitutes for this obscure old saying is obviously not original in this place; he says that David promised to make the first man who conquered the city his general, and that Joab gained this distinction; but Joab was his general already before this. From the interpretation of צִנּוֹר, as *watercourse*, which is accepted without any reason, Consul Schultz draws some wonderful conclusions in his *Jerusalem*, p. 78.

[1] A use to which the Tarpeian rock at Rome was put.

[2] P. 48.

[3] 2 Sam. v. 10, 12. So, after all, it was only *for the sake* of his people!

[4] See the Greek expressions upper- and lower- city in Joseph. *Bell. Jud.* v. 4. 1; *Ant.* vii. 3. 2.

[5] This important information is now only found in 2 Sam. v. 7, 9, 17, 1 Kings viii. 1; cf. 1 Chron. xi. 5. The name ἄκρα, corresponding to the Hebrew מְצוּדָה, is used for this mountain in the description in Josephus, *Ant.* vii. 3. 2, as well as in 1 Macc. iii. 45, iv. 2, xiii. 49 sq.; cf. i. 33. This fortress,

lower-city. This ridge, naturally easy of defence, and, no doubt, additionally strengthened by art in many ways from time immemorial, was surrounded (to use the ancient names) on the south by the deep valley of Ben-Hinnom, or, in the shorter form, of Hinnom [1] (so called, no doubt, after some ancient prince or other possessor); on the west by the valley of Gihon; on the east, and probably in connexion with it on the north also, by a ravine which was known in the time of Flavius Josephus as the Cheesemakers' (Tyropœon);[2] farther east, beyond what was later the Mount of the Temple, streamed from the north-west the brook Kedron, which then flowed to the plain of Jordan. The whole of this extensive ridge, the southern half of which is left outside the city-walls of the present Jerusalem, was certainly, at that time, completely inclosed by strong walls and towers, which David only restored in still greater strength after its capture; and since, as conqueror, he might consider himself the real possessor of this fortress, which he intended to make the strongest bulwark of the realm and of the monarchy in Israel, he laid it out entirely in accordance with his own views, in concert with his general Joab. In this fortress, therefore, he established a large building for the accommodation of his six hundred gallant warriors, of whom more hereafter, apparently on the south-west side of the mountain,[3] and also an arsenal to the south:[4] for his own court, on the other hand, he erected, apparently to the north-east, a palace of stone and cedar-wood by aid of Tyrian craftsmen of every kind;[5] and, in addition, the sacred ark of the covenant, as will be presently explained, now found its resting-place in this well-protected spot. But he also covered a considerable portion of the northern surface of the mountain with buildings for various purposes; while Joab built over the remaining space, perhaps, with a view to letting the houses to foreigners.[6] The chief quarter of the ancient city was thus renewed and beautified during the reign of David to such an extent that we need not be surprised to find it spoken of as the *City of David*; but, although this name was

however, was more strictly distinguished from the whole of the rest of the city, Isaiah xxxi. 4, cf. xxix. 7; and after the name Zion had received its more extended signification in poetical language, poets might even speak of its *mountains*. Ps. lxxxvii. 1, cxxxiii. 3.

[1] The shorter name is found side by side with the original as early as the Book of Origins, Josh. xv. 8, xviii. 16.

[2] *Bell. Jud.* v. 4. 1.

[3] See the description in Neh. iii. 16.

[4] Following the indication given in Neh. iii. 19.

[5] 2 Sam. v. 11; we can only conjecture what may have been the site of this 'House of David' from the single mention of it in Neh. xii. 37.

[6] 2 Sam. v. 9; it is true that the words referring to Joab are now found only in 1 Chron. xi. 8, but they are certainly original, and have only fallen out of the passage in 2 Sam. accidentally.

retained for a very long time,[1] yet it certainly did not arise until the close of David's reign or the beginning of Solomon's. And while this name took firm root in ordinary language, the ancient name of Zion, in the grandeur with which David's reign opened, was celebrated with such various glories, at least in songs and other forms of more lofty utterance, that on the one hand it fell more and more into disuse in ordinary language, and on the other became the proper term in higher style for Jerusalem as a whole.[2]

The lower-city, at that time probably called the *Valley*,[3] had attached itself to the fortress proper, though we cannot exactly tell what position it then occupied; but most likely it was situated for the most part on the north and east—the direction in which the whole city gradually spread in later times. It was in this quarter, probably, that the chief business of the city was transacted; and here were the dwellings of the greater part of the artisan and commercial community,[4] as well as of the prophets[5] and artificers. These two halves, therefore, formed what might afterwards be called the old city;[6] and it will be pointed out below, how far the boundaries of Jerusalem were gradually extended by Solomon.

2) A well-ordered and enlightened government, wherever it acquires power, will always be ready to recognise and protect the existing religion, if at all tolerable, and to enter into friendly relations with its human instruments—the priests. For the rest, it will treat them just like its other subjects, and will not allow itself to be defied by the priesthood. This is the course which we find David adopting; just as Gideon had before attempted to unite a spiritual and temporal supremacy.[7] The priesthood still continued to hold somewhat aloof; at least, this seems to be shown by the fact that the ancient tabernacle remained in Gibeon,[8] so that the central point of all priestly power was not yet identified with the seat of temporal power, although this would be a desirable arrangement for the latter to facilitate the reorganisation of the kingdom. But in other respects, David, in accordance with his own genuine reverence for the old religion as well as his enlightened views of govern-

[1] We often find it in the historical books, as well as in Isaiah xxii. 9, and even 1 Maccabees i. 33.
[2] In such ancient passages as Ps. cx. 2, ii. 6, this name is still used, no doubt, in its strictest original meaning; but when, in 1 Maccabees, the Mount of the Temple, in contradistinction to the 'City of David,' is called Zion, this is the simple result of the frequent use of the Psalter and other ancient writings of high authority.
[3] To judge from the artificial name in Isaiah xxii. 1–5, as well as from other indications.
[4] As indicated in Zeph. i. 11.
[5] Isaiah xxii. 6.
[6] Just as an 'Old-gate' appears Neh. iii. 6, Zech. xiv. 10.
[7] Vol. ii. p. 388.
[8] Ibid. p. 415.

ment, did all he could in this direction, and acted as became the great restorer of the kingdom.

The first step was to remove the ark of the covenant to Jerusalem from the spot where [1] it had formerly been stationed as a mere temporary resting-place; this was certainly effected tolerably soon. This event is narrated with considerable detail by both of the earlier narrators.[2] David assembled for the ceremony, as if for one of the most important national feasts, all the warriors in Israel,[3] and proceeded to Kirjath-jearim,[4] where the ark of the covenant[5] stood on the hill at the house of Abinadab. The ark was set upon a new waggon[6] and escorted by Abinadab's two sons Uzzah[7] and Ahio (the former leading the kine, and the latter preceding the waggon) amid the most joyous songs and sports of the whole people, including David himself.[8] But this procession took no wished-for course; for the kine, becoming somewhat restive at a certain place, kicked the ark, so that it seemed likely to fall off, and Uzzah put out his hand behind it and laid hold of it, unnecessarily and from the precipitate impulse of human nature, for it did not fall; so God was wroth, and he who had rashly touched the most sacred object they possessed, fell down dead on the spot. Such is the account of the second narrator, who is fond of these lofty and austere representations of the Holy.[9] Certainly some event must have happened at this place, which passed for an evil omen, and so broke up the whole festive proceeding. This occurred at Goren Nachon,[10] a place not otherwise known to us and certainly of small importance, afterwards called Perez-Uzzah (i.e. Uzzah's Stroke), and since David, vexed also by the misfortune, was afraid that Jahveh might not choose that the sacred ark should come to Jerusalem,[11] he had it placed in the house of Obed-Edom of

---

[1] Vol. ii. p. 417.

[2] 2 Sam. vi.; the description of the obstacles on the way, vv. 3-12, is specially due to the second, the rest to the first narrator.

[3] 30,000 according to the common reading, verse 1 (cf. verse 15), but 700,000 according to the LXX; 1 Chron. xiii. 1-5, without mentioning any such number, gives more of an indirect description, but this rests on some such number as that given by the LXX.

[4] In verse 2, הִיא בַּעֲלַת יְהוּדָה is a better reading than מִבַּעֲלֵי יְה, for the city is also called Baalah or Kirjath-Baal, Josh. xv. 9 [11], xviii. 14. On the site of the city see ii. p. 289, note, and cf. the remarks of Williams in answer to Robinson (*The Holy City*, pp. 10, 12).

[5] Vol. ii. p. 418.

[6] See what is said ii. p. 417, and cf. further Eckhel *D. N.* iii. p. 369.

[7] Perhaps, according to another authority, 1 Sam. vii. 1, this name stands for Eleazar; just as עֻזִּיָּה exists side by side with עֲזַרְיָה.

[8] Verse 5 must be emended from verse 14 and 1 Chron. xiii. 8.

[9] Vol. ii. p. 416 sq.

[10] The reading of the LXX ἅλω Ναχώρ, and also the בְּיָדוֹ of 1 Chron. xiii. 9, seem to be simply clerical errors.

[11] In the words of verse 9, the narrator would hardly intend to make any allusion to the words of David's song, Ps. ci. 2. That Obed-Edom was a Levite appears from 1 Chron. xv. 18-24, xvi. 5.

Gath (apparently Moresheth-gath),[1] who lived there. It was not until three months afterwards, when he perceived how this man's house was blessed by the presence of the sacred ark, and that the place to which he had brought it was not unlucky, that he decided on completing its transfer to Jerusalem.

The particulars of this procession are described by the earlier narrator. The ark was carried by the Levites[2] (not placed upon a vehicle); as soon as they had taken seven steps forward, a bullock and a fatted sheep were sacrificed;[3] and David, clad like a Levite, performing every kind of sacred dance, took a most active part in the rejoicings of the whole people, who celebrated the day as a grand festival. Thus did the procession move on to Jerusalem; and on its arrival, the sacred ark was at once placed in the new tabernacle which had already been erected for it there; at the same time many magnificent thank-offerings were made, while David performed the duty of a priest and pronounced a benediction on the people. Then he had a cake of bread, a piece of roast meat,[4] and a cake of raisins distributed to every one of the assembled multitude, men and women without distinction, and when the people had separated, he pronounced a fresh benediction on his own house, which would now for the first time receive the lofty blessings conferred by the presence of the sacred symbol. When at the earlier part of the proceedings, his wife Michal saw him thus dancing and rejoicing at the head of the people, and, in particular, approaching Jerusalem in the midst of the female dancers and musicians, who took the most active part in the festival according to the Hebrew custom, this daughter of Saul, considering her royal judgment superior to that of anyone else, affected to despise such a king as soon as she saw him through her window, and now going out to meet him she exclaimed, 'Oh! how the king of Israel covers himself with glory to-day, now that he has stripped himself[5] before the eyes of the handmaids of his servants, just as any vagabond strips himself!'

---

[1] P. 86, *note* 1.

[2] This narrator, in contradistinction to the second, everywhere represents the Levites as carrying the ark; cf. xv. 24.

[3] Instead of שׁשׁה, it is better to read שׁבעה, with the LXX, so as to preserve the sacred number. But it is not clear whether this offering was renewed at *every* seven steps, though this is not probable according to my *Lehrb.* § 342*b*; moreover, this was certainly a sin- and consecration-offering for the happy consummation of the impending journey, not a thank-offering like that described at verse 17 sq.

[4] אשׁפר is best understood in accordance with the context, of meat; and seems to come from שׁפר=שׂרף, 'to burn.' (The ܐܫܦܪ which the Peshito has for μάζα, in Dan. xiv. 26, seems only to be from σφαῖρα.)

[5] *Stripped himself*, i.e. lowered himself, at any rate, while thus dancing and playing he wore somewhat lighter garments (such as the ordinary priestly garb) instead of the heavy royal mantle. For the rest, since Michal finally lays the whole stress of her reproach on this,

But he answered her, 'If before Jahveh who advanced me before thy father and all his house, to appoint me ruler over the people of Jahveh, over Israel—if before Jahveh I play; then I think myself but too mean for this, and appear to myself too humble for it; and from these handmaids of whom thou speakest—from them shall I seek my honour?' No, there is no such need. Thus it is his glory, here as everywhere, to be humble before God; and he knows it to be a true thought that he, equally with the most insignificant of men, is still unworthy to play and to rejoice before Him; how much less can he, in such a position and thus joyfully playing, seek outward honour from even the humblest of men, to whom he rightly feels himself to be but equal! Surely this is the most striking answer which he could have given the princess, and corresponds exactly to the disposition which is also disclosed by his songs. The narrator, however, remarks in connexion with this affair, and not without design, that Michal, till the day of her death, had no children; as though she received her recompense for the proud disposition so conspicuous on such occasions, in never experiencing a mother's joy, in spite of the envy with which she regarded other more fortunate women.

The solemn festivities of this period, however, which certainly formed a great epoch in David's career as king, are the subject of still more eloquent testimony in certain hymns which we are able to ascribe to him without hesitation. Ps. xxiv. 7–10 [1] is a short popular song, which was evidently sung on the occasion of the transfer of the ark of the covenant, while it was yet on the way. It is true that the great hymn of thanksgiving, which must clearly have been sung as a triumphal ode at the close of the sacred ceremony, is lost to us as a whole; but all the indications warrant us in believing that we still possess some important fragments of it in Ps. lxviii.,[2] which is essentially nothing else than an ancient song of victory of this kind revived for the dedication of the second Temple. Next, the short didactic poem Ps. xxiv. 1–6, shows how this consecrated spot must be approached and its blessings won by men. But the most secret thoughts and aspirations of the great king at this time are laid bare in Ps. ci. The whole contents of this poem seem to throw it into these early years, but it cannot have been composed, at the earliest, until after the removal of

---

stripped himself (as only some worthless vagabond would strip himself), the strange combination, כְּהִגָּלוֹת נִגְלוֹת, is fully explained. See my *Lehrb.* § 312*c.* and 240*c.*

[1] I do not think it worth while to show once more that these verses make up a song by themselves, and are independent of vv. 1–6.

[2] Especially vv. 16, 17 [15, 16].

the ark, when Jerusalem had already been 'the city of Jahveh' for some considerable time. Here, at last, the purest feelings and resolves of royalty flow forth free and clear as the open heaven; with that marvellous power of words which belongs to every pure creative truth, the supreme ideal of true kingship which had long been cherished in the holy recesses of the heart, forces itself into utterance; and the language of this hymn exhibits most beautifully the profound impression which the immediate proximity of the consecrated spot could produce, in accordance with the sentiment of high antiquity, on the receptive heart, and so pre-eminently on the spirit of the true king,— and the increased joy and vigour of determination with which David now resolved, in the 'city of Jahveh,' to become, what he had ever before wished to be, a just king, faithful to the true God.

The transference of the ark of the covenant to Jerusalem took place, it appears, before the palace [1] which David was building for himself was completed;[2] and it was sufficient to place it again for a time in a light and portable tent like the Mosaic tabernacle. It has been shown [3] that the old Mosaic tabernacle without the ark of the covenant still existed somewhere else in the neighbourhood, and that a great proportion of the people continued, therefore, still to resort to it. But now that the ark of the covenant had found a permanent seat in Jerusalem, it was but natural that David should not only build himself a palace[4] in the capital of his kingdom, but should also conceive the idea of building for his Lord and God a palace or so-called temple of far greater splendour, and of placing the ark of the covenant within it: in fact, the feelings he expressed to Michal on occasion of the removal of the ark to the capital, would lead us to expect that this scheme would embody one of the dearest wishes of his life, and that he would really feel ashamed of living himself in a more magnificent abode than that of his God. Now if a larger and a permanent sanctuary were built for the Mosaic ark of the covenant, a general cultus, embracing the whole people, might at once be centred in it, and all the Priests required for this might be transferred to Jerusalem from the older sacred tabernacle, which remained at some distance from the capital; and in this way, while the unity of government would be strengthened, the unity of religion also would be more completely restored. Indeed, there are many indications that David made various efforts to build that temple which was not erected till Solomon's reign;

---

[1] P. 124.
[2] This seems to be presupposed in the words of 2 Sam. vii. 1.
[3] Vol. ii. p. 415.
[4] P. 124.

and at first sight it is surprising that the man who accomplished such great works in other directions should never have been able to carry out this idea. It is at any rate partially true, that the heavy wars in which he was constantly involved, hindered[1] or delayed the execution of the scheme, but its abandonment cannot be wholly explained in this way, neither is it the only explanation offered in the Bible. On the other hand, we are driven, by distinct indications, to recognise the cooperation of another cause, of which on further reflexion we may soon discern the nature. The fact is, that the religion of Jahveism, not only in its leading truths but also in its usages, tends far more to simplicity and the clear grasp of essential principles, than to ceremonial splendour and the eclipse of the essential behind external magnificence and inflexible routine. The simple altar under the open sky, which had satisfied the patriarchs of Israel, was still enough for Jahveism, true to its first appearance and development;[2] and though, since the great elevation and the fresh victories of Israel under Moses and Joshua, even the cultus had become in part more magnificent, and in part more closely defined by custom, yet the noble impression of the original simplicity which marked the life of the true religion still retained its hold.[3] But now the ancient freedom and simplicity of the cultus would be still further confined if its head-quarters were such as to bind it down more firmly to a fixed spot and associate it more closely with external splendour. As a matter of fact, we see, from the course of the following centuries, that the results in question did not fail to occur. Solomon's temple epitomised in itself all the splendour of Israel's mightiest days, and then, in subsequent times of need, furnished the community with much firm support and protection; but it also helped to make the old spiritual religion increasingly hard and sensuous. Now, whenever the temporal necessities of an age demand a corresponding innovation, the voice of pure truth makes itself heard first of all more or less distinctly; and therefore, just as once before under Moses, even the first limitation of spiritual religion by the establishment of a Priesthood and a sacred tabernacle had not

---

[1] This is intimated in 1 Kings v. 17 [v. 3]. On the other hand, it is nothing but a later sacerdotal representation of the Chronicler's that David was forbidden by God to build the temple because he had shed much blood, i.e. had carried on many wars, 1 Chron. xxii. 8, xxviii. 3. In a similar way, according to Ulemâ, the funds necessary for the restoration of the Kaabah were not, on one occasion, allowed to be taken from the imperial revenue, because it was supposed not to have been acquired in quite unexceptionable ways (Burckhardt's *Travels in Arabia*, i. p. 253); but according to the older authorities, this conception was quite foreign to the time of David himself.

[2] See the *Alterthümer*, p. 133 sqq.

[3] See ii. p. 180; the *Alterthümer*, p. 361; cf. Isaiah lxvi. 1 sq.

passed unchallenged,[1] so now, when the erection of a magnificent permanent temple was contemplated, the anticipation of the Prophet was fully justified, as he foresaw the great dangers concealed in the project and sought to show how unnecessary was the innovation, at any rate when the strict requirements of the case were taken into account. Great Prophets who, like Nathan, speak in this spirit and thus at any rate succeed, even should the innovation become at last inevitable, in rescuing the purity of the truth for future ages, realise for their time the Grand and the Divine. This prophetic view of the design must also have long delayed its accomplishment. In the last years of his life, indeed, when the great wars had quite subsided, David, according at any rate to some accounts, made some more special arrangements for carrying out the grand undertaking; though it was not until the fourth year of Solomon's reign that a beginning could actually be made, since the preparations and preliminary works must have been very considerable;[2] but moreover, towards the close of David's reign a circumstance occurred, which must have excited afresh the desire to accomplish some such work. This was his happy escape from the great plague, for which the most appropriate thank-offering appeared to be the erection of a temple such as had never before been seen in Israel.

When the earlier narrator began to describe this grand design of David's and the position taken up, with regard to it by the Prophet Nathan (of whose character and greatness there will be more to say hereafter), this temple had long been built, and the happy reign of Solomon was already in the distant past. As he surveyed the whole with comprehensive glance, he sketched the words of Nathan and David, with the object of giving at the same time a prophetic view of Solomon's subsequent career, and thereby conforming to an artistic practice of which he avails himself in other places[3] in his historical delineations. When David (so runs his narrative[4]) sat in his proud palace at Jerusalem, and Jahveh had given him rest from all his enemies round about,[5] he expressed to Nathan his intention of building the temple; and the Prophet, taking a human view of the question,

---

[1] Vol. ii. p. 142 sq.
[2] The probability of this has been since confirmed by investigations on the spot; cf. Vogüé's *Le Temple de Jérusalem*, p. 110 sq.
[3] Vol. i. pp. 143, 145 sq.
[4] 2 Sam. vii.; cf. 1 Chron. xvii.
[5] From this last expression (vii. 1, cf. ver. 9) one might suppose that this oracle would fall into the latest years of David's life; but this is contradicted by ver. 12, according to which Solomon was not yet born; neither can we possibly suppose that David's house, ver. 1, was not built until the close of his life. The expression in 2 Sam. xxii. 1 must, therefore, be specially compared with this. It is true that some more modern writers tell us that

had at first nothing to urge against it. But that very night he was taught otherwise by Jahveh in a vision, and on the following day he told David that as Jahveh had always up to that time dwelt in a tent and had never required of a ruler any other abode, so he too should suffer Him to remain therein ; He who had raised him from the dust to be a monarch would raise him higher yet, and would never suffer His people Israel again, as heretofore, to be oppressed by unrighteous heathens ; [1] He would not, it is true, permit him to build the contemplated temple, but He announced to him instead that his house should endure and be blessed; and when he himself should lie in the quiet of the tomb, a future son of his should build the temple, a prince for ever loved by God as by a father, who, if he sinned, would, like everyone else, be punished at the hands of God, but would never lose the divine favour [2] as Saul had done. On this David went into the sanctuary and offered a heart-felt prayer of thanksgiving for so gracious a promise, which was added to all the divine blessings hitherto enjoyed. Words of thanksgiving were here too weak, for all proceeded from the free grace of God. It was in this that the infinite superiority of the greatness of the true God would appear, viz. that He would sustain His people for ever, and would never again suffer them to fall. Oh that this oracle uttered over David's house might hold for ever ! but the truthfulness of God was the pledge of the fulfilment of the promise, and only because this had been given him by unsolicited grace, had he found courage for this prayer.[3] In reality Nathan and other such Prophets must have conversed with David on the two points now under consideration. In the

this happened in the twelfth year of David's reign in Jerusalem.; see Jalâl-eldîn's *History of Jerusalem*, transl. by Reynolds, p. 32.

[1] Instead of שבטי, ver. 7, we should read שׁפְטֵי, according to ver. 11. The suffixes are sometimes exchanged in this passage, and so in ver. 11 we must read לֹ and אֹיְבָיו, as the context and the comparison of vv. 1 and 9 demand.

[2] In this strict equalisation of all men before God, so that even the king is to be punished for his sins like everyone else, the severe antique spirit of this prophecy is made manifest. Cf. Ps. lxxxix. 33 [32], where this feeling is already weakened. —In vv. 15, 16 it might be preferable to follow the LXX in reading מִלְפָנַי, instead of יִיךָ, in both passages, were it not that in ver. 15 the whole text of the LXX was evidently mutilated, and that

the text of ver. 16 explains itself from the remarks made i. p. 296.

[3] The whole of this prayer, at least in its extension, is somewhat unlike the earlier narrator, so that one may reasonably trace fragments of an older work in this passage; isolated expressions, however, remind us of the style of the earlier narrator: ver. 19 is very like vi. 22, and גלה אֶת אזן, in ver. 27, is peculiar to him ; ver. 19 must be read chiefly in accordance with 1 Chron. xvii. 17, וְהִרְאִתַנִי בְּתוֹר הָאָדָם לְמַעְלָה, 'and lettest me look on the succession of men upwards,' far into the future, as the former member of the verse says. In ver. 23, instead of לַעֲשׂוֹת לָכֶם (which closes the parenthesis from כִּי אֵין forward), we must read לַעֲשׂוֹתְךָ, and also לְגָרֵשְׁךָ for לְאַרְצְךָ, and at the end אֱלֹהִים, partially after the LXX and Chron.

first place, they must have declared from the point of view of the higher truth, whether the building of the temple was necessary or whether it might be dispensed with, and they must have dissuaded David from his design. In the second place, they undoubtedly announced during his life the blessed duration of his house and (a closely connected point in the feeling of antiquity) the transfer to him of the Priestly dignity; this David himself clearly indicates in his last song,[1] nor does the idea present any difficulty. The earlier narrator, in as far as he only gives us in this passage the substance of all these oracles concerning David in a compressed form and brought into a more definite connexion, and sketches the prophetic height of David's career from the point at which he himself learns the highest of all the divine counsels and from which the more distant prospect of the life of Solomon is opened to him as in a mirror, is so far justified in choosing this place for a corresponding answer from David. But the colouring of Nathan's discourse in details and as a whole is exactly that which elsewhere characterises this earlier narrator, so that it is not directly in the words or in their connexion, but only in the thoughts themselves, that we can rediscover the truths to which Nathan once gave prophetic utterance, just as is the case with the discourses of John the Baptist and of Christ in the fourth Gospel.[2]

Again, the reorganisation of the Levites by David was rendered necessary partly by the establishment of the chief sanctuary at Jerusalem, and partly by the confusion into which the affairs of the Levites had fallen during the centuries immediately preceding.[3] In fact, to these men, who had once been the rulers of the community and who were now so weak, it cannot have been otherwise than acceptable to receive powerful protection, and, in as far as the age demanded it, reorganisation at the hands of a man of the people who retained, even when he had become a king, a tender reverence for the ordinances of the ancient religion. The hereditary Priesthood in general connected itself henceforward more and more closely with the rising power of the monarchy, from which it received the protection it expected; although in the time of David it retained a greater degree of independence, from the fact that the sacred tabernacle,

---

[1] 2 Sam. xxiii. 5. The promise of the Priesthood to which Ps. cx. 4 only refers back, may already have been implied on some earlier occasion.

[2] A fact which careful readers have long been able to perceive, and which has been more and more generally recognised in recent times; but I have shown more exactly how it is to be understood in the *Johanneischen Schriften*, i. 1861.

[3] Vol. ii. pp. 347 sqq., 413 sqq.

and therefore a chief part of the religious cultus with it, remained at Gibeon.¹ Since the destruction by Saul of all the descendants of Eli, with the exception of Abiathar who escaped to David,² the highest functions of the Priesthood had once more been exercised by the other high-priestly house³ at this sanctuary; and at the time when all the tribes elected David king, amongst other Levites who came from there to David at Hebron, was a descendant of this house named Zadok.⁴ He was then in the full vigour of youth, and David attached him thenceforth to his court, by appointing him High-Priest in conjunction with Abiathar and causing them both to live together at Jerusalem,⁵ so that probably the one had immediate charge of the new sanctuary at Jerusalem, and the other of that at Gibeon. Now, if the two high-priestly houses were thus put on an equal footing under the monarchy, this arrangement itself would lay the foundation of a fresh organisation of the whole tribe of Levi; and the Book of Chronicles⁶ gives a more detailed description of the manner in which this was worked out, at all events in the last years of David. The explanation of these matters, however, together with that of the temporal offices of the court and the other arrangements of the government, must be deferred to a more convenient place.

The diligent cultivation, in times of peace, of the higher arts of the Muses at the court of Jerusalem is what David's genius would lead us to expect, and is confirmed by a passing reference.⁷ It is true that we have now no particular information on the subject; but we have testimony to the fact, eloquent enough, in the greatness of David himself as a poet, and in the immediate succession of the glorious age of Solomon, which realised a yet higher development of all such arts. That David was skilled in all the arts we have already seen,⁸ and the Gittite style which was so much employed in Israel after his time,⁹ may have been naturalised there in consequence of his former close connexion with the Philistine Gath.¹⁰

---

¹ P. 125. ² P. 91.
³ Vol. ii. p. 409 sq.
⁴ This follows from 1 Chron. xii. 28; cf. xvi. 39.
⁵ Thus the two constantly appear in the earlier narrative, 2 Sam. viii. 17, xx. 25, xv. 24 sqq., 1 Kings i. 7–27; accordingly in the passage 2 Sam. viii. 17 the two names Ahimelech and Abiathar must be transposed, while 1 Chron. xviii. 16, Abimelech certainly stands for Ahimelech, p. 82, *note* 2. It is true that, according to 1 Chron. xxiv. 3 sqq., Ahimelech as son of Abiathar had already become High-Priest in David's last years; but since this contradicts the other authorities, it is better to suppose that the Chronicler in this passage confounds the age of Solomon with that of David; on this more must be said below.
⁶ 1 Chron. xxiii.–xxvi.
⁷ 2 Sam. xix. 36 [35].
⁸ P. 59 sq.
⁹ See the *Dichter des Alten Bundes*, i.
¹⁰ Pp. 83, 99 sqq.

3) But as far as internal arrangements are concerned, a new dynasty is dependent for its ultimate security on the attitude which it assumes towards the surviving members of that which preceded it; and since so many dynasties have considered it impossible to purchase their own safety, except at the price of the destruction or rigorous banishment of every member of the fallen house, we cannot but admire the peculiar greatness displayed by David in this connexion also. As soon as he had taken up his permanent abode at Jerusalem, he enquired whether there yet survived any member of the family of Saul to whom he might 'show the kindness of God for Jonathan's sake;' so they brought him Ziba, an old servant (house-steward) of Saul's, who told him that in the country beyond Jordan, in the house of a wealthy man named Machir, there was still a son of Jonathan's, Mephibosheth by name,[1] who was lame, and on that account, if on no other, hardly capable, according to ancient ideas, of occupying the throne. David immediately sent for him, and returned to him all the family possessions of Saul, with the condition that the old steward with his fifteen children and twenty slaves should administer them as hereditary tenant or copyholder, and should deliver up their produce to him and to his heirs for ever; he himself, moreover, was to eat at the royal table whenever the king was not absent from Jerusalem.[2] How Mephibosheth threw away half of these royal gifts will hereafter appear.

But afterwards, on another occasion, it was shown how little David, with the best intentions, could soften the public feeling which Saul's deeds of violence had stirred up against his house.[3] On the first conquest of the country, the Canaanite city of Gibeon together with its territory was spared,[4] on condition of the performance of certain services for the sanctuary of Israel, and it is possible that the tabernacle was situated for a time, even under Joshua, within its boundaries. When the tabernacle was again placed there under Saul,[5] so that the ancient duties of the city were revived, a dispute may have arisen between Saul and the citizens on this very matter, and the former, with the recklessness so characteristic of his latest years, may have

---

[1] P. 119, *note* 2.
[2] 2 Sam. ix.; from the earlier narrator, who had already prepared us for all these representations, 1 Sam. xx. 14 sqq.
[3] 2 Sam. xxi. 1-14, also no doubt from this earlier narrator. In ver. 5, for נִשְׁמַדְנוּ we must read לְשָׁמְרֵנוּ; also ver. 8 (cf. supra, p. 74), מֵרָב for מִיכַל, although even the LXX found the present readings in both cases. Ver. 5, according to the present text, could at the most be translated 'who thought we were destroyed,' and even that would not suit the meaning.
[4] Josh. ix.
[5] Vol. ii. p. 415.

taken up the quarrel at once with fearful violence, and commenced an absolute war of extermination against all the inhabitants. In fact, many of the Gibeonites must at that time have been put to death, and others driven into exile, amongst whom no doubt were the two chieftains[1] who took such a shameful revenge on Ish-bosheth.[2] When David had reigned several years,[3] a drought and famine of three years' duration terrified all Israel. David had the oracle consulted on the matter; and it answered (no doubt because it was not easy to attribute it to any less remote cause) that the calamity was sent by God to punish the cruelty which Saul had exercised towards the Gibeonites, and which had not yet faded from the popular memory. The oracle usually looked for the cause of offence, under circumstances such as these, in the deeds of the actual government; but the very irreproachable manner in which David had hitherto ruled, rendered it necessary to go further back to find a cause for the calamity; and the feelings of justice and sympathy with which the case of even the Canaanite Gibeonites was taken up, furnish a beautiful indication of the moral position of the people at that time. But the Gibeonites refused either to content themselves with quit-money, or to avenge themselves on Israel, for their very position as serfs would prevent their venturing on this last demand. They required that the king himself should deliver over seven of Saul's descendants to them, to be hanged at the sacred spot already mentioned[4] on the height of Gibeah, the city of Saul, that the divine wrath might thus be appeased. On this occasion David, even against his will, was compelled to yield; but he spared the posterity of Jonathan, and had two of Saul's sons by his concubine Rizpah, and five sons of his daughter Merab,[5] given up to the Gibeonites. The execution took place at Easter, just at the beginning of barley-harvest —a season which had always possessed a certain sanctity in

---

[1] P. 118.

[2] The little place called Beeroth from which they both came, was, as we know from Josh. ix. 17, nothing but a sort of suburb belonging to Gibeon.

[3] It is clear that this event took place *before* the war of Absalom, partly because the outrage against Gibeon must still have been very energetically condemned at the time, as it might have been during the first six or seven years of David's reign at Jerusalem; partly because at the time of Absalom's revolt Shimei plainly referred to this event, and without ground charged David with the guilt of having designedly murdered Saul's posterity, 2 Sam. xvi. 7 sq., cf. xix. 29 [xix. 28]. There are also many of the most modern German writers who will continue to join Shimei in condemning David in this affair; but their want of judgment is evident. How little David desired to destroy Saul's descendants and relations as such, is obvious from the fact that some of them remained quietly settled in Jerusalem itself down to a late period. 1 Chron. ix. 35-44.

[4] P. 22.

[5] P. 74.

Israel in connexion with such events. With touching maternal affection, the concubine seated herself at once on the rock with her mourning cloth, scared away bird and beast from the suspended bodies by day and night, and so continued until a shower of rain came down, with which the divine wrath seemed lifted from the parched earth. On hearing of this, David had the bones of these crucified men, together with those of Saul and Jonathan, which were brought from Jabesh,[1] honourably deposited in the family tomb at Zelah in the tribe of Benjamin.

Thus just and wise was David's internal administration.

2. *David's Wars against the Heathen.*

Of the wars of David against the Heathen, important as they must have been during these thirty-three years, we now possess but the slightest knowledge from detailed accounts. In the oldest writings they were evidently described minutely, but in the works which are still preserved we read nothing but meagre abstracts of their history. What abundant material for the spread of its vain-glorious fame would the nation subsequently have possessed in them, if, like other idle peoples, it had attached any value to such power over foreign races! But since the days of Moses, this people had set a goal before its eyes far other than the vaunting of its earthly victories and conquests, and as its recognition of it became more single-hearted with the advance of time, especially in the period after David and Solomon, the less did the later historical works delight in extensive descriptions of the foreign victories of the national heroes, and of David's in particular, and the more did they contract the ancient records of their achievements.

This general fact, however, is clear at once, that we should be very far wrong if we were to suppose that David stirred up these wars from a simple love of war and conquest, such a supposition being opposed both to the separate accounts which have been preserved, and to the whole spirit of the ancient nation and its religion. How little David resembled the later Assyrian, Chaldean, and Persian disturbers of the world, is most immediately and clearly shown at this point by the fact that he did not, like these great conquerors, seize upon the Phœnician maritime towns, but always remained on the best terms with the little Phœnician states, which were entirely occupied in commerce and the arts of gain. Indeed, he gladly accepted the participation which

[1] P. 110.

they offered him in the more refined arts of life;[1]—so great was the alteration which was now introduced into the mutual relations of Israel and this section of the ancient Canaanites! The time was now fully come for this people, once so greatly dreaded by the Israelites in the field, to be regarded by them simply as a guild of peaceful merchants, so that the name of Canaanite became synonymous with that of the trader; and the pride with which they had once looked down upon the skilful people whom they had overcome in war, manifested itself in nothing but a certain contempt for the commercial cunning which now gained an easy ascendency among them.[2] But in truth there were other causes now at work to produce a closer union between Israel and the Canaanites, who were completely driven back to the strip of land along the northern coast. The Philistines, originally so very different from them, must, from the nature of the case, have been dangerous to them during the last centuries of their great power by land. This supposition is confirmed by certain obscure traditions;[3] and we may well believe that the peril to which they were thus exposed was an additional reason with them for seeking friendly relations with David, as the great conqueror of the Philistines.

The causes of these wars must, then, be looked for in the conduct of the Heathen rather than in that of David. The surrounding peoples, with which Israel had frequently been engaged in war already, could not fail to observe that they would no longer be able to hold Israel in terror and subjection, as they had done so often heretofore, if the nation acquired unity and strength under a vigorous king. They certainly desired to oppose Israel in its powerful movement for increased independence, and attacked it with every weapon of violence or scorn; while Israel, on its side, had in truth to recover from the many losses which it had been compelled to sustain during the preceding centuries, and[4] was able to look back upon a far mightier past. But when once a great war was thus kindled, and the enemy found himself in unexpected danger, he would be ready to seek alliances with more distant nations, and so the flame of battle would spread in a few years over a wider and wider area, until almost all the peoples between the Mediterranean Sea and the Euphrates, between the Arabian Gulf and

---

[1] 2 Sam. v. 11, according to which the king of Tyre sought peace of his own accord after the conquest of Jerusalem.

[2] The first allusion of this sort which is now known to us is found in Hosea xii. 8 [xii. 7]; then the usage becomes fixed, Isaiah xxiii. 8, Zeph. i. 11, Ezek. xvi. 29, xvii. 4, Job xl. 30 [xli. 6], so that from this again an abbreviated noun for *Wares* was actually formed, Jer. x. 17.

[3] Justin, *Hist.* xviii. 3, 5.

[4] Vol. ii. p. 235 sqq.

the Orontes, were caught by it, and it would become a vital question for David, whether he was to subject them all or to surrender the power and honour of his kingdom. If a considerable power were to arise between the Mediterranean and the Euphrates, it would be driven into constant efforts to unite all these countries under its own sway, even contrary to the original purpose of its existence.

1) *David's Military Organisation.*[1]

The forces which David had to oppose to these attacks are fortunately known to us with some precision. The troop of six hundred, the original formation of which we have traced in an earlier period of David's history,[2] still constituted the nucleus of his whole military force. These men were, as a body, not only carefully-trained and well-armed warriors, but had been selected on account of extraordinary valour and love of war; and they formed a sort of model soldiery. On this account they were called *Gibborim*, that is, heroes,[3] a name to which the Italian *bravi* would most nearly correspond. As their sole occupation was the art of war, and they had no further duties, their permanent maintenance of every kind (pay, dwellings free of charge for themselves and their households)[4] was of course drawn from the king, so that they really constituted the first standing army of which we have any special knowledge in such early times. When they were not in the field they were quartered at Jerusalem;[5] they do not appear to have ever been employed on garrison duty. The constitution of this troop can be deduced with accuracy from certain indications. The soldiers appear to have been formed into three divisions of two hundred each; an arrangement which makes our thoughts involuntarily recur to the three companies in which a well-trained army generally made its attack;[6] but we also read

---

[1] Colonel Rüstow's Essay on David as a Soldier (*Militärische Biographien*, i. Zürich, 1858) is profoundly unsatisfactory, and at the same time unappreciative.

[2] Pp. 89, 102.

[3] 2 Sam. x. 7, xvi. 6, xx. 7, 1 Kings i. 8, 10; whence it appears that they are often mentioned with the addition *all*, clearly referring to their considerable number. The number six hundred is never given in these passages; but that the six hundred are meant admits of no doubt, and receives additional confirmation from 2 Sam. xv. 18, if we read גברים here instead of גתים, in accordance with some of the translations of the LXX and Vulgate, which coincide in this passage; and to this reading we are directed by every indication. Even in Isaiah iii. 2, they appear with their special name.

[4] P. 124.

[5] This is clear from 2 Sam. xv. 18, xvi. 6. We have already seen that they were married, p. 101; and so Uriah has his wife Bathsheba in a house at Jerusalem, 2 Sam. xi. 2 sqq.

[6] Cf. Judges vii. 16, Job i. 17, and Gen. xiv. 15; also in David's history, 2 Sam. xviii. 2, where, no doubt, the whole of the main army must be understood; perhaps two hundred of the Gibborim accompanied each division of the army.

sometimes of one of these three divisions remaining behind to protect the baggage.¹ Over every twenty men there must have been placed an officer; so that in all there would be thirty of these officers; for no other explanation can be given of the name of *Shâlîsh* (a thirty-man, one of the thirty) which these officers bore, than that they formed a kind of Order or College.² Over every two hundred men with their ten officers was placed a Colonel; and the three Colonels again had a superior, whom we might call a General. Thus the whole regiment of the Gibborim, including the officers, consisted of six hundred and thirty-four men, to which no doubt a number of retainers made a considerable addition.

Now we are not to suppose that because David was the first to introduce this organisation among the Hebrews, he was also the first to design it. It had probably been already established in still older states in that region, for the name of Shâlîsh has been preserved in a very ancient song,³ and there are other traces not altogether obscure of a similar institution among surrounding nations of still greater antiquity.⁴ But under David this army of heroes certainly earned its title in the fullest sense, and

---

¹ 1 Sam. xxv. 13; cf. xxx. 10, 24.

² The derivation of the word שָׁלִישׁ, where it means much the same as officer, from שָׁלֹשִׁים, *thirty*, is shown by 2 Sam. xxiii. 13, 23, 24, 1 Chron. xii. 4, 18 (Kerî and Kethîb emend accordingly in the last passage), xxvii. 6. The whole college of the thirty is called הַשְׁלִישִׁי, formed according to the *Lehrb.* § 164, 177, 2 Sam. xxiii. 8, 18 (Kethîb), or הַשְּׁלִשִׁים; a Colonel, therefore, is רֹאשׁ הַשָּׁלִישִׁי, 2 Sam. xxiii. 8, 18, or הַשְּׁלִשִׁים רֹאשׁ, ver. 13 (in the plural), or עַל השלשים, 1 Chron. xxvii. 6, xi. 42 (where we must read עַל הָ instead of עָלָיו); cf. 2 Sam. xxiii. 23. The three Colonels are also called, with greater brevity, the three Gibborim, 2 Sam. xxiii. 9, 18, 22; a clear sign that the name of the שְׁלִשִׁים or שָׁלִישִׁים, also was an abbreviation of 'thirty Gibborim;' the General was called שַׂר הַשְּׁלִשָׁה, 2 Sam. xxiii. 18 sq. It cannot surprise us to find, that in times after David, שָׁלִישׁ at last came to be nothing but a general name for an officer in the vicinity and the immediate service of the king. No doubt such an abbreviated expression may admit, from its origin, several very different meanings; for instance, as in recent times a war-chariot, with three occupants, has frequently been discovered on the monuments of Nineveh, and it is also known that in ancient India three men were considered to belong to each war-chariot (according to the *Dhanur-Veda*, cf. Wilson's remarks), we might easily imagine the Hebrew Shâlîsh to have some similar signification. Nevertheless the whole history shows that the word cannot have even the remotest reference to a war-chariot. The LXX probably meant by τριστάτης a man of the third rank, as if none but the first minister as מִשְׁנֶה, of the king, Gen. xli. 43, belonged to the second rank after him. The τρίτης μοίρας ἡγεμών of Josephus, *Antiq.* ix. 4. 4, 5; 6. 3, might mean a commander of the third part of the army (and we might then compare 1 Kings xvi. 9 as somewhat similar); but for this he uses, ix. 11. 1, the more general title of Chiliarch.

³ Ex. xv. 4; cf. xiv. 7. We may consider Gideon's three hundred men, ii. 383 sqq., as a preliminary; and it is curious in how many other passages six hundred warriors are mentioned as the nucleus of the soldiery, Judges iii. 31, xviii. 16 sq., xx. 47 sqq. (in the last place, in fact, as the nucleus for the fresh formation of a tribe), 1 Sam. xiii. 15, xiv. 2.

⁴ The coincidence of the six hundred warriors among the Egyptians, Exodus xiv. 7, and the Indians (*Nala Mahâ-Bhâr.* 26, 2) with those of Israel, cannot be as

HIS MILITARY ORGANISATION. 141

was the soul of all the great victories which were won in this age. We still possess a very ancient catalogue of the most renowned of these valiant warriors, together with some of the exploits of the most distinguished among them.[1] First comes the description of the three Colonels, Jashobeam, the son of Hachmoni, Eleazar the son of Dodo, and Shammah the son of Agee.[2] The first of these, we are told, once brandished his spear over three hundred slaughtered foemen at once; which can only mean that on one and the same occasion, on a single day and as one piece of work, he slew three hundred foes in succession, springing from one to another with terrific speed and fury. Of the second it is related that once, when the Philistines had collected at Pas-dammim,[3] he sustained their attack for a time quite single-handed, and continued to smite them to the ground until his wearied hand clung convulsively to the sword; but then the great victory of Jahveh was already won, and when at last the country people, who before had fled, rallied behind him on the battle-field, they found that there was nothing left for them to do but to strip the booty from the bodies of the slain.[4] Shammah, it is said, when the Philistines on one occasion had assembled at Lechi,[5] was deserted in a similar manner by the flying country folk, but remained nevertheless all alone near a large field of ripe lentils, which the enemy wanted to devastate. He saved it from their destructive purpose, and at the same time won a great victory of Jahveh. We ought, however, to remember, that these single heroes were always attended in battle by their armour-bearers, one or more in number; these exploits will then scarcely appear much greater than that of Jonathan in the battle of Michmash.[6] To the same rank of Colonel belonged the three heroes[7] who,

---

accidental as that of the six hundred in the traditions of the Cid. Cf. also Bruce's *Travels* (ed. 1790), iii. p. 310.

[1] 2 Sam. xxiii. 8-39, where thirty-seven heroes are enumerated; sixteen more are enumerated 1 Chron. xi. 10-47, but partly after the manner of the Chronicler, with still more abbreviated descriptions. Cf. i. p. 136 sq.

[2] 2 Sam. xxiii. 8; the words must be emended according to ver. 18 and the book of Chronicles, although perhaps העצלו really conceals some other word, such as חניתי. 2 Sam. xxiii. 8, indeed, has eight hundred instead of three hundred; and, at any rate, according to the older authority, this hero, as well as his two immediate associates, had displayed much more true warlike valour than his commanding officer Abishai, ver. 18. If

יֹשֵׁב בַּשֶּׁבֶת before the proper name Jashobeam is correct, which is in fact most probable, the first of the three must have had a special additional designation something like μετάθρονος.

[3] See p. 68.

[4] In ver. 9 the unintelligible words must be emended in accordance with 1 Chron. xi. 13; in ver. 10 after הָעָם we must probably restore אֲשֶׁר נָם, as in ver. 11.

[5] In ver. 11 we must punctuate לְחָיָה instead of לֶחָיָה, since a place must be named here; it is the same spot at which Samson attacked the Philistines, ii. p. 406.

[6] P. 33 sq.

[7] Since the description of these three men, ver. 13, is indefinite, we can hardly

when David was still in the mountain fastness near the cave of Adullam, once brought him water at the peril of their lives from the Philistine camp in the neighbourhood.[1] Over the three Colonels was placed Abishai, Joab's brother; a distinction which might be expected to fall to one who is always mentioned next to Joab, David's greatest General, and who almost everywhere acts in concert with him; and moreover he had of course the same advantage that his brother enjoyed, of being nearly related to David.[2] Almost the same story is told of his prowess as of that of the first of the three Colonels. The rank of a Colonel was also possessed by Benaiah, the son of Jehoiada, a man of extraordinary energy,[3] who held the post of commander of the body-guard. He slew the two sons of the king of Moab.[4] Once in the winter, when, after an unusually heavy fall of snow, a lion had taken refuge among the abodes of men and had made his lair near a house in the well, he descended alone into the well and slew him. Another time he engaged in a struggle with a very distinguished Egyptian, who had a spear as long and as heavy as the beam of a bridge;[5] he himself happened to have nothing but a walking-staff in his hand, but he wrenched the great spear from the Egyptian, and slew him with it. This Egyptian was certainly a man of a very different stamp from the slave formerly mentioned[6] (who was probably seized on some expedition for booty), which establishes the noteworthy fact, that the contemporary Egyptian government did not look with indifference upon David's wars for the supremacy over so many countries. Perhaps this Egyptian fell in the war against Edom, of which more hereafter. Such traits of warlike courage are more significant than anything else. They recall to us completely those few periods of history otherwise known to us, in which a marvellous aspiration for the possession of some

---

suppose them to be identical with the three Colonels named above; at the same time it is remarkable that in a passage where *all* the names are given, and indeed, according to the superscription, must be given, these three alone should remain anonymous. Perhaps, therefore, the article has dropped out before שְׁלֹשָׁה, ver. 13. Further, it appears from ver. 22, 1 Chron. xxvii. 6, and 1 Chron. xi. 42, that besides those three heroes whose names are given, others might attain to the same rank, either at some other time or as a mere title.

[1] P. 88.   [2] P. 113.

[3] בֶּן, which is superfluous before אִישׁ, in ver. 20, must be read as בְּנֵי after שְׁנֵי,

as the LXX and to some extent 1 Chron. xi. 22 show.

[4] *Ariel* appears to have been the title of honour of a king of Moab, as Indian princes call themselves Daevasinha (Lion of God). The event occurred in the course of the war with Moab, of which we have very little knowledge from other sources.

[5] This must be inserted from the LXX; we can only suppose it was quite a simple bridge over a wâdi, consisting of nothing but the stout trunk of a tree; 1 Chron. xi. 23 has, instead of this, a weaver's beam, see p. 69. On the other hand, the stature of five ells which the Chronicler assigns him would correspond but ill to Goliath's six and a half ells.

[6] P. 105.

higher blessing, such as freedom or immortality, has taken hold of an entire nation, and so has produced, through special intruments of exceptional power, even military exploits which appear incredible to ordinary men. Such were the times of the first confessors of Islam, of the old Swiss or of the Ditmarshers: the age of Israel under Joshua should be looked upon from the same point of view,[1] but it must be admitted that we no longer possess the record of so many particular features of that era, as in the case before us. Of the other warriors deemed worthy of mention who were not either Colonels or of yet higher rank, we know nothing but the bare names; but the belief that each of them had performed great exploits is justified by the very fact of their being mentioned at all; and of some of them a few details have been preserved accidentally to us from other sources, as for example of Asahel (here introduced at the head of the list), the brother of Joab, who fell so young,[2] and the Hittite Uriah, whose integrity at home and on the field will presently call for notice. And so, just as the names and deeds of Muhammed's many companions were long held in very distinct remembrance and special records were devoted to describing them, David's heroes, too, who had vied with him in valour and self-sacrifice for the community of Israel and the religion of Jahveh, lived on, linked for ever with his memory.

This standing army did not include the soldiers of David's actual body-guard, who were also employed, like the Roman lictors, to execute offenders on whom the king had passed sentence. These were the so-called Cherethites and Pelethites, who were shown[3] to be all foreigners, especially Philistines of every kind. They are sometimes mentioned in conjunction with the Gibborim; but if we compare all the passages in which they appear,[4] we see in the first place that in point of numbers they were, as we could not but expect, far inferior to them; and in the second place, that they were never sent like the Gibborim on actual service. In Saul's time the body-guard were called runners;[5] and it was during his residence at Ziklag that David appears first to have formed a troop of Philistines for the same purpose, and he subsequently continued to recruit it from Philistine prisoners and other foreigners. Their quarters in Jeru-

[1] Vol. ii. p. 241 sqq.
[2] P. 114.
[3] Vol. i. p. 246 sq.
[4] 2 Sam. viii. 18, xx. 23, xv. 18, xx. 7, 1 Kings i. 38, 44.
[5] 1 Sam. xxii. 17, cf. ver. 18; in later times under the kings of Judah they again bore this name. We may conclude from 2 Sam. xv. 1, 1 Kings i. 5, that, according to the ancient custom of that court, there were generally fifty to run before the king.

salem were[1] doubtless not far from the royal castle. This small body could at no time become a source of danger to the state: far more was to be apprehended from the Gibborim, who obviously formed the commencement of a sort of *milites prætoriani* or janissaries, and were already of sufficient importance to play a part at Solomon's accession;[2] to this must be added that they might also be chosen from foreigners, as soon as they conformed (a self-evident condition) to the religion of the country.[3]

The standing army, it is clear, was not very numerous; in all the greater wars the levies had of course to be raised from all the men of the nation capable of bearing arms; and Joab, David's general-in-chief, was therefore appointed in command not only of the regiment of the Six Hundred but also of all the fighting troops. These levies were called out, for instance, by Absalom from all the tribes on the west of the Jordan, when David, with his six hundred Gibborim and his body-guard, had fled from Jerusalem across the Jordan:[4] and in the case of this force distinctive mention is made only of princes, i.e. leaders of hundreds and thousands. Considering how thickly populated the country then was, we could not but expect this army, when actually collected, to be very numerous, 'as the sand of the sea;'[5] but it is difficult to make any more definite statement on this point. According to the accounts of the census instituted by David, the men capable of bearing arms were found to be 800,000 in Israel (the ten tribes) and 500,000 in Judah;[6] but we do not know what age is considered manhood, and the numbers are certainly too round to be accepted as strictly historical. On the other hand, more light appears to be thrown upon the matter by a statement of the Chronicler,[7] that David made an arrangement by which every

---

[1] P. 124.
[2] 1 Kings i. 8, 10.
[3] Thus Uriah was a Hittite, but as far as religion went, a good Israelite; Zelek an Ammonite, 2 Sam. xxiii. 37; Ithmah a Moabite, 1 Chron. xi. 46; and Ittai of Gath, who was appointed commander of one of the three divisions of the army in the battle against Absalom, is expressly designated as a foreigner by David, 2 Sam. xv. 19.
[4] 2 Sam. xv. 18, xvii. 11.
[5] 2 Sam. xvii. 11.
[6] 2 Sam. xxiv. 9. Similar estimates of the numbers of men and soldiers of Israel, which may well appear too great for many of our foregone conclusions, have come under our notice in earlier passages of this history, and others will present themselves further on.

Though we must suppose them to be to some extent round numbers, and in certain places exaggerated, yet there is no reason to doubt their generally historical character. For it is a question in all these cases of a levy *en masse*, to which the whole population without further distinction of religion would be summoned. If, for instance, we reckon the present population of Algeria at 3,000,000, and of these from 300,000 to 400,000 as fighting men (*vide* Dawson Borrer's *Campaign against the Kabailes*), then surely the land of Israel in times of such prosperity as it enjoyed under David and with the extended boundaries of that period, could sustain a far greater population; the question has already been touched upon in vol. ii.

[7] 1 Chron. xxvii. 1–15.

month 24,000 men under a fixed commander were to be in his service; this would accordingly make up a total of 288,000. But this is one of the few pieces of information which we are now hardly able to understand. The names of the twelve commanders, in spite of some variations, correspond on the whole to the names of twelve of the chief Gibborim who are mentioned in the ancient document[1] already noticed;[2] and it is quite credible in itself that the ablest of these trained warriors should be appointed to command the popular levies. The accounts of the other arrangements of the Davidic kingdom which are given in this passage of the Chronicles[3] are in like manner drawn, beyond a doubt, from copious ancient authorities. But it does not appear from this description[4] exactly what service was performed by these 24,000 men, changing with every month; and neither in the rebellion of Absalom[5] nor of Adonijah[6] do they play any part which it is easy for us to recognise. We can only regret, therefore, that the Chronicler has here abbreviated the ancient accounts too much; perhaps every month the corresponding 24,000 men underwent special training in the use of arms, or perhaps they formed in part the garrisons of subjugated countries. It is certain, from a statement of great antiquity,[7] that the Israelites, like all ancient nations, only took the field for spring and summer, remaining at home during autumn and winter, so that every war which was not quite brought to a close had to be begun afresh each year at a fixed time. And for that purpose, it is obvious, David must always have had at his disposal, at any rate afterwards, a larger body of men in addition to the central regiment of the Gibborim.[8]

But the whole force entirely conformed to the ancient Hebrew type in not using either horses or chariots. The ranks fought on foot together, and at the very most the various officers rode mules and asses.[9] Nay, David kept to the old Mosaic custom, and had almost all the captured horses disabled.[10] This

---

[1] 2 Sam. xxiii. 8 sqq.
[2] P. 141.
[3] 1 Chron. xxvii.
[4] To judge from the style of the language, ver. 1 is also entirely from the Chronicler. The fact that Asahel, who was killed by Abner (p. 114), is mentioned, ver. 17, as one of the twelve officers, may be of less importance from the fact that his son is also mentioned in addition; cf. the probably similar case in ver. 6. The supposition that the names of the twelve officers were simply borrowed from 2 Sam. xxiii. 8 sq. is not confirmed on closer consideration; cf. also 1 Kings v. 28 [v. 14].

[5] 2 Sam. xv.
[6] 1 Kings i. sq.
[7] 2 Sam. xi. 1, where, under the designation *the kings*, all together, Hebrew and foreign, are included.
[8] This may be concluded with certainty from the brief words 1 Kings i. 9; cf. ver. 25.
[9] As it had been hitherto; vol. ii. p. 241 sq.
[10] 2 Sam. viii. 4; cf. vol. ii. p. 130 sq., 155. Similarly, even in December 1847, Abdelqâdir houghed the sinews of his horses' feet as a sign of the cessation of all war.

supplies a striking proof of the lofty courage which at that time always armed the people even against those nations which, with great superiority in the arts of war, provided themselves with horses and chariots. In the same way the chief weapon in Israel continued to be the spear, in the use of which many of the Israelites must have attained great dexterity; bows and slings[1] appeared less frequently, and most of the foreign nations were probably better provided with weapons than the Israelites, as the story of Goliath indicates.[2]

2) *Survey of David's Wars.*

A survey of the separate nations with whom war was waged renders it evident that—

a.) Most of the wars were carried on against the Philistines, and most of the separate traditions still preserved also refer to them. If David, while he still reigned at Hebron over Judah only, had paid tribute to the Philistines (as he probably did),[3] we can readily understand the violence of their attack, when, after having firmly established himself in Jerusalem as king of all Israel, he proceeded to throw off every sign of subjection, and to meet their inroads and demands with the same vigour which had been formerly shown by Saul in the prosperous years of his reign. We now possess, in particular, short accounts of these wars in two different styles; and the first is that given from the prophetic point of view of the events.[4] These accounts state that when the Philistines heard that David had been anointed king over all Israel, they all marched out, eager for vengeance, to seek David and to take his life. He heard of their designs, however, in time enough to shut himself up[5] in the citadel of Zion which had been already conquered, and thus to secure himself against their first outburst of rage. When they had spread themselves over the fruitful valley of Rephaim, in search, as usual, of plunder, and had therefore fallen (as we can well believe) into disorder, David, encouraged by an oracle of Jahveh which promised him

[1] 2 Sam. i. 22, 1 Sam. xx. 20 sqq., xvii. 40; cf. vol. ii. p. 282 sq. In the ancient Egyptian pictures we see similar simple weapons; and for the Homeric age consult, among other passages, *Iliad,* iv. 306-9.

[2] Amongst the many little stories which the Koran tells of David, the only new one is that he invented chain armour, Sur. xxi. 80, cf. Tabari's *Annals,* i. p. 43, Dub.; but this is certainly a confusion of David with Goliath, see p. 69.

[3] See p. 111.

[4] 2 Sam. v. 17-25, 1 Chron. xiv. 8-17; cf. i. p. 138.

[5] Since עָלָה is the specific word for conducting a campaign or attack, so its counterpart יָרַד, 2 Sam. v. 17 may very well mean to settle oneself down and remain quiet in a fortress; cf. Judges xv. 8.

success, suddenly attacked and defeated them. This happened at a place otherwise unknown to us[1] called Baal-Perazim (a name which might mean, according to the words which compose it, 'the God of the breaches,' i.e. of the victories), as though the place had received its name from the fact that there David, led on by Jahveh's power, broke through the enemy's lines with a force like that of the floods breaking irresistibly through the dams. This time the Philistines left their idols to their fate, and they were carried off by David and his soldiers;[2] this was the exact counterpart of the previous capture of the ark of the covenant by the Philistines.[3]—On another occasion the Philistines had spread themselves in the same valley, but the oracle opposed David's attacking them openly (for they seem this time to have kept closer round the camp), and told him to take a circuit which might enable him to attack them on the rear, and there take up a position west of them, opposite some lofty Baka-trees;[4] then, if he heard a rustling noise in the tops of these trees, he was to make good speed, for that would be the sign that Jahveh was going before him to smite the camp of the Philistines.[5] David obeyed the oracle, and smote the Philistines from Gibeon to Gezer.[6] This makes it further evident how powerful the Philistines must still have been at the beginning of this period, since they were able to penetrate into the very heart of Israel.

The statements of the other kind of narrative[7] are of a more simply popular nature, setting forth the prowess against Philistine giants of individual heroes who became distinguished in

---

[1] The mountain Perazim, Isaiah xxviii. 21, appears however to be the same place, and if its summit had once been a holy spot like that of so many other mountains, the name Baal-Perazim is explained at once. But Isaiah does not borrow his description from the passage before us, and in general does not take examples out of David's history (see note on the passage in the *Propheten des A. B.*).

[2] Clearly with the immediate purpose of displaying them in his triumphal procession; but this did not seem suitable to the Chronicler, so he makes David have them burned instead.

[3] Vol. ii. p. 412 sq.

[4] A kind of balsam-tree, which grows quite by itself.

[5] This affords us distinct evidence that the Hebrews in early times, like other ancient peoples, believed in omens derived from the rustling of the leaves of sacred trees. צְעָדָה must, like صَعَل signify a heavily ascending sound, gasping as it were, resounding from a mysterious deep; cf. דְּמָמָה, as a sign of the Deity manifesting Himself, 1 Kings xix. 12, Job iv. 16.

[6] If in 2 Sam. v. 25 גִּבְעוֹן is to be read instead of גֶּבַע, according to the LXX and 1 Chron. xiv. 16, since Gibeon, according to Robinson, lies west of Gibeah or Géba (for we can scarcely think that Gibeah in the tribe of Judah is meant), Gezer, which, according to Joshua xvi. 3, must be supposed west of Beth-horon, must indicate a pursuit carried very far to the west; cf. ii. p. 328 sqq. Again, it seems to follow, from Isaiah xxviii. 21, that mount Perazim lay not far from Gibeon. We shall then have to adopt the conclusion that the valley of Rephaim is the one which stretches to the west from Jerusalem as far as Gibeon.

[7] 2 Sam. xxi. 15–22, 1 Chron. xx. 4–8.

these wars; but, like the narratives in prophetic style, which appear to have been cut short at their close, they have clearly been abbreviated in the Books of Samuel, and still more in the Chronicles. Once, we are told, when David was completely exhausted in a battle with the Philistines, a Philistine thought he should find it an easy task to slay him; he was one of the race of giants,[1] by name Ishbi-benob (i.e. probably highlander); his lance weighed 300 pounds of bronze, and he was also girt with a battle-axe.[2] David was already engaged in a fierce struggle with him when Joab's brother Abishai, who has often been mentioned already, sprang to his assistance and slew the giant; but when David's faithful men looked back upon the danger he had escaped, they swore that he should never again go with them into battle, lest he should 'put out the light of Israel,'—a wish which reappeared on another occasion later on in his life.[3] Here we have not even so much as a statement of the place of the occurrence. On two other occasions similar contests took place in the neighbourhood of the Gezer just mentioned;[4] the giant Saph was slain by Sibbechai,[5] and Goliath of Gath, whose spear was like a weaver's beam, by Elhanan the son of Jaare.[6]—In the neighbourhood of Gath itself, one of the five principal cities of the Philistines, Jonathan the son of Shimeah, one of David's nephews, slew a monstrous giant, who had six fingers on each hand and six toes on each foot,[7] and who, in the pride of his strength, had defied Israel.

A short summary of the results of these battles is given in the survey of David's wars against the heathen,[8] which seems to be the work of the last compiler. David, it is said, smote the Philistines and humbled them, and tore from the hand of the Philistines the bridle of the arm, i.e. he tore from them the supremacy by which they curbed Israel as a rider curbs his horse by the bridle, which the strength of his arm controls.[9]

---

[1] Vol. i. p. 227 sqq.

[2] חֲדָשָׁה cannot mean *new* in this passage, because a sword which was only *new* would have been no novelty, and would not have deserved mention at all; it was evidently some unusual weapon, and since the roots חדד, חדף in the Semitic languages give the meaning of *sharp, cutting*, the word may mean an axe, LXX κορύνη; unless we are prepared to correct the word itself to חַרְשָׁה, and compare גֶּרֶן, *axe*; cf. Ps. xxxiii. 1.

[3] 2 Sam. xviii. 2 sqq.

[4] We should probably adopt this reading in both cases in 1 Chron. xx. 4, instead of גֹּב and גּוֹב.

[5] That he was one of the Gibborim is clear from 1 Chron. xi. 29, xxvii. 11. 2 Sam. xxiii. 27 must be emended accordingly.

[6] Since this man came from Bethlehem, he is probably the Gibbor mentioned in 2 Sam. xxiii. 24, 1 Chron. xi. 26, although the name of his father is given differently here. See also p. 70.

[7] Cf. *Journ. As.* 1843, i. p. 264.

[8] 2 Sam. viii. 1.

[9] These words can hardly express any other meaning. If the hand, then the arm also (and especially the fore-arm אַמָּה), must retain a firm grasp of a thing. Although 1 Chron. xviii. 1 states instead,

While this image leaves us almost entirely to guess at the exact means by which they were rendered harmless, it makes it clear that David did not conquer their country in the same way as he conquered Edom, Moab, and other countries, and subsequent history shows that this valiant people retained their own chieftains. Properly speaking, the expression does not even imply that they were made tributary, though this may possibly have been the case; David seems to have been contented for the most part with the peace which they sought under conditions honourable to Israel, and which they seem to have always observed in the later years of his reign.

The conflicts with the Amalekites of the south also were still continued from Jerusalem;[1] but they all seem to fall in the early years, and almost to have annihilated the nation for a long period.

b.) The next place in the survey is occupied by Moab, which appears to have been early involved in war with David, and certainly to have been already conquered before the war with Ammon, during the course of which, though the description is somewhat detailed, no mention is made of it. It is at first sight astonishing that David should have so early engaged in war with this nation when we recall that he had at an earlier period[2] placed his own parents in security under the protection of the king of Moab; to say nothing of the intimate connexion which, in ancient times, united Israel and the three sister nations,[3] and which was still held in distinct remembrance in spite of the many disputes which had from time to time arisen. In fact, if we take a fair view of David's conduct during his early career in Judah,[4] how, when a refugee from the Philistines, the more he was persecuted by Saul, the farther he drew back towards the east,—we are compelled to suppose that his intention in the last extremity was no other than to fall back upon these kindred nations to the east or south-east, and that nothing but the unexpected hostility of Moab finally prevented him from doing so. The various traces of Saul's activity prove that he had, from the beginning, repressed with a strong hand these restless tribes on the other side of the Jordan; and indeed, under him (as the Chronicler only too briefly mentions), many members of the tribe of Reuben had pressed victoriously far to the east,

---

that David took Gath and her daughters, i.e. the cities of her district, out of the hand of the Philistines and thereby entirely destroyed one of the five little Philistine kingdoms, yet the statement is contradicted by the fact, that at the beginning at least of Solomon's reign Gath had still a king of her own; 1 Kings ii. 39 sq.

[1] According to 2 Sam. viii. 12.
[2] P. 86.
[3] Vol. ii. p. 199 sq.
[4] Pp. 84-99.

and settled down in Arabian districts,[1] so that Moab might at first be all the more favourably inclined towards David. In the changeful circumstances, however, of these little kingdoms, it is not surprising to find that at length Moab was drawn again into closer connexion with Saul. It is possible that Ish-bosheth, who took up his abode in the neighbourhood of Ammon and Moab, had secured the friendship of the latter under disgraceful conditions, to which David refused to accede, and that for this the Moabites would seek a bitter vengeance, or would treat the new king of Israel with the same coarse contempt which the Ammonites afterwards displayed.[2] At any rate, it is certain that they must have deeply wounded the honour of Israel, since the punishment which David inflicted on them after the victory was unusually severe. He made the numerous captives throw themselves together upon the ground, divided them with a measuring rod into three divisions, of which he ordered two to be slain and only one to be kept alive.[3] It is true that these severe penalties are brought under our notice elsewhere, and we learn from other passages how the sentence was executed in a manner corresponding to the commencement here described; viz. as the captives lay down like wheat ready for the threshing, sharp threshing-rollers were drawn over them, and they were trampled to death by horses.[4] But since this punishment was inflicted by David on none of the conquered peoples except Moab and Ammon, we may conclude that they must both have wantonly sullied the honour of Israel and provoked the national wrath in some very special manner; for David, no doubt, simply carried out what the excitement of popular indignation imperatively demanded, and this is only another example of the well-known rule that hostility between kindred nations readily assumes the utmost bitterness. Thus, Moab became tributary to David, and for a long time subject to Israel.—Of the other events of this war we know nothing except the solitary fact that Benaiah slew the two sons of the king.[5]

c.) After Moab comes the short review of David's great and rapid victories in the Aramean war of which the chief hero was king Hadadezer of Zobah.[6] No cause is here assigned for this war with these distant nations,[7] but since the kingdom of Zobah

---

[1] Vol. ii. p. 325.
[2] 2 Sam. x. 2 sqq.
[3] 2 Sam. viii. 2.
[4] Prov. xx. 26, Amos i. 3; cf., in the case of the Ammonites, 2 Sam. xii. 31 and ii. p. 387.
[5] P. 142.
[6] 2 Sam. viii. 3.

[7] The words בְּלֶכְתּוֹ לְהַצִּיב יָדוֹ בַּנָּהָר (for we must adopt this reading from 1 Chron. xviii. 3 instead of לְהָשִׁיב), cannot explain this reason. They mean 'as he went to establish his hand at the Euphrates, i.e. to assert and substantiate his power at the Euphrates,' and cannot, from

is nowhere else mentioned as bordering immediately on Israel's territory, it follows that the war must have been kindled by a war going on at the same time between Israel and some nearer kingdom. Now we are actually told in another part of the present second Book of Samuel[1] that a great Aramean war with Israel was brought on by the Ammonites, so that we have every reason to suppose that this was the very war in question; and a closer examination only confirms this conclusion, in spite of certain apparent difficulties. The narration in such detail of the war with Ammon, the development of which cannot be understood without reference to that with Syria, is due[2] to a special cause, its bearing, namely, on the history of Uriah; and it is, no doubt, this fulness which has occasioned it to be passed by in so very cursory a manner in the general review of the great wars,[3] for otherwise it ought to have been described, at any rate in its results, as fully as that with Moab. The picture of this most extensive and decisive of the Davidic wars which we may derive from the authorities still in our possession, is as follows.

After the conquest of Moab, Nahash the king of the Ammonites, with whom David had lived on the best of terms, died. He was probably the same king against whom Saul had waged war,[4] and who might therefore look with favour on the rise of David. He was succeeded on the throne by his son Hanun. On this David sent ambassadors to the Ammonite court to congratulate him on his accession and to condole with him on the death of his father; and if they had been well received nothing farther would have been involved than the solemn renewal, not without obligations for the future being implied on both sides, of the friendly relations which had existed under the late sovereign. But the new king was prejudiced by his counsellors against David, whom he suspected of seeking treacherously to reconnoitre the Ammonite capital by means of his emissaries, so as to be able the more easily to destroy it on the first opportunity. The kindred kingdom of Moab had already fallen before David's power, and the fear of a similar fate certainly appears to have exercised a strong influence on the resolution come to by the new court of Rabbah (i.e. the *capital* of Ammon). Unfortunately, however, in adopting a completely new line of

their very position, refer to David, as though he had actually established himself on the Euphrates, and as though the war with the Syrians had arisen out of it, —a supposition, moreover, which would in itself be quite out of the question. The words refer to Hadadezer, and therefore simply indicate the time and the approximate locality of David's victory over him.

[1] 2 Sam. x.–xii. [2] Vol. i. p. 148.
[3] 2 Sam. viii. 12. [4] P. 24.

THE REIGN OF DAVID.

policy the court lost all self-control. The ambassadors were seized, half of their beards (i.e. one side)[1] shaved off, their clothes cut off as far as the lower half of the body, and they themselves dismissed in this condition. In their persons, therefore, the coarsest insults were offered to their master. David, who had now been king of all Israel for several years, could not help meditating war with Ammon. Meanwhile he sent word to the injured ambassadors, who could not appear in public, to remain in Jericho until their beards had grown again.

The Ammonites would hardly have ventured upon such a deed, had they not calculated on powerful external support; for although their own capital was remarkably well fortified, and the whole nation was still at that time far more powerful than the kindred nation of Moab,[2] yet their territory was certainly hardly as large as that of the single tribe of Judah, and in former times they had always been inferior to united Israel. But they were at no loss for aid against Israel, for Hadadezer,[3] king of Zobah, a prince evidently of great power and military distinction, had doubtless long held himself in readiness to assist them. His importance makes it all the more to be regretted that we have so little trustworthy information about his country or his capital Zobah. This city is not mentioned on any earlier occasion, and even here it is evident that its power was suddenly acquired and of short duration, so that when a later antiquity began to busy itself with renewed eagerness about the history of David, it was no longer possible clearly to identify its site. Accordingly the most contradictory hypotheses have been enunciated about it, and for a long time obtained wide acceptance. Since it is related of the king of Zobah, that he fought with David on the banks of the Euphrates and brought Aramean troops from Mesopotamia into the field,[4] the Christian Syrians early identified Zobah with Nessîbin (Nisibis) in Mesopotamia, which has a somewhat similar sound; an opinion which, even in modern times, J. D. Michaëlis could defend at length. On the other hand, a number of the learned Jews of the Middle Ages accustomed themselves to give this

---

[1] Where the beard is regarded as the man's honourable adornment, such an insult is quite intelligible. It is worthy of remark, that the first ambassadors of Tschingis Khan were similarly treated by the Moslems; cf. Ibn Arabshah, *Fâkihat*, p. 239, 17. 241, 18. Cf. also Kemâl-eldîn apud Freytag's *Loqmân*, p. 48, 6.

[2] Vol. ii. pp. 333, 336 sq.

[3] This is undoubtedly the true form of the name, and is found in 2 Sam. viii. 3–10, 1 Kings xi. 23; it must be substituted everywhere for Hadarezer found in 2 Sam. x. 16–19, and in the Chronicles, for Hadad is the name of a Syrian idol from which a number of proper names are derived.

[4] 2 Sam. viii. 3, x. 16. It has been supposed recently that צוֹבָה is a contracted form of נְצוֹבָה, but this is quite incapable of proof.

name of Zobah to the great and well-known Haleb (Aleppo) on this side of the Euphrates.[1] But any place in Mesopotamia lies too far east, and the situation of Haleb is much too far north for Zobah, as far as there are any safe data for determining its site. The cities Tebah and Berothai, which Hadadezer possessed, and from which David, after his victory, took enormous quantities of bronze, we may reasonably look for not far from Zobah itself.[2] Now, since in Cl. Ptolemy,[3] we find two cities, Barathena and Sabe, close to each other in the same latitude as Damascus, but much nearer the Euphrates; and, further, since the Halamath to be mentioned below, where Hadadezer was finally put down, lay, according to the same Ptolemy, in much the same longitude but much more to the north, (all which falls in exactly with the narratives of the course taken by this war,) we really can no longer entertain any doubt as to the true site of Zobah. According to this supposition the other little kingdoms which were called on this occasion to the assistance of Ammon[4] together with Zobah, lay to the south-west of the latter, and this again harmonises perfectly with the rest of the narrative. They were as follows: Beth-rehob or more briefly Rehob, a little kingdom which must have been founded during the centuries immediately preceding (we know not exactly how) by Arameans who pushed forward far to the south-west, at the expense, therefore, of some of the ancient possessions of Israel;[5] Maachah,[6] and to the farthest south-south-east the land of Tob.[7]

---

[1] Cf. *Journ. As.* 1842, ii. p. 6. *Benjamin Tud.* by Asher, p. 50. The reason of this is, no doubt, that Haleb was also called Berœa in earlier times, and this was connected with the בְּרֹתָי of 2 Sam. viii. 8; cf. also Catalogus Codd. Syr. Mus. Brit. (Lond. 1888), p. 61.

[2] Instead of בֶּטַח, 2 Sam. viii. 8, we must read טִבְחַת after 1 Chron. xviii. 8, which, according to Gen. xxii. 24, was Aramean, and was probably situated not very far from Maachah. Berothai need not be identified with Berothah, Ez. xlvii. 16, which is perhaps the far-famed Phœnician Berytos (the present Beirout).

[3] *Geogr.* v. 19: they were situated in 73° 20′; 33° 0′; Alamatha in 73° 40′; 35° 0′; Damascus in 69° 30′; 33° 0′. (These are Ptolemy's own numbers; the longitude is reckoned from Ferro. See the 'Orbis Terrarum ad Mentem Ptolemæi,' in Kiepert and Menke's *Atlas Ant.*)

[4] 2 Sam. x. 6, 8.

[5] A city of the same name was situated in the tribe of Asher, far to the west therefore, Judg. i. 31, Josh. xix. 28, 30; and this as also the Beth-rehob mentioned as important, Judg. xviii. 28, may be meant here, cf. ii. p. 293, *note* 1. It is true that it is a very common name for Aramean towns, since it signifies nothing but *market*; perhaps one might even think of the رحبة, which, according to Jâqût (apud Schult. ad Salad.), was in later times a simple village in the territory of Damascus, but we have no solid ground for this suggestion. 1 Chron. xix. 6 confuses it with a better-known city of the same name on the Euphrates itself (Gen. xxxvi. 37), and at the same time, therefore, substitutes the Mesopotamians for Rehob; whereas, according to more accurate traditions, the Mesopotamians did not take part in the contest until the following year.

[6] Vol. ii. p. 302.

[7] While the three former kingdoms are all distinctly called Aramean either here or elsewhere in the Old Testament, this kingdom appears likewise to have had Aramean inhabitants; in that case it was the farthest to the south-west of the Aramean kingdoms; since it lay, accord-

THE REIGN OF DAVID.

The fact that Zobah is only mentioned as a place of historical importance in connexion with David and Saul,[1] appears to be due to the circumstance that it was really in itself insignificant, but that just at that time it had attained, through the rare address and good fortune of a distinguished prince, to a position of great power.[2] From this centre the king of Zobah ruled the country far and wide, to the west as far as Hamath on the Orontes, to the east as far as the Euphrates. Nay, even in Mesopotamia he had great authority; many petty monarchs were subject to him, so that mention is made of 'Zobah's Kings,'[3] and the ancient and powerful Damascus, though still no doubt independent of him, was certainly shut in all round by his possessions. In like manner the kingdom of Zobah had already engaged in war with Saul; but now Israel sent against it a hero of a very different calibre.

When David heard of the numerous allies which the Ammonites had secured, and of their having already invested Medeba far to the south in the tribe of Reuben,[4] he ordered all the men of military age to march out with Joab; but while the latter was pushing forward to the very walls of Rabbah itself, intending to give battle to the Ammonite forces which were drawn up before its gates, the allies of Ammon, after raising the siege of Medeba, arrived at the spot, with 20,000 infantry, 1,000 men from Maachah, and 12,000 from Tob.[5] Thus Joab saw him-

---

ing to Ptolemy (*Geogr.* v. 19) who calls it Θαύβα, much farther down to the south-west of Zobah, and so south-east of the land of Ammon, in the wilderness. This position, moreover, exactly suits the few remaining passages in which it occurs (in the life of Jephthah, ii. p. 392 and 1 Macc. v. 13). طوبة, cf. Corp. i. G. iii. p. 234, is different from this place; further investigations are needed as to the connexion with it of Ταβαί, Steph. Byz. Ταβηνοί, Eckhel *D. N.* iii. p. 352 sq., and the present كِطاب *Zeitschr. der Deutsch. Morg. Ges.* 1849, p. 366.

[1] 1 Sam. xiv. 47, but no further information is supplied in this passage.

[2] Hence it follows that Sôphênê (Jos. *Ant.* vii. 5), though similar in sound, must not be identified with Zobah, since it lies much too far north-east according to Ptolemy (*Geogr.* v. 13), Pliny (*Hist. Nat.* v. 13 [12]); even Kommagênê, which Eupolemos (apud Euseb. *Præp. Ev.* ix. 30) understands, would be rather nearer. No trace of the city seems to be apparent any longer; for Zobaiba, as Abulfida

(*Syr.* ed. Köhler, p. 19, 49, 69; the first passage is entirely wanting in the new Paris edition by Reinaud) calls the once celebrated old fortress of Paneas, lies too far to the west; at most, the question suggests itself whether the name of the mountain *Suffa* to the north of Hauran does not bear some relation to it, but the city of Zobah still lay too far east to belong to this. Unsuccessful attempts have also been made to discover Zobah between Lebanon and the sea (*Literary Gazette*, 1855, p. 349). We have no means of discovering how Jâqût knew of Zobah in the ancient history of Israel, and identified with the Syrian Kinisrin (*Zeitschr. der Deutsch. Morg. Ges.* 1864, p. 449).

[3] 1 Sam. xiv. 47; cf. 2 Sam. x. 19.

[4] This addition, 1 Chron. xix. 17, is certainly quite historical.

[5] Instead of these numbers the Chronicles give a total of 32,000; but these were chariot combatants and horsemen; it is surprising, however, that in the statement in Sam. the horsemen are omitted.

self surrounded on all sides, but with prompt decision he selected the bravest warriors to engage the Arameans, handed over the rest to the command of his brother Abishai to hold the Ammonites in play meanwhile, and instructed him to come to his help, should victory threaten to turn to the side of the Arameans, himself in like manner promising to come to the aid of his brother, should he find himself unable to manage the Ammonites. But they could not help mutually encouraging each other to do battle valiantly by the thought that they had to fight for their people (the true community) and for the cities of their God (the many separate cities in which the true God was honoured), that the heathen might not destroy the people and the religion of Israel as they had already almost done at Medeba; but Jahveh would do as seemed good to Him. With such mutual arrangements and exhortations the brother-heroes entered on their task with divided forces; but the Arameans fled before Joab's warriors, and the Ammonites, on seeing it, also retired into the city. But the capital (Rabbah) was very strong, and the Israelites did not succeed in rapidly reducing it; so, when the victors had taken great booty of all sorts, they returned to Jerusalem, and for that year the campaign was certainly at an end.[1]

It was perhaps the first time in his life that Hadadezer had suffered defeat, and he made preparations for the campaign of the following year on a far larger scale. He effected a great union of the Aramean kingdoms, which placed them all in opposition to the threatening growth of the new Israelite power. Damascus, it is true, must at first have hesitated to join this league, but on the other hand Hadadezer succeeded in drawing allies from Mesopotamia, and the Ammonites, who were still in constant danger, certainly fanned the flame to no small extent. But when David heard how Hadadezer was gathering great armies on the Euphrates, and supporting himself on that river, he determined to anticipate his attack. This time he marched in person with his troops over the Jordan to the north-east, and at a place now unknown to us, Halamah,[2] a decisive battle was

---

[1] 2 Sam. x. 1–14, 1 Chron. xix. 1–15.

[2] The LXX see fit to take the חיל of 2 Sam. x. 16 as the name of this place, but this disturbs the sense; on the other hand חלאמה, ver. 17 (which the old translators, whose work is embodied in that of the present LXX, represent sometimes by Χαλαμάκ sometimes by Αἰλάμ), is undoubtedly the name of a place, although in 1 Chron. xix. 17 the reading is altered to avoid the insertion of a name so little known. On the other hand, Josephus, *Ant.* vii. 6. 3, makes it into the name of the king of the Arameans on this side of the Euphrates, and gives him Shobach as his general with 80,000 foot-soldiers and 10,000 cavalry. We may, however, very properly compare the Syrian city Alamatha on the Euphrates, mentioned by Ptolemy, *Geogr.* v. 15; and, no doubt, the Χαλαμάκ which appears in one of the versions of the LXX is a corruption of Χαλαμάτ. Ἄλλεμα or Ἄλλεμοι may be related to it, but only as the name of a country, 1 Macc. v. 26.

fought in which the Arameans from both sides of the Euphrates were completely routed, their commander Shobach mortally wounded, and 1,700 chariot men and horsemen, together with 20,000 foot soldiers taken prisoners.[1]—It is true that now at last Damascus came to the help of king Hadadezer (probably on receiving news of the inroad of the Idumeans), but it was only to crown the triumphant course of David with a final victory of supreme importance. In a second great battle 22,000 Arameans were left upon the field, the great and opulent city of Damascus, together with the other conquered Aramean kingdoms west of the Euphrates, was made tributary to David, and in place of the Aramean princes by whom they had been governed, David everywhere installed his own officers. Thus the Aramean supremacy, which had in previous centuries become so formidable to the Hebrews and even to the Canaanites,[2] was now broken once more by the heroic arm of David; and as a great victory such as this can hardly fail to involve a number of others, Toi, the Canaanite king of Hamath on the Orontes, who had previously been hard pressed by Hadadezer and probably reduced to some sort of vassalage,[3] now felt that he had been unexpectedly set free from his greatest enemy, and sent to David grateful congratulations and rich presents by his son Hadoram. The whole country as far as the Orontes, with the exception of the sea-coast inhabited by the Phœnicians, was subjugated, and one of Hadadezer's generals, Rèzon, the son of Eliadah, broke away from his master and became a rover in the wilderness, as David had been in times gone by.[4]

While David, however, was thus fully occupied in the north, and the strongly fortified city of Rabbah had not yet fallen, the Idumeans had burst upon the extreme south of the land of Judah. They may have thought that David's absence would leave this district unprotected, and were evidently instigated and encouraged by the Ammonites and Arameans. The Idumeans, under whose wing Israel had formerly found shelter in the time

---

[1] According to 2 Sam. viii. 3 sq.; on the other hand, x. 18 gives, with less probability on the whole, 700 chariots and 40,000 horsemen. The number 700 is thus common to both the accounts, which unquestionably refer to the same event.

[2] Vol. ii. p. 302 sq.

[3] Since in 1 Chron. xviii. 3, 2 Chron. viii. 3, Hamath is joined to Zobah so as to make one name, it seems to follow that Hadadezer derived his title from both countries; at any rate, it would be very difficult to explain this conjunction in any other way.

[4] 1 Kings xi. 23 sq., 1 Chron. xviii. 9 sq., where *Hadoram* is rightly substituted for *Joram*. We know nothing of the fate of Hadadezer himself. Nicolaus Damascenus, in a passage from the fourth book of his history (apud Joseph. *Ant.* vii. 5. 2), calls the king of Damascus of that time Hadad, and says that he ruled over all Syria, and was the most valiant king of his age, but was at last slain by David at the Euphrates; many of these statements, however, rest on a confusion with Hadadezer.

SUBJUGATION OF EDOM.

of Moses, had left the latter in peace during the whole period of the Judges, and first took up arms against it, as far as we know, in the time of Saul.[1] Hence it seems probable that the cause of dispute was that the new king allowed himself the exercise of certain rights against the Idumeans which they would not acknowledge; and ever since the successful campaigns of Saul they had probably been ill at ease. In this way the war which had already spread so far now reached the extremest south, where the Idumean possessions were surrounded by a great variety of Arab tribes, Amalekites and others, who had received such frequent provocation in recent times from both Saul and David, that any league formed on their part against Israel might easily become full of danger. Had the Idumeans succeeded in their plans, all the triumphs of David's arms in the north would have been rendered useless at a blow. But the Israelite army was divided with prompt decision into two parts, just as in the campaign of the previous year, and while David himself remained in the north and followed up his victories without interruption, Joab turned back southwards with the other division, marched along by the west shore of the Dead Sea, probably driving the flying Idumeans before him, and defeated them in a great battle in the Salt-valley (somewhere about the southern extremity of the Dead Sea), where they lost 18,000 men.[2] The mountain peaks, however, the caves and the defiles of their country enabled them still to offer a stubborn resistance; and Joab, striving to crush it with his usual severity, exterminated without mercy all the male population (all, that is, who were captured under arms). It was six months before he was able to regard the whole country as subjugated. Some of the members of the royal house were slain, while others effected their escape, and the country was made tributary to David, like all the others which were conquered at this time. David appointed his own officers everywhere, and re-established the ancient division of the country according to tribes.[3]

---

[1] We have no other source of intelligence on this subject than the scanty statement of 1 Sam. xiv. 47; but the incidental information, pp. 83, 90, is instructive.

[2] All this follows from a comparison of the following passages: 2 Sam. viii. 13 sq. where בְּשֻׁבוֹ must be referred to Joab. A great many words which stood in the original passage must have been omitted before ver. 13, just as the whole account of the first campaign against the Arameans has been omitted before ver. 3 of the same chapter. Further, 1 Kings xi. 15–17, where we are compelled to follow the LXX in reading בְּהַכּוֹת instead of בִּהְיוֹת, since David did not himself stay long in Edom. Also Ps. lx. superscr., where the number 12,000 men appears by a clerical error. The omission of all mention of Damascus or Edom at the end of 2 Sam. xii. arises from the fact that the fate of Rabbah came within the view of the present narrator only from its connexion with Uriah.

[3] Vol. i. p. 75 sq.

This year, with its varied and glorious victories, was undoubtedly the time of David's greatest efforts and greatest power—a time of unique exertions and successes, such as never recurred again in the same full measure. Since David took the field in person on this occasion, it may well have been that, as he was previously offering sacrifices and prayers at the holy place, some prophet like Gad or Nathan uttered that wonderfully elevating oracle which supplied a poet of kindred spirit with the starting point of Ps. cx., and in which the royalty of Israel combined with the cheerful valour of the people, shone forth with unsurpassable brightness and purity. When in the far north he received tidings of the unexpected danger which threatened him in the south from Edom, and when for a moment many of those around him were perhaps in doubt, whether it were possible to advance from so great a distance to Edom in time to chastise it, his own unshaken lofty confidence was poured forth, under the influence of a similar oracle, in that hymn to his Lord and God from which we still possess some scattered remains of most glorious poetry in Ps. lx.[1] But when David from the north and Joab from the south, returning with their victorious armies entered Jerusalem, what festivals of rare splendour must have been solemnised in the city! We know from a statement which appears most abrupt as it now stands,[2] that David erected, on Joab's return, a monument of thanksgiving for his victory; and we may imagine how brilliant was the triumphal procession in Jerusalem when we recollect the hundred war-chariots with their horses which were spared when Hadadezer was conquered.[3] David had certainly no intention of using them himself,[4] but merely of leading them in the triumphal procession and then destroying them. In the same way the gilded arms with which Hadadezer's chieftains had adorned their persons [5] were brought to Jerusalem to be preserved as consecrated offerings in the holy place, to-

---

[1] See my *Dichter des A. B.*, ii. p. 374 (2nd ed.), where, however, the occasion of this poem is not as fully explained as it is here; that the Philistines also threatened a revolt at the same time is quite credible. The *perf.* in the second member of ver. 11 [9] follows מִי, as in Ps. xi. 3. The second part of the superscription may be regarded as genuinely historical. It is evidently very ancient, and is borrowed from an older collection of songs. Cf. *Dichter des A. B.*, i.

[2] 2 Sam. viii. 13. The words allow of no other interpretation (cf. also supra, p. 38, for a similar instance), but it is certainly their abruptness which causes 1 Chron. xviii. 12 to omit them while altering the whole passage; moreover, in the latter place, Abishai is mentioned as the conqueror of Edom in opposition to the other authorities.

[3] 2 Sam. viii. 4.

[4] P. 146.

[5] 2 Sam. viii. 7 sq. 10-12. In Jer. li. 11, however, שֶׁלֶט is equivalent to *quiver*, but it seems that this is an Aramean use of the word, and that elsewhere it signifies arms generally.

gether with the weapons of gold, silver, and brass, which the king of Hamath had sent as presents, and the costly articles of booty from so many other conquered nations. Finally we may very well take Ps. xviii. as the great song of victory which David himself sang on this day of triumph; for during the remainder of his life there was never another day of such mighty victory and untroubled lofty joy as we find described in this ode. Indeed, there is no more beautiful picture of the course of David's life, which had steadily advanced to its present marvellous elevation, than is contained in this psalm. It is a hymn of praise and thanksgiving to Jahveh, the rock and the deliverer, as grand in conception as it is perfect in execution, in which David first describes his wonderful deliverance from the utmost danger;[1] then enters into the grounds of this divine deliverance, and shows that, in accordance with the double aspect of the true God, only the God of justice could so elevate the just man who is true to Him,[2] and only the sole and mighty Spirit God so elevate him who has faith in Him, as to make many nations, of the very existence of some of which he was not aware, do homage to him as their royal head.[3]

In the following spring Joab was sent with the army to accomplish the one thing which still remained to be done—the reduction of the strong fortress of Rabbah which had now continued for several years to defy the power of David. This royal metropolis of the Ammonites consisted of a so-called water-city, that is, a lower city on a small river, and the citadel, which was very strong.[4] When, Joab, after devastating the level country, had taken the lower city after a severe struggle, he reported it to David with a request that he would come and preside in person over the final capture which was now imminent, that he might not himself carry off the honour and glory of the reduction of a city of such extraordinary strength. David accordingly advanced with a fresh army, and, after several concluding struggles, succeeded in taking it. The royal crown, the gold and precious stones of which weighed a full talent, he placed on his own head. The captive warriors of this and the other cities of the country he punished with great severity on account of the original cause which had led to the war. He mangled them with saws, iron flails,[5] and iron shearing-machines, or roasted them in burning kilns.[6]

[1] Vv. 5-20 [4-19]. [2] Vv. 21-31 [20-30]. [3] Vv. 32-46 [31-45].*
[4] The sites have been discovered by the [5] P. 150.
most recent travellers, and fully support [6] 2 Sam. xi. 1, xii. 26-31, and, much
the Biblical narrative. abbreviated, 1 Chron. xx. 1-3.

* On the division of the Psalms into strophes, see the remarks in ii. p. 354 sq.

The concluding events of this war enable us to fix its chronology, together with a number of earlier events, at least with approximate accuracy. We know from the history of Uriah, that this conquest of Rabbah took place in about the same year in which Solomon was born; supposing, then, that Solomon became king in his twentieth year,[1] the beginning of the great Ammonite war would fall at the latest in the tenth year of David's rule over all Israel, or perhaps earlier, if it lasted one or two years besides the three which are specified.

3) *The Census.*

So great an increase of external power as David had now attained, is liable to react oppressively upon the masses of the people, unless they protect their ancient privileges against the royal prerogative with an energy which grows with the growing power of the throne. We shall explain hereafter the form which this relation assumed in Solomon's reign; but the account of the numbering of the people (the census) which took place under David, furnishes a conspicuous proof that even when he was at the zenith of his power, the ancient popular liberties did not suffer.[2] That the census really took place, admits of no doubt, though the numbers[3] which have come down to us are very rough. It is equally certain that it was not undertaken till the later years of David's reign, partly because the plague which is mentioned in connexion with it is expressly said to be the second great national calamity of David's reign,[4] partly because a measure of this nature, to which Joab devoted nine months and twenty days, could only be carried out in a year undisturbed by any foreign wars. We can hardly doubt what was David's intention in having it made. He cannot have wished to count the number of his warriors with a view to further conquests, for the army followed him everywhere with sufficient alacrity, and he lived in no kingdom where the citizens shrank from military service, either from simple indifference to a government which had no command of their affections, or from love of commercial and artistic industry. It would be still further from the mark simply to ascribe to him a childish delight in the great number of the population of his kingdom, if for no other

---

[1] It is true that the Biblical sources give us no information on this subject. According to Josephus (*Ant.* viii. 7. 8), Solomon was hardly 14 years old when he became king.

[2] 2 Sam. xxiv.; the additions to this narrative, which appear in 1 Chron. xxi.

1–xxii. 1, are in part derived from some other fuller source to which the Chronicler had access, but are also in part pure remodelling by the Chronicler himself.

[3] P. 144.

[4] 2 Sam. xxiv.; cf. p. 136 sq.

THE CENSUS.

reason, simply because an undertaking of such importance and such difficulty could not have anything to do with childish curiosity. The only satisfactory explanation of this measure is that it was intended as the foundation of an organised and vigorous government, like that of Egypt or Phœnicia, under which the exact number of the houses and inhabitants of every city and village would have to be obtained, so as to be able to summon the people for general taxation. The progress, however, towards some such completion of the development of the royal power in Israel, was so thoroughly in harmony with the tendencies of the age, that under Solomon, at any rate, it was actually accomplished; David might, therefore, project some such census and even commence it, without, strictly speaking, any sinister purpose. But it is well known what a profound aversion and what an instinctive abhorrence certain nations, ancient and modern, harbour against any such design, which they dimly suspect, not perhaps without good reason, is likely to result in a dangerous extension of the governing power and its encroachment on the sanctity of the private home. In Israel especially, where the limitation of the royal power was demanded by the established religion itself, it might lead to a dangerous collision between two sets of efforts and duties; and in the uncertainty as to the possibility of reconciling any such innovation with the ancient religion and popular liberty, any national disaster which happened at the critical moment might very well be interpreted in all innocence by the people, the prophets, and the king himself, as a heavenly voice of warning against so dangerous a proceeding. It deserves notice, though it is entirely in harmony with the whole nature of David's relation to his age, that this novel undertaking was not carried through in his reign, but was given up by him while in progress; nor could anything better illustrate the strength of ancient popular feeling under his rule, and the candour with which he submitted, even in the possession of the great power of his later years, to the oracle which advised him against this questionable innovation.

The account of the earlier narrator is framed from this point of view, and has been but little altered by a second hand. It is as follows. David, led as it were, by some evil spirit, jealous of Israel,[1] into the idea of numbering the people, commissions

[1] In 2 Sam. xxiv. 1 שָׂטָן, which is still retained by the Chronicler in this passage, must be inserted before בָּהֶם; the word is also used with a similar meaning elsewhere by this narrator, 1 Sam. xxix. 4, 2 Sam. xix. 13 [xix. 12]; the connexion prevents our referring it to a man, as in 1 Kings xi. 14, 23. Cf. also the *Jahrbb. der Bibl. Wiss.* x. p. 35.

Joab and the other generals¹ who resided with him at Jerusalem to carry it out. Joab, who here as elsewhere represents the feeling of the common people, answers doubtfully, 'and may thy God increase the people a hundredfold during thy life; but why dost thou take pleasure in this thing?' But as David will not allow himself to be thus dissuaded, they set to work and make a circuit of the whole land of the twelve tribes, pitching a camp, in soldier fashion, wherever they intended to make more than a short stay. They pass from Aroer² on the south-east, and the 'city in the midst of the river,' through the land of Gad and Jazer, as far north as Gilead, and the lower tracts of Hermon;³ then on the north-west from Dan in the forests of Lebanon, down along the Phœnician cities to Beersheba in the extreme south. After an absence of nine months and twenty days, they return to Jerusalem and inform David of the number of men in the whole nation⁴ capable of bearing arms, which they had now ascertained. But immediately afterwards David's heart smites him,⁵ as though he suspected that he might have transgressed; but it is too late, for next morning the prophet Gad appears before him to announce the divine retribution, which only leaves him the choice between three woes—a famine in the land for three successive years, defeat in the face of the enemy for three months, or a pestilence for three days.⁶ He chooses the last, since he can find more consolation in falling directly by the hand of God (for so was a pestilence regarded) than by the hand of man in war, or by the slow ravages of hunger. So from that very morning till the limit of the three days, the pestilence rages through the whole land, sweeping away 77,000 victims; and already the destroying angel stretches his hand over Jerusalem herself, and stands

---

¹ Ver. 2 must be emended in conformity with ver. 4.
² Vol. ii. p. 295.
³ Instead of the unintelligible חדשי in ver. 6, it seems that we ought to read חרמן, and also further on יער, after the Vulgate, instead of יען, in accordance with Ps. cxxxii. 6.
⁴ 1 Chron. xxi. 6 (cf. xxvii. 23 sq.) inserts the statement that Joab, from dislike to David's order, omitted Levi and Benjamin from the enumeration. The exception of the priestly tribe is understood even in the earlier narrative; and Benjamin is perhaps inserted simply as the tribe of Jerusalem, according to Deut. xxxiii. 12.
⁵ This agrees in a striking manner with 1 Sam. xxiv. 6 [5]; cf. p. 96, *note* 6.
⁶ It is easy to see the artificial arrangement by which three woes, each lasting three successive periods (for שבע, ver. 13, we must read שלש, according to the LXX and Chron.) are reckoned by years or months or days. But it is still more striking that these three woes exactly correspond with those which elsewhere actually occur in the course of David's history at Jerusalem, for his flight from Absalom lasted probably some three months, and concerning the famine see above, p. 136. This shows, therefore, that these three woes, as the only ones which were experienced during David's thirty-three years, had long become proverbial when the narrative assumed its present form.

THE CENSUS.

with the pestilence at the threshing-floor of Araunah[1] the Jebusite, when Jahveh, at the agonised entreaty of the repentant king, commands him to refrain, that Jerusalem may be spared. It was just the time of wheat harvest, and this Jebusite was busied about his wheat-threshing under the open sky on the hill north-east of Zion;[2] so David with his chief ministers goes forth by the advice of Gad, to the threshing-floor, buys it from the Jebusite on the spot, together with the oxen which were at work and the wooden implements of husbandry, hastily raises an altar, and offers the oxen to Jahveh. The pestilence was stayed from further ravages, and it was thus universally recognised that there was in the neighbourhood of Zion a place of surpassing sanctity.

The reason for bringing this last circumstance so distinctly forward, is no doubt to be found in the fact that Solomon afterwards replaced the little altar which was hastily constructed on this mountain, by a far larger one in the temple itself;[3] and the choice of this very spot for the site of the temple is unquestionably connected with this occurrence under David, for in the ancient times a temple would never be built on a spot hitherto unhallowed. But the Book of Origins describes the census as being taken under Moses without exciting the anger of God, and a similar measure appears to have been carried through under Solomon, without any such melancholy result; which, it is self-evident, did not spring from any universal necessity; but as if to reconcile the absolute view of the innocence of such a census with the conditional one of its sinfulness, the Book of Origins, after its law-giving fashion, adds that for every man enrolled in the census, half a shekel must be paid as an offering, *in order that* no divine judgment may be inflicted during the census.[4]

3. *David's Temptations.*

If we now go back in imagination to the moment when David, victorious over mighty heathen nations alike in the far north

---

[1] This reading of the name is not Hebrew, but perhaps it is all the more likely to be Jebusite; another reading is *Orna* in Sam. and *Ornan* in Chron. Since he is called king in ver. 22, it would be quite conceivable that he had actually been the king of Jebus before its conquest; but, if so, we must also suppose that the title which appears nowhere but in ver. 22, was, only omitted from the other passages in the later redaction.

[2] This addition, which is found in ver. 15, in the LXX, and 1 Chron. xxi. 20, belongs essentially to the passage, and fits in with the nine months and twenty days of ver. 8, the beginning of the year being reckoned from autumn.

[3] This circumstance is also omitted in the present Book of Samuel, but is found in ver. 25 in the LXX, and in 1 Chron. xxii. 1.

[4] Ex. xxx. 12, xxxviii. 25 sq.; cf. the *Alterthümer*, p. 350.

and the extreme south, successful first in restoring and then in increasing the full power of Israel, celebrated his splendid triumph in Jerusalem,[1] and celebrated it, moreover, not only like an ordinary conqueror, with magnificent processions, but also with so wonderfully noble an ascent of the spirit to the true God as is manifested in the great hymn, Ps. xviii., we might well wish, in our human fashion, that as he stood at this elevation, he had closed a life hitherto (as far as was possible before Christianity) almost entirely spotless, and bequeathed to posterity a wholly unclouded memory and the purest type of true royalty. But the ascent of the dizzy height is always attended by the possibility of a slip and then of a headlong fall. What seems unlawful to the ruler? and what, moreover, to the preeminently favoured, the beloved of men and God? and the fresher the success of life, the greater becomes the power of the temptation. It is true that the strictness of the community of Jahveh, and the course of a life such as David's had hitherto been, a life which owed all its superiority simply to a singlehearted fidelity to the inward and outward demands of the true religion, a life in fact already matured, which in every trial as in every success had only become more deeply conscious of the eternal truth—all this would seem to have disarmed these temptations beforehand; but even if all the coarser temptations before which Saul (for instance) fell, had already lost their power, yet the more subtle ones germinated all the more readily in the secret recesses of the heart, while even the least of them carried all hell within it. As though there were a sort of compulsion upon the Old Testament to supply, in the clear light of history, the most indubitable proof that David had still to take the last step to the perfection of true religion, we see, at this point, the very hero who had till now conferred the utmost glory on his religion by the unblemished purity of his regal life, wavering in his lofty position, and, having once wavered, forced to exert his utmost strength to render as harmless as possible the evil results of his fault, both immediate and remote. In this way the old religion reveals with the greatest possible distinctness both its deficiencies and its grandeur; for after all, David, as the hero of a moral struggle, did overcome, by its strength, the evil consequences of his deed as far as they could be overcome. Thus the evidently intentional omission by the Chronicler of the whole of this aspect of David's life, from a feeling of reserve which was then on the increase, simply shows that he had not conceived the full vitality of Antiquity with the

[1] P. 159.

truth and simplicity of the earlier narrators; for the latter were right in not hesitating to represent along with the real and brilliant virtues of the great hero, this sudden eclipse, the darkness of which the effort of his whole soul could only gradually succeed in dissipating.

1) It was an immemorial custom in all those countries, from which even Muhammed (who certainly showed in this a want of greatness) did not depart, for the magnificence and power of a ruler to display itself in the multiplication of his establishments, that is, of his wives,—for every wife involved a separate establishment.[1] Now the religion of Israel no doubt set forth the ideal of true marriage in all its accounts of the creation as well as in the type of Isaac and Rebekah;[2] but it had not quite strength enough fully to carry out this ideal in practice, and so it tolerated what, strictly speaking, it could not itself approve. This very history of David, however, gives the most striking example of the consequences of such a doubtful attitude.[3] That he should take certain additional wives and concubines in Jerusalem was by no means unexpected; but where was he to draw the line? It was after his great victories, while Joab and the army were absent before the Ammonite capital, that as he was one evening pacing his palace roof, he saw Bath-sheba[4] in the neighbouring house. She was at first unknown to him; but it appeared on enquiry that she was a married woman, and her willingness, in spite of this, to come to him in secret, certainly makes her a partner in his guilt; for the striking example of the Shulamite, in the Song of Solomon, shows how completely even a maiden might in the old community defy the very mightiest. But there is just as little doubt on which side lay the heavier guilt.

2) It shows the utmost depravity when Christians seek to shelter their own unchaste and shameless lives under an appeal to that of David, and that too, although none of their other proceedings show the smallest trace of David's noble spirit, and although they are by no means ready to bear, as David did, the consequences of their shame. The crime of David was certainly one which other rulers in that part of the world then committed freely;[5] but as soon as he had time for reflexion, he

---

[1] As w see from 2 Sam. xiii. 7 sqq. 20.
[2] Vol. i. p. 293.
[3] 2 Sam. v. 13–16; cf. xv. 16.
[4] She is called בַּת שׁוּעַ in 1 Chron. iii. 5; no doubt this is originally only another form of the same name, the intermediate form being בַּת־שֶׁוַע. In this passage she is said to have borne four sons to David, one of whom was called Nathan, but these four names appear in the same order without any information about their mother in 2 Sam. v. 14.
[5] This is proved even by the stories of the wives of the Patriarchs: i. pp. 293, 327.

may well have remembered that his position in Jahveh's community laid on him the obligation of being a very different prince from heathen monarchs; and indeed it was only his dread of the terrible consequences which might ensue, that dictated his conduct towards Uriah. But the Hittite Uriah, one of the 600 Gibborim,[1] may also be regarded from a moral standpoint as a type of the marvellous power and self-control for which these troops, then in their prime, must have been distinguished. Thus the attempts to induce the Gibbor, when recalled from the camp, to sleep with his wife, failed simply because of the soldierly sense of duty, which made him declare that as long as his companions remained on the field with the holy Ark and bore the hardships of service, he would not avail himself of any special privilege. So far David had attempted to hush up his solitary lapse, and evidently intended then to have nothing more to do with the woman; but now his growing sense of the shame of detection drove him on to commit to the unlettered soldier when he returned to Joab, a despatch which provided for his being stationed unsupported in the front of the battle. It is certainly true that Saul had once laid a similar plot against himself;[2] and also that the requirements of service make it necessary that some of a besieging party should be more exposed than others; but all this cannot excuse the action of David. The valiant Uriah appears consequently to have fallen by a stone hurled from the besieged city to which he had approached too near. He perished before he had fully learned the relation in which the king stood to him, happy only in his ignorance; but since David married his wife when the period of mourning was over, and she bore him a son, it is not surprising that the secret leaked out in more than rumours.

This broke the powerful spell which had hitherto bound the whole nation to the name of David, for we can readily understand that a moral nation such as Israel then was, so far uncorrupted and just, filled once more with aspirations towards a grander life, must have been cruelly undeceived by such real stains on the character of a hero whom it had hitherto regarded with unqualified admiration. Every morally reprehensible action involves an infinite series of fatal consequences, partly through the relaxation of the strength and purity of the sinner's own soul, partly through the influence of the bad example on others and the breaking of the spell which knits the uncorrupted, by a strong bond, all to each; nor can anything be of avail in such a case except a genuine penitence accompanied by the

[1] P. 139 sq.   [2] P. 74.

complete removal of the cause of the offence and fall, if it rests on a real imperfection in existing arrangements.

In the present instance the austerity of the old religion gave proof of the great vigour of its life in the whole kingdom, in the fact that David's fault was neither palliated nor endured in gloomy silence, but was laid before him on the right occasion with the utmost power, and then fully recognised in its true colours and deeply repented of by himself. All the good which the old religion could effect by its own energy, without founding a completely new order of things, was in this case accomplished with the most wonderful consistency and the noblest results. The Prophet Nathan, who was descended [1] from a priestly family, and was probably also somewhat younger than the king, met David after the birth of his son with a combination of firmness and judgment which I shall not here attempt to reproduce in my own words, since the account in 2 Sam. xii. is as easy to understand as it is inimitable. But if in this matter Nathan shows himself great, David is no less so. Though he had but now fallen so low, the cutting truth of the Prophetic word shakes him out of the hollow passion in which he has lived since first he saw this woman, and rouses him again to a consciousness of his own better self. He is still too full of the better feelings of his earlier life intentionally to resist the truth which, once revealed to him, tortures him so inexorably, and against which no dull torpor can any longer hold out; nor is anything wanting except the forcible shock of the Prophet to awaken in a spirit like David's a perception of the abyss which yawns at his feet, and a deep yearning to retrace his steps. Not that after he had long stubbornly endeavoured to conceal his first fault and had thereby sunk deeper and deeper, the return to a profound and genuine repentance was as easy to him as we might conclude from the narrative, which is only too brief.[2] On the other hand, we see very clearly from Ps. xxxii. how bitter were the inward struggles he endured, before he allowed himself to be reformed by the divine chastisement and became strong enough openly to acknowledge his sins before God. His greatness, however, is shown in the fact that, king as he was, he soon humbled himself like the lowliest before the higher truth, and although his penitence was as deep and as sincere as possible, it did not cause him either to lose his dignity or to forget his royal duties. When the new-born son was struck with sickness in which it was not altogether groundless to see a result and divine penalty of the sin of his parents, David, fasting and alone,

---

[1] P. 89, *note* 2.   [2] 2 Sam. xii. 13.

prayed to God for his life with such earnestness, that the elders of his house (his uncles and elder brothers) could not persuade him to desist. When the child died on the seventh day, no one had courage to tell him, but he perceived from the whispering of his servants that his worst fears were realised. He appeared before them composed, went out into the sanctuary to pray, and took food once more, pointing out to those whom his conduct surprised, the truth that further pining could no longer avail anything. That his repentance brought with it a genuine and complete reformation is proved by his subsequent history: in all the rest of his life he never again fell into a similar transgression. Indeed the man who has felt, with the intensity expressed in the wonderfully moving hymn, Ps. xxxii., the horror of sin and the blessing of complete redemption from its power, cannot easily lose again the truth so hardly won and so clearly perceived. Nor was Bath-sheba without comfort, for she subsequently bore to him another son, Solomon, and him (we are told) Jahveh loved, and did not slay him. The pious father in his happiness entreated the oracle, through Nathan, to confer on the new-born child some name of lofty import, and Solomon, as his parents called him, received through the Prophet the glorious additional name of Jedidiah, i.e. Beloved of God.[1] The sadness of the fate of the first child rendered the omens under which the second stepped into its place all the more auspicious, and we can easily understand that of all his sons this one became the dearest.

In this manner the guilt, as far as the guilty man himself could remove its consequences, was certainly atoned for in the proper way, and sensible men in Israel would neither recollect it against the king nor suffer themselves to be seduced by his example into similar crimes. But the only adequate means of preventing the further consequences would have been to improve as far as possible the social arrangement which supplied a provocation from which there was no escape, to these and

---

[1] Thus we see from 2 Sam. xii. 25, that a loftier significance may have been attached to proper names formed in *-jah* as such (cf. *Lehrb.* p. 671 sqq.); this is why the expression used is 'he called him Jedidiah because of Jahveh,' to call him after the meaning of Jahveh; for the words 'because of Jahveh' are certainly intended to contain an explanation of the second element of the name. This is how every Muhammedan, besides his so-called baptismal names, may have an additional name of loftier significance ending in *-eldîn*, which designates the man in his religious capacity. Indeed *Jedidiah* was a newly-invented name, and does not occur elsewhere, whereas *Solomon* was an ancient and common name (cf. the similar names Lev. xxiv. 11, Numb. xxxiv. 27, 1 Chron. xxvi. 25 sq.); so that nothing is more untrue than that Solomon first received that name from the 'peace' of his time. This double name, therefore, has nothing in common with the custom which may be observed among the later kings of Judah, of changing their names at the beginning of their reign, as if to secure an auspicious commencement.

similar offences; that is to say, polygamy ought to have been abolished, both among the people generally and especially in the royal household. This institution is the absolutely irrepressible source of numberless evils of this decription; it ever furnishes a ready stimulus to unbounded sensual desire in the sovereign; and, should he be exalted above it, is likely to introduce a dissolute life amongst the very different children of different mothers, by bringing the pleasures of sense so prominently and so early before their eyes. Moreover, the more completely the children of different mothers are kept apart, the more readily is sensual desire kindled between them; and finally, if they are kept, by strict supervision, in chaste separation from each other, threatening evils still remain in connexion with the choice of one of the various sons for the succession to the throne; for the son of a favourite wife might suppose that such a relationship gave him the first claim to the crown, or a wife who enjoyed the king's preference might beg the same preference for her son. In this lies hidden an inextricable tangle of the most mischievous evils, and no sooner is one set aside than two or three others spring up; and any single one is enough profoundly to disturb the peace of a whole kingdom. If, therefore, the royal polygamy had been abolished on this occasion and the whole household of the king arranged on principles of stricter chastity, this first lapse would hardly have been followed in the dominions of the kings of Israel by others of a like nature. But neither David nor Nathan nor any other sage of that period would be likely to think of a radical cure of an evil which the whole of Antiquity was yet too far from recognising as such, either in the royal house or in that of the humblest subject. Thus the evil, even if it could no longer offer any temptation to David himself, still retained all its strength for everyone else, so that the monarchy in Israel remained exposed to the same perturbations to which it is still subject in all polygamous countries; and even in the freshness of its prime the germ of destruction might already be detected, ready to cooperate sooner or later with other causes for its dissolution. Thus the subsequent troubles which Amnon, Absalom, and Adonijah brought into David's house—and they were the only ones which temporarily clouded the clear sky in which his star shone—were all of them connected with this fundamental wrong, and on the same thread hung many of the evils which were felt under David's successors. Hence the account of Nathan's severe rebuke to David might appropriately assume the form under which we now possess it. Because he had availed himself of war to kill Uriah, Nathan threatens that war shall never cease from his own house, and because he had taken his wife secretly for himself, his own wives should be violated in the open face of day by another (Absalom). When David manifests penitence, Nathan, it is true, withdraws the sentence of instant death which hangs over his head. He shall still live; but because he has furnished cause of offence to the enemies of Jahveh his new-born son shall die,—and this actually happens. Experience of the sequel, especially the history of Absalom, may have imparted its very distinct colouring to this short narrative, thereby enabling the earlier narrator to give a prophetic forecast, according to his custom, of all the history to come; but yet there is certainly an internal connexion between the subsequent troubles of the house of David and that which breaks out on this occasion for the first time, and it must be considered allowable to give it a corresponding prominence and force in the representation of the whole affair.

3) We do not know exactly how long it was after these events that Absalom found the first motives for his own guilty conduct in his brother Amnon's infamous deed, but it is probable that no long period intervened.[1] Amnon was David's eldest son, and his mother Ahinoam, who does not appear to have been of specially noble extraction, was David's first wife. He was a man of very violent and insolent disposition, a character which is often found in the first-born sons of families such as David's, and which is attributed by tradition to Reuben himself as a typical example.[2] He was also still further corrupted by the low cunning of Jonadab, the son of his paternal uncle Shimeah, who was ready to truckle to the eldest-born. This Amnon fell desperately in love with his half-sister Tamar, the daughter of David's third wife, and though an old Mosaic law laid a strict prohibition on such attachments, he paid no heed to it, since this law was at all events not very rigorously enforced[3] at a time when the children of different mothers

---

[1] The chronology of the following history depends almost entirely on the number forty in 2 Sam. xv. 17; but this number immediately involves the greatest difficulty and obscurity, for it does not in any way suit the case. Perhaps אַרְבָּעִים is a mistake for אַרְבַּע, arising from the fact that this numeral, being lower than ten, was originally connected with a following *sing.*; which, though very rare, was yet not quite impossible in the popular language (see my *Lehrb.*, § 287*i*). A further example of this confusion of four and forty is certainly found in 1 Kings v. 6 [iv. 26] and 2 Chron. ix. 25. If, then, we adopt this reading of the number, some ten years would elapse between Amnon's outrage and Absalom's rebellion, see xiii. 23, 38, xiv. 28, xv. 7. Supposing, then, that Absalom's rebellion took place some ten years before David's death, Amnon's crime must have been committed not long after the affair with Bath-sheba.

[2] Vol. i. p. 373 sq.

[3] This results clearly from the whole tone of the narrative 2 Sam. xiii. 1-16;

lived, as in the royal court, in separate houses, although it is quite improbable that David would have sanctioned such a marriage. The absolute impossibility of obtaining an interview with the maiden who led a modest life in another house, only depressed him more and more every day, until at last he began actually to pine away.[1] When Jonadab at length drew his secret from him, he advised him to take to his bed as though he were ill, and, when his father came to see him, to beg him to send Tamar to him to bake some cakes suited to a sick man's palate and give them to him to eat. The monster was successful in his trick, although the maiden resisted to the uttermost, and reminded him in his fury of the special moral law of Israel. But no sooner is his lust appeased than his love is changed in a moment into yet more violent hatred, for he now feels for the first time the sinfulness of his deed, and the impossibility of his love being ever reciprocated; and the unhappy girl is instantly thrust violently out of his house. Uttering loud lamentations she goes to her own brother Absalom, who bids her keep silence, and she remains desolate but quiet in her house. Even David, though greatly incensed, would not punish the wretch, in consideration of his being his first-born son;[2] just as Reuben, according to the Patriarchal tradition, remained unpunished up to the close of his father's life.

This outrage, which no doubt brought back the sad memory of his own former offence, must have weighed heavily on the king's heart. An ancient custom enjoined on the brothers the duty of running every risk for the honour of their sister,[3] in cases where their parents were negligent or silent; and although it was quite unheard-of for one of the brothers to attempt anything contrary to the king's will, yet Absalom was not the man to sit quietly down, even in the presence of his royal father. Absalom was David's third son (of his second son we never hear anything, and therefore conclude that he was a person of no importance), and moreover, his mother was not of plebeian origin like David's other wives, but the daughter of the king of Geshur.[4] He was a man of daring character, and inherited from his father nothing but his regal pride. Accordingly

---

and the ease with which such exceptions might be made is seen from the remarks in the *Alterthümer*, p. 226 sq. So quickly would the customs of heathen courts infect that of Jerusalem also.

[1] Instead of התחלות in ver. 2, which according to ver. 5 sq. has another meaning, it is better to read הִתְדַּלּוֹת, according to ver. 4, formed from דַּל, according to my *Lehrb.* § 121a. The name Jonathan, p. 148, is easily interchangeable with Jonadab.

[2] This addition to xiii. 21 must be supplied from the LXX.

[3] Cf. note on Cant. i. 6, viii. 8, in the *Dichter des A. B.*

[4] P. 115.

he observes the profoundest silence towards Amnon, but two years afterwards, when all might be forgotten, he invites all his brothers and David himself to a shearers' feast at his estate at Baal-Hazor several miles to the north of Jerusalem,[1] and is delighted to find that David, whom he is not really anxious to include in his invitation, while declining for himself, will allow him to be accompanied by his brothers, and, at his special request, by Amnon. At the feast, when they are all at their wine, Absalom's slaves, by a preconcerted arrangement, suddenly break in on them and slay Amnon with the sword. The princes all mount their mules and fly in consternation, but the report that Absalom has slain them all reaches David at Jerusalem before them. The cunning Jonadab alone suspects the truth, and strives to comfort David, and he soon sees his conjecture confirmed by the arrival of the princes and their attendants hurrying in precipitate flight along the road from Beth-horon. This young man who probably desired to make himself of some importance as David's nephew, was clever enough to guess the truth from the first, but it is sad to think that his thoughts and his advice were never founded on anything but a knowledge of the devil in man. In this case he had observed that ever since the violation of his sister, there had always been a look of dark revenge on Absalom's face.[2] Meanwhile Absalom had fled to Geshur, to his maternal grandfather Talmai, son of Ammihud, who could very well protect him, though only a petty monarch, and doubtless dependent on David. On the other hand David himself, even when the first bitter pang, was over, continued for a whole year to wear mourning for Amnon.[3]

---

[1] The addition of Baal shows that in early Canaanite times this place must have been consecrated, and therefore at one time of some importance, but at the time of which we are speaking it had certainly become very insignificant, though it is still mentioned, Neh. xi. 33, as a Benjamite place, but without the addition of Baal. According to 2 Sam. xiii. 23, it appears to have been situated on the skirts of the eastern desert near the larger city of Ephraim which is mentioned as late as John xi. 54; and if, as we might conclude from the reading עֶפְרוֹן, Kerî, or עֶפְרוֹן, Kethîb, 2 Chron. xiii. 19, this were identical with the עָפְרָה which lay near Bethel, it might perhaps be identified with Robinson's عصور, Bibl. Res. i. p. 448, ii. p. 264, in which case it would lie to the north-east of Bethel. But were this so, the narrative in 2 Sam. xiii. could not be derived from the earlier narrator, since he himself calls the city עֶפְרָה, 1 Sam. xiii. 17. A still greater objection is, that the troop of fugitives could not in this case have returned along the road from the western Beth-horon as they are said to have done in an addition to ver. 34 in the LXX which is certainly genuine. We must suppose, therefore, that the place lay to the west on the borders of Benjamin and Ephraim, and that this would be expressed by the words עִם אֶפְרָיִם; were there no city אֶפְרָיִם, this interpretation would be given as a matter of course.

[2] It seems necessary to read שְׂטָמָה for שִׂימָה, in ver. 32, unless it can be taken something like شوم, as formed by contraction from שְׂמָאל, and signifying something *left-handed*, i.e. foreboding misfortune.

[3] A long pause in the narrative must be supposed at ver. 37.

THE WOMAN OF TEKOAH.

When Absalom had lived three years at a foreign court in a sort of exile, David, who was at length consoled for the death of Amnon, ceased to express himself with indignation against him,[1] while in secret no doubt he felt a yearning to see him once more; but before a complete reconciliation could be effected, a further step still remained to be taken; and it was of a nature which a king had to consider far more seriously than the simple head of a family. But Joab, whose own daring made him fond of daring wherever displayed, and who was especially attracted to it in a probable heir to the throne like Absalom, no sooner observed this change to be taking place in David's mind, than he formed a project by which the king, in his very capacity of chief judge, should find the glimmering fire of paternal love suddenly fanned into a burning flame. It was a common practice of antiquity to preface the truth which had to be inculcated by an easily intelligible example which might serve as an introduction. In this way a powerful person who had been guilty of a serious delinquency, might himself be appealed to as the judge of a case brought forward as a parallel, so that his judgment, caught in this snare, might be transferred, without the possibility of escape, to the real matter in hand; and this method was in special favour in the case of kings, the supreme judges, with reference even to their own actions. Accordingly, just as Nathan had come before David on a previous occasion with the words 'Give judgment!'[2] and a narrative which simply served as an illustration, so now Joab sends a wise woman from Tekoah, having previously arranged with her the course she was to adopt. She came to David dressed in deep mourning, fell down before him with a cry for his royal help, and then explained that she was a widow whose two sons had fallen out with each other in the field, and one had slain the other; on this the whole body of her relatives demanded that she should surrender her only remaining son to vengeance as his brother's murderer; but were she to do so, she would have no heir to continue her husband's family; she would be like a cinder utterly burnt out! After hearing this case, which was certainly well calculated for impressing the truth that there must be something yet higher than blood-vengeance and the capital punishment of every murder, the king replied, somewhat indifferently, that she need only go home

---

[1] After וַתְּכַל (for this is the proper form) in xiii. 39, some such word as חֲמַת, cf. ver. 21, must have fallen out; אֶל is interchangeable with עַל, as is so often the case with this narrator; 'the anger of David ceased to manifest itself against Absalom.'

[2] These words must certainly be added in 2 Sam. xii. 1 from the Vulgate.

again, and he would at once give the proper orders. On this, with the cunning semblance of drawing back, she expressed a fear that she might perhaps be troubling the king too much, since, even if the dreaded blood-vengeance were exacted, the guilt would still pertain to herself and her relations only, not to the king and his throne; but David only promised the more emphatically to punish the first of her relatives who harassed her any more, even with words. Upon this she became bolder, and wished that the king would, if such a thing might be, swear by God that, since the destroying avengers of blood were so numerous, they should not be allowed to put her son to death; and David at once swore that not a hair of her son's head should be touched. Had she really desired nothing further from the king than what she had already brought forward, her object would have been now completely gained. Moved by the combined tact and persistency of her entreaties, the king had at last promised her the most complete protection for the prosecuted murderer, and in so doing had acknowledged the possibility of an exception to the general rule. But it was only now that she could come to the application to David's own case, which was all the more difficult, because she could not use the same openness and boldness of speech as a Prophet, but on the other hand, her only course was to allude slightly, and apparently incidentally, but yet clearly, to the case of Absalom. So she begged permission to lay yet another matter before him, and suddenly adopting a higher tone, she continued, 'How then can the king find it in his heart (since he is shown to be guilty himself by that very sentence of his own) to be so cruel to the people of God (that is, to members of the true community, who have a right to a share in its blessings), as not to recall his banished son? The life of all men is so transient, and as water when spilt cannot be gathered up again, so they, when once they have sunk into the nether world, can never return thence; but may God never take away before its time the soul of that man who cannot find it in his heart to banish any exile from before his face.'[1] In this way she had touched upon her real object with a firm but cautious hand, and now, fully conscious of the position in which she stood towards the king, she turned rapidly back in conclu-

---

[1] This is the way in which the difficult words 2 Sam. xiv. 13 sq. are to be understood; כּזֹאת, ver. 13 refers to the following לבלתי השיב; and for וחשב we must read חוֹשֵׁב, in close subordination to נֶפֶשׁ. In this participial formation the ו is elsewhere occasionally written before the first radical in a remarkable manner; see notes on Ps. vii. 10 [vii. 9] in the *Dichter des A. B.*, and on Ez. xiii. 7 in the *Propheten des A. B.* The whole discourse of the wise woman may have furnished the historical occasion of such proverbs as Prov. xxv. 15, which would be an additional reason for giving it so fully.

sion to the opening of her discourse; 'the facts she had come to lay before the king were these: the people had made her afraid on account of her son, so that she had resolved to implore the king's grace for herself and him, in the hope that he would be sure to help her and her son together; the king's word would set her at rest, for he was like an angel of God in the just hearing of complaints, and she wished him every blessing.' Since David could hardly fail after all this to perceive the real drift of her petition, he asked her whether she had been instructed by Joab to address him thus: and she confessed that she had been told by him exactly what she was to say, since he desired to present the affair of Absalom in another light; but surely the king was like an angel in wisdom, to know everything upon earth. Upon this, David sent for Joab, and to his great delight gave him permission to bring his friend Absalom back; accordingly, Joab fetched him immediately from Geshur to Jerusalem.

But it was still impossible for David to take him fully into favour, as though he had committed no great offence against his king and father; while, therefore, he allowed him once more to live quietly in his former house in Jerusalem, he did not permit him to appear at court. Treatment like this, however, wounded the young man's pride, for he no doubt thought that he had already gained a victory in his recall to his own country. His vain young heart was now quite unsettled by the previous alternations of his fate, for, ever since the death of Amnon, as he was probably David's eldest son, he must have regarded himself as his successor; and the present intermingling of good and bad fortune, of honour and disgrace, was as little as possible calculated to effect a radical reformation in his restless heart. This seems soon to have originated in his disordered mind the abandoned project of revenging himself for the imagined slight, even if it were by expelling his father and seizing his crown. Many circumstances may have given secret encouragement to this design, mad as it appears at first sight. That the probable heir to the throne should be early surrounded by all sorts of flatterers and malcontents is only what we should expect. He was (we are told) the handsomest man of his age, faultless from head to foot, and wonderfully graced by flowing locks,[1] and exceptional personal beauty and stature were considered [2] one

---

[1] The exact equivalent of the 200 lbs. imperial weight, which the hair which was cut off each year weighed (2 Sam. xiv. 26) cannot be accurately fixed, as long as we have no exact knowledge of this scale of weights. But see above, p. 69.
[2] Pp. 18, 23.

of the first marks of royal dignity. No reasonable or right-minded man had any ground of the least importance for being dissatisfied with David's rule. The indications of history lead us to an opposite conclusion, and, to judge from the earnestness of his penitence for his first display of tyranny, he was by no means likely ever to return to a similar course. But we now learn to appreciate the extraordinary difficulties with which royalty itself had still to contend in those days. A king at that time had to undertake in person an unlimited amount of work and trouble of a kind which would hardly be thought of in the present day; for instance, he had to pronounce judgment in person for everyone who came to seek justice at his hands, and we can easily understand that the increasing extent of the kingdom of Israel rendered this task the harder to perform, and that many a petitioner for justice must have departed not over well pleased. In addition to this, the feeling of unrestrained liberty which had been developed in such strength during the preceding centuries still retained a powerful hold on the whole people; and it shows how very gentle David's rule had been, that he had never yet made any attempt to confine it within narrower bounds; but there still remained a great deal of the old lawlessness, and what was to prevent the people from being carried away by the idea that as they had been the gainers by the new supremacy of David in comparison with that of Saul, so they might profit yet more by a further change? Moreover, the transgression of David, which, as has been said, had broken the early spell of his rule, may have continued to work to his disadvantage among many of his younger contemporaries.

But it is yet undeniable that, however powerfully such causes might contribute to accelerate the progress of any revolutionary and seditious movement, they were inadequate of themselves to furnish its primary incitement. We must, therefore, avail ourselves of sure indications to infer a still deeper cause. When we reflect that the men who played the most important parts under Absalom—his general Amasa, who was actually a near relative of Joab and of David, and Ahithophel a citizen of Giloh—belonged to the tribe of Judah, and that the insurrection itself sprung into being at Hebron, the ancient capital of Judah, it becomes certain that some discontent in David's own tribe here came into play. In fact, after Absalom's death, Judah remains resentful and apart, when the rest of the tribes have returned to their allegiance. This proves clearly that the hereditary jealousy among the tribes and the early antagonism between Judah and his brethren is not yet eradicated. Judah, accustomed from the earliest times to independence and preeminence, stood proudly apart under David even after Saul's death,[1] and now probably offered some opposition to the growing unity of the kingdom, and fancied itself put too far in the background in various ways, while the northern tribes likewise uttered occasional complaints. And as at such times of complicated grievance the most radically opposed parties often form a momentary alliance in order to gain some object which promises them mutual advantages, some of the malcontent northern tribes appear to have followed the impulse given by Judah. This is confirmed by the sequel of the rebellion, for the ten tribes, from early experience no strangers to the evils of division and anarchy, were the first to return to their allegiance, and Judah followed after some delay. According to this view Absalom was at the beginning at once tempter and tempted.

While Absalom, however, lived in half-exile excluded from the court, and was thus deprived of freedom of action, he could not hope for success in his secret plans. Accordingly, after he had endured this state of humiliation for about two years, he sent to entreat Joab to admit him into the royal presence. Joab, however, as the king's first minister and representative, feared to venture on so decided a step. After a second unsuccessful attempt of the same nature, Absalom had recourse to his favourite weapon of revenge, and he employed his servants to set on fire Joab's large barley field, which was now in full ear, and bordered upon his own estate.[2] When Joab's servants with their garments rent brought him this aggravating news,[3] he hastened to Absalom, who now reproached him with not fulfilling his reiterated request, and actually succeeded in inducing him to procure his re-admission to the king's presence. Thus was Absalom brought before David: and, falling at his feet, he received from him a kiss of reconciliation.

But from this moment he knows no bounds to his ambition. In imitation of heathen monarchs he sets up a chariot and horses and fifty runners.[4] And as persons were constantly coming from every tribe to seek justice at the court at Jerusalem, he zealously receives them at the city gates, and does not permit them to make the prostration customary before a member of the royal family, but prevents it by shaking hands with them and kissing them. He informs himself sedulously of the matter in dispute, assures every suitor that justice is on his side, but that he will scarcely be able to obtain it, and he even intimates, with

---

[1] See p. 109 sqq.
[2] As Samson had done, Judg. xv. 4 sq.
[3] According to the addition of the LXX in 2 Sam. xiv. 30.
[4] P. 144.

an occasional word, how superior would be the administration of affairs were he only king. After thus flattering the people and ingratiating himself in their favour during four years,[1] he decides upon the execution of his cunningly planned project. He alleges as a pretext that he is obliged to hold a festival in his birthplace, Hebron, in fulfilment of a vow which he made during his exile in case of his happy return to his native land, and he obtains the king's permission to carry it out. At the same time, he privately despatches his emissaries through all the tribes to his friends with instructions to proclaim him king, as soon as they hear the first trumpet-note of warning. He himself then marches to Hebron with two hundred men who were ostensibly only to be guests at the sacrifice, and were, therefore, doubtless taken for the most part from the poorer and more dependent classes; these were not in the secret of the conspiracy, but from their dependent position it could not prove difficult, at the sacrifice, to induce them publicly to espouse their benefactor's cause. But the main point was that a person of considerable importance, Ahithophel, David's chief councillor, whose sagacity made him the object of general dread, and who must have been in concert with the conspirators, had withdrawn beforehand to his native city Giloh somewhat south of Hebron,[2] and there awaited the outbreak of the rebellion. We do not know what was the cause of his estrangement from David, who was in ignorance of his defection. Apparently it was nothing but the ambition to play a new and higher part; but his importance and his crafty nature evidently made him the soul of the whole enterprise. While the sacrifices were proceeding, Absalom sent for him from Giloh, and the presence of this influential personage appears to have brought to a head a conspiracy which immediately spread with amazing rapidity through the preparations which had already been made, and, pouring like a wild mountain torrent from the ancient capital of Judah, threatened to flood the whole country.

4) We cannot blame David for not bestowing any special notice on these proceedings until the alarming tidings were brought to him that the favour of all Israel was turned to Absalom; for the monarchy, in that early and unsophisticated age, possessed none of that police organisation which is now regarded

---

[1] On the reading in 2 Sam. xv. 7, see p. 170, *note* 1.

[2] Cf. 2 Sam. xv. 12 with ver. 31, xvi. 23; it appears there necessary to read וַיִּשְׁלַח for וַיִּשְׁלַח. Giloh lay south of Hebron, according to Josh. xv. 51, although its exact situation is still unknown to us. A son of this eminent personage was in the regiment of the Gibborim, 2 Sam. xxiii. 35; he is not named, however, in 1 Chron. xi.

as essential to the security of a government. It may rather be viewed as a sign of the noble, large-hearted confidence which we have observed in him throughout his career, that he granted such complete freedom of action to his favourite son, who, being now the eldest, was probably popularly designated as his successor, and whose active nature was doubtless peculiarly congenial to him. It thus came about in a moment and without any direct fault on his part, that matters reached an extremity which could not fail to prove the very touch-stone of his rule; for it supplied the test not alone of the fidelity of his immediate friends as well as of his subjects, but also of the capacity of his own spirit, in spite of earlier failures, to collect and sustain itself by the strength of the true God in the contest against such unexampled calamities.

Without losing his self-possession David formed the instant decision to quit Jerusalem, not however alone, but accompanied by his servants and guards as well as by the whole of his royal household. This, under the circumstances, was the wisest course; for it was otherwise quite possible that the city might be stormed by the approaching rebels in the first fury of the sedition, a useless massacre take place in the streets,[1] and David himself be made prisoner. The best weapon against an insurrection so violent, but in reality so groundless and unreasonable, was to draw back as quietly as possible, with the intention of gaining time; for if only the first alarm were successfully overcome, in many quarters presence of mind would soon be restored. Even the departure from Jerusalem, for which David now gave orders, was an admirable means of testing the real strength of both parties. Only ten concubines [2] were left behind to protect his royal palace in Jerusalem; all the other members of his household, together with their attendants, he took with him. Among all his officers of state no one refused to follow him, and, in addition to the body-guard, the six hundred Gibborim marched out perfectly loyally, so that David had at his disposal a military force far superior to any which Absalom could bring into the field against him, especially when the first alarm was over. Among these was Ittai of Gath, who with other brave compatriots had but lately left his own country to enter David's service; and as he had probably in earlier days taken a leading position in his native city, he had also received from David a high appointment. David now courteously advised him either to remain

---

[1] This is hinted at as David's feeling, 2 Sam. xv. 14.
[2] That others besides these ten accompanied him in his flight follows from 2 Sam. xix. 6 [5].

with the new king at Jerusalem, or to return with his countrymen to his own home, as it was not right to draw a comparative stranger into so insecure a position, and make him the companion of his wanderings.¹ But the valiant Philistine declared his unswerving resolve to follow David in life or death, and we shall see what important service he rendered in the subsequent battle.

The road taken by the fugitives led towards the desert on the east on the way to the Jordan meadows. The king's first halt was at the last house on the eastern side of the city. His bodyguard with the Gibborim passed on before him over the brook Kedron, and came to a halt under the first olive tree at the foot of the Mount of Olives. When the king himself followed them over the brook, all the people burst forth into loud lamentation.² It is true that the Levites, with Zadok of the branch of Eleazar at their head, were also removing the ark of the covenant from the spot which David had appointed for it,³ in order that as of old it might protect him in the field; while Abiathar the second High-Priest, of the house of Eli, did not follow until all the rest had left the city. But when they had set down the sacred ark at the spot where David had commanded the first halt, the king advised Zadok to take it back to its own appointed place, for, if God led him back to the city, He would also permit him to see His sacred ark and its resting-place again; but if He had no delight in him, he would still bow with calm submission to His will. On the other hand, he requested the High-Priests Zadok⁴ and Abiathar quietly to observe the course of events in Jerusalem, and, when there was any important news, to send word of it to him in the Jordan plain by the sons of one or other of them; a stratagem of war allowable at all times, which David must not be blamed for employing.—The procession now ascended the Mount of Olives, David and all his followers weeping, and with their heads covered in token of their grief. The king himself walked barefoot as a penitent. When he was informed of Ahithophel's defection he only exclaimed 'May God turn his counsel into folly.' And as if this wish were to

---

¹ According to the LXX, after עִמָּךְ, in 2 Sam. xv. 20, must be inserted the words וַיהוָה יַעֲשֶׂה עִמָּךְ; and in the same way in ver. 22, הַמֶּלֶךְ after הִגַּתִּי.

² All these local details are derived from vv. 17 sq., 23, 30, but according to one of the versions of the LXX, after הפלתי in ver. 18, we must insert וַיַּעַמְדוּ עַל הַזַּיִת אֶת הַמִּדְבָּר; and, according to one in the Hex., הַזַּיִת after דֶּרֶךְ, in ver. 23.

³ P. 129. מִבֵּית הָהָר, which should be inserted, according to the LXX, after הָאֱלֹהִים in ver. 24.

⁴ In ver. 27, instead of הֲרוֹאֶה we should read הָר, as an exclamation 'thou seer!' i.e. thou prophet, since a High-Priest might certainly bear this higher but at the same time ancient designation.

receive its immediate fulfilment, when he reached the top of the
mount which had often served as his place of prayer, he was
overtaken by his long-tried friend Hushai of Erech in Ephraim,
who, in the garb of a mourner, was prepared to accompany him.
But David advised him, as he was no warrior and could only prove
a burden to him, to return to the city, and say to Absalom 'that
his brethren and David himself had withdrawn to a distance,
while he had turned his back upon them;[1] and now, in the place
of the father he would serve the son, were his life but spared.'
Should he be received into favour, Hushai was to do all in his
power to frustrate Ahithophel's proposals, and to communicate
to David any important tidings by the two sons of the High-
Priest. So Hushai returned to Jerusalem, which he had scarcely
reached before Absalom arrived.—When David had begun to
descend the mountain and had thus lost sight of Jerusalem, he
was met by Ziba,[2] who brought with him a handsome present,
doubly welcome at the moment of an enforced flight,—a pair
of asses saddled ready for any members of the royal household
who might wish to ride, and bearing likewise two hundred
loaves, one hundred pounds of raisins, and one hundred pounds
of other fruits and a skin of wine. Upon enquiry he stated
that Mephibosheth his master remained in Jerusalem, in the
hope that in the present troubles the people would restore to
him the kingdom of his grandfather Saul, whereupon David,
not apparently unfairly, presented to Ziba himself the whole of
his master's estate of which he was then the manager.[3] Continuing on the other side of the Mount of Olives their direct
way to the wilderness on the Jordan, they reached the insignificant town of Bahurim,[4] where one of the inhabitants, Shimei,
son of Gerar, belonging to Saul's family, advanced to meet
them, cursing and throwing stones, and loudly asseverating
that Jahveh Himself brought this misfortune upon David as a
punishment for his many murders and other cruelties against
Saul's house; what might be said in support of such a charge
has been already explained.[5] As he thus insulted the king
before his own troops, Abishai, Joab's brother, proposed to cut
off his head on the spot; but David sternly rebuked these two
violent sons of Zeruiah, in words which sufficiently indicate
his perfect composure and submission to the Divine will in
the depth of his misery, and his elevation above every base
passion: 'Let him curse! if Jahveh prompted him, how could

---

[1] In ver. 34 we should, according to the LXX, insert after אֲרִשָׁלוֹם the words עָבְרוּ אַחֶיךָ נַיַעֲבֹר הַמֶּלֶךְ אָבִיךָ אַחֲרֵי.

[2] P. 135.
[3] Ibid.
[4] P. 116, note 3.
[5] P. 135.

any man oppose him!' and then turning to all around him he added, 'if his own son sought after his life, how far more pardonable was this Benjamite; let him curse, for God had prompted him: possibly God would yet look upon the depth of his sorrow,[1] and recompense him for it with good!' Thus they passed on, while Shimei long bore them company upon the hill side, cursing and throwing at them dust and stones. At length, full weary, they reached the wilderness, where they rested, for the present moment at all events secure against surprise.[2]

We are obliged to assume that David's departure from Jerusalem took place in the morning, so that he could readily reach the Jordan on the same day; for our present authorities indicate that it was also on the same day tolerably early that Absalom arrived at Jerusalem, probably towards noon. Among the first to tender his congratulations was the crafty Hushai. Absalom received him at first with some surprise at his desertion of his friend; but the accomplished courtier, following David's hint, readily excused himself, and soon made his presence acceptable. 'Was it not his duty to remain with him whom God and the people had chosen king? besides, did he not thus serve the son of his late master and not a stranger?' This satisfied Absalom, and he now asked Ahithophel what he would advise him to do next? Ahithophel recommended, properly enough at least from the popular view, that he should take the concubines left behind by his father (in contradistinction to wives proper, these women might readily be transferred to a successor[3]), and openly treat them as his own; all the people would then understand that he was irreconcilably at enmity with his father, as he had seized on his house and his whole power, and thus his adherents would be enabled to act more decidedly. For this purpose the festal tent was erected on the palace roof, and Ahithophel thus succeeded in severing completely and irremediably all connexion between father and son. A councillor of such experience, however, was also well aware that other measures of a very different character must at once be taken, and David annihilated with the least possible delay; he therefore told Absalom that he would pursue David that very night with 12,000 chosen men, in order to surprise him while his army was weary and dispirited, put his followers to instant rout, and only slay the king; thus, he hoped, he should easily be able to divert the affections of

---

[1] For the *Kethîb* עוני, 2 Sam. xvi. 12, the sense at any rate requires that we should read עֲנִי; the explanation of the writing of the ו is given in my *Lehrb.* § 15*b*, note.

[2] After עֲיֵפִים in ver. 14 some word like

הָעֲרָבוֹת has disappeared, although it was not in the copies of the ancient translators; the *Arm.* has it, probably only from conjecture, at the end of the verse.

[3] P. 115.

the people from the father to the son, as a bride is easily persuaded to return to her husband; only one single man's life would have to be sacrificed to restore peace to the whole nation.[1] But although this plan commended itself to his most sagacious advisers, Hushai contrived, with consummate skill, when Absalom asked his opinion, to throw doubt upon the possibility of carrying it into execution; 'Absalom could not be ignorant of the desperate bravery of his father and his warriors, like the she-bear in the wood robbed of her cubs, or like the wild boar in the field,[2] and such an experienced commander as David would never allow his men to go to sleep; therefore if he were hidden in any defile or other refuge, and at the first onset turned upon his pursuers even though with but partial success, the report would spread of a great defeat of David's enemies, and terror would seize even the most lion-hearted warrior, for the bravery of David and his troops was already well known. His advice, on the other hand, was, that it would be better for all the levies of Israel to gather round Absalom, that he might lead them into the field; then, wheresoever they met with David, they could fall upon him as the dews fall on the earth in drops innumerable, overpowering in a moment his whole army, or if he retreated to a fortified city, then a countless multitude could lay cords upon it and pull it down into the trenches, so that not one stone should rest upon another.'[3] The new-made king gave the preference to a proposal which promised him, at any rate for a few days, the enjoyment of complete repose and the gratifications of his high position, as if God had deluded him into rejecting Ahithophel's council. And as if Hushai was destined to turn everything in David's favour, he gains for him a third advantage on that very same day. He is anxious by the instrumentality of the two High-Priests to inform David of the aspect of affairs, and of the desirability of his crossing the Jordan with all possible speed, lest he be swallowed up and all the people that were with him. A maid from the priest's house carries these tidings to the two young priests Jonathan and Ahimaaz, who remained the whole day at the Fuller's well south-east of Jerusalem, waiting for a message. As they set off to convey their tidings, their movements are watched by a youth who betrays them to Absalom. They, however, proceed in haste to Bahurim, the small

---

[1] The words in 2 Sam. xvii. 3 are clearly to be emended from the LXX, כְּשׁוּב הַכַּלָּה אֶל־הָאִישׁ אַךְ נֶפֶשׁ אִישׁ אֶחָד אַתָּה and then וְכֹל.

[2] In ver. 8, we must, according to the LXX, insert בַּיַּעַר יְכַחֵיר אָבְזָר after שָׁכוּל.

[3] That is, the city must first be conquered, and then demolished as a penalty.

town already noticed,[1] and there at a friend's house they descend into the dry well in the court. The mistress of the house then places the cover over it, upon which she spreads out some pulse to dry, so that nothing should be observed. When Absalom's spies make enquiries of this woman, she directs them on a wrong track to a small stream (from which they subsequently return without result); David's faithful messengers then come up out of the well, and succeed in reaching the king with their tidings; on the receipt of which, David with all his retinue crosses the Jordan before the next day dawns.—Ahithophel, however, who thus unexpectedly saw his advice overridden by other counsel, and his influence with the new king shaken in such a wholly unexpected manner, was acute enough to foresee the final issue which was now become inevitable, set off in haste for his own city, there made his last will, and hung himself; a clear proof that he had been impelled by nothing else than a mad ambition, so that life itself became insupportable, when the attainment of the position he had hankered after proved insufficient to satisfy his desires.

Thus full are the details supplied to us by the earlier narrator of the most extraordinary day of David's reign. Of the subsequent events up to the day of the decisive battle we do not know so much, as the account of the earlier narrator has obviously been very much abridged at this point by a later hand. There remain, however, many traces to show that this battle did not take place at once, but that the intervening period was crowded with events, among which we may name the solemn anointing of Absalom in Jerusalem;[2] and, as we have already pointed out,[3] probably three whole months elapsed before David actually returned to Jerusalem. Our knowledge of these events may be summarised as follows.

David took refuge, with his followers, in Mahanaim, on the eastern side of the Jordan. It was an important city, and[4] had already served as a royal residence about twenty years before; and it was certainly strong enough to endure a long siege. We have already seen[5] that the country on the east had, from of old, been somewhat indifferent to the movements on the other side of the Jordan; but on this occasion, it must have taken David's part against Absalom with great decision. This was all the more important, as Moab, Ammon, Zobah, and other of David's conquests, were thus kept true in their allegiance to him. When David (we are told) reached Mahanaim, Shobi, son

---

[1] P. 116, *note* 3.   [2] Cf. 2 Sam. xix. 11.   [3] P. 162.
[4] P. 112.   [5] Vol. ii. p. 323 sq.

of Nahash of Rabbah (and therefore probably some member of the royal house of Ammon, favoured by David[1]), Machir, son of Ammiel of Lo-debar, already mentioned,[2] and Barzillai of Rogelim in Gilead, the venerable old man whom David ever after held in such high esteem, joined together in supplying him with all kinds of necessaries for the use of his court and his troops, from feelings of simple loyalty and affectionate regard. They brought ten fine mattresses, household utensils of metal and earthenware, wheat, barley-meal, parched corn, beans and lentils, honey and cream, flocks and fatted oxen.[3] The military levies of these districts seem, likewise, gradually to have gathered round him. Undoubtedly his position here was at first one of extreme danger. Absalom gathered the levies of all the tribes on the other side of the Jordan, and appointed Amasa, a near relative of David's who was much esteemed, in command;[4] with this large force he crossed the Jordan, and occupied Gilead almost before David could establish himself in Mahanaim. At that time, Mahanaim itself must have undergone a siege. This fact is necessarily involved in the progress of the campaign, and is besides presupposed by David's two hymns, Pss. iii. and iv. These glorious mementoes of this heroic soul during a season of deepest trial[5] belong to this period, and breathe the same high confidence in God which characterises the recorded utterances of David on the first day of his flight. Absalom's army, however, compelled, as the result proves, to raise the siege, received a check well calculated to destroy the courage of the troops of this upstart king, notwithstanding the superiority of their numbers.

The decisive battle was undoubtedly fought in a wooded region many miles distant from Mahanaim, but on the same side of the Jordan.[6] The attack must, therefore, have proceeded

---

[1] P. 157.   [2] P. 135.

[3] In 2 Sam. xvii. 28, according to the LXX, מַרְבַדִּים עֲשָׂרָה must be inserted after מִשְׁכָּב. The connexion, however, shows that שְׁפוֹת בָּקָר must have the meaning of fat cattle, as the Vulg. translates; we ought, therefore, to compare وَسِفَ, which is connected with יסף and indicates the excrescences of beasts growing fat.   [4] P. 87.

[5] Ps. xxiii., however, does not belong to this age, and was not indeed originally among David's songs, as has been explained in the *Dichter des A.B.*, ii. pp. 67 sqq. 2nd ed.

[6] The supposition that the 'wood of Ephraim,' 2 Sam. xviii. 6, was on the other side of the Jordan seems, at any rate, to be rendered impossible by the name, and, according to xviii. 23, the messenger of the victory seems to turn from the battle-field towards the meadows of the Jordan in order to reach David. After the battle, however, the army returns to Mahanaim, while, if the battle had been won on the west of the Jordan, it would plainly have been much better for it to have remained there and occupied Jerusalem. Moreover, a wild and extensive forest is with more reason to be looked for in the districts on the other side of the Jordan. We must, therefore, interpret דֶּרֶךְ הַכִּכָּר, xviii. 23, 'he ran in the style of the Kikkar-running, and thereby overtook Cushi,' so that בָּכָר

on this occasion from David's side, this being the natural result of the retirement of the enemy from the siege. The troops despatched to follow up the retreating foe probably numbered about 20,000 men,[1] and were distributed by David in three equal divisions under the command of Joab, Abishai, and Ittai.[2] David himself was anxious to go with them as commander-in-chief, but to this the army offered a strenuous opposition: 'if they should flee, no one would regard it, or care if half their number fell; his life was worth ten thousand of theirs, and what would happen should he fall in the battle? Better that he should be prepared to aid them from the city, and afford them protection in case they came back beaten.' The aged hero was obliged to yield to these representations, and took up his position at the gate, while the troops marched out before him in excellent order, in detachments of hundreds and thousands; and in the hearing of the whole army he publicly charged the three generals (among whom Joab now of course assumed the supreme command) to deal gently with his son Absalom, and, at all events, to spare his life. The encounter of the two hostile armies speedily resulted in the decisive defeat of the much stronger forces of 'Israel,' i.e. of the numerous tribes united under Absalom, but, as they were not wanting in bravery, their loss was enormous. Twenty thousand is roundly given as the number who fell on the battle-field before David's heroes, but, in the wild flight which ensued, a far larger number were lost in the thickets and bogs of the extensive forest near which the battle was fought. A like fate overtook the royal pretender, for, as he was trying to urge his mule through a thicket close to the largest terebinth tree of the forest, he became entangled among the branches, owing to his height and great profusion of hair, so that his mule ran away from under him, and he looked like a person who had hung himself, his terror and despair no doubt rendering him thus awkward.[3] A common soldier discovered him, and brought the tidings to Joab, who reproached the messenger for not having dispatched him at once, for which he would have given

would here mean a special style of swift running, cf. כִּרְכֵּר, 2 Sam. vi. 16; and although there is a difficulty in the simple word דֶּרֶךְ in this connexion having the meaning of 'style,' these words must be understood to mean not the direction but the manner in which he ran, by which the runner was able to overtake Cushi, as it is clear from xviii. 27 that he ran in a particular way. We must, therefore, apply the name 'forest of Ephraim' to some wooded district on the other side of the Jordan; what made such a title appropriate may be seen from ii. p. 321 sq.

[1] This follows from the words of the troops, ver. 3.
[2] P. 179.
[3] Calderon's tragedy, 'the Locks of Absalom,' is not only a composition of great ignorance, but is in the highest degree unworthy and weak.

him ten pieces of silver and a rich military girdle; but he
replied, 'had a thousand pieces of silver been his guerdon, he
would not have laid his hands on the king's son, since the king
had so publicly charged all to spare him; even were he willing
against his conscience to tell a lie, yet nothing could remain
concealed from the king, and Joab himself would be certain to
hold aloof so as not to give any support to the lie.' So
genuine was, at that time, the reverence with which the loyalty
of even a common soldier invested the regal dignity! But the
violent Joab, sagacious enough to see that Absalom's death
was the most speedy and certain method of putting an end to
these disturbances, had no inclination to dwell upon such considerations. He snatched up three spears, and drove them
through the heart of the still living prince, whereupon his ten
armour-bearers closed around him and finally dispatched him.
Joab then gave the signal for ending the pursuit, and the
defeated rebels, on hearing of their king's death, were completely
dispersed and withdrew to their own homes. Some of the
victors, however, succeeded without any interruption in laying
Absalom's dead body in the deepest pit the wood afforded; they
then raised a great heap of stones over it, an ancient mode of
exhibiting the highest hostility to the departed. Such was the
melancholy monument accorded to a prince, who, having lost
all his three sons,[1] had already during his own lifetime erected
with royal splendour at a spot which probably owed to this
circumstance its name of King's Dale,[2] a very different mausoleum, which was long after celebrated as 'Absalom's' tomb, and
was certainly adorned with a magnificent inscription recording
his name.

The communication of the news of this great victory to
David gave rise to a strange rivalry. Ahimaaz, the priest's son,

---

[1] According to 2 Sam. xiv. 27 comp. with xviii. 18, he must have lost three sons in some disaster of which we have no record in our present narratives.

[2] The only other mention of this 'King's Dale' is in Gen. xiv. 17, and is certainly only an addition of the third narrator. It was situated not far from Salem, which must not be confounded with Jerusalem (i. p. 307), but was a northern city on the Jordan, and is to be identified with ὁ αὐλὼν Σαλήμ, Judith iv. 4, cf. ver. 6. According to Gen. xiv. 17, it was formerly called Shaveh; the later name was perhaps given to it from Absalom's preference for it. In the Middle Ages, it is true, among the older monuments on the east of Jeru-salem there was one shown as 'Absalom's monument;' and it is at this day still called 'Absalom's tomb' (see Carmoly's *Itinéraires*, p. 441, cf. p. 472, and espe-cially the exact description in Tit. Tobler's *Siloahquelle und der Oelberg* (1852), p. 267 sqq.); but this assumption, although it occurs in Jos. *Ant.* vii. 10. 3, rests on nothing more than a misconception of the words in 2 Sam. xviii. 18, Gen. xiv. 17, as though the place were to be looked for close by Jerusalem; and yet Williams (*The Holy City*, p. 374 sq.) chooses to consider this monument as genuine, and Saulcy (*Voyage*, ii. pp. 288 sqq.) leaves the matter undetermined.

who[1] had on a former occasion brought to David the news of Absalom's earliest acts in Jerusalem, and who must have excelled the numerous skilful runners of the time,[2] offered himself to Joab as the bearer of the joyful tidings to David that God had avenged him of his enemies: but Joab, who was better acquainted with David, and foresaw how violently the news of his son's death would act upon him, withheld him, as too good for this employment, and gave it to a man named Cushi.[3] But when Cushi had departed, Ahimaaz was anxious, at any rate, to prove his skill, and after Joab had once more unsuccessfully attempted to dissuade him, by assuring him that he undertook a thankless office, he finally gave way to his urgent entreaties, and the young priest started on his course; clearly not with any expectation of reward, of which no hope could be entertained, but out of affectionate loyalty to the king. Meanwhile David remained at Mahanaim in the inner court of the gateway, on the side nearest to the battle, awaiting the tidings: and when the watchman standing upon the roof of the gate near the wall observed a single runner approaching he communicated it through the warder to the king, who was seated below. To him it seemed a good omen that but a single messenger was in sight, as in defeat and flight many always hasten onwards; but as, when the runner came nearer, the watchman saw another behind him, and judged the first messenger to be Ahimaaz from the particular style of his running, David thought both circumstances auspicious, for the second messenger also came alone, and Ahimaaz never brought any but good news. In fact, Ahimaaz by his peculiar skill in running arrived before his competitor, although he started later. On reaching the king he kneels before him, announcing that God has given him the victory over the rebels; but when the king makes instant enquiry respecting Absalom's welfare, he cautiously states that he has only seen Joab and Absalom let loose the great tumult of battle, and knows no further particulars,[4] upon which he

---

[1] P. 183.

[2] News was still conveyed by men on foot; and even at the present day, separate Arab tribes are famous as swift runners; cf. Petermann's *Reisen im Orient*, ii. p. 301.

[3] In 2 Sam. xviii. 21 this Cushi is treated as a well-known person, although he is not mentioned anywhere before. This simply confirms what we know from other sources, that many passages from the work of the older narrator have been omitted in the present redaction. Probably he was one of Joab's ten armour-bearers, xviii. 15, another of whom is mentioned in xxiii. 37. By descent he may have been an Œthiopian; cf. p. 144, *note* 3.

[4] The first clause of the speech in xviii. 29 has been very variously and yet quite erroneously understood by the ancient translators, although the cause of the mistake lies not in the text which is evidently correct, but in the misapprehension of a rare connexion of clauses, which is explained by my *Lehrb.* § 336*b*, and 307*c*. At most, the word אַבְשָׁלוֹם may have been left out after עַבְדְּךָ; at any rate, the *Pesh.* and *Arm.* add it.

receives the simple command to stand quietly by the king's side. When, however, Cushi thereupon enters with similar congratulations, and, on David's quick question respecting Absalom, cannot conceal his sad fate, the unhappy father tremblingly ascends to the small chamber on the roof of the gate, that in solitude he may give unmeasured vent to his tears and lamentations, desiring but one thing—that he might have died for Absalom.

The tidings of David's intense and apparently inconsolable grief could not remain a secret, either from Joab or from the rest of the army. The day of victory became one of bitter humiliation to the victorious host; and returning to Mahanaim, it stole silently into the city, as though it had itself sustained defeat, and had been driven to a shameful flight. As the king with covered face still continued his loud lament, Joab at length ventured to approach him, and as a sort of interpreter of the feelings of the army, declared that 'by acting thus he deeply disturbed the joy of his faithful followers, who had ventured their all for his safety and that of his numerous household, for it appeared that he loved his enemies and hated his friends; he cared nothing for his officers and faithful adherents who had sacrificed everything for him, for it was now plain that it would have pleased him well had they all fallen and only Absalom survived: he must rouse himself and show himself publicly, and speak a word of heartfelt encouragement to the people, for he could most solemnly assure him that, if he did not, the troops would all desert him that very night, and a greater evil would then befall him than any he had ever experienced since his youth.' Thus earnestly adjured, he descended from the solitary chamber on the roof, and taking his seat by the open gate, he passed the whole army in review before him.

5) It was indeed high time for David to attend to affairs of state; for, despite the general flight of the defeated foe, the country on the west of the Jordan was very far from being once more in his possession, and as Absalom had been solemnly anointed king, it was open to choose as his successor whomsoever they desired. Western Israel (that is, all the tribes excepting Judah) soon, it is true, recovered its senses, as it perceived that in the whole course of the revolution Judah had greatly disappointed the expectations which it had aroused. In periods like this of great excitement, public opinion is liable to rapid fluctuations; and so a general movement now spread through Israel in favour of the aged hero-king, whose many acts of kindness in early days were once more gratefully remembered;

and a solemn deputation from this most important portion of his kingdom invited him to return immediately.[1] Welcome as this must have been to David, the tribe of Judah still remained obstinately aloof, and kept its forces together under Amasa, Absalom's late general. But David was too cautious and placable in temper not to try the plan of conciliation, and he accordingly sent to the elders of the tribe the two High-Priests, Zadok and Abiathar, and put the matter directly before them: 'Why should they his nearest relatives be the last to recall him home, when he has been already invited back by all the other tribes?' To Amasa, in particular, he sent a most solemn assurance, that 'as he was his nearest relative, he should be immediately appointed commander-in-chief in place of Joab,' which was not simply a measure of prudence and conciliation, but one which, when strictly considered, involved no injustice towards Joab himself, for he had long been notorious for too great severity in war, and had just acted with such direct disobedience to the royal command in Absalom's case, that it was impossible to overlook his offence without endangering the royal prerogative. By this astute conduct he quickly brought all Judah also round to his side, so he was invited with all his faithful adherents to return, and a solemn deputation was despatched to meet him at Gilgal, the point at which he intended to cross the Jordan.

This deputation from Judah was accompanied by Shimei, the Benjamite who had so grossly insulted David during his flight,[2] and also by Ziba,[3] with his fifteen sons and twenty slaves. Not satisfied with coming to meet David at the Jordan, they crossed the river to do homage to the king on the other side; and while the ferry-boat which the deputation had prepared to convey the royal household across and do anything else the king might desire, was passing backwards and forwards, Shimei seized the favourable moment on the farther bank to fall at the king's feet and entreat his pardon for the crime which he now so deeply repented: 'he was the very first of the house of Joseph (i.e. of all the tribes excepting Judah) who came to render homage, and he trusted that this also would soften the king's heart.' Abishai, indeed, wished to make short work with him,—'Ought not he who had cursed Jahveh's Anointed to suffer death?' But David, in the moment of present happiness, as in that of recent misfortune, severely reproved the heat of Zeruiah's sons: 'What had he to do with them, that to-day

---

[1] The conclusion to 2 Sam. xix. 11 has preserved in the LXX. dropped out of the Hebrew text, but is still   [2] P. 181 sq.   [3] Ibid.

HIS RESTORATION.

they desired to be his tempters? Was it on that, of all days, that one should fall in Israel? Was he not right in believing that he was now once more king over Israel, and he would not throw away his privilege of showing mercy!' Accordingly he granted Shimei his life, though he would have been perfectly justified in taking it, and swore to spare him. Saul's lame son Mephibosheth also came down to the Jordan to proffer his homage; Ziba had already been presented[1] by David with Saul's estates on the day of his flight; and at this very time had anticipated his former master in rendering his allegiance to the king. Mephibosheth appeared in deep mourning, as from the first day of David's flight he had not washed his feet, nor cut his nails,[2] nor dressed his beard, nor washed his clothes. On David's enquiry why he had not on that occasion accompanied him, he excused himself by saying, 'His servant had deceived him; as he was lame, he wished to mount on his ass, that he might ride after him, but his servant had left him secretly in order to traduce him; but the king, kind as an angel of God, would do as seemed to him right. All the members of his father's house were as dead men before him [i.e. in his mighty power he could have put them all death], and yet had he deigned to admit him to his table; he had nothing more to say in justification or complaint before the king.' It could not be difficult to decide which of the two was in the right, the master or the servant, who had approached David as if he had an easy conscience, as in reality Mephibosheth had not denied that he had cherished hopes of being able to recover Saul's dominion, while his mourning admitted of the ready explanation that he undoubtedly had cause to be less contented with Absalom's rule than with David's. But though he was not entirely blameless, yet as there was now no reason for punishing severely so foolish a purpose, David cut the matter short by ordering him to divide his estates with Ziba; and overjoyed at this, he replied that he would willingly part with all, now that he had seen the happy restoration of the king.—From the provinces on the east David's retinue was also increased by the arrival of Barzillai, the octogenarian who had brought him such generous assistance in his distress.[3] He came to escort the king across the river, and to take leave of him on the other side. This venerable old man pleased David so much that he entreated him to accompany

---

[1] P. 181.
[2] According to the LXX, the words וְלֹא נִצְּפַּר should be inserted in 2 Sam. xix. 25 after רַגְלָיו; in ver. 26 מִירוּשָׁלַם should be read. In ver. 34, for אִתָּךְ read more expressively שִׁיבָתְךָ according to the LXX, cf. 1 Kings ii. 9. In ver. 38, בְּנִי is wanting after כְּמוֹהֶם, and is still found in the *Pesh.* and *Arm.*
[3] P. 185.

him to Jerusalem, and spend his last years in honourable maintenance at the court. This gracious proposal the hoary prince modestly declined, on the plea that his age had deprived him of all taste for such pleasures, and for himself his only wish was to die in his native city and to rest by his parents' side; but let the king take his son Chimham with him to Jerusalem, and show him whatever kindness he thought fit. David willingly assented, and after their passage over was fully completed he parted from his aged friend with hearty expressions of good-will. This full account of Barzillai is evidently introduced here because his son Chimham and his family were afterwards famous at Jerusalem, and contributed much to the prosperity of the kingdom.

But while David delayed at Gilgal, having crossed the Jordan with the help of the members of his own tribe, who were joined by a number of Benjamites and other persons of different tribes who lived in the neighbourhood, the bands of the northern tribes reached the Jordan full of disgust and astonishment that the men of Judah, who had been later than themselves in deciding to recognise David again as king, had yet been the first to bring him home and pay him homage, apparently desirous to secure by these means a monopoly of the royal favour, and obtain for themselves exclusive privileges. In the disordered state of the nation west of the Jordan, this dissatisfaction soon found vent in open reproaches against the king himself. It was in vain that the Judahites reminded them that the king belonged by birth to their tribe, and assured them that there was no legitimate cause of discontent, as they had not received any advantage or gift of any kind from the king. The Israelites still maintained that the right of the initiative belonged to them, because they possessed ten-twelfths of the kingdom and therefore of the king, besides which they had the advantage of the birthright;[1] why, then, had the men of Judah despised them and not fulfilled their wish to restore the king, which they had been the first to express? Thus the internal strife, which had been apparently brought to a close, threatened to burst forth with renewed violence; for undoubtedly this was no mere war of words, as the northern tribes might well be afraid that such a course of action at the re-establishment of the kingdom might involve the loss of still more essential privileges. It was not possible for David to condemn the men of Judah for what had just occurred, as there had in reality been no question about

---

[1] According to one of the versions of the LXX, בְּכוֹר should be read for בָּדְוֹך, in 2 Sam. xix. 44, since many counted Joseph as the first-born, and Judah at any rate could not be so considered; i. p. 422 sq.

losing or conferring any real privileges; but he had no sooner
declared that he could not blame the Judahites than an ambitious
leader on the other side, Sheba, son of Bichri, a Benjamite,
sounded the trumpet with a call to instant revolt, in words often
re-echoed in after times :

> We have no part in David,
> No inheritance in the son of Jesse!
> Every one to his tent, O Israel!

And in fact, in the distraction of the moment he found much
encouragement. The Israelites deserted to his side, while the
men of Judah gathered more closely round David, and escorted
him in safety to Jerusalem. Here it was scarcely possible for him
to attend even to the most pressing of his own affairs, but he
nevertheless at once placed his ten concubines, whom Absalom
had violated, under guard in a separate dwelling, where they
were to remain confined for life in a state of widowhood, in-
eligible for re-marriage. It was necessary for him to give his
undivided attention at once to Sheba's revolt, the gathering
strength of which might obviously render it even more dangerous than that of Absalom. He accordingly commissioned
Amasa, who had just been appointed commander-in-chief, to
assemble the levy of Judah within three days, and then to
present himself again to receive further orders about the war
which was now become inevitable. But, as the event proved,
he had not in such matters the skill and success of his predecessor Joab, and he remained absent beyond the appointed time :
David, consequently, without the slightest idea of displacing
him, but to prevent loss of time, gave orders to Abishai, Joab's
brother, to march at once with the forces ordinarily retained in
Jerusalem, in order to prevent Sheba from taking possession of
any fortress, and clouding the king's eyes.[1] Abishai accordingly departed with the 600 Gibborim, with which were united,
owing to the urgent necessity, the royal body-guard, and 'Joab's
men.' These last were evidently a band which Joab had quickly
collected in Jerusalem at his own charge; they were to serve
as volunteers, and he desired, himself a volunteer, to serve with
them in the war. The king could have no reason for refusing
this, as, ever since he had surrendered his office to Amasa
at the Jordan, he had been on very friendly terms with him,
and, besides that, he was his near kinsman. When these
troops, on their way to take the field, arrived at Gibeon, a little

---

[1] I.e. causing him trouble and anxiety, because these make the eyes dim, throw- ing a sort of shadow over them: Ps. vi. 8 [7]; הָצִיל from צַל.

north of Jerusalem, which, together with Jerusalem and almost the whole of the territory of Benjamin, must be reckoned as at that time part of Judah, they were met at the great stone in the city by Amasa, who, after summoning the levies all over the country, east and south of Jerusalem, had passed on to the north and west, and was now on his return to Jerusalem, having completed his mission, at the head of the large force which he had raised. Joab, dressed in his long military cloak, with his girdle outside it, in which he wore a sword made fast on his hip, addressed Amasa with the utmost cordiality, taking hold of his beard with his right hand to kiss him. At the same moment, apparently by accident, this movement of his arm turned up the scabbard, and the sword fell out; and as Amasa was not upon his guard, Joab skilfully seized the sword in his left hand and ran him through the body, dispatching him by this single stroke. The friendship and tranquillity of this rough warrior thus proved to have been mere hypocrisy while he waited to take the first opportunity of revenge; and he might well rejoice that he had rid himself of so important a rival sooner than he could have hoped, just as he had formerly done with Abner.[1] He was determined that no one should surpass him in zeal for David's cause; and, in fact, he showed himself on that occasion also the only man capable of bringing the war to a speedy close. Without any delay by the corpse, the two brothers continued the pursuit of Sheba; and, indeed, the dispatch of Amasa seemed the shortest way of attaining their object. Standing close by the corpse, one of Joab's armour-bearers called out loudly, 'Whoever wishes to serve with Joab, and is for David, let him go after Joab!' As Joab's name no doubt inspired far more general confidence of victory than Amasa's, all were ready at once to transfer themselves to his command; those, however, who were going to range themselves with his men, stopped at first on seeing the corpse still weltering in blood, but when the armour-bearer had moved it aside and covered it over with a cloth in an adjoining field, Joab's banner was followed by all.

Sheba was now swiftly pursued, and he found no place of rest until he reached Abel, in Beth-Maachah, which was situated in Dan, in the northernmost nook of the country, and was well fortified, and even here he seems to have owed his reception more to compassion or to the misconception caused by some false report, than to any determined opposition to David. As soon as it became known that the expedition was directed solely

[1] P. 117 sq.

against Sheba, all the free-born men of the surrounding tribes gathered round Joab.¹ He accordingly began the siege; threw up a wall around the city, on which he took his stand, while the entire army set to work to undermine the city walls. But a wise woman desired to speak with Joab from the wall, and after obtaining permission she thus addressed him: 'In old time there used to be a proverb—Ask in Abel and in Dan whether anything has fallen into disuse, which the God-fearing men of Israel had once ordained! Such had been the fair fame of this city and the neighbouring Dan; and even now they were the most peaceful and the most devoted men in Israel, while Joab was trying to destroy a city and a mother in Israel: why was he desolating Jahveh's inheritance?'² Thus referred to the eternal divine laws of the true community, Joab defended himself, as in duty bound, from any intention of destruction, and simply required that the rebel should be given up; which was agreed to by the woman. The result was that the citizens, upon the representation of the wise woman, cut off the traitor's head, and threw it over the wall to Joab, who at once drew off all his troops.—Our present authorities do not supply the conclusion of this story, or tell us what sort of reception David accorded to the victorious Joab on his return: but he probably felt obliged to show some indulgence to a man who was indispensable to him as a soldier, and who, notwithstanding his culpable ferocity, never lost sight of his master's interests. The ancient liberties and privileges of the Israelites doubtless remained unaffected after the victory.

4. *Close of David's Career.*

1) Thus was the heaviest trial of David's royal career overcome. But a man who can, like David, in the roar of a sudden storm display such lofty composure and submission, and then, as it spends its force, sing hymns like the third and fourth Psalms, penetrated with the purest trust in God, is already raised in an eminent degree above human weakness and frailty, and whatever be his outward fate, he can only quit this life as

---

¹ In 2 Sam. xx. 14, for הברים (LXX ἐν Χέρρι) it appears necessary to read הַבַּחֻרִים, 'the young men;' and, according to ver. 15, the ו before בֵּית מַעֲכָה should be struck out. The word מַשְׁחִיתִם in ver. 15, must be derived (if the reading is correct) from שַׁחַת, *pit*.

² In 2 Sam. xx. 18 sq. the reading and the sense should, partly in accordance with the LXX, be restored as follows; בְּאָבֵל וּבְדָן הֲתַמּוּ אֲשֶׁר שָׂמוּ אֱמוּנֵי יִשְׂרָאֵל and then for אָנוֹכִי perhaps אֲנַחְנוּ, or better עֶרְנוּ with a ו before אַתָּה. There was certainly an old proverb about the good repute of the town, to which she refers. Ver. 22 must be completed by the LXX.

one of God's victors. Yet, since he triumphantly outlasted the fury of the storm, not only had he suffered severely enough in his old age to atone, humanly speaking, for the fault in which a great part of these disorders originated,—not only had he been tried as no other individual of his time could have been tried and proved,—but the nation likewise had learnt, by the severe discipline of events, how terrible a punishment followed each fruitless ill-advised effort to introduce an imperfectly considered improvement. With growing unanimity and prudence, it adhered to the benevolent rule of its hero-king, whose many trials had purged his heart and left only the purest piety. The result thus proved advantageous to each party, though it had certainly not been the object of human desire and pursuit; and as many evils were removed as the circumstances of the age permitted.

The remainder of David's life, a period, probably, of ten years, flowed on, so far as we can collect, in a bright calm and an undisturbed course of improvements, of which history furnishes but few examples. These improvements must have taken deep root in the soil, as they were carried on without any essential change under Solomon. The scanty records of this period in our present historical books do but attest what happy tranquillity was from that time enjoyed by the monarchy, in the midst of its great extent and splendour. In the Chronicles [1] it is stated that David was much engaged in the latter part of his life with preparations on a large scale for the erection of the temple, and this statement not only possesses intrinsic probability, but receives confirmation from the fact, that Solomon began at once to carry out this magnificent undertaking during the first years of his reign. The details of this are, however, better reserved for Solomon's reign. Considering the extraordinary labours and struggles of his early life, it is not surprising that David showed signs of old age rather early; and as his bodily frame, with its burden of seventy or indeed seventy years and a half,[2] seemed at the point of death, and no warmth could be produced by means of bedclothes, his attendants cast about anxiously for some means of prolonging his life, and (as they found no other mode left to them for communicating to him vital heat) they selected for this purpose a maiden from Shunem, named Abishag, whom they caused to rest on his bosom, to revive with her youthful warmth his decaying frame.[3]

---

[1] 1 Chron. xxviii. 2 sqq., xxix. 1 sqq.
[2] According to 2 Sam. v. 4 sq., 1 Kings ii. 11; cf. ii. p. 369.
[3] 1 Kings i. 1–4; the infamous insinuations of Bayle and others about this simple affair scarcely deserve mention.

Turning away, however, from all these external events, in order to gaze once more into the soul of this great king as it is revealed to us during the concluding period of his life by the clearest testimony, we see in it the completion of a change affording the highest evidence of the true greatness and elevation of his spirit, as well as of the glorious termination of his earthly labours. In his youth, a close spectator of the prophetic life, and occasionally yielding himself to its inspiration, he had never, in his maturity, amid the numerous cares of war and government, desired to be, or to assume the least appearance of being, a Prophet (in this, exhibiting a striking contrast to Mohammed). Now, however, as age advances, he becomes one, not by any intention of his own, or with any public display of prophetic faculty, but involuntarily, and therefore with all the greater purity and earnestness; nor was it for the sake of others, or to exercise a Prophet's sway, but simply because the power of his spirit impelled him to it, and directed his regards with the greater singleness of purpose to the future alone. Prophetic intuition and speech, which were regarded in antiquity as life's most elevated expression, were now developed as the ripe fruit of a long and varied career in the spirit of one whose position in the kingdom was enough to have adorned the close of his life without this distinction; but, filled with its power, he reached almost the highest possible culmination of kingly glory. Even the hymns which poured forth from the very depth of his soul during the pursuit by Absalom, are often illumined with involuntary flashes of fire from the true prophetic spirit which alternately displays the utmost energy and gentleness: so crushing is his word against the ungodly designs of the enemy, filled as he is with the clear consciousness of his own election, and so calm is his subsequent composure in cheerful submission and supplication for the good of all;[1] and even earlier than this, in the wonderful elevation of his song of gratitude for the recovery of peace of mind after his aberrations with Bath-sheba, the deep emotion of his utterance reaches occasionally a prophetic height.[2] But in that song, which an ancient tradition justly designates as 'David's last (poetic) words,' the poetic and moral spirit of the aged king is finally transfigured into the prophetic. Gathering himself up at the approach of death for a poetic flight, he feels with unmistakable clearness that he is a Prophet of Jahveh, and, looking back on his life now near its close, as well as freely glancing forward to the future, he ex-

[1] Ps. iv. 3–6 [2–5]; iii. 9 [8]; iv. 7–9 [6–8].   [2] Ps. xxxii. 6–9.

presses the God-given assurance of his soul that the rule of his house, being firmly established in God, will continue after his death.[1] No prince, and certainly no one who had not acquired his kingdom by inheritance, could possibly close his life with a more blessed repose in God, and a brighter glance of confidence into the future.

This is the real stamp of true greatness. For if, standing at its conclusion, we form a complete picture of his life, we are forced to admit that his career constitutes the culmination of that general advancement towards which the people of Israel had been aspiring with increasing energy for more than a century, and it is as successful a realisation of this ideal as the circumstances by which they were then surrounded rendered it possible for them to attain. The age did not require in its leader and representative a man gifted with special spiritual activity, though it might be of the very highest kind, and hence it was not a Prophet that it demanded, for its most pressing want was the completion of the undertaking begun by Moses at the close of his career and carried on by Joshua, which the centuries that had since elapsed had not, however, accomplished; it needed, that is, the possession of an earthly fatherland in which unity might be firmly established among all the members of the nation, and which would secure for that people in which the highest religion had taken root, that perfect independence and tranquillity in which its nationality and its religion could alike find free room for the utmost expansion. True religion, if it was to appear on earth at all, could not but be implanted in the bosom of a given nationality, and it then became requisite for its higher development that the people destined to be its organ should first attain a more complete position as a nation among the other nations of the earth. Strengthened by its unity and self-consciousness, the nation might then address itself to higher and heavier tasks; just as the individual, however great may be his spiritual powers, must first reach manhood before these can operate in him with their full force. Only a warrior, that is, a man of the people, could serve as the instrument for raising up the nation to that matured strength which became more and more urgently necessary for its existence. But on the other hand, no man of the people could satisfy the demands which had been loudly made in the community since the last spiritual movement of Samuel, who did not at the same time embody all its sacredness. 'If but a hero might spring forth from the people whose strongest

[1] 2 Sam. xxiii. 1-7; cf. the *Dichter des A.B.* i. p. 143 sqq. 2nd ed.

weapon is his pure trust in the spiritual God, on which he never relaxes his hold;'—this was the cry of the age, and in answer to it appeared David, the warrior who never alienated himself from the prophetic and other supreme truths of the community, but sympathised vividly with them, and gradually brought his own spirit, as well as the entire national mind, more and more completely under their penetrating influence. Only a man thus gifted could succeed in uniting for the prosecution and attainment of this object the whole power of the people, at that time so highly strained, and in completing that undertaking for which the noblest efforts had long before laid a firm foundation. The new enthusiasm and elevation of the community was not the creation of David. It met him as his noblest incentive, but it is the completeness with which he suffered it to take possession of him, the fidelity which prevented him from ever being untrue to it, and the energy with which he overcame even the one error of his life which threatened permanently to alienate him from it, so that he was finally brought only more decidedly under its power,—it is all this that constitutes the secret of his peculiar greatness, and the charm which never failed to attach to his struggles and triumphs all the strongest and purest spirits of his age.

2) The general results of such labours in such a period were necessarily greater than any other individual could produce in the whole course of the national history; and although, from a purely spiritual point of view, Samuel's elevation was far higher, yet the full glory of the age inevitably falls upon the mighty consummator of its own aim.

a.) In the first place, Israel has now acquired greater strength and stability, and takes its place among other nations as a distinct nationality; and it has gained what it had been unable, since the last days of Moses, to obtain completely—a beautiful country of which it is not to be so easily deprived. And as it did not conceive the idea of universal conquest, the number and extent of territories and peoples which now submitted to its sway might well appear sufficient to assure it a powerful and influential position among the nations of the earth.

b.) In the second place, as the nation now attains, for the first time, firmer unity and power, its monarchy, transfigured in the person of David, does what a genuine earthly monarchy should do, and includes within its own range all the diverse efforts, powers, and ranks of the nation. David is warrior and poet; ruler, and yet ready to listen to the popular voice; a man of the people, yet, if necessity demands,[1] he acts and is recognised as Priest;[2] a powerful monarch, and yet, without prejudice to his own dignity, ever attentive to the voice of great Prophets, and willingly acting in accord with them. Thus all the various elements of the nation find their centre of unity in him: he is a true king, and it seems as if civil discord might be rendered for ever harmless. It is even in this respect an advantage that he is neither a Prophet nor by birth a Priest, but a simple man of the people. In early times Israel needed both the marvellous spiritual force of isolated great Prophets and the constant supervision of an hereditary Priesthood to train it to be 'God's people;' but now a simple man, sprung from the people, has completed in it a regenerating work, which will contribute more to the continuous development of the community than anything which has preceded it,[3] and will bind together all members of the nation into the most compact whole. Thus the popular element in Israel was ennobled by him, and every cause of division removed which might have embittered the different classes against each other. Although there still existed strong remains of the class distinctions which had sprung up during the earlier history, their permanent existence for the future now became dependent upon the actual or possible benefit which they conferred, and they could never, as before, become injurious in consequence of their one-sided pre-eminence. With David for their great example, there was no aim, not even the highest, which did not now come within the compass of the efforts and aspirations of everyone, even the most insignificant, who possessed the power and aid of the true Spirit of Jahveh;[4] and the one-sided supremacy of the priesthood which was so powerfully extended at the commencement of the Theocracy, was now broken through by the whole career and administration of David, with far more lasting results than had attended the earlier efforts of the Judges. With the prophetic faculty of the true religion, however,—this fundamental power in the community of Israel,—there was now associated a monarchy penetrated by its spirit, and so far on an equality with it that the prophetic voice could no longer lay claim in its presence to utter

---

[1] P. 127.
[2] As Ps. cx. shows past dispute.
[3] Hence the honourable appellation 'servant of Jahveh' which David gradually receives (as early as 1 Kings viii. 66, in the Book of Origins), and which he shares with very few great historical personages of the Old Testament. For there is propriety in the feeling of the Old Testament that this name, so simple yet so elevated, is only merited by the few who have made some special great divine work the task of their lives, and achieved it as true servants of God in His community.
[4] Cf. such expressions as that in the ancient song 1 Sam. ii. 7 sq., and many others which became current afterwards.

the decisive word for the guidance of the people. In David we already see realised the relation of the true king to the prophetic power, in so far as he, on the one hand, voluntarily follows its direction only where it seems to him to coincide with the fundamental laws of the community of the true God, while, on the other, the prophetic power demands nothing more from him; and while these two deepest powers of the community of Israel thus hold each other in check, David completes in his own person the Basileo-Theocracy, so that the next question which arises is, whether this constitution is able to maintain itself as supreme and final.

c.) In the third place, as David feels himself to be Jahveh's true king, so the nation, with a prouder consciousness than heretofore, learns to regard itself as 'Jahveh's people,' a favourite appellation in the narratives of this period;[1] and while it never forgets who is its actual and immortal King, it renders a cordial and willing obedience to its earthly ruler, and, deriving glory from his glory, affords him in return the support of its affection and fidelity. Thus the necessary changes in the ancient constitution appear to be happily accomplished, and the Basileo-Theocracy is completed. Throughout history there are found two sorts of sovereignty among mankind,—one over the humbler beginnings or even the insoluble embarrassments of life, in which the king is only the warlike leader or possibly the dark tyrant of his country; and a second one of higher stamp, refined by the effort to conquer its own deficiencies, and hence, in spite of the difficulties which beset its establishment, developing its powers and acquiring permanence. By the assistance of the Theocracy, monarchy in Israel was enabled to pass over the earlier of these two stages, and at once attained the higher form, the only one which could venture on the attempt of blending itself with the Theocracy. In David, a king sprung from its own flesh and blood, the whole nation feels that it attains to a nobler and royal existence. Moreover, through all the sufferings and changes of life, he found only more and more strength in Him 'who redeemed him out of all distress;'[2] and so a new and higher spirit passes from him alike into the nation and the individual, and his influence in this respect is rendered more permanent by means of his nervous eloquence and the grandeur of his imperishable

---

[1] As in 2 Sam. xiv. 13, 16; a similar feeling revived, for instance, in the first ages of Islam, cf. the narrative in Freytag's *Chrestom.* p. 40.

[2] Cf. the standing expressions, 2 Sam. iv. 9, 1 Kings i. 29, ii. 26, Ps. iii. 8 [7], and many similar ones.

hymns, which had secured for him a home in the hearts of the people.

d.) Finally: it was David and not the earlier military heroes of Israel who first rendered it possible for the nation permanently to entertain the idea of gaining an imperial power, i.e. a position of importance and influence, commanding the respect of the other nations of the earth. In far other ways than Moses and Joshua had employed, he made the Heathen feel the real significance of the connexion of the national power and the compact kingdom of Israel with its extremely peculiar religion; and as it was among the Heathen that he himself took the greatest pride in singing Jahveh's praise, and by his whole career proclaimed to them His unique greatness,[1] it thenceforth became at once the privilege and the duty of every member of the community of Jahveh to take up the same position towards them. And besides, all Israel had now become accustomed to the wonder-working influence of the royal power and to an enthusiastic devotion to 'Israel's king,' and it was at the same time transformed, as it were, into a school of heroes ready to fight against the Heathen; nor could the Persians after Cyrus, in the assured expectation of their continuous supremacy, have clung with more magic reverence to their royal house and its members [2] than that which a large portion of Israel, at any rate, thus early learned to cherish without wavering towards David and his house, so far as concerns the sort of imperial dominion of which it dreamed. The destiny of David, whom God had made a mighty ruler over the nations, is to be realised again by Israel, and like an inexhaustible treasure the divine mercies which it has already experienced are in reserve for it in the future. Such was the prophecy, at the close of the exile, of the great Unnamed,[3] who only expressed once more the permanent basis of all the *Messianic* hopes to which this era gave birth: and the only great question which could arise in the future was this, *by what means* should Israel maintain the world-wide supremacy towards which it had now made its first assured step, or regain it in case of its loss? While they are not without a deeper basis of intrinsic necessity, it is

---

[1] Ps. xviii. 50 [49] sq. In this David followed, but with incomparably more force, the example of Deborah, Judg. v. 3.

[2] This point is strongly brought out by Xenophon in the *Cyropædia*, and with especial clearness in the *Anabasis*.

[3] Is. lv. 3–5. This Prophet intentionally chooses the word עֵד, rare in antiquity, in the meaning of a *prophetic ruler*, i.e. one who announces God's will (cf. the *Alterth.* p. 142), as the कवि: becomes the old Persian $. What perversity it is to refer the words ver. 4 to the Messiah of the future, ought by this time to be self-evident.

David who, without intending it, supplies the personal foundation of all the Messianic hopes which from this time contribute with increasing power to determine Israel's career; and so he stands at the turning-point in the history of two thousand years, and separates it into two great halves.

Such, in its main features, is the bearing of David's reign on the subsequent course of the nation. He was a king who could never be forgotten by his own people, but he also possessed a unique importance in the history of all true religion. His life also was not a little glorified in his death. Few kings, have departed amid such universal veneration and with so direct a prospect of the successful prosecution of their life's work. He had fixed upon his beloved mount Zion as his last resting-place, and upon its southern slope had erected, in accordance with ancient royal usage, a magnificent mausoleum, which also served as the burial-place for most of his successors. His funeral obsequies were celebrated with the greatest pomp ever yet known in Israel, and his arms were preserved as sacred relics in the temple.[1] But the lapse of time only increased the reverence in which his memory was held in the national heart, until it finally culminated in a glowing desire to behold him once again upon the earth in human form, and to see the advent of a second 'David.'

---

[1] According to the casual remark 2 Kings xi. 10.

SECTION II.

The Splendour of the Monarchy; The Age of Solomon.

If we now take up again the continuous thread of the history at the point where we let it fall, it conducts us at once, in the life of the great King Solomon,[1] to one of its most intricate knots, which we must attempt rightly to understand and to disentangle, if we are to pass it and then to follow the altered direction of the history of this second period. We have seen what elevation and glory the people of Israel had attained when its great hero David expired. 'When a man rules over men justly and in the fear of God, it is as when, after long and dismal rain, the sun some morning rises the more cheerfully, and causes the grass to spring up more vigorously:' thus David had sung before he died,[2] in just retrospect over all the days he had passed through of Saul's reign and his own, as well as in tranquil hope for all the future; and this brightest day long seemed to the nation the high noon of its whole earthly history, and tempted forth into blossom everything for which the seed had been so richly scattered in the former period. Under the long reign of David's son, who, although very differently trained and situated, was really scarcely less great, the people maintains its already powerfully-awakened aspiration towards a still higher elevation, and by turning to new directions of activity and culture, acquires a multitude of possessions hitherto wanting, yet necessary to complete the finer half of a nation's life. But while all the best that was possible under the strong protection of human monarchy in the ancient people of God presses with the greatest speed and versatility towards its culmination, there is already germinating unobserved in the

---

[1] The LXX (according to the best editions and MSS.), spell the name quite correctly in all the books with an ô, Σαλωμών; so also Ecclus. xlvii. 13, 23 (but not so the Complut. Pol. in the preface); the pronunciation Σολομών, produced by shortening this long vowel, is first found in the Sibylline poet, iii. 214, in the N.T., in Josephus, in the later Greek translations and other later works. The Syrians and Arabs, however, have preserved the length of the vowel, but have transformed the name of the favourite king into a diminutive form, *Shelaemûn, Sulaimân.* On the other hand, in the feminine name Σαλωμή the long ô has been always retained.

[2] 2 Sam. xxiii. 3 sqq.

midst of this splendour that corruption which we shall see break forth openly at the conclusion of this great king's reign, and from which the succeeding ages of the monarchy in Israel could never entirely recover. Thus the strongest contrasts become here apparent; the highest development of national prosperity possible under the monarchy and Theocracy, and the beginning of a canker, which constantly grows, and ends by incurably corroding everything within its reach. Still, during the long days of Solomon, the star of Israel with its mighty aspirations rises yet higher, but only within the very same period to fall into a decline which nothing could arrest. And it is on this account that this period of forty years exactly marks the lofty centre of the second period of the ancient people, with its two directions of ascension and decadence, and is sharply enough distinguished alike from the unrestrained efforts of the earlier times and from the even deeper decline of the later. The origin of the two-fold tendency—at the first glance so hard to explain—of this elevated era, which determined the character of the four following centuries, is the enigma that lies before us for solution; and if an age like this, in which an entirely new and powerful tendency is germinating in secret, is in itself more difficult to comprehend, the difficulty is in this case rendered greater by a corresponding deficiency of adequate historical sources.

That our existing historical books describe Solomon's life at far less length than that of David, is owing certainly to the fact that the memory of his age, taken as a whole, did not preserve to posterity a picture of such pure delight as his father's. Originally, it is true, it was otherwise. The youth of Solomon, unlike that of David, fell in the most brilliant daylight of the history of the monarchy. The literature, which was then powerfully developing itself, early sought to embrace in their utmost variety all the circumstances of the life and government of this great monarch, as we may still recognise with sufficient clearness from some large fragments of such works. Such are indisputably to be found, on closer inspection, woven in with the existing account of Solomon in the Books of Kings. The earliest, which, according to all indications, were already composed within the first half of the reign of this king, appear to be the fragments of the Book of Origins relative to the temple,[1]

---

[1] According to i. p. 76, the description of Hiram's works in bronze for the furnishing of the temple, 1 Kings vii. 13-17, as also the fragment viii. 62-66, are to be derived from the Book of Origins. First, on account of their great resemblance to similar descriptions of the Book of Origins of the Mosaic sanctuary, alike generally

then scarcely completed, pieces with which this book probably concluded. From the annals of his government, which were certainly written soon after Solomon's death, is drawn the important survey of his household;[1] and perhaps to the last source is due the brief but precise description of his buildings,[2] although there are many clear marks that this last has not come into the present text without many *lacunæ*. Other important fragments have been preserved from the oldest Book of Kings, which had described with admirable minuteness the events of Solomon's history till his death, in the way in which its leading portions seemed to the author already conditioned by David's history.[3] Yet another narrative of Solomon's life must some time later have followed this. It was not quite so detailed as the former; it already took up a special and more lofty standpoint, from which it included and artificially arranged the three main stages of the history of the great monarch; yet it did not fail to narrate in due proportion and with most attractive circumstantiality the many remarkable occurrences of his reign. A good many fragments of it have been preserved,[4]

---

and in single passages, as ver. 14; cf. Ex. xxxi. 3. Next, because this description is very perceptibly distinguished in its style and colouring and in part in its contents, from the remaining descriptions of Solomon's buildings, vi. 2–7, xii. 48–51; an example of this is given below. Finally, because the present account from vii. 13 forwards, plainly takes up from a fresh MS. source the description of some of the articles belonging to the temple, after having conducted the thread of the narrative in quite a different direction by the description of the building of Solomon's palace, vii. 1–12. This interruption is in fact so plain and palpable, that even the LXX. have thrown the description of the building of Solomon's own house to the end of cap. vii.; just as they might have placed the piece still more correctly after cap. viii. The description of Solomon's house, vii. 1–12, which the Book of Origins could not in accordance with its design incorporate in itself, may have been composed like the similar one of the temple, cap. vi., some time after Solomon's death.

[1] Namely, the passages 1 Kings iv. 2–19, v. 2 [iv. 22] sq., 6–8 [iv. 26–28]; the remaining clauses from iv. 1, which are now woven into the others, may have been first arranged in this order by the last composer, while the former, by their contents and language, are closely connected with each other, and are sharply enough distinguished from these.

[2] But, in accordance with the brief remarks already made, only the passages vi. 2–10, 14—vii. 12, 48–51 are here meant: how incomplete these are in themselves will be further pointed out below.

[3] Vol. i. p. 149. According to 2 Sam. vii., cf. p. 131 sq., the passage 1 Kings v. 15–25 [v. 1–11], and, with this, the other, ix. 10–14, belong to this narrator, just as ix. 25–28, x. 28 sq., and the words xi. 11, 12, with the exception of the clause inserted by the last author וחקתי אשר צויתי עליך, by their contents and style, point to the same source.

[4] Especially the two passages which by all indications belong exactly to each other, 1 Kings iii. 5 (where the narrative appears quite broken off)–28, ix. 1–5, xi. 9; further, the passages viii. 24–26, x. 1–13, 14–27; cf. more on this below. Besides these there may be many other shorter passages from this work; to this must not be ascribed, on the contrary, by its language and manner (cf. i. p. 157, *note*), the fragment vi. 11–13. This last passage comes in now so very abruptly and so disturbs the connexion of the description of the building of the temple, that it is altogether omitted in Cod. Vat. of the LXX. But since the last author, even in this description of Solomon's buildings, arranges his materials somewhat loosely together, it cannot be maintained that these have not been here inserted by him.

and since they are interwoven with the other older accounts, just as we saw in the lives of his predecessors, they may be ascribed, as other points of resemblance are not wanting, to the author who is named[1] the second principal narrator of the history of the Kings.

But such ancient and circumstantial representations proved less and less pleasing to later writers; and if some aspects of the work of this extraordinary monarch remained always so remarkable that they could be better described in the exact words of the ancient sources, or specially presented in a fresh and circumstantial form, much else, on the other hand, fell into the background, while at the same time many a new glance was thrown over those periods. After the older Deuteronomist author had thus worked up Solomon's life for his own time, the second, coming after all the rest, put together from the various written sources that lay before him the present account of his life, with more or less abbreviations of its various parts, but with only few additions of his own.[2] In this last composition the single fragments, whether larger or smaller, of earlier works, are only loosely connected together, and frequently the last author apparently intends to conclude a subject, while he has still something or other to bring up about it subsequently; a practice which is certainly peculiar to this narrator whose method is one of selection, but is nowhere so constantly repeated as in this case. The very loose arrangement which thus arose, clearly became the occasion for the Chronicler[3] to re-arrange a great deal of it, though he himself does not strictly carry out his alterations,[4] and certainly, many transpositions of whole passages in the Septuagint[5] have no other origin than the attempt to introduce a more cohesive order into these fragments of narrative, although it cannot be said that by this process the proper arrangement has been everywhere restored. But few additions of importance for the ancient history are contained in the Chronicles.

Only a few more detailed narratives, accordingly, remain to us now, of that history of Solomon which exercised such decisive influence on the following centuries. Yet along with these are many compressed traditions and brief indications of important events. The difficulty of composing out of these materials a true picture of the whole of this long reign, is all the greater because our existing sources supply us with

---

[1] Vol. i. p. 150 sqq.
[2] Vol. i. p. 156 sqq.
[3] 2 Chron. i.–ix.
[4] Cf. 2 Chron. i. 14–17 with ix. 25–28.
[5] Cod. Vat.

For some accounts of Solomon outside the Bible, see below.

but few *data* of time. If, however, we put together, in as life-like a form as possible, all the surviving traditions of that glorious noon of Israel's whole history, and combine with them the traces of its events which are scattered in the poetical books (and of these last there are many more, when closely inspected, than would be conjectured on a superficial view), it will not be possible to remain entirely in doubt, at any rate, about the chief causes of the main tendency of that period, and consequently, of the entire history of the ancient people. And for this purpose, it is precisely about the beginning of the reign of this king, which, in his case, as in that of every other sovereign, conditions the whole subsequent course of his history, that the most detailed and trustworthy traditions have been preserved.

I. The Beginning of Solomon's Reign.

1. Solomon grew up in the last and more peaceful years of his father's reign, and, when he was called to the throne, was probably not more than twenty years of age.[1] At that primitive period, however, of the monarchy in Israel, the king's sons, as indeed the history of Absalom proved to us, were not generally shut out from free participation in public life, and the possible opportunities it offered for the cultivation of a firm and healthy disposition; and Solomon's first step towards sovereignty was destined to afford an immediate test, in more ways than one, of his capacity for it.

That the sovereignty should be carried on in David's line, could not be seriously doubtful after the complete revolution effected by him in the dominant opinion alike of the Prophets and of the entire people. A rule which, like David's, closes with increasing external splendour and internal prosperity, transmits its sacredness to the ruler's house, and thus preserves the blessing of its own uninterrupted continuance in the same line. But more precise legal prescriptions about the succession were then still wanting; and this gave rise, towards

---

[1] Cf. p. 160. That Solomon could not be much younger, follows also from 1 Kings xiv. 21, according to which his son Rehoboam, at the commencement of his reign, was forty-one years old. When, on the other hand, Josephus makes Solomon begin to reign as young as possible, viz., at fourteen years of age, this is plainly connected with his supposition of an eighty years' reign of this monarch; this doubling of the number forty, however, is explained ii. p. 371, and according to 1 Kings iii. 11–14, a remarkably long life was by no means among the blessings which antiquity regarded as divinely bestowed upon this monarch. Further, it was believed by many that, even in the fourth year of his reign, that is, at the beginning of the erection of the temple, he was only thirteen years old, and had altogether only lived to fifty-three; see Jalâl-eldîn's *Hist. of Jerus.* ed. Reynolds, p. 288.

the end of David's life, to a complication which might easily have become very injurious, had not one of the contending parties displayed incomparably more firmness than the other.

1) After Absalom's death, Adonijah,[1] the son of Haggith, was David's oldest surviving son. As he had been born towards the end of his father's reign in Hebron, he was now more than thirty-four years old. Judging from the reminiscences of him, he must have borne much resemblance to Absalom; he was of handsome figure, imperious and ambitious, yet mentally scarcely qualified to rule; his disposition was reserved, and he was, besides, afraid of open struggle. That he was no very capable ruler for a kingdom such as Israel then was, could not fail to be obvious to the more intelligent. Guided by Nathan, the greatest Prophet of the time, and Zadok, the honoured chief of the Priests of the house of Eleazar, this party cast its glance upon Solomon, the son of Bath-sheba, whose birth had taken place under strange circumstances.[2] David himself inclined to this side. He had (so it was asserted) assured Bath-sheba that her son Solomon should be his successor.[3] The early and public nomination of a successor, however, was not yet at that time among the royal customs of Israel; and David, accordingly, had made no sort of arrangements for the public recognition of Solomon as his successor. He had always been an indulgent father towards all his sons, and had consequently never said an angry word to Adonijah, now his eldest son, when the latter, with growing boldness, assumed new outward signs of royal state, such as horses and chariots, and fifty runners. Expectation and endeavour might, therefore, gather round Adonijah as well as Solomon; and while the two rivals with their partisans were in open opposition,[4] their claims would not certainly have been settled until after the death of the aged hero, had not Adonijah allowed himself to be carried away by his desires somewhat too soon. Whether he thought that David, in an advanced stage of disease, was too incompetent really to continue to reign, or to offer any opposition to a new king, or whether he could not

[1] 'Ορνίας, a name which, according to Joseph. Gen. *Hypomnest.* c. 63, is equivalent to it, has arisen merely out of a mistaken reading of the Hebrew. [2] P. 168.
[3] This must have been described by the older narrator in an earlier passage, but is now wanting.
[4] This follows clearly from 1 Kings i. 12, 21, ii. 22, as well as from the entire position of affairs; and, in order not to judge unfairly of Solomon and his party (as has been so often done in modern times, even at this day), it must be above all things carefully kept in mind that if Adonijah had triumphed, he would certainly have put Solomon and all his chief adherents to death. Much rather may it be said that Solomon's conduct was subsequently proportionately mild, and that he let the rest of his brothers live follows from Luke iii. 21.

any longer restrain his followers,—to be brief, he invited his adherents to a suitable spot, south-east of Jerusalem, where there were numerous springs,[1] and here solemn sacrifices were offered, and he caused himself to be proclaimed king. His party was large and full of courage. The aged Joab, who had lost none of his early rashness, had, like the High Priest Abiathar,[2] yielded to his solicitations, probably because he had received from Adonijah promise of future impunity for his former offences. All the other sons of the king, moreover, except Solomon, followed the call of the eldest; and Joab, as commander-in-chief, was accompanied by all the military officers of Judah[3] who were in the neighbourhood. Already, at the boisterous sacrificial feast, success seemed assured. But the important old regiment which was the nucleus of the army, the Gibborim, with their brave leader Benaiah, as well as the royal body-guard and probably the two still surviving brothers of David, remained on Solomon's side;[4] and aid still more valuable than even these warriors could render, was derived from the wisdom and swift determination of the great Prophet. At his instigation Bath-sheba first of all went into the sick king's chamber, entreating his assistance in placing her son upon the throne. After her the Prophet himself was admitted to audience. He did not go so far as to call upon the king for Adonijah's destruction, but simply wished to know whether he had concurred in Adonijah's plans. Thus driven to the necessity of decisive action, the feeble old hero felt all his power once more return. With swift determination, he summoned Solomon's mother before him, and, swearing by Him 'who had redeemed his soul out of all distress,' he announced to her his firm resolve to uphold her son. He then called in the three strong supporters

---

[1] 'The serpent-stone by the well,' 1 Kings i. 9, does not occur elsewhere, but this well must have lain on quite a different side of the town from the Gihon, where Solomon was to be anointed. We cannot, however, doubt, according to all indications, that the Gihon lay on the north side of the city (see below), the Rogel far to the south, for this latter once formed the boundary of the tribe of Benjamin towards Judah, and lay south of Gehinnom; Josh. xv. 7, xviii. 16. It corresponds also with the later so-called well of Job, or rather of Joab, who here as good as met his end. How it was still called after Joab in the Middle Ages may be learned now from Carmoly's *Itinéraires*, p. 442. That running water was needed for such a sacred ceremony is certain, just as in later ages these were favourite spots for the places of prayer (Proseuchæ); see *Jahrbb. der Bibl. Wiss.* p. 56 sq.

[2] P. 180.

[3] The indeterminate expression 'the men of Judah, David's servants,' ver. 9 comp. with ver. 33, ver. 47 with ver. 38, is further explained ver. 25; see p. 144 sq.

[4] The two men Shimei and Rei, who, ver. 8, are prominently named as important adherents of Solomon, were probably the two only surviving brothers of David; his six brothers are enumerated 1 Chron. ii. 13-15. שמעי may well be the same as the third, otherwise written שמעה, 2 Sam. xiii. 3, 32, 1 Chron. ii. 13, or שָׁמָּה, 1 Sam. xvi. 9, xvii. 13, and רֵעִי appears to coincide with the fifth, written in the Chronicles רַדַּי.

of Solomon—Zadok, Nathan, and Benaiah, and ordered them to conduct Solomon on the well-known royal mule, on which he himself had always ridden in public processions, down to the Gihon, which lay north of the town, where there were numerous springs. After Zadok and Nathan had anointed him and proclaimed him king amid the blast of trumpets, they were to escort him back into the palace, and solemnly place him on the royal throne, that everyone might see that Solomon would reign with the king's consent. As it turned out, the great majority of the people at once joined this procession with loud acclamation and joyous dance.[1] All the officers of the Gibborim and many other powerful personages attached to the court, hastened to offer to David their thanks and congratulations; and the aged king sank on his knees upon his couch, to thank his God for the happiness of being able with his own eyes to see the successor he had desired. Jonathan, the son of the High Priest Abiathar, who was among the conspirators, hurried off to carry this news to Adonijah and his friends; and as Adonijah at first thought this fine young Priest a messenger of joyous omen, the speedy disappointment of this hope was the more bitter; and all those who had engaged in the undertaking separated hastily and fled in terror.

This last public act of the dying king proved once more in the clearest manner how completely the whole people had accustomed itself readily to follow him. Whether in Solomon he had chosen the fittest of all his sons to reign over such a kingdom it was for the succeeding period to disclose; and Solomon must at once have had sufficient call to reveal the nature of his own character.

Deserted by his terrified adherents, Adonijah had fled in great alarm to the steps of the sacred altar in the house of Jahveh, and would not be torn from it even with violence, unless 'King' Solomon would agree on oath to spare his life. Solomon magnanimously promised not to injure a hair of his head if he would remain loyal for the future; if not, he must die. He accordingly quitted his consecrated place of refuge, did homage to the young king, and received orders from him to stay quietly at home. But after David's death the infatuated man was seized with a fresh longing. Knowing very well what great influence is customarily possessed by the queen-mother in

---

[1] For מְחַלְלִים בַּחֲלִלִים, ver. 40, should be read more correctly, according to the LXX, מְחֹלְלִים בִּחִילִים, because the artificial flute-playing which the former reading suggests could not be the action of the first moment, nor of the whole people, which the connexion, however, presupposes.

courts in which polygamy prevails, he entreated Bath-sheba, in the most submissive language, to grant him but one single favour and obtain for him from her son the possession of the concubine Abishag of Shunem, who had been given to David [1] in his last illness, but had not been used by him, ostensibly that he might have some consolation for the diversion of the sovereign power from himself, the elder son, to the divinely favoured Solomon. Too simple to perceive any mischief in such a request, the queen-mother conveyed it to her son. The latter, however, with instant penetration, immediately recognised what claims Adonijah and his party could and certainly would base on the possession of this last wife of the great monarch who was but just dead, since the possession of the woman must in itself be a matter of complete indifference to a man already somewhat advanced in years, like Adonijah; for in those periods it easily excited the belief that it was accompanied by a right of succession on the part of the possessor in the house of the deceased.[2] But Solomon himself had already founded a royal house, which was moreover the only one that had received the consent of David and the adhesion of the majority of the nobles, and above all of the Prophet Nathan, and he could not tolerate the attempt to establish a second alongside of it in Israel.[3] He swore, therefore, by the God who had hitherto strengthened him and had established his house, that Adonijah, after having so deceitfully broken his previous promise, and clearly revealed afresh his heart's desires, must at once die; and Benaiah executed the sentence of death. This proceeding involved no excessive or unnecessary severity. In such circumstances and at such a time every clear-sighted and resolute ruler was obliged to act in this way; as the artificial means which are resorted to in similar cases in the present day, e.g. imprisonment for life, were in that age still entirely unknown.

2) Whether the unfortunate Adonijah was led away to this last attempt by the special advice of his powerful friends Joab and Abiathar we are not informed; it is, however, clearly indicated,[4] and is in itself obvious, that they had kept themselves at a distance from Solomon, and had only waited for the first oppor-

---

[1] P. 196. [2] P. 115.

[3] This is the sense of the words 1 Kings ii. 24: 'As Jahveh liveth who hath established me and set me on the throne of David my father, and who hath made me an house, as He promised:' that this cannot mean the private establishment (harem) of a king, as in Ex. i. 21 the language applies by the connexion to private houses, is here self-evident, as in the similar cases, 2 Sam. vii. 11, 1 Sam. ii. 35; cf. also Ps. ci. 2, Is. vii. 2, 13.

[4] In the words 1 Kings ii. 22, and ver. 28, where, however, according to the LXX and Josephus, Ant. viii. 1. 24, as indeed the facts of the case demand, שלמה is to be read for אבשלום.

tunity to declare themselves publicly for Adonijah. Solomon was compelled, therefore, in their case also to punish any further attempt to create disturbance in the kingdom; and the Chief Priest Abiathar was commanded to withdraw to his patrimonial estate at Anathoth, north of Jerusalem; 'he was worthy of death, yet would he at that time spare him, because in former years he had ever faithfully served his father as Chief Priest, even in adversity.'[1]—Of the subsequent fortunes of this personage, who must have been at that time considerably above sixty years of age, we have no further particulars. If it be considered, however, that the narrator indicates clearly enough that it was only for this occasion that he was spared, and if it be further taken into account how the same narrator in another preparatory passage of still greater clearness and detail, lifts the veil from the approaching tragedy of the final ruin of the house of Eli,[2] it becomes evident that the blow which at this time fell upon this member of the house of Eli, who had been so long and so highly honoured, was only the beginning of a long series of terrible disasters for him and for his family. For the present, the High Priesthood which had been administered under David by Zadok from the one house and Abiathar from the other (the latter however with a slightly higher rank), was transferred solely to the former,[3] and all subsequent High Priests to the time of the Maccabees belong to his house. Whether it was that Abiathar could not brook his banishment from the capital, or from whatever other cause he may have given offence, it is at any rate evident that he and his house subsequently incurred with much greater severity the royal displeasure. Not only did he himself fall by the sword, but to those who looked back from the end of the reign of Solomon or of his successor, it seemed as though some ancient divine curse, resting on Eli's house, permitted none of its members to die in the tranquillity of age, and extirpated by the sword its last remnants, so that scarce one was saved, reserving even these only to supplicate the more prosperous house of Zadok for the alms of charity or else a scanty maintenance as Priests. Such was the fate in after times of the once powerful Priestly house of Eli.

---

[1] P. 91 sqq.
[2] 1 Sam. ii. 31-36, cf. vol. i. p. 144; ver. 33 is to be understood as follows: 'But every man (אִישׁ, according to *Lehrb.* § 278*b*) will I not remove for thee from my altar, in order not to darken thine eye, and grieve thine heart; but all the residue of thy house shall die by the sword of men (LXX).' The words play, therefore, on the ancient popular belief that the ancestor of the family had, even before his death, mourned over the complete ruin of his posterity; cf. i. p. 296.
[3] 1 Kings ii. 35, cf. iv. 2; 1 Chron. v. 34-41 [vi. 8-15]. The remark in 1 Chron. v. 36 [vi. 10] belongs properly to ver. 35 [vi. 9].

Joab, likewise, would certainly have then met with nothing worse than banishment from the capital, had not other and more weighty considerations attached themselves to his case. It was said that upon his dying bed David had recommended the successor he had already named not to let Joab's grey hair descend unscathed into the under world, because he had taken base revenge on the two great generals Abner and Amasa,[1] had shed the blood of war in the midst of peace, and had stained himself over and over with the blood of the noble, ' from the girdle about his loins to the latchet of the shoes upon his feet.' If, however, our present customs render the very notion of such a commission offensive to us, we must recollect that in that primitive age of the monarchy, the king possessed the power of protection which had formerly belonged to the sanctuary, so that everyone whom he had promised to spare, was secure of his life. But we must further remember that this right of asylum expired with the king's death, as it had formerly done at the end of the High Priest's life, and that consequently, if the king had for any reason pardoned a criminal, this personal forbearance extended only to the death of this individual king, and could in no way bind his successor. The actual undeniable guilt was regarded as still there in spite of a sovereign's temporary lenity, so that a new king was not necessarily held to any promise of indulgence made by his predecessor; nay, it was rather esteemed his duty at length to eradicate the uneradicated guilt, and free his royal house from the obligation of punishment.[2] As these considerations were not wanting in Solomon's case, he did not now feel bound to exercise any further mildness towards Joab, who, in fact, on the first report of Adonijah's fate, fled of his own accord to the altar. To this he clung when Benaiah came to carry out sentence of death upon him, and Benaiah had to send for further orders whether, in spite of his resistance, he should execute him on the spot. Solomon, however, determined even under these circumstances upon his death. He was accordingly slain by Benaiah, yet interred with full honours on his estate in the south-east of Judah (in the 'wilderness'); and his office of commander-in-chief was bestowed upon Benaiah. For Joab's posterity, however, this blow proved the first of a series of disasters, as in those ages the misfortune of the head was always dreaded as the precursor of that of the whole house, which in fact so often resulted from it; and long

---

[1] Pp. 117, 194.
[2] Cf. the *Alterthümer*, pp. 197, 425. The true import of this narrative is quite clear, especially from ii. 5 sq. 31–33. Only a superficial observer can here reproach Solomon with unnecessary cruelty.

EXECUTION OF JOAB AND SHIMEI.

afterwards it was told that the only reason why so many loathsome diseases, bloody deaths, and extremities of distress prevailed among his descendants, was because their ancestor Joab had in former days twice so deeply erred.[1]

David's royal prerogative of mercy had been extended to the Benjamite Shimei in the same way as to Joab:[2] and his treatment, also, was said to have been the subject of a dying charge committed by David to Solomon. Since, however, he had remained quiet during the change of sovereigns, Solomon only ordered him to stay where he was in Jerusalem; and solemnly swore that 'if he should pass over the brook Kedron (i.e. should go beyond the city bounds), his life would be forfeited.' To this requirement Shimei submitted; but when, three years after, two of his slaves (perhaps Philistines) ran away to the king of Gath,[3] he pursued them and brought them back from there. He may thus have broken his promise to the king unintentionally and inconsiderately, and certainly Solomon had not much cause to fear him as a relative of Saul and as a rival, since the weakness of the party of the house of Saul had been sufficiently proved at the rising of Absalom. But in this fatal forgetfulness which had befallen the aged arch-traitor against David, there was then discerned with certainty a divine token that the ancient guilt still clung freshly to him, and he must suffer the penalty, for otherwise he would not have acted thus madly as if God had forsaken him. Solomon accordingly had him executed, too, plainly not from desire of revenge or any other passion, but in pursuance of the belief which then generally prevailed, as though a divine decree demanded that even the very last should fall who had once deeply transgressed against David. This proves at the same time what high sanctity was then attached to David's memory.

Such firmness of resolution and such vigour of action but few had expected beforehand from the young prince. If, in the empires of those days, immediate execution of justice which had the sanction of custom, and severe treatment of every offence against royal sanctity were fundamental conditions of all successful action on the part of the king;[4] and if every new government was obliged to deal with such efforts with increasing rigour as it acquired more firmness and wisdom, or else to recover at the

---

[1] This follows from 2 Sam. iii. 28 sq.; cf. p. 118.
[2] P. 190 sq.
[3] This king is called (1 Kings ii. 39) son of Maachah. Maachah, however, being a common name, is probably only a confusion with מָעוֹךְ, 1 Sam. xxvii. 2; and either that old friend of David was still living, which is not quite inconceivable, or it was a grandson of similar name.
[4] For the further elucidation of this period much help is afforded by proverbs so clearly belonging to it as Prov. xx. 8, 26, xvi. 14, xvii. 11, xix. 11, xx. 2.

proper season much that had been in this aspect neglected before, it is easy to estimate what a deep impression these first acts of the young king must have produced upon the whole people.[1] David's throne must have appeared not overturned, but endowed with fresh youth and new energy of existence. And as the new prince began his reign with judgments and punishments quite in the spirit of his great sire, and thus enjoyed the grand prerogative of inheriting that reverence on the part of his subjects for the royal sanctity which his father had so firmly established, without being bound to the imperfections which had been gaining ground in the previous reign,—he felt himself under just as sacred an obligation to continue his father's marks of favour and beneficence towards such as had at any time rendered him distinguished services. Accordingly he continued to maintain at his court Chimham and the other descendants of Barzillai the Gileadite[2] at his own cost, and granted them other significant favours, so that they became long after a celebrated family, and again contributed much to the prosperity of the country.[3]

Such is our knowledge of the beginning of this reign, derived from the words of the first narrator, which have been fortunately preserved to us; and we may safely infer from them how Solomon strengthened his kingdom from within, and what principles he followed in reference to the people of Israel itself. That the new king was then recognised by all the tribes of Israel with a solemn ceremony at which he swore to maintain intact the laws of the kingdom as his father had done, is in itself quite probable, although no definite statement to that effect has been transmitted to us.

2. Of the mutual relations between the young king and the numerous foreign nations subdued by David, the existing historical narratives give but a few brief indications. That so many strong warlike peoples, after a subjugation of only a few decades, should have at once done homage to the new monarch without any resistance, a consideration of all the circumstances renders quite improbable. Others besides the son of the king

---

[1] Hence the conception of the royal wisdom of Solomon enters quite involuntarily, but also very justly, into the representation of those events, 1 Kings ii. 5, 9.

[2] P. 191 sq.

[3] This is certainly only briefly indicated 1 Kings ii. 7; but the narrator must have been intending to detail more fully in some later passage, now lost to us, what is here intimated beforehand. Since the Chimham named in Jer. xli. 47 seems, by the rarity of this name, to be the same, it appears that through the establishment of a Caravanserai he had rendered not unimportant services to the country; and such great undertakings for the promotion of commerce are most easily conceived to have arisen in Solomon's age. Moreover, from Ezra ii. 30, it is clear how much this family continued to be respected through long ages.

of Edom, who had taken refuge in Egypt, may have thought that now, after the fall of the dreaded David, the irresistible Joab, and so many others of those valiant conquerors, the right moment must be arrived for throwing off the yoke of Israel.[1]

The following account includes all the details which we now possess of the efforts of the separate nations in this direction.

1) When Edom[2] was subdued by David's troops after an exceedingly bloody struggle, one of the youngest members of the ruling house, Hadad, probably the eldest grandson of the last king, succeeded in escaping from the country. Some of the most devoted of his father's servants had first of all brought him down south-east to the free commercial town of Midian on the gulf of Elath,[3] and then crossing the sea to the peninsula of Sinai, had made their way by desert-tracks to Paran[4] and had there been so fortunate as to find some trusty guides, who conducted them to Egypt. Since Egypt had not yet formed any alliance with Israel, the Egyptian monarch received the young fugitive favourably, bestowed on him a house for his own, with an annuity and estates, and subsequently even gave him in marriage the sister of his own first consort Tahpanes. This was clearly with the intention of being able to avail himself of his aid in the future against the powerful aspirations of the kingdom of Israel, and is quite in accord with another tradition already alluded to.[5] This exalted lady bore him a son Genubath, who was brought up at the Egyptian court quite like one of the royal princes, and who must subsequently have played in Asia a not unimportant part, or otherwise he would not have been mentioned. On hearing of the change of sovereigns in Israel and the death of Joab, Hadad demanded his dismissal from Pharaoh, to return to his native land. But the feeling towards the kings of Israel had already essentially altered, so that (as will be immediately explained) the friendship of these monarchs had now become rather an object of desire. The Idumean prince, accordingly, received an evasive answer, but, like a true, intractable Edomite, would not suffer that to withhold him. He fled secretly to the mountains of his fathers, was there recognised as king by many of his countrymen, and, though never entirely victorious, he yet occasioned Solomon many embarrassments in a country which from its many mountain-summits and caves was always difficult to subdue completely, and the inhabitants of which had perhaps by that time somewhat recovered from the bloody defeats they had sustained under Joab.[6]

[1] 1 Kings xi. 21 sq. [2] P. 156 sq. [4] Vol. ii. pp. 189, 194. [5] P. 142.
[3] Vol. ii. p. 335. [6] 1 Kings xi. 14-22, cf. ver. 25, and

2) This revolt in the far south certainly began (according to this account) shortly after the accession of Solomon. At the same time a still more violent rising must have taken place in the extreme north-east. While David was still on the throne, an Aramean, by name Rezon,[1] had come forward in that quarter as leader, had broken loose from the king of Zobah whom David had conquered, and with a body of troops, collected from the forces which had been dispersed in all directions after the dissolution of the kingdom of Zobah, had roamed as a freebooter through the deserts. When Solomon, however, assumed power, Rezon marched with gathering hosts to Damascus itself, occupied it, and was proclaimed king there. At any rate he cannot have maintained himself with his troops very long undisturbed, as we see Solomon in the middle of his reign occupying many other distant countries north and east of Damascus; but that for a long period he caused him many embarrassments is expressly asserted.[2]

3) Lastly, we still see clearly that in the west, also, soon after Solomon's accession, considerable disturbances arose. The little kingdom of Gezer (or Geshur) between the territories of Israel and those of the Philistines, which had certainly been long dependent on its more powerful neighbours, but had still preserved a certain independence, was in full insurrection against Israel, supported probably by the Philistines, who, when the other enemies of Israel were astir, would not have remained quiet.[3] The Phœnicians certainly, long since devoted only to the sea and to peaceful commerce, and completely separated from their ancient brethren, remained tranquil; but the rest of the Canaanites, headed by the little kingdom of Gezer, which

---

the remarks vol. i. p. 76 sq. This passage is evidently incomplete at ver. 22, and the LXX have some sentences more which would entirely suit here, although the last appear in the 25th verse of the masoretic text; and certainly it is better to refer these to Hadad and read אָדָם for אֲרָם; 'but as for the mischief that Hadad did (*Lehrb.* pp. 683 sq., 737, *note*) he abhorred Israel and reigned over Edom;' then all that is wanting in the masoretic text after ver. 22 is that he secretly escaped. The LXX put Ἀδέρ for Hadad, since the copyists preferred making of this name a proper Hebrew word; the same change is found Gen. xxxvi. 39 in the MS.; cf., also, p. 152, *note* 3. The LXX call the queen Θεκεμίνα. Josephus, *Ant.* viii. 7. 6, only places the events 1 Kings xi. 14-25 in the last period of Solomon's reign, because they are now narrated after xi. 11-13; but this arrangement proceeds only from the last author.

[1] A genuine Aramean name, corresponding to that of the later Damascene king Rezin, Is. vii. 1 sqq. The LXX spell it Ἐσρώμ, at least in Cod. Vat. ver. 14; but Cod. Alex. has Ῥασώμ; for further remarks see below.

[2] 1 Kings xi. 23-25; cf., however, the remarks already made on ver. 25. The words are then, at any rate, intelligible in themselves, although we must lament their great brevity. That Rezon's revolt against Solomon began before the second half of the latter's reign, is clear from the fact that he was at least from twenty to thirty years older than Solomon.

[3] 1 Kings ix. 16 sqq.; comp. with ii. p. 328 sq. and further remarks below.

had with difficulty maintained itself in the south on their ancient power, and by Hamath in the north, appear to have attempted at this period to make a last combined effort to defend themselves against Israel: a fact which explains how under Solomon the last remnants of their ancient independence were taken from them, and how from that time they might sink into a degradation completely outside the pale of the law.

From these traces we cannot doubt that the nations conquered by David combined either to revolt, or to threaten revolt against the new and untried king, as soon as they heard of the death of David and Joab. We do not need to gather this historical truth only from the second Psalm, although, since we cannot refer it to any other king than Solomon, this poem would in itself afford sufficiently clear evidence of the fact; it stands firm independently.

A second severe trial was thus imposed on the young king at the very threshold of that exalted position which he was to occupy so long. But if only the lofty spirit grew young again in him with which David had felt himself true king in the community of Jahveh, he could not fail to find in it the safest inward help and power. The feeling by which David had become the mighty victor over so many nations was not that of an ordinary warrior and conqueror, who seeks power and honour only for himself and his house, or at most for his people. The true Mosaic feeling worked powerfully in him that Israel should not find its aim in itself, but in everything should serve the True above it. And in maintaining the paramount ascendency of this over every other object in the king of Israel, he had found it the source of a royal consciousness infinitely purer and stronger than that of ordinary kings; for the human king is then only the mightiest tool of a necessary divine purpose, and he can always think and act in this wonderfully elevating trust. With a frame of mind thus truly royal, inspired by the solemn anointing and encouragement of so great a Prophet as Nathan, and elevated in spirit by the lofty position which a king of Israel then assumed among the nations of the earth, Solomon could encounter the threatening storm of the revolt of many subjugated nations with that divine courage and that admonition sprung from prophetic trust, to which the second Psalm gives utterance.[1] A more expressive monument of the elevation of that period and of the wonderful firmness of spirit of

---

[1] Cf. further the *Dichter des A. B.*, vol. ii. (2nd edition) pp. 61–66. How this Psalm may have been understood Messianically in far later times, will be mentioned below.

the new ruler, it is not possible to conceive; and we may well feel that if the young king looked the evil in the face with such purely divine confidence, one of the main weapons of his threatening foes was already torn from them.

Yet foreign affairs, too, seemed to promise well. The only kingdom which, under the circumstances, might, in alliance with the discontented nations, have become dangerous to the powerfully aspiring monarchy in Israel, was Egypt; and Egypt was much more inclined to friendship with the royal house of Israel. Egypt was then ruled by the twenty-first dynasty, which had its seat in the extreme north of the country at Tanis, and could not fail from there carefully to survey the international relations of the countries as far as the Euphrates. Since the days of Moses the feeling of Egypt towards Israel may well have undergone great alteration through the lapse of time and the change of its ruling houses; while Israel, in its final position of dominion over many nations, necessarily entered into new relations even with distant peoples. What more pressing considerations moved the reigning monarch of Egypt to seek the friendship of Israel, we do not certainly know. Meanwhile the accession of Solomon falls in the thirty-fifth year of the reign of the last king of the Tanitic house, whom Manetho calls Psusennes,[1] and it may well be conjectured that that dynasty had already, during the whole reign of this, its last king, become so weak that it was glad to seek the friendship of a great foreign power. But to no nation in anterior Asia would Egypt then more naturally direct its attention than to Israel, which was at that time aspiring to a really imperial supremacy. And it is quite probable, although we have now no evidence of it, that after David's great conquests over the surrounding nations, Egypt had already sought to cement a closer alliance with Israel, in whose dominion, after the Philistines had lost their power, it saw the nearest check upon its own. Immediately after David's death, the Egyptian king refuses[2] to the Idumean prince at his court all cooperation against Israel, and will not so much as let him quit the country at will; which would have been impossible had he not already resolved to make a firm stand in favour of the royal house in Israel. We even see him at once in full activity come to Solomon's aid. He espouses him to his daughter, and assists him to put down the rebels in the south-west. With an Egyptian army, which evidently

---

[1] Cf. Bunsen's *Egypt*, vol. iii. p. 120 sq. with the original authorities at the end. Unfortunately in 1 Kings xi. the name of a reigning Egyptian queen is mentioned but not that of the king.
[2] P. 217.

advanced by sea and landed at Joppa, he reduced and set on fire the fortified town of Gezer, treated its Canaanitish inhabitants with the severity of a conqueror's rights, and then bestowed the territory of this city upon his daughter as a dowry.[1] This Egyptian princess, before Solomon could erect for her a more fitting residence, had to take up her abode in the ancient chambers of the palace in the city of David upon Mount Zion.[2] This, as well as every remaining indication, proves clearly enough that the new event of a matrimonial alliance with Egypt falls in the beginning of Solomon's reign.

Against the northern rebels, however, Solomon marched in person, and conquered Hamath.[3] This originally Canaanitish kingdom had attempted under David[4] to free itself from its Aramean enemies, and through judicious behaviour had been able still to maintain a sort of independence. But now it appears to have been involved in the revolt of the southern Canaanites and of Rezon against Israel,[5] and was incorporated in the kingdom of Israel. The disturbances of the nations were everywhere composed, and although the fire of rebellion still gleamed in the ashes only to break out again at a more opportune time, yet in general the entire Davidic empire, in some places even extended, was restored to the sway of the great son of David. From the Euphrates to the Egyptian border, from Thapsacus on the Northern Euphrates, where powerful commercial caravans crossed the river, to Gaza close to Egypt, with an equally flourishing trade, the whole country belonged to Israel.[6] And assuredly this speedy result was brought about not only by the firmness of disposition which was soon observed in the new king, but also by the dread of the name of the scarce departed hero, who might almost be believed to have become once more alive in his son.

3. The young king, in short, thus became, alike from within and from without, master of all the difficulties of his situation: and the question arose in what direction he would now develop his assured dominion. A new direction would in any case have to be struck out, since the most pressing want which had evoked the establishment of a monarchy in Israel had been

---

[1] 1 Kings ix. 16 sq., cf. above, p. 218, a detached but very important statement.

[2] 1 Kings iii. 1, ix. 24. The feeling to which the Chronicler (2 Chron. viii. 11) refers the later removal of the Egyptian princess to another palace is quite foreign to the spirit of antiquity.

[3] 2 Chron. viii. 3 sq., a statement which has only been preserved here, but must be quite historically true; it is confirmed also by 2 Kings xiv. 28.

[4] P. 156. [5] P. 218.

[6] Only the last composer of the Book of Kings, it is true, expresses himself thus, 1 Kings v. 1, 4 [iv. 21, 24]. The fact itself, however, generally understood, is correct; cf. also passages like viii. 65 Gen. xv. 18-21, Ps. lxxii. 8.

satisfied by David. David took up the work which Saul's royal house had let fall before its completion,—the deliverance of Israel from the supremacy of foreign powers, and its training in unity and courage to follow the true national aim. But David completed also the next task of any monarchy in Israel, as is proved by the proportionately great ease with which Solomon maintains the inheritance of his father in spite of some great momentary dangers. Henceforth, therefore, the monarchy in Israel was compelled to strike out a new direction, inasmuch as, after surmounting the difficulties of its first problem, it stood already essentially on a higher elevation, and found everything prepared for entering on a fresh path.

But if everything was then pressing forwards in a new direction, it was in Solomon that the right king had arrived to guide the course of events as skilfully and as prosperously as possible. Brought up in the full splendour of the latter days of David, and thus accustomed to the real elevation and unity of a truly royal career; distinguished from his birth by great mental gifts; keen of insight as well as of poetic disposition; swift to resolve, yet possessed of artistic sensibilities; enjoying the pomp of royalty and all the arts of peace, while at the same time he took an active part in increasing in every way the prosperity and power of the kingdom; in his maturity full of reverence for the sanctity embodied in Israel, although certainly without his father's deeper experiences of life;—he was in almost every respect the right instrument to conduct the monarchy in a new direction, and to supply what had not yet been attempted under David.

It was open to him to pursue further the military career, and to consummate the universal dominion for which David had laid a firm foundation. This would have been somewhat of a novelty, since David had waged only defensive wars; and pretexts for wars of attack would have been then much easier to find in Israel than they were for that miserable Christian Louis XIV. But the moderation of the true religion of Jahveh, as it was represented under David by great Prophets, had long since offered a sufficiently forcible opposition to such a beginning,[1] and under those Prophets and other powerful personages who promoted Solomon's accession, this tendency had become dominant over every other,[2] so that there was the less opportunity for the young king to devote himself to it.[3]

It remained, therefore, the better task of the new reign to

---

[1] P. 160 sqq. [2] P. 209 sqq.
[3] See further the essay 'Ueber die Wendung aller Geschichte Israel's in ihrer hohen Mitte,' *Jahrbb. der Bibl. Wiss.* p. 29 sq.

make wise use of the lasting peace which had been won through great victories, and as there is every appearance that this had already been the sole object of David during the last more peaceful years of his reign, Solomon applied himself to it with confidence.[1] Here was almost boundless room to recover what had hitherto either never been attempted or left entirely imperfect in Israel. And while the young king, after the first establishment of his power, unfolded in this direction all his activity and strength, and by his own creative fancy and energy as well as by his own lofty example advanced before his people in all the arts of peace, there was developed at the same time a prosperity shared alike by the monarchy and by all classes of the people in Israel, which had never been possible before and could never again return.

But in the midst of the great changes involved in this development, a new danger lay concealed. Continous war, had it become the business of life for the people in their aspirations after imperial dominion, would have constantly tended to drive to the outside the fermenting elements of popular power. Peace, on the other hand, were it elevated into the main principle of this powerful kingdom, might develop with greater purity all its different aspirations, yet in the very process of doing so might urge them the more sharply against one another; so that the contradictions which lay still unreconciled in the entire mass, would step forth the more openly, and might break out into a struggle previously unknown. A long prosperous peace after great national victories, a period like that in the Roman empire under Augustus or under the Antonines, in Germany since 1763 or again since 1815, invariably acts as a test whether such a people can maintain itself at the elevation it has once attained or not; and that Israel was not then capable of this is already proved clearly enough by certain indications towards the end of Solomon's reign. For above all, it would inevitably lead the new king of Israel into a severe temptation. Through the arts of peace Egyptian monarchs, too, had often sought renown and honour, and the reigning king in Egypt, who allied himself with Solomon by his daughter's marriage, ruled in this spirit. But do not they, too, conceal, as soon as they are pursued one-sidedly, a crowd of the most dangerous seductions, which act first of all on the king himself, who is the immediate centre of all the splendour and charm of such periods, so long as nothing

---

[1] But this is by no means the reason why their king first received the name of Solomon, i.e. Peaceful, since the allusion 1 Chron. xxii. 9 depends only on the free representation of the Chronicler; cf. p. 168.

else than the example of peaceful Egyptian monarchs lies historically before his eyes?—But we will consider first that side which in this long era of peace displayed itself earliest and with most brilliancy, the organisation and greatness of his government.

II. The Organisation and Greatness of Solomon's Government.

The forty years of Solomon's reign stand out unique as the period of most tranquil and powerful development of all the arts of peace, in the long history of Israel. The destiny of that nation not only placed it in opposition to the aspirations of every other nation of antiquity, but obliged it to sustain an almost uninterrupted struggle with them, and caused it, while called upon to solve one of the loftiest problems of the human mind, to suffer severely from violent internal disputes. This period of Israel's greatest power externally witnesses the fruit of David's labours; and for a considerable time almost all inward struggles are silent, and the speedy development of all the arts of peace is rendered possible. It seems as if this history were intended in the tranquil elevation of its brilliant noon to teach us under what conditions the arts of peace may be successfully unfolded, and how they early rose in Israel to a position of eminence.

It is indeed surprising to observe what rapid progress was made in Israel in the cultivation of the arts at a period when, in Europe, the possibility of their development was still far distant. The first condition needful to enable them to flourish with vigour and stability is in all cases (and on this too great a stress cannot be laid) a national power which rests outwardly on firm foundations, which permits activity of mind to exercise itself at once undisturbed and unrestrained in such aspirations as are concerned with what are or seem to be the most urgent wants of life, and seeks in this a source of pride and emulation in which the rough soldier finds only what is unnecessary and unworthy of honour. This first condition existed at that time in Israel. But that it might not exist without result much besides was indispensable. It needed the rule of a religion which should at every moment remind man of the divine claim standing over him, and thus impel him rather to inward composure than to wild unrest. It needed, further, the seeds of love for the peaceful improvement of the fertile soil, as well as for the general spread of culture and skill, which had been long ago introduced into Israel, and had been most powerfully promoted by the labours of such creative minds as Samuel and David.[1] It needed, again, the proximity of nations who had already in earlier ages acquired a still higher familiarity with the arts of peace, like the Egyptians, and still more the Phœnicians, the latter of whom were induced by their own advantage to promote culture and arts of every kind in Israel, and who during the last centuries had been continually attaching themselves more and more closely to Israel. The influence of Egyptian civilisation does not appear to have been equally great, for, in spite of Solomon's matrimonial alliance with Pharaoh, no definite trace of it is to be found.[2] And it needed, lastly, the prosperity which accrued to the people from the circumstance that David was succeeded by a monarch who was no less great, who had the wisdom to enter entirely into the real needs and the better aspirations of the age, and who, by the splendour of his own genius, was capable of promoting them.

When, however, a nation devotes itself at such an opportune season, in alliance with its sovereign, to the arts of peace, the long-existing elements of activity in the arts spread themselves in every direction. But the result can only be injurious if, at those rare times when a nation is awakened to the full sense of its powers, an injudicious compulsion and control should promote some arts, but restrain others no less necessary, and thereby succeed only in disturbing the cheerful development of the whole higher life. Under Solomon, who served to posterity as the pattern of a wise king,[3] we observe the higher art of life unfolding itself freely in every possible direction. It does not proceed one-sidedly merely from the sovereign, although from his natural disposition he has the greatest taste for the arts, but the entire nation participates in it also, so far as the age permits. Moreover it displays itself not only in splendid buildings, it seeks also to extend the welfare of the whole people, and in those spheres where it must be freest, because it there becomes most delicate and spiritual, it meets with no unintelligent restraint. Let us observe this more closely in detail, as we may deduce it from our historical memorials.

[1] Cf. vol. ii. p. 353 sq., 423 sq., and above, p. 134.
[2] What Eupolemus (Euseb. *Præp. Ev.* ix. 30) or Al. Polyhistor (Clem. Al. *Strom.* i. 21) says of the assistance of an Egyptian king Vaphrés in the building of the temple, supported by allegation of the letters exchanged between the two kings, is plainly in imitation of 1 Kings v. 16 [2] sq., and may be derived from an Apokryphon. Not much significance is to be attached to a slight similarity between the plan of Solomon's great buildings and Egyptian temples and palaces, since it appears elsewhere in high antiquity.
[3] See p. 215.

1. *The Sacred and Royal Buildings.*

1) In the case of the Egyptians and other ancient nations we are able to recognise their modes of paying honour to their deities, and of ordinary life, almost solely from their buildings, which have defied all the devastations of time; but the buildings erected in the era of Solomon possess, it must be admitted, no such high significance for the history of Israel, a nation which was destined to immortalise itself among mankind by far other monuments. Nevertheless they not only afford speaking witness of the lofty power to which Israel had then risen, but they exercise so much influence on the course of this history that we must consider them here more closely.

a.) It had been a firm determination of David in the last years of his career,[1] to erect at Jerusalem a house for Jahveh, the exalted God and proper Lord of the realm, which should be suitable to the new splendour of the kingdom. And as he had employed Tyrian artists for all his magnificent erections, Solomon followed his example, and very early in his reign applied to the Tyrian king Hiram[2] for the aid of skilled Sidonian artists of various kinds, for the execution of all the necessary works.[3] This Tyrian king was then, at least as Josephus[4] declares, in the eleventh year of his reign. He had been already on terms of friendship with David, and now readily acceded to Solomon's wish. Sidonian artists mixed with those of Israel, since Israel during the last century of war had remained far behind the Tyrians in the higher arts. Besides them, however, there came as specially superior, almost as scientific architects, Phœnicians from their city of Gebal—or in its Greek form Byblos—so celebrated for its science.[5] The

---

[1] Pp. 129-133.

[2] This name was originally pronounced Hirom or Hurom, as its written form still shows, 1 Kings v. 24 [10], 32 [18], vii. 40, and that in the first syllable there was, according to my *Lehrb.* § 163c, originally an *u* is proved by the spelling Χιράμ and Χειράμ in the LXX, Εἴραμος in Josephus, with Huram in the Chronicles; it has got corrupted into Σουρών in Eus. *Præp. Ev.* ix. 30 sqq., and, stranger still, into *Hyperon*, in Clem. Al. *Strom.* i. 21. The Phœnician name Σιρῶμος in Herod. v. 104, vii. 98 certainly proves how easily *s* and *h* were exchanged at the beginning of a word.

[3] The correspondence between the two kings is given, 1 Kings v. 16-23 [2-9], entirely in the language of the first person, as history writers, universally, easily complete the proper form. Josephus, *Ant.* viii. 2. 8, asserts very earnestly that these letters were to be found in his time with precisely the same tenor in the Tyrian public libraries; but, unfortunately, we have no more precise knowledge of his proofs of it: the letters, as he gives them, are only free reproductions of the Hebrew.

[4] *Ant.* viii. 3. 1. According to 2 Sam. v. 11, he might seem to have been reigning already at the time when David built his palace in Jerusalem (which certainly took place soon after the conquest) and to have helped David in its erection; this is indeed assumed 2 Chron. ii. 3, and Jos. *Ant.* vii. 3. 2 does not definitely distinguish two Hirams. But if the mention of the eleventh year of the thirty-four years' reign of the Hiram who for the most part lived in Solomon's era, is correct (Jos. *Ant.* viii. 5. 3, *Contr. Ap.* i. 18, according to Menander and Dios), the other Hiram must have been his grandfather. Hiram's father is named by Josephus from the oldest sources, Abibal.

[5] The term *Giblites*, so far as they are mentioned 1 Kings v. 32 [18], must have

Tyrian king had already himself erected in his native city several celebrated buildings:[1] and the two sovereigns appear almost to have rivalled one another alike in wise proverbs (of which more below), and in splendid edifices. Much of the proper Tyrian architecture was unquestionably transplanted in consequence to Jerusalem, as the few traces of Phœnician style still known to us attest. For the metal work an artist was obtained who was descended on one side from Israel, though from his Phœnician father he derived his regular Phœnician name Hiram—like that of the reigning Tyrian king. His mother, however, was a widow of the tribe of Naphtali on the Sidonian borders: he obeyed, therefore, the more readily, the summons of Solomon.[2]

That the Sidonian artists, however, could only give free play to their peculiar art so far as the Jahveh religion permitted it, was the natural result of the position of this religion at that era. Yet it seems as if later writers had felt the need of making this truth as prominent as possible; for the Chronicler, venturing here on a freer representation, relates how David handed over to his beloved but still too youthful son Solomon the design for the erection of the temple, drawn by the hand of God Himself, with all its parts, furniture, and Priestly ordinances, with the commission to execute everything according to this divine plan.[3] For it was not Solomon but David alone who was generally regarded at the time of the Chronicler as the great and noble originator of all the sacred regulations in Jerusalem; as though even the first works of Solomon had only been executed in exact accordance with his father's design, and thus what the Book of Origins described as having taken place first of all in the Mosaic sanctuary[4] might seem to have been similarly repeated in the

some such meaning, with which also Ezekiel xxvii. 9 agrees. Moreover it appears now more and more clearly, that much as the Canaanitish- (or Phœnician-) Hebrew style may have borrowed from the Egyptian as the earlier developed, it yet possessed very much that was peculiar; cf. the *Jahrbb. der Bibl. Wiss.* x. p. 269 sqq., *Gött. Gel. Anz.* 1864, p. 1783 sq.

[1] According to the exact Phœnician accounts of Menander and Dios in Jos. *Ant.* viii. 5. 3, *Contr. Ap.* i. 18.

[2] 1 Kings vii. 13 sqq. from the Book of Origins. That the later Jews took offence at the name and descent of the man who made the vessels of the sanctuary, we see from Eupolemus, in Eus. *Præp. Ev.* ix. 34 (cf. Jos. *Ant.* viii. 3. 4) where he is reckoned in the family of David; besides, in 2 Chron. ii. 14 the tribe of Dan is put for Naphtali. Yet the old Chronicler (2 Chron. ii. 14, iv. 16) calls him *father*, i.e. master, workmaster of king Hiram as also of Solomon. On the other hand, while according to the old account, he understood nothing but metal work, the Chronicles make him acquainted with all possible arts. In giving him the surname Abiv or Abif, later writers have misunderstood 2 Chron. iv. 16; the name 'Εχίας in Jos. Gen. *Hypomn.* c. 63 is only a corruption of 'Εβίας.

[3] 1 Chron. xxviii. 11–19; ver. 19 is to be read עָלָיו הִסְגִּיר עַל הַהַשְׂכִּיל אֲשֶׁר לוֹ instead of עָלַי הִשְׂכִּיל כֹּל לְמֵךְ as the sense shows (comp. with the reading of the LXX). The similarity of הַסְגִּיר and הִשְׂכִּיל may have misled the transcriber.

[4] Vol. i. p. 87.

Solomonic through the instrumentality of David. As in all such supernatural representations, only one side of the great event is brought prominently forward; it is not without its truth, but may easily lead anyone entirely astray who ignores the remaining historical truths by its side.

In considering the external resources which were at Solomon's command for the execution of his undertaking, the prior question arises how much he may have already received from his father. That David had accumulated very large treasures by his great victories and the tranquillity of the concluding years of his reign, and had destined much of these for the erection of the temple which he had already resolved upon, is quite credible, although the older of the accounts of his reign now preserved to us are entirely silent on the subject. At his funeral, moreover, there were doubtless immense sums expended, in accordance with the custom of antiquity, and yet we should know nothing of it, had not an account of it been preserved in Josephus, which, in spite of its late composition, contains nothing improbable.[1] The Chronicles, however, supply more particulars about the treasures destined by David for the future temple. Immediately after the great plague, David (it is related) disclosed to his son how he had made every preparation for the erection of the temple which was to be begun after his death, had engaged stone-masons and artificers of every kind, and had collected 100,000 talents of gold,[2] 1,000,000 talents of silver, as well as an immense quantity of bronze, iron, costly wood, precious stones and marbles.[3] He had then shortly before his death proceeded to summon all the nobles and officers of every class from the whole of Israel, together with Solomon, to a solemn diet, and had made known to them how, besides all the royal preparations and the divine design of all the sacred buildings and ordinances which he then handed over to Solomon, he further spontaneously, and from pure love for the cause, devoted to the erection of the temple what might be called a private fortune of 3,000 talents of the best gold, and 7,000 talents of the finest silver. He then

---

[1] The High Priest Hyrcanus opened the tomb of David, and took from one of its chambers three thousand talents. Similarly later, Herod took large treasures from another, Jos. *Ant.* vii. 15. 3; cf. xiii. 8. 4, xvi. 7. 1. There is no doubt that the tomb of David could still be distinguished at those periods (Acts ii. 29), and certainly no king of Jerusalem, not even Solomon (see below), was buried with such treasures as David. The grave of David was (1 Kings ii. 10, Neh. iii. 16) on Zion; cf. Williams, *The Holy City*, London, 1845, pp. 415-20.

[2] A talent of silver is about 375*l.*, from which the proportion of a golden one may be reckoned. The shekel was about 1*s.* 8*d.*, but varied in value very much at different periods.

[3] 1 Chron. xxii. 2-19, cf. especially ver. 14 with the further explanation xxix. 2. The Chronicler begins from 1 Chron. xxii. 2 to describe the ordinances of David which were to serve as a pattern for the future.

called upon all assembled to make similar donations, upon which they also devoted to the same object 5,000 talents of gold, 10,000 (gold-) drachmas, 10,000 talents of silver, 18,000 talents of bronze, and 100,000 talents of iron, as well as precious stones.[1] It is certainly unmistakably clear that the whole of this representation is connected with the fundamental conception of the Chronicler already mentioned, that it was rather David than Solomon who had been the true spiritual founder of all the sacred buildings and ordinances in Jerusalem, so that he had even already engaged all the stone-masons and artificers (which, according to the older accounts, Solomon was the first to do). And not only is the peculiar language of the Chronicler everywhere apparent, but the whole representation of these last acts of David presents itself as an imitation of many acts and words of Moses in the existing Pentateuch. In particular, David commits to his son the execution of all the sacred works which he is himself no longer able to carry out, a charge similar to that of the dying Moses to his successors; and although a voluntary contribution to the sanctuary was certainly an ancient usage, yet the one here described reminds us strongly of that laid by the Book of Origins in the Mosaic age.[2] The round numbers, as well as the mention of Persian drachmas, lead to the same conclusion. Still it cannot be doubted that the Chronicler is here reproducing the ancient tradition of great treasures being destined by David for the building of the temple, only, in his usual fashion, he has worked it up more freely; and, without finding such treasures, Solomon would never, so far as we know, have been able to set to work in earnest at the erection of the temple so soon after his accession. The quantity of bronze which David[3] had won by his conquest of Zobah, might now find its most suitable use.

b.) Such treasures, however, were chiefly needed only to procure the building materials which had still to be obtained, and to pay the Tyrian and other artists. Labour, that important aid in the work, Solomon obtained for this, as for his other edifices, with scarcely any expenditure of money; and, at any rate at the beginning, he could boast, like Sesostris in the Egyptian story,[4] of having been able to complete this and the other great architectural works of his reign, without exacting any bitter labour from any of his own nation. Israel had risen with great force against all the remnants of the ancient Canaanites, except the Phœnicians, and had reduced them to subjection even in those

---

[1] 1 Chron. xxviii. sq., especially xxix. 3-9.
[2] Exod. xxv. 1 sq.
[3] P. 158.
[4] Diod. Sic. *Hist.* i. 56.

districts where during the period of the Judges they had again become dominant. These Canaanites, completely subdued for the first time by the monarchy, were now compelled, wherever they were not yet willing to transfer themselves to the religion and nationality of Israel, to perform forced service for the king, a practice which had been already begun under David.[1] Solomon accordingly raised for the preliminary works in Lebanon and other places, where the requisite stone was quarried and the timber felled, a levy of thirty thousand men, a third part of whom in turn worked continuously for a month, while the two others were sent home for two months to procure the necessary subsistence for themselves and their families. Subsequently, it is true, when the buildings of various kinds became more numerous, there are unmistakable signs that Solomon claimed even from the people of Israel themselves certain forced services. The entire number was reckoned at 70,000 porters and 80,000 wood- and stone-cutters in Lebanon and elsewhere, with 3,300 overseers, who were only partly taken from the dominant race.[2] The preliminary works for the temple were finished in three years, so that the building itself could be begun in the second month of the fourth year of Solomon's reign.[3]

c.) The locality in or near Jerusalem where the temple should be placed, could not be a matter of doubt in the king's mind. It was the Mount Moriah,[4] north-east of Zion, which David

---

[1] According to the brief but important account 2 Sam. xx. 24, with which the account 2 Chron. ii. 17 agrees. If 2 Sam. viii. 15-18 is compared with it, the result is that the forced service was not instituted till the later years of David. With this agrees also the statement that Adoniram, or shortened, Adoram, who already under David occupied the important post of superintendent of all these services, was still (according to 1 Kings xii. 18) living at the beginning of Rehoboam's reign.

[2] In the complete impossibility of verbally harmonising the passage 1 Kings v. 27 [13] sq., partly with ver. 29 [15] sq., partly with ix. 15-23, 2 Chron. ii. 17 sq., viii. 7-10, it must be assumed, (1) that only 1 Kings v. 27 [13] sq., 31 [17] originally describe the preliminaries of the building of the temple; on the other hand, ver. 29 [15] sq. is originally from another source, probably such a general survey of the circumstances of Solomon's reign as the fragment iv. 2-19 supplies; and (2) that the expression 'all Israel,' v. 27 [13], means only the country and kingdom, not Israel in contrast to the Canaanites; the LXX have, at any rate, introduced quite a different arrangement of the sentences v. 27 [13]-vi. 1; and (3) that the 550 (1 Kings ix. 23) were actual chief-overseers, while the 3,300, 1 Kings v. 30 [16], (3,600 2 Chron. ii. 18 by mistake), include at the same time sub-overseers; of those 550 chief-overseers, however, 300 were taken from the Canaanites themselves, and only 250 (2 Chron. viii. 9 sq.) were born Hebrews. The expression that Solomon had employed *only* Canaanites on forced labour, and Israelites *only* to command (1 Kings ix. 22), is, in the face of such clear evidence as 1 Kings xi. 28, xii. 3 sqq., too general, but proceeds only from the last author. Yet I cannot see that the assertion of the last narrator is entirely groundless; elsewhere also it is the custom of this narrator, in treating of Solomon, to express himself somewhat too generally, as 1 Kings v. 4 [iv. 24].

[3] According to the unquestionably correct additions of the LXX after 1 Kings v. 32 [18], with which the fourth year fits in properly, vi. 1.

[4] The name occurs, except in Gen. xxii. 2 (where the place is intentionally called somewhat generally 'the land of Moriah'),

had already consecrated after the great plague by an altar,[1] a spot which had previously been nothing but a field. That this mountain possessed no other sanctity before that memorable event under David, is proved by the fact that it is not more closely interwoven in the traditions of the times of the patriarchs.[2] Only the fourth and fifth narrators of the primitive history venture on a novelty in assigning the highest event in Abraham's life, the offering of Isaac, to that spot which had in their day become the most sacred in all the holy land, and thus attempt at the same time to explain the ancient name Moriah from a truth of the higher religion which had there, as it were, become localised.[3] But that it was especially sacred in consequence of the great plague, and was on that account chosen as the temple-mountain, follows also from the fact that a mountain should have been then selected which, in comparison with the Mount of Olives and other summits of that district, was so low, —while in other cases the loftiest summits of a district were fixed upon in preference for such purposes;[4] the lofty Mount of Olives, for instance, lying somewhat farther to the east, had already been used by David before the plague as a place of prayer.[5] To this it may be added that a mountain which (as will soon be further explained), on account of its steep and uneven summit, could not be readily adapted for a temple, would never have been selected for it if other causes had not made it appear the only suitable one. Its proximity to Zion was a further reason for choosing it, since it might be so easily attached to the ancient citadel.

d.) For this site further preparations of peculiar difficulty were needed before the erection of the temple itself could be begun. The ground must be made properly level and firm, as the weight and extent of the various edifices required. Unfortunately, the sources preserved in the Old Testament give us no

only in 2 Chron. iii. 1; but these two passages are quite sufficient to identify it. It cannot, moreover, be asserted that this mountain did not lie (according to Gen. xxii. 4) sufficiently far north from Beersheba, since Abraham might depart the first day late, and on the third see the land of Moriah early. The name is lost subsequently in the 'Mount of the Temple,' but is certainly ancient, and connected with the Canaanite proper name Moreh, Gen. xii. 6, cf. Judges vii. 1.

[1] P. 163.
[2] Vol. i. p. 305 sqq.
[3] According to Gen. xxii. 17, the name is twice (but differently) derived from seeing; (1) 'Jahveh sees,' provides, properly Jahveh's seeing, from the main contents of the narrative; (2) passive, properly 'Jahveh's appearance,' with reference to a similar expression in a temple-hymn (now, it is true, lost to us, but then assuredly often sung), 'This is the place of which it is said this day, "On the mountain where Jahveh appears" . . . . (perhaps, "let us sing to Him ").' יְהוָה יֵרָאֶה, connected according to my *Lehrb.* § 333b., yet with previously-named subject, as in Ps. iv. 8. This affords fresh proof how clearly Jerusalem is intended.
[4] A hymn of David's own time alludes to this, Ps. lxviii. 15 sq.
[5] P. 180 sq.

information about it; further details are supplied by Josephus, although, in the different passages where he refers to it, his description must be received with some caution, as the distinction is not drawn with sufficient clearness between what was accomplished in this matter by Solomon himself, and what by his numerous successors.[1] Following the Mosaic model, several forecourts had to be erected round the sacred house proper. The house, therefore, could be placed on the actual summit of the mountain, while the forecourts might be arranged beneath it in stages;[2] but for every separate space which the fundamental idea of the edifice required, the ground had to be levelled beforehand; where it was too high the soil was removed, and where it was too low or wanting in firmness, it was raised or strengthened by substructures. At first, relates Josephus, certainly from some ancient source now unknown to us, the level space on the summit of the rock was scarcely sufficient for the erection of the house and the altar, that is (since it is unquestionably the altar in the Priests' court that is meant),[3] the first or inner forecourt. The extent of the second or outer forecourt, that is, of the entire sanctuary,[4] was, of course, necessarily determined with accuracy from the first, because, without such a plan to determine the main parts, the building could never have been begun. We have, moreover, every reason for assuming that this outer forecourt surrounded the temple in a large square, each side of which was 500 paces inside;[5] it was so arranged, however, that the temple, with the

---

[1] The clearest passage is the oldest, *Bell. Jud.* v. 5. 1; shortest and least satisfactory is the description in Solomon's life itself, *Ant.* viii. 3. 2. 9; much that is important in reference to Solomon may be recovered from the building of Herod's temple, *Ant.* xv. 11. 3.

[2] Hence in Jer. xxxvi. 10, the *upper* is the same as the inner forecourt.

[3] Just as in the expression 'between the porch and the altar,' Joel ii. 17; for this must mean 'in the Priests' forecourt.'

[4] For the original temple of Solomon had certainly only two forecourts, as Ezekiel only presupposes and describes these two. A third court, which the second temple had, might seem to have existed in the Solomonic also, as in the life of Jehoshaphat, 2 Chron. xx. 5, the *new* court is mentioned; if only this could have been the third or so-called Gentiles' court, and if only the successors of Solomon had laid the foundation for such an one!

[5] The historical books of the Old Test. are certainly silent on the point; but Ezek. xlii. 15–20, xlv. 2, has plainly not invented this statement arbitrarily, since the stadium which, according to Josephus also, *Ant.* xv. 11. 3, cf. viii. 3. 9, was the length of each of the four walls, may describe about the same space when it is remembered that Josephus usually prefers general expressions. According to the recent measurements the present platform of the ancient temple-mountain is on the east 1,520, on the south 940, on the west 1,617, and on the north 1,020 feet long (cf. the exact description of Catherwood, in Bartlett's *Walks about Jerusalem*, London, 1844, p. 174), which Robinson, *Bib. Res.* i. p. 431 sq., attempts to explain by the supposition that the Castle of Antonia had included the entire north of the present platform; while G. Williams (*The Holy City*, London, 1845, p. 329 sqq.) assumes, with somewhat more probability, but yet without adequate certainty, that the platform had been extended to the south in the erection of the church of St. Mary, the present Mosque El-Aqsâ, undertaken by the Emperor Justinian. But

court nearest to it, lay more to the west, since on the east as the most sacred quarter was placed the chief entrance into the temple, in front of which it was desirable to have a larger space.¹ Solomon himself, however, according to this account, only completed the substructure of the mountain on the east, the quarter which must have been the nearest to him for that purpose, while later kings carried out the plan of the building on the other three sides also.² Still better proof than the descriptions of Josephus of the gigantic size of the walls with which Solomon and his successors supported and enclosed the space destined for the sacred buildings, is afforded by the remains themselves, which have been preserved to this day and appear almost indestructible. Some of the latest travellers have begun to examine and describe them with somewhat more exactness.³ They show us clearly that it was not the oldest races of Greece and Asia Minor only that executed Cyclopean walls, for the Solomonic may with equal or still greater propriety be so designated.⁴ Repeatedly have those buildings which were erected on the levelled spaces of Moriah,

---

¹ according to Josephus, *Bell. Jud.* v. 5. 5, cf. *Ant.* viii. 3. 9, we are obliged to imagine the second forecourt, but not necessarily the third, a rectangular square. The platform might, therefore, have been extended in the ages after Solomon to admit the third forecourt, especially towards the north and south; as we actually know from later times that the whole platform from south to north, including the adjacent castle of Antonia on the north-west, was six stadia long, Jos. *Bell. Jud.* v. 5. 2.

¹ In fact, there still remains a smaller square which rises, well preserved upon the hard rock, above all the remains of the artificially levelled platform of the mountain, but it is situated more to the west than the east; cf. Williams, *The Holy City*, p. 323 sqq. There stands now upon this smaller square the house venerated by the Mohammedan next to the Kaaba, the Mosque for which Omar prepared the ground on the capture of Jerusalem, commonly called the Mosque El-Sachrâ, i.e. of rock. It is probable that it does not stand quite upon the site of Solomon's temple, but I have no doubt that this very square enclosed the ancient temple together with the Priests' forecourt; cf. 2 Chron. xxix. 4, xxxi. 14. From the most recent accounts we learn that in the midst of this Mosque, hitherto inaccessible to Christians, there stands a real rock; whence, however, this comes, deserves further investigation.

² As we know that king Joash built a good deal, 2 Chron. xxiv. 27, which is evidently mentioned as a very difficult work, 2 Kings xv. 35; cf. further on the subject below.

³ After what Robinson says, *Bib. Res.* i. p. 415 sqq., the description of Catherwood, a professional architect, should be consulted, especially on this point, in Bartlett's *Walks about Jerusalem*, pp. 161-178. In this work the beautiful and apparently very trustworthy drawings are especially noteworthy. Other observations and conjectures have been collected by Williams, *The Holy City*, pp. 315-362. According to Bartlett, p. 23, the southern side even of the smaller square, which extended beyond the space already levelled, had to be supported by similar gigantic walls.

⁴ Similar walls are found in the ancient Phœnician buildings in Gebal or Byblos (*Athenæum Franc.* 1854, p. 1090), in Cyprus, Asia Minor (*Revue Archéol.* 1865, July, p. 2 sqq.), Malta, and elsewhere; also in Baalbek, as already Wood and Dawkins had remarked, cf. John Wilson's *Lands of the Bible*, ii. p. 381 sqq. 400. Elsewhere in Palestine also scattered examples are to be found (Tobler's *Denkblätter aus Jerusalem*, p. 652); Saulcy's *Voyages*, i. p. 46 sq., 318, 326, ii. p. 159, 534 sqq.; those in Hebron are touched on in Hâjji Chalfa's Jihân-Numâ): Herod constructed similar walls for his great buildings in Jerusalem and Cesarea, Jos. *Ant.* xv. 9. 6. 11. 3.

firm and strong as they were, been violently destroyed. The Solomonic temple with its forecourts and halls was succeeded by the second (that of Zerubbabel) and the third (that of Herod) with yet more splendid surroundings. This under Hadrian gave place to heathen temples and other buildings, and these in their turn to Christian and Mohammedan structures, which, after many changes, are standing to this day; and of all the earlier erections on the level platform, there is now not the smallest trace any longer visible. But through all these great and various demolitions and restorations on the surface, its foundations, with their gigantic walls, for the most part unseen, have been indestructibly preserved, to prove even at this day how much assistance art must here have rendered to nature, and with what astonishing resources Solomon prosecuted his designs. The style of the subterranean vaults, the entrance to which is found on the south, renders it improbable that they were begun by Solomon. But we may with all the more confidence regard as the work of Solomon and the other ancient kings those enormously large jointed stones which tower up from a great depth below the surface of the ground into lofty walls, and above which may be seen, in many places, layers of smaller and differently cut stones, which must have been laid over them at a proportionately later period.

The erection of these gigantic supports and walls was certainly not unaccompanied by the noise of work. Complete stillness on the other hand marked the putting together of the stones for the actual house of God. The ancient dread peculiar to the nation of Israel of making their sacred buildings too artificial even then operated so far that the sacred house was put together on the spot without any noise of hammers, axes, and other tools of the kind.[1] The stones were accordingly so prepared where they were quarried, that they could be put together on the summit of Moriah into the walls of the sacred house without further labour; and if (as is in itself probable) they were provided like the enormous blocks of the walls on the mountain with jointed edges, there would be no difficulty in putting them together without noise. The quantity of cedar and cypress wood required for the building was conveyed, with the aid of the Tyrians, the nearest way from Lebanon to the sea. It was then bound together in rafts, floated to the harbour

---

[1] 1 Kings vi. 7, comp. with ver. 18; according to the last passage, some sort of hewing of the stones for the sacred house, at any rate, took place. On the other hand, the words, ver. 17, allude to the above-mentioned stones for the foundations, of which we know otherwise, from 1 Kings vii. 10 sq., that those used in Solomon's palace were eighteen cubits long, and even longer.

of Joppa, west of Jerusalem, and thence brought up to the capital.[1] On these rafts the stone also was probably conveyed, if it was quarried in Lebanon; but of the place of its excavation we have now no information, and where Lebanon is mentioned in this connexion, it is always with reference to its costly wood. The necessary bronze work was cast in earthen moulds in the middle of the Jordan valley, in the district between Succoth on the east, and Zarthan on the west, where there is a fine clay soil; and the quantity of it was so great that the king would not have it weighed at any stage of its preparation, and the weight of the cast-metal work was not, therefore, recorded.[2] All this bronze was polished.

e.) The sacred house itself (the *Naos*) was, in length and breadth, half as large again as the Tabernacle. It was, therefore, only sixty cubits long from east to west, and twenty broad, and always remained, accordingly, a house rather for God Himself than for His worshippers, like the temples of all ancient nations, which were, in fact, mere habitations for the gods, or rather for the images of the gods, and hence cannot be remotely compared with our large churches, which are adapted primarily for the congregation.[3] But in two respects the building attained larger proportions. In the first place, the height of the house was fixed at thirty cubits (that is, twice as great as the height of the Tabernacle), plainly on account of the chambers to be erected round the house, of the height of fifteen cubits, the purpose of which will be described below. But the Holy of Holies was left now, as in its earlier model, a perfect cube, and its height was consequently limited to twenty cubits.[4] And,

---

[1] 1 Kings v. 23 [9], comp. with 2 Chron. ii. 10, where Joppa is named. This Joppa does not appear (ii. p. 329) in the history of Israel during the earlier centuries, and belonged, according to all probability, to the kingdom of Gezer, first subdued at the beginning of Solomon's reign, p. 220.

[2] According to the Book of Origins, 1 Kings vii. 46 sq. The Egyptian potentates certainly acted very differently, who, as we see in the Egyptian sepulchral pictures, preferred to have all their glories described with the greatest accuracy.

[3] The cubit measures are all to be understood, however, of the space within the walls, which at the bottom were generally very thick; cf. 1 Kings vi. 6, and the more precise statements of Ezekiel's temple.

[4] Neither the discrepancies of the numbers in the LXX, 1 Kings vi. 2 sq., cf. ver. 16 sq., 20, nor those in Josephus, can obscure these plainly true proportions; the only thing open to question is the cause of these differences.—Solomon's temple has been made the subject of closer investigations in recent times by Hirt, Stieglitz, Fr. v. Meyer, Grüneisen, and Kiel, which have been noticed by C. Schnaase (*Geschichte der bildenden Künste*, Düsseldorf, 1843, vol. i. p. 241–286), but this last writer himself goes far wrong when he proposes anything new, and in general has too mean ideas of his subject. One main cause why the numerous important questions on this subject have not yet been answered with sufficient certainty, is unquestionably to be found in the incompleteness and want of precision in our existing accounts in 1 Kings, of which I shall immediately bring forward an instructive example in the case of the two pillars. Nowhere has etymology failed in its duty so much as here. For the latest essays on

secondly, the simple entrance on the east was widened into a splendid portico, which was of the same breadth as the house, yet measured only ten cubits (in depth) from east to west, but, according to a later statement, rose to a height of 120 cubits.[1] In this a freer scope was given to art, which in the house proper had been more strictly tied down to the ancient sacred proportions. With it, accordingly, was combined a truly splendid piece of work, which was to adorn the entrance to the whole building. These were two gigantic bronze pillars,[2] each of which was twelve cubits in circumference. They were each fluted, and the depth of the fluting was four inches. Each was

the subject see the *Kunstblatt*, 1848, st. 5 sq., *Theol. Stud. u. Krit.* 1850, and *Jahrbb. der Bibl. Wiss.* i. p. 65 sqq., iii. p. 262. The investigations about the temple most recently commenced by De Saulcy, De Vogüé, and Renan, are still far from complete (*Rev. archéol.* 1861, p. 322 sqq., 1863, p. 12 sqq., 281 sqq.)

[1] This height of 120 cubits is wanting 1 Kings vi. 3, and occurs only 2 Chron. iii. 4. Objections may be easily urged against this towerlike elevation, on the ground of the disproportion of its length and breadth. But inasmuch as the rest of the dimensions in the Chronicles are in perfect harmony with the older accounts, an exaggeration in this alone is not in itself very probable. It might further be thought that the thickness of the two columns at the entrance, without any great height, would be sufficiently accounted for by the weight they had to support. The Phœnician temple at Paphos, especially as it is represented on the copper coins of the Empress Julia and of Caracalla (cf. the essay of Fr. Münter about it, Copenh. 1824), appears similarly to have possessed a far higher portico. But the two still higher pillars in front of it, which are represented on the Paphian coins, bear no similarity at all to those of the Solomonic temple. Since, however, the temple of Zerubbabel was sixty cubits high and broad, Ezr. vi. 3 sq., and that of Herod 120 cubits high, the Solomonic appears, at any rate with the addition (according to what has been said) of its upper chambers (see below), to have been towards 120 cubits high, and hence the statement of the Chronicles may have arisen. Cf. also the *Jahrbb. der Bibl. Wiss.*, ix. p. 256.

[2] The description of them, 1 Kings vii. 15-22, was originally in the highest degree clear and satisfactory, but has become much mutilated and consequently obscure in the present text. If it is, meanwhile, compared with the extracts in ver. 41 sq.

and in the description of the destruction of the temple, Jer. lii. 21-23 (the latter is again still further abbreviated 2 Kings xxv. 17), as well as with the text of the LXX, which, though in most passages much more complete, was elsewhere even more defective, no uncertainty can remain on the whole. To name the chief points here: the gaps in ver. 15 are easily supplied from the LXX, comp. with Jer. lii. 21, where בַּעֲבָיו וְכֹל בָּתרוֹ אר should be read, or something similar, for בתר. At any rate, the thickness עָבִי, can only mean that of the whole pillar, since if the thickness of the bronze wall alone was four inches, and the pillars themselves were hollow (which was, at any rate, what Josephus meant), then the thickness of their wall or of the bronze would have had to be named. Ver. 18 is perhaps to be read "וַיַּעַשׂ מַעֲשֵׂה רוּחָה רִמֹּנִים שְׁנֵי; for 'to the wind,' Jer. lii. 23, must mean the same as exposed to the wind, hanging loose, ἔργον κρεμαστόν as the LXX correctly understood it here, but not in Jer. The meaning of ver. 19 follows from ver. 22, where the 'lilywork' is the same as the capitals; hence the mention of the 'belly,' ver. 20, or (what is the same) ver. 41 sq. its 'bowl.' Ver. 20, painfully imperfect in the LXX, only becomes clear when the first words are struck out as a repetition from ver. 19, and וְרִמֹּנִים is read instead (while, ver. 18, this word occurs wrongly for עַמּוּדִים). The two columns before the Paphian temple also, according to some Paphian coins, possessed loose hanging ornaments, but certainly fastened quite otherwise athwart from one to the other; and on the *Ti* of the temple of Gautama at Pegu, just as on Japanese temples of Buddha, swing little bells made to sound by the wind (see the pictures in Seebold's *Nippon*, ii. 4).

eighteen cubits high;[1] but above their shaft (which, as in other ancient sorts of pillars, was left smooth beneath) rose a capital five cubits[2] in height, and very ornamentally constructed. It was in the beautiful form of a lily in blossom, swelling out at the top and with overlying leaves. Its smooth bowl was, however, covered over and held together with a network of seven ingeniously linked threads; and below, where the bowl was more slender, as well as on the top of the network, a double wreath of artificial pomegranates[3] was introduced. Four of these in each wreath, directed to the four quarters of heaven, hung quite fast on the capital, and probably stood straight upright; but the remaining ninety-six, or every twenty-four between two fixed ones, hung more loosely, and could be set in motion by the play of the wind, like a real wreath of flowers on a man's neck. All this, as it appears, was of bronze. Over these triply-adorned capitals of the two pillars extended the beam which joined them both above. But above this beam a new decoration was repeated on both sides, of the same breadth as the beam;[4] until, above the whole of this ornamental entrance, which may have been from thirty to thirty-five cubits high, the upper stonework of the portico rose into the air.[5] This work was magnificent enough to be immortalised by special names. The pillar on the right received, on its erection and consecration, the name of Jachin, that on the left the name of Boaz, doubtless, after some favourite persons of the time, perhaps, young sons of Solomon;[6] just as the first Herod called

---

[1] For this 2 Chron. iii. 17 and the LXX, Jer. lii. 21, put thirty-five cubits, perhaps including the ornaments on each pillar explained below.

[2] 'Four cubits,' ver. 19, and in the LXX, ver. 22, like 'three' in 2 Kings xxv. 17, is evidently only a different reading.

[3] Such have been found in many varieties in Phœnician art, *Revue archéol.* 1863, Jul. p. 1-6.

[4] This important fact follows clearly from ver. 22, according to the more perfect text of the LXX, and since in ver. 21 sq. only the putting together of the parts of the whole structure is described, mention must have been made of it earlier with every detail. A lofty ornament above the capital appears also on the Egyptian and Assyrian pillars;. cf. the pictures in the *Description de l'Égypte Antiq.* vol. i. and in Loftus' *Chaldæa and Susiana* (p. 366).

[5] From a correct comprehension of the perfect text, it of course follows that the two pillars are not to be conceived of as standing detached in front of the temple like obelisks. What, in that case, could have been the use of the beam above them, and the new capitals? Moreover in ver. 21 they are clearly called 'the pillars of the porch,' as the LXX rightly translate. If any independent Propylæa had been meant, these would have required quite a different designation. The position of the two pillars in the temples of Heracles at Tyre and Gades, Herod. ii. 44, Strab. *Geogr.* iii. 5. 6, would then be more suitable for comparison.

[6] Jachin occurs elsewhere also as a proper name, and Boaz is even found among David's ancestors. It is incomprehensible how even now anyone can look in regular Rabbinical fashion for a typical sense in the names of these two pillars, as though they referred to the attributes of God. For other improbable meanings see, for example, R. Rochette in the *Mémoires de l'Acad. des Inscript.* vol. xvii. 2, p. 54; cf. the *Jahrbb. der Bibl. Wiss.* viii. p. 225.

his two splendidly built mural towers at Jerusalem Phasael and Mariamne.

Except on the side of the portico, the sacred house was surrounded by an outer three-storied house, not much more than fifteen cubits high. Each story was five cubits high, and the lowest was of the same breadth; but each story was a cubit broader than the one beneath, because the wall, which was several cubits thick at the bottom, was made a cubit thinner with every five cubits of height, so that the cedar-beams of the ceilings of all the three stories of the outer house rested directly upon each of these ledges in the temple wall. This outer house was divided into a number of chambers, the entrance being in the south-eastern chamber of the lower story, from which a winding staircase led to the two upper stories.[1] What purpose these numerous small side chambers were to serve, is not explained; but certainly they were not in any way for the use of the Priests, since they had their chambers in their forecourt. When it is remembered that they were connected as closely as possible with the innermost sanctuary, it must be supposed that they were to contain the offerings and other treasures of the sanctuary, for which no room could be found in the house itself. Hence it is narrated that after the completion of the building of the temple, Solomon immediately brought the various gifts of his father into the sacred store-rooms.[2] Besides, as has been remarked, the actual sacred house rose still to a considerable elevation above this structure.

The Holy of Holies and the Holy Place, separated within by a wall, formed outside, according to all descriptions, only one whole, covered by one roof.[3] Since, however, the former was only twenty, the latter thirty cubits high, the question arises how the space of ten cubits above the former was employed. It was probably left quite empty, so that the Holy of Holies appeared from the Holy Place quite like a house by itself. The roof over the whole house, which was sixty cubits long, was in that case the only roof of the Holy Place, the length of which was forty cubits; and consisted, as in Grecian temples, of an ornamental ceiling in squares,[4] with small pieces of cedar wood

---

[1] 1 Kings vi. 5 sq. 8, 10; these clauses only should be taken together, vv. 7 and 9 belong in another connexion. In ver. 8, for the first תיכנה it is better to read תַּחְתֹּנָה, and in ver. 10 יָצִיעַ for בַּיִת, as the LXX show; or at any rate before the latter word the former should be inserted; ver. 10 then treats of the roof of every story of the outer house and is properly connected with ver. 9.

[2] 1 Kings vii. 51, comp. with xiv. 26, and other similar passages. That David's consecrated gifts also included arms, follows from 2 Kings xi. 10.

[3] That the roof of the Holy of Holies might have been lower, and consequently distinguishable from outside, is against the evidence of all the descriptions.

[4] גֵּבִים, 'cavities,' 1 Kings vi. 9, clearly

as dividing beams. Whether the roof was flat or sunk, we do not know from the ancient books; but the Chronicles [1] speak of gilded upper chambers, which would presuppose a flat roof.[2] The windows were probably placed in the lofty sides of the house which rose above the surrounding external structure, and consisted of mere air-holes, with strong gratings, which did not admit any great quantity of light.[3] The awe which the gloomy interiors of their temples inspired, was dear to all antiquity, and, according to the foregoing remarks, the Holy of Holies must even have been quite dark.

Whether the sacred house was ornamented outside, and if so in what way, we do not know.[4] Inside, the walls were overlaid to their whole height with boards of cedar-wood,[5] which were further adorned with carvings. These consisted partly of common ornaments, such as palm branches, coloquintidas (egg-like fruits), and beautiful flowers, partly of cherubs as the ornament most proper for the Sanctuary.[6] All these were overlaid with strips of the finest gold. The wall which separated the Holy of Holies from the Holy Place, as well as the altar which stood exactly opposite the Holy of Holies, and as it were belonged to it,[7] was adorned in like manner. But the floor both of the Holy Place and of the Holy of Holies was planked with cypress-wood, and overlaid with gold.[8]—Both the doors were ornamented in precisely the same manner with carvings and gold. The door of the Holy of Holies, which was clearly the smaller, consisted of two leaves, and was made of the wood of the wild olive-tree; it was in five squares, with projecting posts of the same wood. The larger door of the Holy Place was in four squares with projecting posts of the same wood, while its two leaves, each consisting of two folding boards (an upper and an under), were of cypress-wood. Both doors moved on golden

gives this sense, which must also lie in the κοιλοσταθμεῖν of the LXX; Lat. *lacunaria*. Φατνώματα at any rate in the outer forecourt are mentioned by Jos. *Ant*. viii. 3. 9.

[1] 2 Chron. iii. 9.
[2] Cf. also the erection of idols upon it by Ahaz, 2 Kings xxiii. 12.
[3] 1 Kings vi. 4.
[4] It will always remain a singular thing that the outside is so little mentioned; and no one can fail to perceive in this circumstance a mutilation of the text.
[5] This is now made out to have been the case in Egyptian temples also. *Athen. Franç.* 1854, st. 153.
[6] See the *Alterthümer*, p. 139 sq.
[7] *Ibid*. p. 374 sq.

[8] This seems to be the safest meaning of the words vi. 14–22, 29 sq., which are now wrongly interrupted by the description of the cherubs, vv. 23–28, which does not belong there. In vv. 14–17, 19, is described the first overlaying with cedar-wood, cf. vii. 2 sq.; in vv. 18, 29 the second overlaying with carving; in vv. 20–22, 30, the third with gold; and although scarcely given in their original order, the words are yet clear. The לִפְנֵי הַדְּבִיר, ver. 20 sq., is accordingly the fore-part, i.e. the fore-wall of the Holy of Holies; but the first should then stand after קוֹמָתוֹ. 2 Chron. iii. 6 adds precious stones to the decoration.

hinges;[1] that which led into the Holy of Holies was further secured with golden chains, which stretched across the whole breadth of the door and projected on the wall.[2]

About the internal and external decoration of the portico our existing accounts, which are unquestionably very much abbreviated, give us scarcely any information. Only accidentally has a statement been preserved[3] from which we must conclude that its inner walls were decorated with lily-work, just as the capitals of the pillars of the porch terminated in the shape of lilies;[4] and the same decoration reappeared, as we shall observe, on the temple vessels. Lilies and lotos served at that time in the countries from Sinai to Asia Minor for our roses, which were unknown. The walls themselves were built like those of the inner forecourt, which was surrounded by a wall of three rows of large squared stones laid one on another, upon which were placed shoulder-pieces of cedar wood.[5] In it, or at any rate close by it, Solomon also erected the buildings necessary for the Priests.[6] About the arrangement of the great or outer forecourt, our ancient accounts are silent. Our knowledge of it is derived only from other sources, as has been already explained.[7] In it however, were erected, in course of time, the beautiful large halls where the Prophets so often addressed the assembled people, and the cells or chambers where disciples gathered round a teacher.[8] How many teachers of eminence in their time may here have founded schools, of which we do not now know even the names! In such a one in Jeremiah's time assembled the sons, i.e. disciples, of the 'man of God' Hanan,[9] who, to judge by this title of honour, must have lived long before Jeremiah, but is now completely unknown to us.[10]—Especial splendour doubtless marked the construction of the numerous gateways; and, besides the main gateway on the east, we know of the 'Gate of the founda-

---

[1] 1 Kings vi. 31–35, vii. 50; cf. the *Jahrbb. der Bibl. Wiss.* i. p. 66 sq. In 2 Chron. iii. 7 sq. the gold in the Holy of Holies alone is estimated at 600 talents, and the value of the golden nails at 50 shekels.

[2] According to the words 1 Kings vi. 21. According to 2 Chron. iii. 14, the ancient Mosaic curtain also had been stretched in front of the Holy of Holies (probably outside the door), made of variegated linen with representations of cherubs on it; but the description reminds us too much of Ex. xxvi. 31, and may have been borrowed from the second temple which the Chronicler always had in his eye. Similarly the Chronicles extend the golden chains of the pillars much farther, vv. 5, 16.

[3] 1 Kings vii. 19, and in the LXX, ver. 22, according to which the description of the lilywork of the porch must already have preceded, though it is now wanting.

[4] P. 237.

[5] 1 Kings vi. 36, and vii. 2, 12; cf. viii. 64, 2 Chron. iv. 9. פְּרֻתוֹת are fragments cut off, i.e. projecting, aptly rendered by the LXX. ὠμίαι.

[6] As may be seen with more detail from Ez. xl. 33–47.

[7] P. 232 sq.

[8] Jer. xxvi. 2 sqq., xxxvi. 10, 20, 2 Kings xxiii. 11, 1 Chron. ix. 26, 33.

[9] Jer. xxxv. 4.

[10] P. 14, *note* 1.

FURNITURE OF THE SANCTUARY.

tion,' which must have lain to the north;[1] the upper, called also the upper Benjamin Gate, or, after it had been rebuilt by Jotham, the new Gate,[2] which lay at any rate towards the north, but perhaps in the inner forecourt; the Gate behind the 'guard,'[3] in the south, where, lower down between the temple and palace, were the quarters of the body-guard; finally, on the west, the 'Gate of cells,' the least clearly distinguished of all, so-called because behind it there stood, as in a sort of suburb, a crowd of small cells, chiefly such as the Levites occupied in their hours of release from temple duty.[4]

f.) The furnishing of the sanctuary with the appropriate vessels was marked by the same union of feelings as the erection of the temple; and reverence for the prescriptions of antiquity was combined with that moral and artistic liberty which generally distinguishes this elevated age. Thus much we may, on the whole, still recognise with certainty; but we cannot help deeply regretting that the ancient detailed accounts of it have been most imperfectly preserved to us.[5] At one time, soon after their construction, all these sacred vessels were of sufficient importance to be described with realistic precision; so great a novelty in Israel was the art involved in them, and so great the astonishment excited by this art-power, which

---

[1] For סוּר, 2 Kings xi. 6, cf. ver. 11, we should certainly read יְסוּר according to 2 Chron. xxiii. 5.

[2] Ez. ix. 2, Jer. xx. 2, xxxvi. 10; cf. 2 Kings xv. 35.

[3] 2 Kings xi. 6, cf. ver. 19, according to which the opposite gate of the palace was called that of the 'guard,' or according to 2 Chron. xxiii. 30, by an equivalent name, the upper, i.e. northern: on the situation of the palace, see more below. Outside, in front of this gate, lay (according to 1 Chron. xxvi. 15, 17) two special guardhouses for the porters or doorkeepers, one opposite the temple, the other towards the palace (that אֲסֻפִּים probably means this, becomes clear from Neh. xii. 25, cf. *Jahrbb. der Bibl. Wiss.* iii. p. 123).

[4] This results from a comparison of 1 Chron. xxvi. 16-18 with ix. 26, 33, 2 Kings xxiii. 11; according to this, in 1 Chron. xxvi. 16, for שַׁלֶּכֶת we should read (as the LXX also give) לִשָׁכוֹת; and it appears that this is almost identical with the expression פַּרְוָרִים or פַּרְבָּר, which, according to Jos. *Ant.* xv. 11. 5, is pretty much the same as προάστειον, and reappears with a similar meaning in the Tal-mudic אֲבְרוָר or בְּרוָר, while ܒܣܘܡ (Pers. برواز), meaning *roof*, is found now only in Syrian dictionaries. The assumption of Lightfoot and others that the Solomonic temple had four doors on the west, like the Herodian (Jos. *Ant.* xv. 11. 5), is without foundation.

[5] The Book of Origins gives (1 Kings vii. 40-47, from וַיַּכַל to the end) a survey of all the metal-works of Hiram. The single works here named must of course have been previously described in detail; but the pots (in ver. 40 we should read סִירוֹת, according to ver. 45), shovels, and basons, are only enumerated ver. 40, as they are in ver. 45, whereas they should have been here described in detail. In addition to this, this book had certainly given a detailed description of the rest of the vessels also, which had not been made by this one artist, but we now only find a brief enumeration (and that, too, from the hand of another author) of *all* the vessels, including those not constructed by Hiram. The statement that all these vessels were golden, involves no necessary contradiction of the Book of Origins, which makes Hiram construct everything of bronze. The bronze works might be gilded before they were set up in their places.

employed such extraordinary means to produce its splendid works. But later ages found much of it neither so novel nor so notable; and while the ancient descriptions of these vessels, as of the erection of the temple itself, are already greatly abbreviated in our present Books of Kings, the Chronicler has still further contracted them. Subsequently, on the other hand, towards the period of the New Testament, a new impulse was roused after clearer conceptions of this among the other Solomonic glories. In the absence, however, of more ancient and reliable information, it was left for mere imagination to describe them as of that completely marvellous character which was then attributed to the whole age of Solomon, while at the same time an effort was made to balance the accounts in the Old Testament of Solomon's temple with those of the Mosaic tabernacle. In the statements of Josephus [1] about those details of the temple which have been left indefinite in the canonical books, we possess a clear picture of such later poetical representations; and since he unquestionably drew his accounts of Solomon from apocryphal sources, we may safely assume that whatever bears the marks of this play of fancy was also derived from such writings. What may be safely affirmed in this condition of the accounts of the temple furniture is as follows.

The Holy of Holies, as in the Mosaic tabernacle, received nothing but the ark. No attempt was made actually to renew this supremely sacred relic, rendered so venerable by its antiquity and its vicissitudes, but it was left essentially unchanged. It was, however, furnished with a new lid, on which occasion it appeared that the ark contained nothing but the two tables of stone of Moses. The lid, or rather the splendid footstool,[2] was renewed, because a pair of new cherubs was to be fastened to it; and this ornament was the only addition which was permitted, since the greater space of the Holy of Holies enabled the two cherubs to be represented on a much larger scale. They were carved out of olive wood and overlaid with gold; their heads were fastened again, as before, to the two ends of the footstool, which was extended to a length of ten cubits.

---

[1] *Ant.* viii. 3. 7, 8. To bring forward only some of them here: Solomon had one large golden table (the Mosaic) made, but together with it 10,000 other similar ones, 80,000 wine-pots, 100,000 golden vases, 200,000 silver ones (2 Chron. iv. 8 only 100 golden basons are named); and so it goes on, even with the adornments of the priests. It may, however, be assumed as a general fact, that this historian explains in his own fashion and further paraphrases much of what he found more briefly indicated in his materials, but he never ventures actually to invent such definite numbers and events. Quite different and peculiar is the description of the whole temple in Eupolemus (Eus. *Præp. Ev.* ix. 34), the sources of which we do not now know, but which contains some remarkable statements.

[2] [A. V. *Mercy-seat.*—ED.] See the *Alterthümer*, p. 165.

FURNITURE OF THE SANCTUARY.

Their height, moreover, was now fixed at ten cubits to correspond, and the two mighty wings that were attached to each well showed how much higher the aspiration of the whole national spirit of Israel now soared. Each wing was extended five cubits wide; and while one wing of each was turned towards the middle of the footstool, and these two met in the centre, the others were extended to the wall on either side, so that the whole space of the Holy of Holies, twenty cubits in length from east to west, was occupied by these mighty forms. This large and splendid group was certainly erected at once in the Holy of Holies itself[1] and was placed ten cubits above the floor, so that from the Holy Place it was not seen through the door. On the other hand, the carrying-poles of the ark which was to be placed beneath, were seen projecting from the Holy Place by anyone who placed himself right in front of the dark Holy of Holies, although, as they were covered by the golden chains stretched[2] immediately in front of them, they were not seen any further outside.[3] At the consecration of the temple, the ark was brought up with solemn procession, bearing on the way a corresponding image of the cherubs, and was then placed in this position.

In the Holy Place stood a gilded altar and a holy table.[4] Instead, however, of the single candlestick of the tabernacle, there were here placed five gilded candlesticks on the south side and five similar ones on the north, but we do not know in what order, nor why there were exactly ten of them.

In the Priests' forecourt, the great brazen altar, which certainly stood in the middle, measured twenty cubits square, and ten cubits in height.[5] In detail we know only of two bronze works which belonged to this court.[6] On the south-east was placed the great laver for the officiating Priests, the extra-

---

[1] This follows from the words 1 Kings viii. 6, and agrees very well with what is remarked in the *Alterthümer* about the floor of the cherubs, and the independence of this work.

[2] P. 240.

[3] 1 Kings viii. 6-9, vi. 23-28. The obscure expression viii. 8, with difficulty permits another meaning, only it must then be assumed that the description viii. 6-8 was composed before the door of the Holy of Holies (described p. 239) was put on, which is conceivable, since it may be derived from the Book of Origins. Later representations are given in the Mass. *Middôth*, i. 6, ii. 6.

[4] Instead of the single table, which is clearly meant in 1 Kings vii. 48, the Chronicler (2 Chron. iv. 8) puts ten tables arranged like the ten candlesticks; but it is difficult to see what purpose these ten tables were to serve in the Holy Place itself.

[5] This is certainly stated only in 2 Chron. iv. 1; but is meanwhile quite in harmony with the rest of the proportions of the Solomonic vessels to the Mosaic, cf. Ex. xxvii. 1, and hence is certainly from an ancient source. Cf. Ez. xliii. 13-17.

[6] 1 Kings vii. 23-39, cf. with 2 Chron. iv. 2-6; whereas, on the contrary, the bronze laver cursorily mentioned 2 Chron. vi. 13 is plainly named and described with precision by a copyist's mistake instead of the speaker's stage.

ordinary circumference of which is alone sufficient to show how far these ages were in advance of the Mosaic in their splendour and the multitude of superior Priests. It was an enormous round cauldron, called the *bronze sea,* five cubits high, but measuring ten cubits across, and a handbreadth thick. Its brim was shaped like that of a cup, with overhanging lily-flowers. Round the outside of it ran two rows of coloquintidas, all cast in the same piece with it; twelve bronze oxen served to support it, three set towards each quarter of the heavens.[1] In order, however, to convey from this temple-reservoir a larger quantity of water to any part in the wide courts of the temple where it might be needed on account of the sacrifices, ten beautifully ornamented bronze trucks were prepared, which might be called cauldron-trucks; their common name, however, was simply *bases*; five of them were placed on the south, five on the north side. These were destined for the most direct use in the sacrifices as sacred vessels, and they were therefore not merely made of bronze, wheels and all, like other temple vessels, but in the ornamental representations of cherubs, lions, bulls, and palm-branches, which all formed part of the casting, together with a wreath of flowers beneath, they bore the mark of their sacred purpose.[2] It is very remarkable that, in our own time, in many places of Europe, bronze movable caldrons of a high antiquity have been excavated, which bear an unmistakable resemblance to those of Solomon.[3] These productions of art were doubtless spread by the Phœnicians in the most remote ages as far east as west. But at the same time those of

---

[1] As in the Alhambra; see the pictures in Murphy, pl. 33 sq., or like the recently discovered similar art forms of the ancient Assyrians (Layard's *Discoveries,* p. 180).

[2] Cherubs and flowers or palms were found (according to pp. 239, 242) elsewhere, also, as decorative forms in the temple. If, however, lions and bulls are here added, it must be remembered that the lion was the ancient emblem of the tribe of Judah (as will soon be made still clearer); but the bull (ii. p. 183) had, as a type, ever since the earliest ages, possessed some sanctity for Israel. The sacred fourfold form of Ezekiel, i., is not to be thought of here; it is much more likely Ezekiel himself was subsequently guided by recollection of the temple-forms here enumerated.

[3] The most probable picture of this base which we can form from the description of it, I have, after the attempts that have been communicated in the two previous editions of this work, finally presented in a separate essay in reference to those discoveries (see the *Nachrichten* in the *Gött. Gel. Anz.* 1859, pp. 131–146, cf. also the *Jahrb. der Bibl. Wiss.* x. p. 273 sqq.). I here refer to that more detailed representation and only remark, (1) that the sense of מסגרור and שלבים, according to Ex. xxvi. 17, xxv. 25, cannot be matter of doubt; and (2) that from a correct insight into the construction of these bases it is explained how Ahaz, according to 2 Kings xvi. 17, could cut off the panels of the ten bases, in order to pay the Assyrian tribute with them; for the panel formed the greatest part of the metal of the base, while the latter could be used in case of necessity without the former. Perhaps the later editor of the Books of Kings abstained for that reason only from abbreviating the descriptions of these bases and of the bronze sea, that the following narrative of Ahaz might be more intelligible.

Solomon have their peculiar Israelitish marks; and even in these comparatively minor temple-articles, it may be seen with what great art and splendour Solomon carried all his designs into execution.

g.) To a sanctuary of wood and stone, however, there was always attached, according to the representations of antiquity, a sacred grove. Nor was the Solomonic temple without one, as we may conclude from the poetical allusions to it,[1] even though our historical narratives are silent on the point. It consisted, no doubt, of cedars and palms.

h.) The whole temple, as far as Solomon intended carrying it for the present, was completed in the eighth month of the eleventh year of his reign; its erection had lasted, therefore,[2] precisely seven years and a half.[3] Since, however, the great annual autumn festival at which the people were accustomed to assemble at the sanctuary in their largest numbers, occurred in the seventh month, the king determined to arrange the festival of the actual consecration of the new sanctuary in this month, so that the dedication of the temple should take place the week before that in which the autumn festival would otherwise be celebrated. With this should be joined, in the following week, the regular autumn festival,[4] which might easily give rise to the idea that the one or the other feast had lasted fourteen days. For this solemn dedication of the temple, Solomon made arrangements on a grand scale. All the heads of tribes and families in Israel (whether by birth or by election) were summoned to Jerusalem for it. The superior and inferior Priests, besides, assembled for a festival which could not take place without their most active participation. The ceremony doubtless began with the removal of the ancient tabernacle which had been left in Gibeon,[5] as well as of the rest of the ancient sacred vessels which still remained there. All these, together with the ark of the covenant, which had been for more than forty years preserved at Jerusalem in a tabernacle erected for it by David, were brought in solemn procession by the Priests to the new sanctuary. Only the ark, however, found there its destined home; the other remaining relics

---

[1] Ps. lii. 10 [8], xcii. 14 [13].
[2] P. 230.
[3] 1 Kings vi. 37 sq., comp. with v. 1 and vii. 1, ix. 10.
[4] All the circumstances require that the relation indicated 1 Kings viii. 65 sq., cf. ver. 2, should be more precisely understood in this way. It then becomes intelligible how, 2 Chron. vii. 8–10, the 23rd day of the month should be named as that on which the people were dismissed. That the feast of atonement fell, on that occasion, in the middle of the feast of dedication affords no important objection. That the consecration did not take place till after Solomon had, in the course of twenty years, completed all his erections, is a foolish addition of the LXX before viii. 1, with words which are borrowed from ix. 1.
[5] P. 125.

of the Mosaic age, on the other hand, must have been stored up
as a perpetual memorial in other appropriate places, e.g. in the
chambers of the temple. An enormous number of sacrifices was
consumed. The king alone offered up twenty-two thousand
oxen and one hundred and twenty thousand sheep solely as a
thank-offering, of which all those who took part in the festival
might eat if they chose. Many other persons doubtless made
similar voluntary offerings; and so great was the number of
sacrifices that, as the large altar in the inner court did not
suffice to receive them, the king was obliged to consecrate for
the same purpose the entire space of this forecourt. What an
impression, however, the whole festival made upon the assembled
crowds, and with what feelings they returned home from the
combined feasts, we see clearly from the description of the
Book of Origins. After the removal of the ark to its new home,
with which the chief part of the solemnity was successfully
concluded, the shining fiery cloud, the sign of the presence of
Jahveh, settled, it was said, with such power upon the house,
that even the Priests were compelled to withdraw before it, and
for a moment to quit the house.[1] Thus deeply were all suddenly penetrated with the feeling, that just as the bright
smoke of the vast sacrifices was rising with favourable auguries
over the house, so surely would Jahveh descend from the clear
heaven and graciously dwell there, as He had in earlier days
tarried in other sacred spots. But though throughout the
whole festival the Priests had necessarily the most laborious
share of the duties, Solomon, no less than David on a former
occasion,[2] in virtue of his genuine sovereignty, assumed the
supreme direction of the whole solemnity. He himself took an
active part in speaking. After the Priests had performed their
functions, he gave thanks in the solemn assembly with a loud
voice to Jahveh, that He had graciously enabled him to finish an
edifice in which Jahveh had promised with favouring omens ' to
abide for ever ; ' and in conclusion uttered a solemn address to
the congregation, in which he reminded them of the good promises (oracles) of God made in former days to his father David,
pointed out how gloriously these had hitherto been fulfilled, and
entreated their further accomplishment for the future.—Such
is the information afforded by ancient sources.[3] Later writers,
however, availed themselves of this lofty situation in their
ancient history, to attach to it some other truths of greater

[1] Cf. ii. p. 218 sqq., and the *Alterthümer*, p. 379.
[2] P. 126 sq.
[3] 1 Kings viii. 1-11, and vv. 62-66 es- sentially after the Book of Origins; on the other hand, vv. 12-21 after the older narrator of the history of the kings, like 2 Sam. vii.; vv. 24-27 after the later.

significance to them. The first Deuteronomic editor makes Solomon in a long speech pray that Jahveh, who was actually exalted far above such an earthly dwelling-place, would hear all the prayers addressed to Him by His servants within and without the temple,—an address which is of extreme beauty in spite of its length, only it belongs by its ideas to the seventh and not to the eleventh or tenth century.[1] The Chronicler, on the other hand, completes the picture of the auspicious consecration by representing that fire from heaven kindled the sacrifices; and, with this exception, limits the detail and eloquence of his usual style to the description of the festive processions.[2]

i.) As the great sanctuary had now become the centre of the whole religious life of Israel, where the sacred usages were solemnised with a splendour unknown before, and where gifts and consecrated offerings flowed in from such an extraordinarily large multitude, the position of the Levites necessarily assumed a new shape and entered on a more steady development. It was upon them first that the whole splendour of this new house of Jahveh fell. They found in it a point of union, an actual citadel, such as they had not possessed since the age of Joshua,—nay, such as they had never before attained with equal power and consolidation. Their duties and occupations, moreover, increased to such an extent, that they were certainly in need now of more thorough reorganisation and in part of more complete transformation than had been previously effected by David.[3] Some of the particulars of this new organisation in the case of the Levites who were to be employed at Jerusalem, are known to us chiefly through the Chronicles. It is true the Chronicler describes everything appertaining to it in reality only in the shape to which it had been developed towards the conclusion of the whole history of the monarchy at Jerusalem,[4] because his sources supplied him only with such materials. Further, he refers the origin of the organisation to the precepts of David,—nay, even of Samuel.[5] But as this is only the result of his general view (which will be explained below) of Solomon's career, we have no ground for doubting that the basis of the

---

[1] The words 1 Kings viii. 22 sq., 27–61, belong clearly by their origin to a far later composition, that, namely, of the first Deuteronomic editor; cf. i. p. 158.

[2] The most important additions of the Chronicler are to be found in 2 Chron. v. 11–13, vi. 41 sq. (from Ps. cxxxii. 8–10), vii. 1–3, 6.

[3] P. 133.

[4] This is evident, e.g., from 1 Chron. ix. 11, comp. with v. 37–40, after an older source; the Azariah there named was, according to that, one of the last High Priests before the destruction of Jerusalem.

[5] To David, 1 Chron. xxiii.–xxvi. and in other passages; to Samuel also, 1 Chron. ix. 22. On the other hand, it is by no means to be concluded from expressions like 2 Chron. xxxi. 2, that the Chronicler did not assign the origin of this organisation till Hezekiah's time.

whole of this new organisation of the Priesthood was laid in the age of Solomon, which omitted nothing from its creative arrangements. The essential features of it were as follows. For the performance of the principal temple duties there were formed out of the two ancient families immediately descended from Aaron twenty-four smaller families (divisions), each of which was to provide the service for a week.[1] To assist these, twenty-four families were appointed from the lower ranks of Priests, each of which was to furnish the proper number of ministrants required for a week.[2] For the temple music twenty-four families were appointed, each of which was to send twelve of its own men.[3] All such series of twenty-four were immediately, however, divided into three groups;[4] and accordingly the musicians, too, were traced back to the three fathers Asaph, Heman, and Ethan or Jeduthun, as will be further explained in considering the development of the arts in the Solomonic period. Other Levites were engaged in considerable numbers for service as porters at the different gates and guard posts of the temple,[5] others again received the hereditary duty of guarding the treasures of the temple;[6] and similar provision was made down to the most minute details of the lower temple services.[7] The basis of these arrangements was maintained without interruption from that time to the latest ages. That many Levites and Priests should now be provided with dwellings in the immediate precincts of the temple, either permanently or for the periods of their service, was inevitable; but their means of subsistence they still continued to derive chiefly from the tithes and estates which[8] they had hereditarily possessed from ancient times, and to which they could also retire for residence.[9] In addition to this, the High Priest with his whole suite retained the extensive quarters on Zion, which[10] David must have assigned to him.[11]

2) After the completion of the sacred edifice so far as was needful for its consecration, Solomon began the erection of a

---

[1] 1 Chron. xxiv. 1–19. How the weekly service was conducted may be partly gathered from 1 Chron. ix. 25.

[2] 1 Chron. xxiv. 20–31. The twenty-four here are to be counted thus: Shubael, Jedeiah, Isshiah, Shelomoth, Jahath, Amariah, Jahaziel, Jekameam, Michah, Shamir, Isshiah, Zechariah, Mahli, Mushi, Jaaziah, Shoham, Zaccur, Ibri, Eleazar, Ithamar (according to the LXX), Jerahmeel, Mahli, Eder, Jerimoth.

[3] See the principal passage 1 Chron. xxv., cf. besides the *Dichter des A.B.* i. p. 274. sqq.

[4] Cf. the three chief guards of the temple threshold according to the annals of the realm in Jer. lii. 24. Hence the Mass. *Middôth*, i. 1, reckons three Priests, twenty-one Levites.

[5] 1 Chron. xxvi. 1–19.

[6] 1 Chron. xxvi. 20–28, ix. 14–27; cf. 2 Chron. xxv. 24, Ezr. viii. 29, Neh. x. 38–40 [37–39].

[7] 1 Chron. ix. 28–32.

[8] Vol. ii. p. 308 sqq.

[9] Cf. 1 Kings ii. 26, Jer. xxxii. 7 sqq., xxxvii. 12, Luke i. 23, 39 sq.

[10] P. 124.

[11] After the High Priest of the time, this palace is called 'Eliashib's house,' Neh. iii. 20 sq.; cf. the *Alterthümer*, p. 328 sq.

house which should contribute to the glory of the second power in Israel, viz. the monarchy, which had then reached its highest splendour. The house which David had erected for himself soon after the conquest of Jerusalem,[1] appeared too small for the dignity as well as for the treasures of the king, considering the lofty elevation which the power of Israel and its monarch had, since that period, attained. The site of this house we do not certainly know by any express testimony: but it was probably erected on the southerly continuation of the temple-mountain, commonly called Ophel, i.e. hill.[2] This structure, of which we possess only a short description, was, alike in its extent and its magnificence, a monument of the greatness of that age no less exalted than the temple itself. As it was to serve several purposes, it consisted really of a row of different large buildings, the construction of which occupied a period of thirteen years, far longer, that is, than the erection of the temple.[3] The chief edifice, a hundred cubits long, fifty cubits broad, and thirty high, consisted of three stories, each of which rested on fifteen columns. These columns, however, were not arranged at intervals in the different stories which each contained but a single chamber, so as to serve to support the roof; but they seem to have been placed in front in three rows, one above the other, all the columns being first covered over with cedar planks, and then with a ceiling of cedar wood; and as the whole appeared to be constructed of lofty cedars, it was called 'the house of the forest of Lebanon.' No story was further divided, so that the windows, which from their height let in an unusual amount of light, stood opposite one another; the doors were made with posts of four-cornered beams. The style of this house clearly proves that it was to serve only as a place for storing up and preserving the royal treasures and

---

[1] P. 124.

[2] That it was not built on Zion proper, is proved from the passages about the settlement of the Egyptian princess, p. 221; but as a royal castle it would certainly not have been placed out of the way in the lower town. That, on the contrary, the royal castle lay to the south of the temple, follows clearly from Neh. iii. 25 (see below), as well as with great probability from Micah's words about the Messiah, iv. 8; moreover, the words Is. xxxii. 14 show that magnificent buildings lay on this portion of the town. Other proofs are afforded by the situation of the horse-gate of the old town, of which more below; by that of the gate of the royal runners (on which see above, p. 241), and by that of the tombs of the latest kings, on which see below. This is further confirmed by what we know otherwise about the carefully made water-conduits which Solomon constructed on this quarter of the town (see below). Cf. further, the remarks in the *Gött. Gel. Anz.* 1865, p. 1776 sq., following the work of Theodoric *De Locis Sanctis*. Thomas Lewin is also in favour of this situation for Solomon's palace; see his *Jerusalem*, Lond. 1861, and his later work *Gött. Gel. Anz.* 1864. p. 726. In the times of the New Jerusalem many places on the Ophel were certainly assigned to the temple-servants and traders; Neh. iii. 26, 31, xi. 21.

[3] 1 Kings vii. 1 comp. with ix. 10 and above, p. 245.

valuables, and several indications still show with sufficient clearness what great treasures were there accumulated.[1] But besides the first and independent forecourt, Solomon erected a porch, which probably consisted only of colonnades, and was on that account called the porch of pillars, fifty cubits long and thirty wide, of the use of which we have no definite information. Eastwards, separated by a second court,[2] there rose the porch to the royal palace proper, with columns the capitals of which were ornamented with foliage. This porch was wainscoted from floor to roof with cedar-wood, and received, from the purpose to which it was destined, the name of the throne- or judgment-hall. Here doubtless stood the throne of Solomon, elsewhere[3] described as a marvellous work, made of ivory and overlaid with pure gold. It stood on six steps, on both sides of which were placed, in the ancient sacred number, twelve splendid lions, unquestionably because the lion was the ensign of Judah;[4] on each of its two elbow-pieces, also, was a lion, and it terminated above, in a round crown.[5]—Close on this porch abutted the actual residence of the king; and finally, behind it (just as the Harem always occupies the most retired place) was erected another for the Egyptian princess, both in similar style. A large court, the walls of which were constructed like those of the inner temple court,[6] surrounded the whole. All portions of it, from the foundations to the roof, were constructed with large stones of the best kind, from eight to ten cubits in size, which, not only where they were visible but where other parts of the building covered them, were smoothly polished. The walls on the inside were overlaid with cedar-wood, just as in the temple.[7]

---

[1] There lay, according to 1 Kings x. 16 sq. the 200 golden shields, mere objects of display, and according to ver. 21 many other costly vessels besides. We know, therefore, now where the royal treasure-chambers were, mentioned 1 Kings xiv. 26; further, where the armoury of the forest, i.e. of the Lebanon-house, lay (Is. xxii. 8), which besides must have been distinguished from the arsenal on Zion which was the older, Neh. iii. 19.

[2] This inner court is also noticed 2 Kings xx. 4, according to the *Qerî*.

[3] 1 Kings x. 18-20. According to 2 Chron. ix. 17-19, on the top of the steps overlaid with gold, was a footstool overlaid in the same way; this is, at any rate, the sense of the words ver. 18, if the second לְכִסֵּא be placed before בַזָּהָב.

[4] This follows from the ancient image applied to Judah, Gen. xlix. 9, as well as from Is. xxix. 1, Ezek. xix. 2 sqq.

[5] Cf. *Zeitschr. der Deutsch. Morgenl. Ges.* 1861, p. 153.

[6] P. 240.

[7] This is the most probable aspect of the whole royal edifice, which results from the words 1 Kings vii. 4-12. It will be generally found that such descriptions, where they are at all completely preserved, give a very clear sense. In ver. 2 three should be read instead of four. Ver. 6 I read רָאשֵׁיהֶם for the last פְּנֵיהֶם, and strike out the ו from the first אוּלָם in ver. 7, so that this becomes the second accusative; otherwise, the last six words in ver. 6 would give no sense at all, and no indication would be afforded of the situation of the portico. In ver. 7, for the last קַרְקַע we should rather read (according to vi. 15) קִירוֹת, and this is to be understood here in the same way as there.

The palace was erected on a somewhat lower level than the house of God which adjoined it, and was connected with it by a staircase. This was reserved for the use of the king alone, to make his solemn entry into the temple, and must have been constructed with great magnificence, although we have no further information about it.[1] In the temple itself the king had a special stall to which this royal entrance led up. It was a covered seat, placed on a strong pillar, from which on Sabbaths the king might survey or address the whole assembly, and which was hence called the 'Sabbath-pulpit,' in contradistinction to the court-pulpit where the king gave judgment.[2] This raised stall was certainly placed in the inner, not the outer forecourt;[3] for round it were drawn the boundaries of the sanctuary, formed probably in an arc by an ornamental balustrade.[4]

3) But both these edifices, the royal and the sacred alike, unquestionably required, in addition, a number of other costly works, in part for their completion, in part for their corresponding embellishment. To a large royal castle appertained extensive gardens, parks, and beautiful grounds of every description; nor could these be easily kept up without the most costly water-conduits; and in the same way the requirements of the temple, also, with its numerous sacrifices and priestly purifications, necessitated an artificial arrangement for the constant supply of water, at once abundant and clear. Of Solomon's further works of this kind in connexion with those great edifices, our present historical books give only a very imperfect and scarcely intelligible account;[5] but that antiquity, in ac-

---

[1] This follows from 1 Kings x. 5, where עֹלָה, or rather (according to 2 Chron. ix. 4) עֲלִיָּה, cannot possibly mean 'sacrifice,' either according to the connexion of the words or the nature of the case itself. This approach is hence called similarly (2 Kings xvi. 18) the 'king's entry without.'

[2] This follows from 2 Kings xvi. 18 comp. with xi. 14, xxiii. 3.

[3] This is, at any rate, clearly required by Ez. xlvi. 2; the words in 2 Chron. vi. 13 (p. 243, note 6) point to the same conclusion, and the words of a Psalm probably composed by King Josiah, xxviii. 2, receive in this way their best explanation.

[4] Somewhat as in the forecourt to the Paphian temple, according to the coins mentioned above. The boundaries were called שְׂדֵרוֹת, properly rows, and are mentioned 2 Kings xi. 8, 15 (cf. further below); this is clearly required by the connexion of the words, and מִסְדְּרוֹן has a somewhat similar meaning; the name γεῖσιον, in Jos. Ant. viii. 3. 9, is not Hebrew. That the royal stall was by the great laver we learn from the description (p. 242, note 1) in Euseb. Præp. Ev. ix. 34, which is quite independent of 2 Chron. vi. 13. According to Ezekiel the 'prince' might only remain at the gate of the inner forecourt.

[5] In the words 'and all Solomon's desire (i.e. all his edifices) which he was pleased to do,' 1 Kings ix. 1, cf. ver. 19, where it is not Jerusalem alone (as in ver. 1) that is referred to. But the original Hebrew text clearly named as works of Solomon the *sea* and the *wells of the forecourt*, as the LXX at 1 Kings proves, just as the *bases* and *pillars* here named must also be works in the temple.

cordance with a fixed tradition, ascribed them to this monarch, may certainly be concluded from the short enumeration of the great undertakings and estates of Solomon in the Book of Koheleth[1] (Ecclesiastes) : we must therefore investigate how far indications, otherwise scattered, will enable us to recognise with precision this side of Solomon's activity.

a.) In the history of ancient Jerusalem nothing is at once more important and more obscure than the arrangement of its water-supply, which all traditions[2] unite to represent as always copious and derived from different sources, yet which in its origin remains to a great extent incomprehensible to us. The most recent investigations have led to the two important observations that many of the pools and wells were connected with one another by subterranean conduits; and that even in the present day, as in the age of Christ, a copious spring of the best water must be concealed beneath the summit of the temple-mount.[3] Nor can any doubt be entertained that even from the time of Solomon all the needs of the temple were supplied from these subterranean streams of constantly-flowing water. Prophetic imagination contemplates this with greater freedom than reality would allow, when it anticipates that in the fullness of time a mighty stream may issue from the house of Jahveh far and wide, to quicken every waste place and to cleanse everything unclean;[4] but without such a cause, the fundamental idea of the prophetic conception could never have arisen. We know, from the ancient history of the holy city, of several open pools, of the sources of whose supply we are ignorant; and modern travellers have described similar tanks, some as still available at the present day, others as dried up. Some of these also, we have every reason to refer to Solomon. Unfortunately, however, we do not now possess any passage with any pretensions to antiquity in which a connected and clear account is

---

[1] 'I planted me vineyards; I made me gardens and orchards, and I planted trees in them of all kinds of fruits; I made me pools of water to water from them a thick forest of trees,' Ecc. ii. 4–6. Herein lies unquestionably a historical reminiscence which the composer may even have derived from older books.

[2] The expression in Tacitus, *Hist.* v. 12, 'fons perennis aquæ, cavati sub terra montes,' by no means refers, by the connexion of the words, merely to a spring under the temple; the description of the temple-well in the book of Aristeas is, however, very remarkable, cf. also Philo, in Eus. *Præp. Ev.* ix. 37.

[3] See Robinson's *Bib. Res.* i. p. 341 sqq.; Williams' *The Holy City*, p. 385 sqq.; and, of the most recent date, W. Krafft's *Topographie Jerusalem's,* 1846; but especially Tit. Tobler, *Die Siloahquelle und der Ölberg*, 1852.

[4] The most ancient words are in the prophecy of Joel, iii. 18; later on this is carried out further, Zech. xiii. 1, xiv. 8; Ezek. xlvii. 1–12; Rev. xxii. 1. For with these anticipations were unquestionably mingled the images of the water of life in Paradise. But without some local cause they could never have taken the form in which we find them first of all in the priest Joel.

given of all these reservoirs of Jerusalem. And what in particular was the source of the copious flow of water under the temple-mount, cannot—even so far as it is at the present day capable of being determined—be satisfactorily investigated so long as the Turks are allowed to treat the Christians and their scientific explorers like dogs. We might be tempted to derive that subterranean temple-well and the supply of other pools from springs outside the city-bounds. In that case, the aqueduct from the three so-called wells of Solomon south-west of Bethlehem would suggest itself, the remains of which are still clearly to be traced. The style of these three great tanks at Bethlehem certainly proves them to be very old.[1] There is no reason in the nature of things why Solomon should not have constructed them; and it is pleasant to think what delight the great king might take in providing and embellishing the residence of his ancestors with magnificent works. It is true that it cannot yet be proved that the aqueduct, which was repaired and restored in the fourteenth century after Christ, had been constructed before the age of Pontius Pilate;[2] still less can we prove that Solomon had provided Jerusalem or the temple with water from those very reservoirs at Bethlehem;[3] yet probability preponderates in favour of this supposition. Our definite knowledge, however, on this point, is limited to the following. The city had at all times in its environs some inexhaustible springs of water, while the brook Kidron, which flows by on the east, and was certainly formerly much larger, is now always without water, at least in the dry season. In particular may be named here the two springs, which, according to the explanations already given,[4] must have lain in opposite directions outside the city; the well Rogel on the south-east,[5] and Gihon on the north. If we now reflect that the ancient and certainly Canaanitish name for a well, Rogel, entirely disappears just after the age of Solomon, we are led to believe that Solomon formed it into a reservoir, which (because the Kidron flows from north to south) was called 'the lower.' From this doubtless proceeded many water-conduits for the irrigation of the gardens laid out by Solomon on the south of the town. But it was not in any way connected by Solomon

---

[1] See Robinson's *Bib. Res.* ii. p. 164 sq.
[2] Cf. Williams' *The Holy City*, p. 411 sqq. That Pilate built something may be concluded from Jos. *Bell. Jud.* ii. 9. 4; *Ant.* xviii. 3. 2; but the measure of distance there given would extend far beyond Bethlehem (see on this point more below).
[3] Zschokke tries to prove this in detail in an essay on '*die versiegelte Quelle Salomo's*' in the *Theol. Quartalschrift*, 1867, pp. 426–442.
[4] P. 210 sq.
[5] Its water has a different taste from that of Siloah.

with the more northern reservoirs, and king Hezekiah was the first to unite its water with the Siloah in the valley, in order to draw it off in that direction.¹ The Gihon, on the north,² however, probably had from Solomon's time a double outlet. One of these was called 'the upper,' which was certainly the same as the upper or ancient pool, the waters of which were first brought into the city in the reign of Hezekiah, by an artificial conduit on the west.³ This upper outlet Solomon clearly left as he found it, as its name 'the ancient pool' in fact indicates. He may, however, have drawn off one or more streams from the spring, and conducted them eastwards towards the temple, so that perhaps the pool of Bethesda was fed by it; perhaps, too the subterranean temple-spring as well as the Fount of the Virgin south-east of the temple, and what is now called the spring of Siloam at the outlet of the valley of the Tyropœon, were derived thence; for the more recent investigations have proved that these two were connected with the temple-well by subterranean passages.⁴ On the other hand, the ancient spring Siloah may have originated on the south-western slope of Zion, and thence flowing open in numerous conduits, may have formed the pool of Siloah, or King's pool, as well as another called the 'artificial pool,'⁵ until it descended to the

---

¹ This follows from Is. xxii. 9 comp. with 2 Chron. xxxii. 3 sq. The connexion of the reservoirs of modern Jerusalem according to the traces hitherto discovered may be best seen from the plan of the city published at Berlin in 1845 by Kiepert and the consul Schultz. The ancient Siloah in the valley is best regarded as included within the ancient city walls.

² To look for the Gihon on the west in the present pool Mamilla is certainly wrong, if only because the Serpent's pool must have been situated there, as is explained below. It is true that valley is often called Gihon (see Burchard in Laurent's *Peregrinatores*, p. 63, 65, 76), but that this name had no other origin than among the monks of the holy sepulchre close by is seen from the fact that formerly the whole western valley was called Gehinnom, cf. Bahâeldîn's *Life of Saladin*, p. 73, and Kemâleldîn, in Freyt. *Chr. Ar.* p. 122 sq. That the Gihon lay on the north of the city, west of the Kidron valley, follows also from 2 Chron. xxxiii. 14.

³ This is according to Is. xxii. 11, comp. with vii. 3; 2 Chron. xxxii. 30; 2 Kings xx. 20. From this it is clear that this was a very extensive structure, and since the 'double walls' may be understood of the western corner, where the northern walls of the city of David and the later walls abutted on one another, the passage applies well to the large reservoir within the city, which is now still called after Hezekiah. The old reservoir may be imagined to be the great northern cistern of which the consul Schultz speaks, p. 35 of his *Jerusalem* (Berlin, 1845). Those 'double walls' were not the same as the wall by the king's garden on the south-east, where the walls of Zion and Ophel met, 2 Kings xxv. 4.

⁴ Judging by the colour, the present water of Bethesda is certainly different; the taste of the water in the temple, however, is the same as that of the Fount of the Virgin and of Siloam, as Williams goes on to describe. Recent investigators have already discovered a subterranean conduit from the Fount of the Virgin to Siloam.

⁵ The proof of this lies especially in the description of the ancient walls and gates, Neh. iii. 1-32. On closer consideration it appears that this begins north of the temple, and makes a complete circuit from the north-east. If it be observed further, that in such descriptions the expression הַגַּיְא can only mean the valley west and south

east nearly opposite to the entrance to the valley of the Tyropœon, and was here united with the water from the north in the basin now known as the spring of Siloam. This conduit of the Siloah was certainly an excellent work of Solomon's. It was the only open flowing stream in the ancient city, and in addition to this it flowed right round the city of David,[1] while its water was in some way or other connected with the temple. And so in succeeding ages it easily became, with its gentle yet never-failing flow, a type of the dominion—at bottom equally mild and gentle—of that kingdom of God and that royal house which now appeared to be for ever firmly bound to the rock of Zion.[2] Whether Solomon also excavated the two great reser-

(Hinnom), and הַנַּחַל only that on the north and east (the Wâdi Kidron); further, that הַמִּקְצוֹעַ, 'the corner,' Neh. iii. 19, 24, probably means the later so-called valley of the Tyropœon, the whole passage is not so obscure as it appears. The sheep-gate, on the north-east of the temple, was followed by the fish-gate farther north, ver. 3, in the neighbourhood of which, it is clear, was a pool from the spring Gihon. The old gate, ver. 6, cf. Zech. xiv. 10, lay then to the north-west. After a long interval this was succeeded by the valley-gate, ver. 13, evidently towards the northern end of Hinnom, and further south, almost at the beginning of the city of David on the north, was the dung-gate, ver. 14 (no doubt the same as the potsherd-gate, Jer. xix. 2). Then came the 'gate of the fountain,' which was plainly the source of the Siloah, which then a little further south formed 'the pool of Siloah of the king's garden,' ver. 15, hence called more briefly 'the king's pool' (Neh. ii. 14), where steps led down from the city of David into the valley of Hinnom. In the next place we hear, for the first time, ver. 16, of the spot called the 'sepulchres of David,' which are now shown on the south-west (cf. above, p. 228 sq.) with the artificial pool, the name of which indicates that it was a new pool. After a long interval, where the wall turns right round to the south, there follows (ver. 19) 'the staircase to the armoury at the corner,' evidently at the southern entrance of the valley of the Tyropœon. The wall now proceeds on the western side of this valley northwards until the point at which the valley ceases south of the temple, ver. 24; continues on its eastern side, where Solomon's palace on the north abuts on the southern out-buildings of the temple, ver. 25; goes round Ophel, including in it the eastern water-gate and horse-gate, which led down into the valley of the Tyropœon, vv. 26-28, until it gradually comes to the east gate opposite the Kidron; and here taking a northerly direction, finally reaches the sheep-gate, vv. 29-32. With this the shorter description, Neh. ii. 13-15 agrees, where the valley-gate serves for exit, as well as the somewhat longer one, Neh. xii. 31-40, where two processions start from the temple and march through the town to the dung-gate, from which point one makes the circuit of the city on the south, the other on the north, and both at last meet again south of the temple. These remarks may suffice to correct the numerous errors about the position of the various gates and reservoirs of the city, which are still to be found not only in Robinson and Williams, but even in the map of Kiepert and Consul Schultz. If closer investigations should procure us more precise knowledge than we now possess about the site of the sepulchres of David, we should be able to pronounce with greater certainty about details. As to Siloah, it is clear from Is. viii. 6 that it was originally a running stream, not merely a pool, that it may have been connected with the present Siloam, but was something more than this reservoir; perhaps the present Sultan's pool south-west of the city was formerly derived from the spring. Cf. also the explanation of Jer. xxxi. 37-40 in the *Propheten des A. B.* 2nd ed. ii. p. 266.

[1] P. 124.

[2] Is. viii. 6, Ps. xlvi. 4, both passages are of the same period. The name הַשִּׁלֹחַ, Is. viii. 6, modified by the Hellenists into Σιλωάμ, is pronounced rather differently in Neh. iii. 15, הַשֶּׁלַח; at any rate, both names must certainly mean the same water. The name denotes by itself only fountain,

voirs in the valley named Gehinnom on the west side of the city, we cannot determine with equal certainty.[1] Thus much, however, is clear—that the general artificial water-supply of the city and its neighbourhood[2] is to be referred in its essential features to Solomon, and that it remained as he had arranged it, until under king Hezekiah it underwent some important changes to accommodate it to the altered requirements of the age. In the meantime, however, with all these artificial reservoirs the ancient city could not entirely dispense with the collection of rain water in large wells, although this was not certainly so necessary for it then as it is at the present day, since the destruction to a great extent of the artificial water-supply.

b.) Aided by these elaborate water-works, Solomon now laid out on the broad southern slope of the city,[3] gardens of every kind, vineyards, orchards, and these again in every variety. We may reasonably imagine that he sought to grow in them specimens of most of the species of plants 'from the cedar to the hyssop,' on which he composed a book. How far these gardens, which belonged to the palace, extended to the south, we have no precise knowledge. Five miles farther to the south, however, by the three reservoirs at Bethlehem, he seems to have had similar ones. Of his splendid parks and a sort of gymnasium at Etam in the same district, to which Solomon often made pleasure excursions, a vivid remembrance, drawn certainly from ancient writings, was preserved even to the times of Fl. Josephus.[4] Similar parks probably gave to the mountain-city not far eastwards—the situation of which the Arabs still know as *Fureidîs*, i.e. little Paradise—the genuine Hebrew name Bethkerem, i.e. House of Vines.[5]

stream; that it signifies the extensive aqueduct, mentioned p. 253, is rendered quite improbable by every indication.

[1] The 'Dragon-well,' Neh. ii. 13, lay opposite the valley-gate, possibly, therefore, on the same spot where now the great reservoir Mamilla lies. But this reservoir, as it now appears, does not belong (according to Williams, *The Holy City*, p. 410 sq.) to earlier antiquity.

[2] That the Phœnicians were acquainted with similar arts of irrigation and had brought them to a high pitch of perfection, is proved even now by the traces in Malta; see Raumer's *Hist. Taschenbuch*, 1844, p. 261 sq.

[3] It was principally there that the royal gardens lay, 2 Kings xxv. 4 (and again xxi. 18), Neh. iii. 15 (where all the divergence of the explanation of the LXX rests on a false reading), and also the royal wine-presses, Zech. xiv. 10.

[4] *Ant.* viii. 7. 3. Williams asserts (*The Holy City*, p. 413 sq.), that the valley at the entrance of which lay the three celebrated reservoirs south-west of Bethlehem, is still called Wâdi Etân; of this Robinson says nothing.

[5] The Bethkerem, named Jer. vi. 1, lay, according to this passage, as well as according to the Fathers of the Church, not far north of Tekoa; it agrees with the position of the hill which is now called Fureidîs, and where a crowd of remains attests the existence of ancient cultivation. It is now called, after Christian tradition, the hill of the Franks.

c.) Solomon further undertook the erection of similar palaces, for purposes at once of pleasure and utility, in other spots in his wide dominions, as we may gather very clearly from some historical traditions. He seems to have found especial delight in the forest-clad heights of Lebanon, with their crown of snow;[1] and his father's conquests and his own afforded him, in the beautiful northern districts, plenty of room for such parks, without obliging him to subtract from the estates of his countrymen. It was there, in Antilibanus, that he built the towers (alluded to in the Canticles), which proudly looked towards Damascus, and were adorned with glittering ivory; for such towers as these are clearly enough distinguished in this song from the towers of David with their military appurtenances.[2] To the north, not far from Lebanon, the slopes of which produced always the best wine, lay also Baalhamon, where he laid out a celebrated vineyard; and for every thousand stocks a tenant could get a thousand pieces of silver, four-fifths of which must be paid into the royal treasury.[3] How the king would make excursions of pleasure from Jerusalem to such favourite spots; how he would sometimes ride in a chariot, surrounded by the most practised horsemen, or sometimes would be borne on a litter of two seats, constructed of the most costly materials; how he would be guarded by sixty of David's Gibborim, once so terrible, now but little occupied with war, and how a numerous suite would accompany him,—all this the Canticles describe from faithful reminiscence with great vividness.[4]

2. *Measures for the Security and Prosperity of the Realm.*

Solomon, however, would have been but a sorry king had he merely contented himself with erecting these royal and sacred edifices. But we find him equally zealous in taking measures on the grandest scale for the security and prosperity as well as for the orderly administration of his vast dominion. We may, therefore, supply at this point much information which has general reference to the condition of Israel during the ages of the monarchy.

[1] To which the historical work, 1 Kings ix. 19, especially refers.
[2] Cant. vii. 5 comp. with iv. 4.
[3] Cant. viii. 11 sq. comp. with the proverbial expression Is. vii. 23. As to Baalhamon I still hold to the probability of my observation in 1826, that it is the same with Hammon in the tribe of Asher, Jos. xix. 28, as Baal-shalisha, 2 Kings iv. 42, is shortened into Shalisha, 1 Sam. ix. 4; there is no reason at all for referring it to Baalbek, i.e. Heliopolis; it would be better to identify it with the place βελαμών in the tribe of Ephraim, Judith viii. 3.
[4] Cant. iii. 6–10 comp. with vi. 12, i. 9; and Jos. *Ant.* viii. 7. 3.

The security of the kingdom did not certainly require Solomon to take the severer measures which became necessary in a later and more oppressed age,—for King Hezekiah, for instance, who, in order to protect the capital from hostile attack, either stopped up or drew off all the supply of water outside its walls. The age of Solomon felt itself too powerful and too prosperous to need such precautions. Still he did not neglect anything to this end. He even attempted to confirm it by new means which had never before been employed in Israel, as though greater security externally should become a lasting guarantee for the unusual prosperity internally, which was now spreading undisturbed in peace.

1) The capital, accordingly, was newly fortified; and we further know that this undertaking was not commenced till the second half of the king's reign.[1] The fortification of the city at the time of David was limited, as far as we can recognise, to the broad mountain of Zion on the south, which became the nucleus of the whole city. In the walls of this 'city of David,' however, a weak point must have been observed, which Solomon improved at considerable expense.[2] This was probably to the north-east, westwards therefore of the temple, not far south of the spot—perhaps even upon the very spot—where the later fortress of the city lay.[3] Zion, as well as the mountain north of it, appears here to have sloped down rather low into the valley of the Tyropœon, so that Solomon had an earthwork thrown up there, and within the lines erected a fort, which might serve as a powerful defence alike for Zion and the temple. This fortification, which derived from the earthwork the name of Millo, or more fully, Beth-Millo, was evidently of considerable extent, and took some years to complete; moreover, it is still spoken of in the following centuries. Later

---

[1] This is clear from 1 Kings ix. 24 comp. with vv. 10, 15.

[2] This follows from 1 Kings xi. 27, for the words here 'he closed the breaches of the city of David,' cannot, according to the clear connexion of the words, be anything else than an explanation of the foregoing 'he built Millo.'

[3] The only passage besides that just adduced from which we may gather a little more definitely the situation of Millo, is that in 2 Kings xii. 21 [20]: 'Beth-Millo which goeth down to the steps,' for Silla or Sulla is probably abbreviated from סֻלָּם, 'steps,' so that it results that from this structure a flight of steps led down into a deep valley. Now such a flight certainly led down from Zion on the west, and another on the south into the vale of Hinnom, Neh. iii. 15, 19 (where עָלִית, as in v. 31 sq. is to be read for עָלה), but Zion itself was there of considerable height, while on the north-east it still shows traces of an artificially-raised mound (see the *Jerusalem* of Consul Schultz, p. 28: he makes a great mistake, however, with Williams, in confounding (p. 81) the 'high street,' 1 Chron. xxvi. 16, 18, which lay on the temple-hill, with the Silla in the valley); cf. 1 Macc. xiii. 52. The mention of Millo so early as in 2 Sam. v. 9 is plainly only a brief description in the language of a later day of the part of the city intended. That *Millo* is much the same as *Akra* is proved also by the version of the LXX, 1 Kings xi. 27, and elsewhere.

still, Solomon appears to have carried the wall round the mountain on the north and east;[1] since the eastern hill with the temple and palace, and the northern, on which the population of the capital was rapidly increasing, formed one whole with Zion, and required defence. Of course, besides this, the temple, as such, had its own walls. The most northern portion of the city, however, which was so closely connected with Zion,[2] bore from that time the name of Mishneh, i.e. second city, which we might translate by New-Town.[3]

Solomon further sought, however, to protect the whole of the kingdom by erecting a new chain of forts. He was clearly the first who endeavoured to defend the ancient boundaries by selecting a series of fastnesses to form a sort of girdle round the land; as though he had a presentiment that hereafter new dangers from countries then subdued might threaten the territory of Israel. Accordingly, in the extreme north he fortified Hazor;[4] farther south, Megiddo, in the plains of Galilee; next, west of Jerusalem, the city of Gezer;[5] the two towns of Upper and Lower Beth-horon,[6] which lay in dangerous and narrow passes, and Baalath, situated not far from Gezer. This chain is evidently deficient in towns in the south; and probably Solomon had no time to complete the series in this direction, so that it was left to his successor to carry out this part of the plan. If we reflect, moreover, that Gezer[7] had been taken in war, and that the neighbouring cities alluded to may have been involved in its revolt, and further that, in the north, Megiddo and Hazor were for a long time in the possession of the Canaanites,[8] it will appear that Solomon first of all transformed into new fortresses only such towns as might have been claimed as royal conquests.

Still more violent was the innovation on which the king ventured in the style of arms, in introducing, contrary to all ancient Israelite custom, horses and chariots, not merely in small numbers and for his own pleasure, but in large quantities

---

[1] For the words 'and the walls of Jerusalem,' 1 Kings ix. 15, cf. iii. 1, must mean a different wall from Millo, and it is also naturally to be expected that Solomon carried the wall round the rest of the city. From his time till its first destruction Jerusalem does not seem to have increased much in circumference.
[2] P. 125.
[3] At least, this is the most probable meaning of the name; Zeph. i. 10, 2 Kings xxii. 14, Neh. xi. 9.
[4] Vol. ii. p. 253.
[5] P. 221.

[6] The upper town, which is even more important than the lower, is wanting in the present text, 1 Kings ix. 15-18, but occurs in the LXX in place of the latter, and together with it 2 Chron. viii. 5 sq. In the two Beit-ûrs Robinson still found remains of ancient fortifications. The situation of Baalath is given by Josephus in agreement with Josh. xix. 44; the city is, moreover, the same as the Baalah mentioned p. 126, *note* 4.
[7] P. 221.
[8] Cf. Judges i. 27, iv. 2.

for military purposes. In this the Egyptian monarchy was evidently his pattern; and this fact is attested by the proverbial expression, 'Pharaoh's chariots at Solomon's court.'[1] He imported fourteen hundred chariots, of course with the necessary horses, and twelve thousand trained horses for cavalry; the proportion of which clearly discloses how much more horsemen were then beginning to be employed in Egypt, compared with chariot men; for in the oldest times, Egypt, as its monuments prove, possessed only fighting chariots, not fighting horses. These Egyptian forces, with their novel arms, were in part kept by Solomon in the capital, in part stationed by him in the country round; for the latter he was obliged to build separate little towns (barrack villages).[2] From this time onwards, the question whether or not such chariots and horses were to be introduced contrary to the ancient customs of the community of Israel, forms a subject of contest, the importance of which may be estimated from what has been already said.[3] The great Prophets,—those, at any rate, whom we know in the ninth and eighth centuries,—always kept in view only what was essential for the true religion; but there had been a contest once.

2) Great, however, as was the king's care for the security of the kingdom, his efforts to promote the commerce and trade of his country were equally prodigious; and these he certainly commenced at once, after securing the stability of his power. These arts of peace, it is true, had already taken root in Israel during the period of the Judges,[4] but during the excessive military activity of the last century they must have been severely repressed. A combination of prosperous relations, such as had never before been witnessed, now invited the nation to pursue them with zeal; and if the king himself entered upon the work with the greatest activity, he assuredly did so, not (like many other princes) to divert the proceeds from the pockets of his subjects into his own, but because these arts of

---

[1] Cant. i. 9. This is plainly the meaning of the expression.

[2] According to 1 Kings ix. 19, x. 26; on the contrary, in v. 6 [iv.26] instead of 40,000 chariot-horses we must of necessity read 4,000, according to 2 Chron. ix. 25, cf. i. 14; more properly 4,200, supposing that to every chariot, besides the two regular horses, there belonged another in reserve. Moreover, the chariot horses (according to 1 Kings v. 8 [iv. 28], Micah i. 13) had the special name רֶכֶשׁ, while the Syrian ܪܟܫܐ, and still more the Arabic رَخْش of the Rustem, in the Shahnâmeh, signifies the war-horse proper; between the two significations stands that of the fleet-horse, in Esther viii. 10, 14. Josephus, *Ant.* viii. 7. 4, turns the towns where chariots were stationed into commercial cities with chariots upon fine military roads constructed by Solomon. In this as in other fanciful embellishments he probably follows some apocryphal work about Solomon, of the use of which distinct traces appear in his writings.

[3] Vol. ii. comp. with p. 145 sq. above.

[4] Vol. ii. p. 354.

EFFORTS TO PROMOTE TRADE. 261

peace needed the stimulus of a more energetic impulse, which could not possibly be successfully imparted without the whole weight of royal power and royal will. In the broad extent of the possessions of Israel at that time, it lay open to the king to develope traffic alike by land and by sea. He promoted both with courage and success.

a.) To increase the land-traffic, he had small cities built in advantageous localities, in which goods of all sorts in large quantities were kept in suitable storehouses; a practice similar to that which had from ancient times prevailed in Egypt.[1] Such commercial centres had, therefore, for the most part, to be erected on the boundaries of the country, where an active exchange of commodities between remote nations easily sprang up. We have not many particulars, but we know, at any rate, that they were established chiefly in the most northern districts of Israel, towards the Phœnician boundaries, as well as in the territories of the kingdom of Hamath, which was first conquered by Solomon himself.[2]—The main road for the land traffic between Egypt and the interior of Asia must have been the great highway leading past Gaza and further west of Jerusalem to the Northern Jordan and Damascus. Here it was joined by the road from the Phœnician cities, and continued as far as Thapsacus, on the Euphrates.[3] This was entirely in the dominions of the king; and here, under the peaceful banner of a great and powerful monarchy, commerce could flourish as it had never flourished before. It was clearly for the improvement of this route, which had to traverse the Syrian desert on the north, that Solomon built, in a happily chosen oasis of this wilderness, the city of Thammor, or Tadmor, of which the Greek version is Palmyra. There is not a single indication that this city was of importance before Solomon's time, but from that era it flourished for more than a thousand years.[4] A little more light is thrown, by one single example,

---

[1] Cf. ii. p. 13. That a similar custom exists even at the present day in the interior of Africa may be seen from W. Munzinger's *Ostafrikanischen Studien*, pp. 567-9. From Spence Hardy's *Eastern Monachism*, p. 182, we learn that it existed also in ancient India.

[2] According to 1 Kings ix. 19, 2 Chron. viii. 4, 6, xvi. 4: for the cities of this description in Naphtali named in the last passage may have been founded only by Solomon; and perhaps this is referred to in the sentence 'Solomon began to open the δυναστεύματα of Lebanon,' which occurs in the LXX, 1 Kings ii. 46, to which nothing now corresponds in the Hebrew. The reading in the passage 2 Chron. xvi. 4 has certainly been altered from another, 1 Kings xv. 20, not, however, without the precedent of an ancient account of such cities.

[3] 1 Kings v. 1, 4 [iv. 21, 24].

[4] 1 Kings ix. 18, where the Kethîb תמר is to be read. The pronunciation Tadmor (2 Chron. viii. 4) which prevailed later, has not, however, arisen through the spread of Aramaic, but is original (cf. a Tedmor in Lebanon, in Seetzen's *Reisen*, i. p. 244); inasmuch, however, as that ancient pronunciation appeared to call *Palms*

upon the way in which commerce was conducted upon this route. The desire for Egyptian war-horses and fighting chariots was at that time very generally spread, even among the petty Hittite (i.e. generally Canaanite), and Aramean kings, whether they were dependent upon Solomon or not. But the key to this traffic with Egyptian arms was in the hands of Solomon alone, especially so long as he continued on friendly terms with the sovereign of that country. He accordingly had it conducted by his own merchants, who were bound to deliver up the profits to him for a fixed salary, an arrangement somewhat similar to that which we have already noticed [1] in the case of the newly laid-out vineyards; and it is remarked that the profits (of course after reckoning all expenses) on a war-horse amounted to one hundred and fifty shekels, on a chariot with its three horses,[2] to six hundred shekels.[3] How many horses and chariots of the kind may have thus passed northwards and crossed the Euphrates!—The laying-out of great army-routes, which met in Jerusalem,[4] and the establishment of convenient travelling-stations (caravanserais),[5] could not be neglected. Of both of these operations we still possess some indications.

b.) For any distant navigation, however, Solomon was obliged to rely on the aid of the Phœnicians, inasmuch as they were in that age the only nation which possessed the necessary ability and inclination for it. It is true that the idea of competing with the Phœnicians upon the Mediterranean could hardly have occurred to him, since they had long before that time attracted all the commerce upon it to themselves, and would

---

to mind, Tadmor passed the more easily in Grecian mouths into Palmyra. No great weight is to be attached to the belief of its later inhabitants, mentioned by the Arabian geographer Jâqût, that the city had already existed before Solomon. On the otherwise correct reading, 1 Kings ix. 18, see below; on other points, the *Jahrbb. der Bibl. Wiss.* vi. p. 89.

[1] P. 257.
[2] P. 260.
[3] This is the meaning of the words 1 Kings x. 28 sq. They are certainly made rather obscure by the word מִקְוֵה (which made the LXX think of a country Κουε), which does not again occur in such a connexion, but since it is wealth and profit which are here spoken of, no one can be tempted to compare the Arabic قُوى, which in some of its derivations is used of the rise of prices or the surplus and profit of trade (cf. *chaúe* or *chúe* in Seetzen's *Reisen*, ii. p. 325). The whole passage then means, 'as for the export of horses which Solomon got from Egypt, and the profit of the royal traders which they received as clear profit, the carriage and export of a chariot from Egypt amounted to &c., and thus they were exported by means of these traders for all &c.' The mere carriage and export, therefore, of a horse or chariot cost the sum named, independently of the price at which it was purchased in Egypt. The Chronicler repeats the passage, only with the transposition of a word (similar transpositions occur elsewhere in his work), 2 Chron. i. 16 sq., but in ix. 28 reproduces its meaning with a change which makes the horses exported for the king from Egypt and all other countries. Cf. besides, Layard's *Nineveh*, ii. pp. 359-61.

[4] Jos. *Ant.* viii. 7. 4.
[5] P. 216, *note* 3.

scarcely have either desired or tolerated such a rival.¹ The only small harbour, however, which was easily available for the ancient Israelite territory upon this coast, was now opened in Joppa;² while cities like Cæsarea, Dora, and Acco (Ptolemais) north of Joppa did not acquire any great importance for Palestine till a much later age, when the special efforts and requirements of the Greco-Roman period brought them into prominence. But the Red Sea, which had been thrown open to the kings of Israel by the conquest of the Idumeans, offered the finest opportunity for the most distant and lucrative undertakings, the profit of which might perfectly satisfy a nation in the position of Israel in the dawn of maritime activity; and on their part, the Phœnicians could not fail to be most willing helpers in the promotion of undertakings which it lay in the hands of the powerful king of Israel entirely to cut off from them, or at any rate to encumber with great difficulties. In this way the mutual desires and needs of two nations coincided without any injury to the one or the other; and nothing but such a combination can give rise to advantageous and lasting alliances. Except the erection of the temple and its consequences, no external event throughout the whole reign of Solomon was richer in its results for Israel than this successful attempt at navigation to far-distant lands. Phœnician sailors were at first, it is true, the teachers of the Israelite. It was they who aided them in constructing and manning the tall ships, which, destined to distant voyages upon uncertain seas, needed to be stoutly put together; but yet how many new ideas and what varied knowledge the nation would in this way acquire! The ships were built in Ezion-geber, the harbour of the town of Elath (or Eloth), probably on the very spot where Akaba now stands.³ The cargo brought back each time from the three years' voyage consisted of four hundred and twenty talents of gold, besides silver, ivory, red sandal-

---

¹ Certainly the ships 1 Kings x. 22 are named Tarshish-ships. But we see, from passages like Is. ii. 16, Ps. xlviii. 17, that in ancient times nothing more was intended by this than great and strong ships; the name is therefore no more to be taken literally than ships of Hiram, x. 11, only we must admit that the contents and style of the clauses x. 11 sq. 22 show them to have been derived from an older source than the passage ix. 26-28. In the repetition of these passages in 2 Chron. viii. 17 sq., ix. 10 sq. 21, the reading 450 for 420 talents may certainly be correct; but if the ships of Tarshish be turned into ships which then sailed to Tarshish, i.e. Spain, this can only have arisen through a misunderstanding of the subsequent narrator, as all more exact investigators in modern times since Th. Ch. Tychsen and Bredow, have recognised.

² P. 221.

³ Akaba, i.e. *back*, is certainly only a dialectic variation and at the same time an abbreviation for the Hebrew and ancient mythological Ezion-geber, i.e. giant's back; and the name of the present Wâdi el-Gudjan, farther north and deeper in the interior, still perhaps contains a reminiscence of the former glory of the maritime city.

wood, apes, and peacocks, probably also nard and aloe.¹ The sandal-wood had never before been introduced into the country, and was used by the king in the same way as in India, partly for making balustrades before the doors of the temple and the palace, partly for the decoration of lyres and harps. The term Ophir itself, the goal of these long voyages, is to be extended, according to all these indications, to the most distant coasts of India,² and the 'gold of Ophir' became from that time a proverbial expression in Israel.

c.) The royal revenues were further increased by the customduties which the merchants not in the royal employ were obliged to pay out of their profit,³ as well as by the presents of subject kings or of petty princes seeking protection, and the tributes of the governors of conquered countries; and no inconsiderable accession was derived from the resort of numerous rich pilgrims to Jerusalem. Independently, however, of all such sources of income, which were more or less accidental, the total revenue of the king in ready money, which accrued chiefly from the tributes of subjects and the proceeds of the maritime trade, was estimated at six hundred and sixty-six talents of gold annually.⁴ We shall subsequently investigate somewhat more closely what proportion of this was contributed by the tribes of Israel themselves.

Thus the splendour of the royal rule of Israel extended even to the arms and household furniture of the king. The rich Aramean monarch Hadad-ezer had once provided his body-guard with golden arms;⁵ and Solomon in like manner had two hundred

---

¹ The passages of the O. T. where these two occur were none of them written before Solomon, while their Indian origin is indisputable; see Lassen, *Indische Alterth.* i. p. 285, 288.

² Even if Ophir originally (according to Gen. x. 29) lay on the south-east coast of Arabia, it might, after the voyage was extended from there to India, just as well include this land in common usage, as the quite similar name Havîlah, Gen. x. 7, 29, designates many more eastern countries. The most recent exact investigation about Ophir is that of Lassen, *Indische Alterth.* i. p. 538 sq., only it is not necessary to limit oneself to the Indian *Abhira*. For proof that India in ancient times was rich in gold, see *Journ. As.* 1846, i. p. 371.—The pronunciation Σοφίρ or Σουφείρ in the LXX merely depends on a habit, in other cases also widely spread among the Hellenists and other Greeks, of putting an s before foreign proper names: an example of this we have already observed, p. 226, *note* 2. The reasons by which Quatremère in his essay on Ophir (*Mémoires de l'Acad. des Inscriptions*, 1845, t. xv. 2, p. 349-402) tries to make out that not India but Sofala in Africa is meant, possess little depth. We pass by, among others, the strange statements in Wellsted's *Reise nach der Stadt der Khalifen*, p. 278 sqq.—The island of Urphé in the Red Sea, where, according to Eupolemus and Theophilus (Eus. *Præp. Ev.* ix. 30), David had already had gold buried, has probably arisen out of the name Ophir.

³ As the sense of the words 1 Kings x. 28 sq. has been correctly determined above, it becomes clear how in x. 15, 2 Chron. ix. 14, two different kinds of merchants can be named together, and מִסְחַר, as distinguished from מְקוֶה, appears accordingly to mean the custom-duties.

⁴ 1 Kings x. 14.   ⁵ P. 158.

great shields prepared, each of which was overlaid with six hundred pounds (or rather six minæ), and three hundred smaller, of which each was overlaid with three hundred pounds of artificially wrought gold. These golden shields were carried before him by the guards in solemn processions, especially when the king went in state [1] from the palace into the temple.[2] All the drinking vessels and a quantity of other furniture in his palace were made, in the same way, of pure gold; and silver seemed to be of no value anywhere in his eyes.[3] All Israel then, as a later narrator expresses himself, ate its bread with joy, every man sitting peacefully under his own vine and fig-tree.[4] We probably still possess from the midst of that contented and happy age an important fragment of a song which, in its higher flight of gratitude to God, glorified with eloquent and picturesque words the universal prosperity of these long days of peace.[5] Through the inhabitants even of the whole kingdom was diffused the contented tranquillity and cheerfulness of a life satisfied with itself, to which we see in the Canticles a brilliant testimony still preserved from the age immediately after Solomon. Jerusalem, however, was the chief receptacle of all this wealth and splendour; and while the other inhabitants of the capital sought to rival the king in the magnificence of their residences and equipments, silver seems to have taken the place there of stones, and cedar-beams of the common sycamore planks otherwise used in building.[6] Nay, so deep an impression was made upon the nation by the remembrance of the extraordinary prosperity and long tranquillity of the age of Solomon, and so slight was the extent to which in succeeding centuries similar circumstances ever reappeared, that the nation always looked back to this period with a longing which increased with every generation; just as, naturally, in the remembrance of those who came after, the unexampled prosperity of this age was blended into a single image with the glory of the age of David.

---

[1] P. 251.
[2] This clearly results from the narrative 1 Kings xiv. 27 sq., 2 Chron. xii. 10 sq.
[3] 1 Kings x. 16 sq., 21, 23; cf. 2 Chron. ix. 15, sq.
[4] 1 Kings iv. 20 sq., v. 4 [iv. 24] sq. The beautiful expression of the vine and the fig-tree has certainly first passed into this narrative from the Messianic description of Joel, and Micah iv. 4, and it is only the second Deuteronomic narrator who ventures on thus transferring it.
[5] The fragment Ps. cxliv. 12–14, of a style in every respect rare, belongs in all probability to this period; there is a clear allusion in ver. 12 to the newly flourishing architecture of that age.
[6] 1 Kings x. 27.

3. *The Administration and the Manners of the Monarchy under Solomon and his Successors.*

Even prosperity like this would have been destitute of stability, had it not been supported by a well-arranged and careful administration of the realm. Such a mode of government had already long existed in Egypt, and much of the royal usage of Israel was unmistakably derived from this source. And even of the necessary reflection of the prosperity of the whole people in that of the king and his court, Egypt had long ago supplied the type. Certain customs of the monarchy and the court accordingly now grew up, which were sedulously maintained in every succeeding age in Israel, and which we must here describe in more detail, with reference to their origin.

1) The simplest method of conducting a monarchical government is for the sovereign to associate with himself one or two 'friends,'[1] on whom he publicly confers his entire confidence, and who preside over and administer everything in the realm, the one perhaps over the civil, the other over the military department. Nay, in the simplest form of all, the king appoints only one single friend, in whom is placed the highest trust; in which case it is of course the commander of the army who is selected, inasmuch as the strict order, unity, and protection of the realm alike within and without constitute the object of all kingship, and so far everything in it proceeds from the sovereign. This was the arrangement in the petty kingdoms round about Israel in the earliest times;[2] and the same simple organisation of the supreme administration still prevailed in Israel also under Saul.[3] But such a representative of the king easily acquires only too much power, and stands forth as sole master in government and war.[4] When the enlargement of the state increases the difficulties of its administration, the different departments are necessarily more subdivided, and new offices of 'friends' or ministers of the king assume a sort of independent importance by the side of the simpler organisation. This change was already effected in Israel under David. The foremost place was then occupied by two offices, which, in contrast to the ministry of war, may be called properly civil. Their creation appears to have been a matter of necessity, and they

---

[1] Cf. the names Gen. xxvi. 26, 1 Kings iv. 5, and the beautiful description of what such a person ought to be, Prov. xxii. 11.

[2] Gen. xxi. 22, 32 comp. with xxvi. 26; see above, p. 103.

[3] According to 1 Sam. xiv. 50; comp. with the similar remarks (soon to be mentioned) about the government offices under David and Solomon.

[4] As Abner under Ishbosheth, according to p. 111 sqq.

subdivided between them all the rest of the administration of ordinary affairs. The first was that of the *Mazkîr*, i.e. 'the reminder,' who was to act like the mouth of the king, or as chancellor. It was his duty to bring before him all more important questions, the complaints, petitions, and suits of subjects, or of foreigners; but he had besides to lay before the king the proper papers and memorials; and it was specially required of him that he should be skilled in the art of composition, for he had to prepare the actual royal records and commands.¹ The second was that of the *Sôpher*, i.e. 'the writer,' whose duty it was to prepare the decrees in all civil matters, especially about the revenues. This appears at any rate the safest interpretation of these two words, of which the first especially has now become somewhat obscure. The Mazkîr was accordingly required to be well acquainted with all the treaties with foreign nations,² and had the superintendence of the record-office (the archives). The business and authority of the Sôpher, who is mentioned far oftener, were certainly more extensive. He could sign the judicial decisions,³ but the whole accounts of the realm also passed through his hands, the rating-lists of the people,⁴ as well as the money matters (finance) which were most closely connected with them.⁵ We shall not, therefore, be surprised to find that under Solomon there were two Sôphers appointed at once,⁶ who probably divided the business between them according to these two different departments.

The basis of the ancient arrangement of the Priesthood, which served as the hereditary protection of the existing Jahveism, remained unchanged under the monarchy, and consequently the office of the High Priest, as the representative of the entire Priesthood, could not fail to be now brought into closer

---

¹ It cannot certainly be expected that the names of the royal court-offices of Israel should still have been everywhere easily intelligible in the last centuries B.C.; but it is to be noticed that the LXX translate these names in 2 Sam. and Kings quite literally ὁ ἀναμιμνῄσκων, in 2 Sam. viii. 17, however, with still greater clearness, ὁ ἐπὶ τῶν ὑπομνημάτων, and Is. xxxvi. 3 as in the Chronicles, ὁ ὑπομνηματογράφος; this name recurs in the Ptolemaic period in the city-administrations (Strabo, *Geogr.* xvii. 12), and its holder is named *qui e memoria Augusti*, according to the best reading, Suet. *Aug.* c. 79. The nearest parallel is in the name now found in inscriptions, μνημονεύων; cf. Sauppe in the *Gött. Gel. Nachr.* 1863, p. 310 sqq.

² This must be concluded from his part in the negotiations about war or peace; 2 Kings xviii. 18 sqq., Is. xxxvi. 3 sqq.

³ In the most ancient times a Sôpher appears accordingly as supreme judge himself; Judges v. 14.

⁴ Just as, again, every single tribe might have its Sôpher for the family-lists, and every commanding officer his Sôpher for the army lists; 1 Chron. xxiv. 6, 2 Kings xxv. 19.

⁵ He appears clearly as minister of finance and public works, 2 Kings xii. 11, xxii. 3 sqq., in like manner also xviii. 18 sqq.; cf. 1 Chron. xxvii. 32. The γραμματεῖς or γραμματισταί occupied elevated posts at the Egyptian and Persian courts; and הסופר at Carthage was, no doubt, as others have already remarked, the Carthaginian Quæstor.

⁶ The words 1 Kings iv. 3 cannot be understood in any other way, certainly not as if these two had successively administered the office.

connexion with it. The first act of the monarchy, when it was quite firmly established in Israel, was to confirm the High Priest; this was already done under David.[1] It was now his duty, accordingly, to take care both by his knowledge and character to maintain his authority and power erect at once towards king and people. And inasmuch as the events of the age of David[2] left room for choice between the two most illustrious High Priestly houses, the connexion between the Priesthood and the Monarchy was more easily made closer. Moreover, the division in the High Priesthood itself, which continued to exist[3] under David, ceased[4] under Solomon. The family of Zadok, as far as we can conclude from later accounts, retained from this time onwards without break the High Priestly dignity in Jerusalem;[5] but it was still open to the king to choose in addition to this High Priest by hereditary right a House Priest to be his special 'friend,'[6] and it was this personage certainly who laboured as his proper 'minister of spiritual concerns,' while the High Priest continued to retain the rest of his ancient privileges.

As it was under Solomon that the monarchy attained its highest splendour, it was he who completed the circle of the principal government offices already introduced by David with the post of a Governor of the royal house, or *chamberlain*.[7] The duties of this officer were certainly limited at first to the superintendence over everything relating to the royal palace, as well as the royal etiquette; and nothing indicates so well the great importance which Solomon, following the example of the ancient and highly developed court usage in Egypt and Assyria, attached to such things, in striking contrast with David. But this post came to be one of special and increasing influence. The chamberlain readily acquired the right of introduction to the king, and thus easily became the chief minister; nay, himself the representative of the king, to be compared with the Hâjib[8] in Arabian courts. And in later

---

[1] P. 125 sq. [2] P. 134.
[3] Ibid. [4] P. 212 sq.
[5] 1 Chron. v. 34-41, unfortunately the only passage in the O. T. where the line of these High Priests is recorded. According to this, from Zadok under David to the Hilkiah known to us from 2 Kings xxii. sq., there were only ten High Priests, perhaps nothing but a round number, see i. p. 23 sq.
[6] This is clear in Solomon's case, 1 Kings iv. 5 comp. with ver. 2 (the clause about Zadok and Abiathar, ver. 4, on the contrary, does not belong here, and is only repeated from 2 Sam. xx. 25); probably, however, the Ira at David's court, mentioned in 2 Sam. xx. 26, was such an officer. At the court of the Indian kings there was the *Purôhita*, see *Laws of Manu*, vii. 78, and that he was a minister as well we know from Sômadêva (cf. Brockhaus in the *Berichten der K. Sächs. Ges. der Wiss.*, 1860, p. 158).

[7] עַל־הַבַּיִת, 1 Kings iv. 6, xvi. 9, xviii. 3.

[8] الحاجب.

times he had certainly won for himself this position in Jerusalem, by the side of which the earlier Mazkîr remained simply minister of foreign affairs and master of the rolls.[1]

It is inevitable that among the principal ministers of the king, one should stand nearest to him, that the unity of the administration may not be impaired. The only question that arises is, who this is to be? and it is instructive to observe how this foremost position shifted about in the course of the history of the monarchy in Israel.[2] Under David, just as in the simplest times[3] and in the actual necessities of war, Joab, as commander-in-chief of the army, still stands also at the head of the various high court officials. Under Solomon, it is the High Priest who fills this post of honour,[4] in accordance with the high external respect which[5] the ancient religion then enjoyed. In still later ages, when the power of the kingdom sank lower and all its forces required to be held together with a firm hand, we see the chamberlain occupying the first rank;[6] while from ancient times in Egypt lofty wisdom came to be more and more looked for as the qualification for this supreme dignity.[7]—When, however, a kingdom is either not yet sufficiently civilised, or is already advanced in its decline, a chief officer and representative of the king like this easily becomes, with all his household and dependents, a power only too dangerous to the well-being of the state. Such a personage may even seek so to aggrandise and confirm the power of his own house that the wish may well be formed that his place should, at any rate, be filled by a better man, with an extended family influence and a powerful party. Even David found in Joab, with his family and adherents, a burden which he was obliged to carry till his death. Solomon's kingdom was preserved, so far as we can see, from this evil; but in later days, when Shebna had come from a foreign country and was installed as chamberlain under King Ahaz, Isaiah could find it worth while to exert himself, under a sovereign like Hezekiah, to displace him

---

[1] Hence in 2 Kings xviii. 18, Is. xxxvi. 3, he occupies the last place among the three first ministers.

[2] We can recognise this with great certainty, especially from the arrangement in the three short lists of the chief offices, as they existed with their holders in the earlier and later years of David, and during the very long reign of Solomon, 2 Sam. viii. 16-18, xx. 23-26, 1 Kings iv. 2-6, comp. with the valuable fragment of a very minute list (a court-calendar) from the later period of David, 1 Chron. xxvii.

[3] P. 266.

[4] 2 Sam. viii. 16, xx. 23, 1 Chron. xxxvii. 34, comp. with 1 Kings iv. 2.

[5] P. 211 sqq.

[6] As we may conclude from his position, 2 Kings xviii. 18, Is. xxxvi. 3, comp. with xxii. 15. The most civilised kingdoms in Egypt and India returned to the practice of nominating a regular representative of the king, Gen. xli. 40-44; *Laws of Manu*, vii. 141, comp. with cl. 54.

[7] Gen. xli. 41-45; cf. Is. xix. 11.

with his party, and to secure the appointment to his post of a more suitable person.¹

Together with these regular government officers, there were besides many mere court officials and persons charged with special affairs of importance. The commander of the royal body-guard² always received his orders direct from the king, and is, consequently, always placed in the same list as the ministers of state.³ The compulsory service which⁴ became so important, was, in David's last years, placed under the charge of a high commissioner; and in Solomon's time another was appointed over the rich domains,⁵ the twelve superintendents of which had in turn each month to provide the court with all the needful supplies.⁶ Already under Saul,⁷ a principal overseer had been placed over the king's flocks, which formed the simplest and firmest foundation of the royal economy which the age and the country could afford; and he continually appears in all similar passages as in charge of one of the court offices.⁸ Under David the number of such overseers over the stationary or movable treasures of the king was immensely increased, and we still possess an instructive court calendar about them dating from that period.⁹

All these higher royal officials still bore the ancient name of 'princes,' i.e. heads, or superior officers. The king might besides associate with them 'counsellors,' in any number he pleased, of whom one was specially distinguished as his 'friend.'¹⁰ Following the ancient custom of the royal courts in Asia and Egypt, a court historian was certainly appointed in Israel also, whose function was to record all important occurrences affecting the royal house and kingdom, and at the close of a sovereign's reign to give perhaps a public survey of its history. But although some traces of his activity are certainly still preserved,¹¹ we no longer know his title.

---

¹ Is. xxii. 15-25.
² Pp. 75, 143.
³ 2 Sam. viii. 18, xx. 23; under Solomon he is only apparently omitted, since in 1 Kings iv. 6, before Adoniram are to be inserted (following the LXX) the words וְאֱלִיאָב בֶּן־שָׁפָט עַל הַמֻּשְׁמָעַת, only the LXX have incorrectly confounded the last word with מִשְׁפַּחַת, πατρία, just as in the passage 1 Chron. xi. 25, adduced p. 75, note 5. ⁴ P. 230.
⁵ 2 Sam. xx. 24, 1 Kings iv. 6.
⁶ 1 Kings iv. 5, cf. vv. 7-19; see more on this point below.
⁷ Pp. 83, 90.
⁸ The Turkish K'ôpân-Sâlâri in the Qirq Vezîr, p. 128 sqq. of the Paris edition.

⁹ 1 Chron. xxvii. 25-31, containing very instructive particulars as well for the provincial affairs of Palestine in that age.
¹⁰ See above, p. 178 sqq.; cf. with 1 Chron. xxvii. 32-34, and the instructive proverbs, Prov. xi. 14, xv. 22, and such expressions also as Is. i. 25, xxxii. 7.
¹¹ See i. p. 136 sqq. Many attempts have been made to identify him with the Mazkîr, p. 267; but this officer must at least originally have had a much higher office in the administration of the kingdom, and passages like Ezra iv. 15, Esther vi. 1, do not warrant the positive

In all these arrangements, however, the point of greatest importance was this—that the king originally selected all such assistants in the administration of the kingdom from his own people alone, and so far not the least ground was afforded for the existence of any jealousy or discord between court and people. This was still the case under Solomon, according to all that we have hitherto been able to learn. Not till a much later age did a king, under the influence of caprice, or dependent on foreign powers, engage a foreigner as his first counsellor.[1] Moreover, the introduction of eunuchs first into the royal harem, and thence into the court at large, and the entrusting of the most important affairs and offices to them by the side of the ministers, was an immorality which crept from the Assyrian (Syrian) and Egyptian courts little by little into Israel also,[2] but it jarred most severely against the true religion.[3] This custom was certainly started by the princes of the kingdom of the Ten Tribes who, in this as in other cases, wished to make a public display of their royal glory;[4] yet they were gradually followed in this practice by David's successors, so that this canker continued to exist to the latest days of the monarchy in Jerusalem.

2) It will be readily understood that as the monarchy in Israel rose in civilisation after the age of David and Solomon, even the outward marks of its power would be more and more derived from those heathen monarchies whose civilisation had been much earlier developed. Solomon still appears at the commencement of his reign[5] riding just as David had done, following ancient Israelitish custom, upon a simple mule; but at an early period the foreign usages of kingly state began to be imitated.[6] To this tendency must be ascribed the assumption of a new royal name on the day of accession to the throne, a practice which had long since been introduced in Egypt and elsewhere. In Israel it does not occur[7] until later, but it appears then to become fixed in Judah,[8] though it was never introduced into the kingdom of the Ten Tribes; yet these new names always remained in this nation at any rate

---

conclusion that he was also the court historian although from the nature of his other occupations he would not have been ill-qualified for the work.

[1] As Ahaz appointed Shebna, Is. xxii. 15 sqq.

[2] If *Sârîsîm* (eunuchs) are already mentioned in the statement cited above, 1 Sam. viii. 15, and by the Chronicler also 1 Chron. xxviii. 1, once in David's time, we are not warranted in concluding thence that they were only introduced under Solomon.

[3] See the *Alterth.* p. 187.

[4] With their introduction was connected the new style of building *Armenôth*, of which more below.

[5] P. 211.

[6] Pp. 177, 209.

[7] P. 168, *note*.

[8] See the examples below. Had not such a practice existed, Isaiah could never have anticipated that instead of the child's

THE REIGN OF SOLOMON.

very simple. The sort of servile adoration for the human king which easily acquired the force of custom in heathen states, was never likely to become general in this.

The polygamy of the king would almost inevitably exercise an influence, which could not fail to be prejudicial, on the course of the administration and the well-being of the community in this as in every other kingdom, whether old or new, which suffered from this evil. How quickly the evil consequences revealed themselves in Israel has been already pointed out.[1] This was the origin of the high importance which in this kingdom too was very soon acquired among the royal wives by the king's mother, particularly if he himself were young,[2] and which once enabled a woman, contrary to every national custom, to succeed even in seizing the reins of government.[3]

No mention is made of the coronation in the case of the three first kings of Israel. The unction alone, when received from the proper hand, possesses from the beginning of monarchy in Israel,[4] a high significance. The crown as a royal distinction was transferred from foreign kings to the sovereigns of Israel. David placed on his own head that [5] of the Ammonite king. Solomon, who did not at first wear it,[6] assumed it for the first time on his Egyptian marriage. From that time, however, it remained in both kingdoms the clearest mark of royalty,[7] for which the sceptre only [8] had hitherto served.—On the other hand, the king of Israel enjoyed from the first, like every other heathen monarch, the right of having a tall servant, whose duty it was to carry a basin behind him everywhere both within and without the house, and to look after his quarters for the night.[9]

On the whole, the court manners became already under

---

name Immanuel, a still loftier one would be assigned to the Messiah at his real entrance on his dominion; Is. ix. 5.

[1] P. 169 sqq.

[2] See what has been already said above (p. 210); hence the Books of Kings, even in their present shape, name the mothers of every successive king. She received also the special title of honour הַגְּבִירָה, 'the reigning queen,' 1 Kings xv. 13, 2 Kings x. 13, Jer. xiii. 18, xxix. 2. In Egypt, on the other hand, according to the monuments as well as according to 1 Kings xi. 19, the first consort of the king already acquired this lofty designation.

[3] Athaliah, 2 Kings xi.

[4] P. 6.

[5] P. 159.

[6] P. 211.

[7] Ps. xxi. 3; here probably, it is true, of a king of the kingdom of the Ten Tribes; cf., however, Cant. iii. 11, also my *Alterthümer*, p. 394 sq. and remarks on Ez. xxv. 9.

[8] P. 73.

[9] Cf. above, p. 96 sq. We have here, accordingly, the chamberlain, the Byzantine *Accubitor* (cf. Matthias of Edessa, *Arm. Hist.* p. 368, and the *a cubiculo* or *cubicularius* in Friedländer's *Röm. Sittengeschichte*, pp. 92 sqq. 170. It was formerly the duty of the hereditary Chamberlain of the German Empire, when a public court was held, to offer the Emperor the basin and towel. His Hebrew title is later שַׂר מְנוּחָה, Jer. li. 59.

Solomon more Egyptian; and the effect which this change must have had will be made clear further on. But however the manners and modes of life of the kings of Israel gradually departed from the primitive simplicity of a Saul and David, they could hardly, especially in Judah, abandon that elevated type which had been exhibited to them in David, alike in the character and aspiration, and in the habitudes and honour of the monarchy. How the precedents of his life and spirit operated on the majority of his successors in the most varied relations, will subsequently appear by numerous examples. At least in death and burial, his descendants wished to be associated with him alone. Even Solomon, who had erected for himself a splendid new palace, would still choose no other place for his remains to repose in than by David's hereditary sepulchre; and there in the 'city of David,'[1] on the same consecrated spot on Zion, all the kings of Judah down to Hezekiah, as the historical books state with significance in every case, built their last resting-places close by one another, so that this spot was called 'the sepulchres of the kings.'[2] Unquestionably these were once splendid structures, and their position will perhaps hereafter be discovered with a certitude greater than the present tradition[3] about them can justify.[4] Why king Manasseh was the first to introduce a change into this practice, and erect for himself a monument at a quite different end of the city,[5] we no longer exactly know. Perhaps he did so less from his well-known disinclination for good old popular customs than from want of space in the ancient consecrated ground: at any rate, he was followed in it by his successors.[6] A spot was, however,

---

[1] 1 Kings xi. 43 comp. with ii. 10.

[2] Yet this name does not occur till the Books of Chronicles; see besides the passages mentioned p. 254 *note* 5, 2 Chron. xxi. 20, xxiv. 25, xxviii. 27. The Chronicles here represent the three kings, Joram, Joash. and Ahaz, as being buried in the city of David, but not in the 'sepulchres of the kings,' as though this was the work of the popular will. But since in Asa's case, 2 Chron. xvi. 14, it mentions a special monument which he had erected for himself in the city of David, and the monuments, according to this evidence, lay at some distance from one another, this representation has no better foundation than a later opinion about those whose remains reposed in each tomb. Hezekiah, according to one account, wanting in 2 Kings xx. 21, but preserved in 2 Chron. xxxii. 33, was interred 'by the steps,' consequently on the boundary of the space 'of the sepulchres of the sons of David' close by the descent of the mountain, as though there had been here no further available space.

[3] P. 228 sqq.

[4] The efforts hitherto vainly made by Saulcy and others, since 1852, to discover with certainty these *sepulchres of David* are well known; cf. *Jahrbb. der Bibl. Wiss.* v. p. 223, vi. p. 82.

[5] 2 Kings xxi. 18. 'The garden of his own house, the garden of Uzza,' can only be the name of one of many royal gardens, which, perhaps, derived its name from one of Solomon's sons (p. 257), hence ver. 26, more briefly, simply 'Uzza's garden.'

[6] Amon, 2 Kings xxi. 26, and Josiah, according to the still shorter expression, xxiii. 30; this is not contradicted by what is said of Jehoiachim, xxiv. 6. 2 Chron. xxxiii. 20, 25 speaks much less definitely.

now chosen, evidently intentionally, which appeared to be in other respects much better adapted for such a purpose, in one of the royal gardens which lay north of Solomon's palace; and hence[1] it was very near the temple on the south side, and in fact abutted closely upon it.[2] But when the kings formed the design of thus resting almost under the same roof and protection as the Holy of Holies, this proximity of human remains to the sanctuary appeared to others, who took the opposite point of view, in the highest degree reprehensible; for there still prevailed the ancient abhorrence of any dead object as the easily polluting contrast of all that was pure, divine, and holy.[3]

4. *Progress in Science, Poetry, and Literature.*

Although the remarks already made point to many unequivocal signs that the sovereignty of Israel was even already in danger of becoming like an Egyptian or heathen one, yet these signs were little noticed amidst the splendid prosperity of Solomon's long reign. Such times, at first, could not but add a powerful impulse to all purely intellectual efforts. No people that has not, like Israel, overcome the true difficulties of life in the actual world, and, advancing from victory to victory, learnt to carry its head high among its neighbours, can easily lift its thoughts above the world of sense, and attain those acquirements and capacities which only such an elevation can secure permanently to a whole people. It is, indeed, possible, in a nation already sunk or sinking, for individuals to resist degeneracy, and to make wonderful new acquisitions—as we shall see in the next stage of this history. But no entire people can add new capacities and intellectual possessions to its pristine store, and judiciously employ them, unless it has achieved and still continues at a certain general elevation. Through a century of struggles Israel had gone on raising itself with increasing success; and while it now enjoyed a long peace and unprecedented prosperity as the reward of stubbornly fighting out so many contests, and thereby acquired the knowledge of many new countries, objects, and relations, and at the same time the thirst for fresh enquiry, it nevertheless continued—in the first half of Solomon's reign, at least—sufficiently moderate and uncorrupted, in spite of its power, to throw itself with fresh energy into the

---

[1] P. 249 sq.
[2] That that garden, as was to be expected according to p. 249 sq., actually lay in this direction, results from the remarkable words Ezek. xliii. 7-9, which at the same time show that several kings, and those the latest, lay buried there; and if the question about the propriety of it was then much agitated, such an expression as Jer. viii. 1 sq. can be the more easily explained.
[3] See the *Alterth.* p. 169 sqq.

new intellectual path which this period opened to it. Thus a new era also for science, poetry, and literature dawned on the people, the rich effects of which still lasted long after the wealth and superfluity which the age brought with it had vanished together with the national power.

The direction imparted in this new era, however, was necessarily very different from that of the early beginnings of poetry and science. Lyrical poetry, as the earliest species, was then as good as completed, in its direct development, by David, and had at any rate begun its artistic applications;[1] and although music and song, and possibly poetic composition also, were, in the ruder times before David and Samuel, rather left to women,[2] yet they were now, through David's genius and example, so vigorously as well as tenderly developed, and so ennobled, that they were henceforth esteemed the most dignified occupations of men, nay of princes and kings, rendering it hard for any nation of antiquity to surpass Israel in this branch. The foundations of an historical and legal literature also had already long been laid;[3] and the establishment of pure religion had itself also set up the beginnings of a kind of science; thus, for instance, the history of creation according to the Book of Origins, Gen. i. 1–ii. 4, distinctly refers to earlier theories of the nature of mundane things which prevailed long before the date of that work. But as the whole nation during the preceding centuries had been rather exclusively occupied with its self-preservation against many powerful enemies, so its mind also, in all relating to thought, poetry, and art, was chiefly absorbed in itself, and had not, therefore, as it was then situated, warmly embraced any subjects except those of religious or popular interest. But now, in the long peace, the mind first gained the leisure, while, in the fortunate elevation and power of the nation, it acquired the courage, and, in the stream of so many new experiences and traditions from foreign lands, found the incentive and the summons, to investigate secular things also with keener eyes, and to roam beyond its former narrow horizon. Of what kind were the many wonderful impressions from foreign lands with which Israel was now flooded? What relation did the religious traditions and legends of other nations, with which Israel now had much freer intercourse, bear to its own? What is kingly rule, which now arrived at its highest stage; and what is the dominion over other nations, to which Israel is now called, after a long and extraordinary career? What, in fine, is a laudable

---

[1] Vol. ii. p. 356.   [2] Vol. ii. p. 355.   [3] Vol. ii.

and noble influence, a dignity of human life, which Israel was now pledged to maintain, and if possible to develope? Many such questions then presented themselves; but they all turned the mind to a more searching scrutiny of all things, especially of the world of man, and all outside man. Thus the new tendency sets vigorously and steadily to the end which we are accustomed to call philosophy, and which, in conformity with the Bible and the simple fact, we might just as well call wisdom.

Every new mental energy like this, if only directed to a grand subject, and persistently exercised, leads to an art corresponding to itself. But in those bright days, when art sought to elevate all the lower sphere of life, it was also more zealously attempted and more happily exercised in new essays of purely intellectual skill. The new intellectual impulse succeeded, therefore, in also creating a new species of art, as the plastic body of those profound ideas to which it was necessarily led by its present task of penetrating into the mysteries of the universe.

All this was, indeed, visibly fostered by the active rivalry in which Israel was now engaged with those neighbouring nations of the day which were most eminent for science and art, the Egyptians, Phœnicians, Sabeans, and others. Of the historical reality of this rivalry we possess the surest evidence. Of all the advantages which a nation derives from a noble independence, none is perhaps greater than that of being able, by virtue of that independence, to enter into close, honourable contact with the best and most cultivated of its contemporaries, and thus to compete with them in arts and sciences also; nor is there any emulation that more evokes the noblest national efforts. We do not, indeed, now possess the means of discerning what constituted the great 'wisdom of all the sons of the east and of Egypt,' which Solomon surpassed.[1] Nevertheless, we can draw some conclusions from the few examples explained below; and there are indications which distinctly show us what new traditions and theories subsequently poured into the holy land from foreign countries. How much expanded and enriched, for instance, is the primitive history of this earth and of man, in the form which it gradually assumed under such influences, when compared with the much simpler form in which the Book of Origins first exhibits it;[2] the Book of Proverbs also shows that the more definite representations of Paradise, of the Tree and Fountain of Life, and others, were now introduced.[3] But

---

[1] 1 Kings v. 10 [iv. 30] compared with x. 1–9.
[2] See the *Jahrbb. der Bibl. Wiss.* ii. p. 136 sqq.
[3] Cf. vol. i. p. 38 sq.; the *Dichter des A. B.* iv. p. 2.

Israel's strong and sound national feeling prevented the merely external adoption of the newly imparted elements, and did not suffer that rivalry to lead to weak imitation.

Philosophy does not only exist where it struts in the ostentatiously worn fetters of the strict laws of thought (logic), or where it tries to bring all truths into an ordered whole (a system). We may admit that system is its completion,—although this completion, like every other that vaunts itself among men, is often wholly erroneous and misleading,—but it is neither its origin nor its permanent and vital principle. Its origin and very life is rather the restless and insatiable desire to examine, and to examine all subjects without exception, high and low, near and far, human and divine. When the enigmas of things no longer allow a thoughtful man any rest, and an indefatigable zeal to solve them is kindled in the most gifted minds of a nation, or of several nations simultaneously, the auspicious youth of all philosophy is already begun. At that early period, when the Greeks had by no means even once advanced so far, the noblest Semitic nations had evidently arrived at this stage; and Israel, which received through its higher religion a special summons to ponder on the relations of all things, now entered, in this nobler arena of honour, into the most equally matched competition with them. The queen of Sheba came from afar to try the king of Israel with problems. When, after a few preliminary trials, she found him prepared to answer her, she poured out her whole heart to him in questions, drew forth even the greatest mysteries that were still wholly dark to herself, and penetrated deeper and deeper into his inmost mind, revelling in their joint unwearied researches; while he did not disappoint her in the smallest question, but solved all her difficulties.[1] Happy is the time when mighty princes whose realms are encompassed by the sacred peace of God, are thus able to visit each other, and to compete in wisdom, and, what is better, in the zealous pursuit of it!—Menander relates a similar incident in Phœnician history. A Phœnician, younger son of Abdêmon, solved all the problems that Solomon laid before him; and Dius recounts more circumstantially that Solomon used to send difficult questions to his royal brother Hiram, with a request to have similar questions sent to him in return, on condition that he who failed to solve them should pay the other a penalty in money, and that Hiram, acceding to this proposal, had to pay these fines, until he reversed his fortune by employing a Tyrian

---

[1] This is the meaning of 1 Kings x. 2 sq.

Abdêmon against Solomon. We see no reason to question the general veracity of these accounts preserved by Josephus.[1]

According to the prevalent tradition, the man to whom the whole renown of the new wisdom of this era in Israel belongs was none other than the remarkable sovereign of the time; but we must take care not to understand Solomon's proverbial wisdom too slavishly in an historical sense. The whole age had the most powerful impulses in that direction; and, even in the last ten or twenty years of David's reign, everything favoured the happy development of this zeal for wisdom. It is, indeed, difficult to recognise the beginning of it before Solomon, for the surpassing intelligence, the magnificence of the king himself, and the great change which subsequently came over all the tendencies of the popular mind, united to exert a common influence in obliterating all exact recollection of the wise men of this era. Nevertheless, we can still discover some reliable facts on this subject.

The brief narrative itself asserts that Solomon was wiser than Ethan and Heman, Chalcol and Darda, the sons of Mahol. However little we now know about the wisdom of these once famous sages,[2] we must assume that, as elder contemporaries of Solomon, they cultivated nearly the same kind of wisdom as that for which he himself subsequently became still more famous; for no discreet writer could compare any men with Solomon but such as resembled him in quality, and who therefore were not much anterior to him in date. But we must also suppose that the Canaanites, with whom Israel had long enjoyed the most peaceful intercourse on almost all sides, were far ad-

---

[1] *Ant.* viii. 5. 3. According to the Phœnician history of Theophilus (in Euseb. *Præp. Ev.* ix. 34, 19) they had also competed with each other in presents of gold.

[2] They occur elsewhere than in 1 Kings v. 11 [iv. 31], but not quite so distinctly as we wish. We find all four in 1 Chron. ii. 6 in the same order, as sons of Zerah the son of Judah, for 'Dara' there is probably only a mistake for 'Darda.' But although Zerah may be equivalent to Ezrah, from whose family Ethan and Heman were descended (cf. Ps. lxxxviii. 1 [title], lxxxix. 1 [title]), yet the Chronicler has probably only inserted the other three names there, from 1 Kings v. 11 [iv. 31], because he could conveniently annex them to Ethan (who, according to ver. 8, originally stood there). For, according to 1 Kings v. 11 [iv. 31], the four could hardly belong to such a remote period; and Chalcol and Darda are, on the contrary, called sons of Mahol in 1 Kings v. 11 [iv. 31]. They might, however, have all belonged to the tribe of Judah, and, in that respect, the Chronicler may have rightly inserted them there. According to this, the Chronicles themselves distinguish those there named from the celebrated musician Ethan, a grandson of the great Samuel, and from Heman. Yet in Ps. lxxxviii. 1 [title], lxxxix. 1 [title], they are evidently identified; and when we consider that both the musicians and sages of this name must have lived in the same time, as also that, in the time of the Chronicler, music and wisdom were still near each other, it seems probable that the Levitical schools of music adopted these two into their guild, and therefore into their family, only because they really were the fathers of this knowledge; and this may have been done at an early period. Cf. *Dichter des A.B.* i. p. 274 sq.

vanced in wisdom and art long before the time of Moses; and that as Israel was obliged, during the long stormy period of the Judges, to maintain itself against its enemies in the land by other means than the sword, it had also begun to compete with them in intelligence and knowledge. Samson had discovered [1] how to subdue his enemies by devices of the intellect also, and with him the mind of the whole people had more freely developed itself in this direction, in the last century before David. Wit, riddles, poetry, and legend are the signs of these fresh efforts of a new intellectual life that is just ready to grapple with higher problems; and we have already seen how Solomon competed in these with Hiram.[2]

And, if we look beyond this sort of books of wisdom like Solomon's, and survey the general character of the literature of the age, we discern at any rate one writer, although no longer known to us by name, who was an elder contemporary of Solomon, and who has a just claim to be called a sage in the wider sense of the term,—the author of the Book of Origins.[3] He was a Levite, and, as such, his task naturally was to compare Israel's great past with the splendour of its present, and to point out all those things which had acted in ancient time as the germs of its existing greatness. The lofty wisdom and genuine royal dignity, which had become naturalised in Israel in the first half of Solomon's reign, are brilliantly displayed in his representation of the eminent men of antiquity: and his work shows most admirably with what exuberant art and finish, with what comprehensiveness and order, a very detailed historical narrative could be then written. We could not wish for a more striking proof of the high development of literary art in the beginning of Solomon's reign than we can find in the Book of Origins, judging by the abundant remains in which we are still able to recognise it distinctly.

Now 'God gave Solomon very much wisdom and intelligence, a mind capacious as the sand on the sea shore,' as the last narrator comprehensively expresses himself.[4] But it was only because this richly-gifted mind fell in the midst of such an era, such an already thriving garden of many similar spirits, and was thus impelled from all sides to more vigorous development and complete maturity, that he became the great sage who surpassed his predecessors, and who—because the whole tendency of the popular mind underwent so great a change after his death—remained for all subsequent time the unique exemplar of wisdom in Israel.

[1] Vol. ii. p. 400. [2] P. 277. [3] Described in vol. i. [4] 1 Kings v. 9 [iv. 29].

It is in reality difficult for us now to estimate the compass of Solomon's wisdom, as expressed in writing. For these writings of the wise king, whether he composed them himself or availed himself of the assistance of others, are now lost to us, some of them altogether, others at any rate in their original form; and they had probably already disappeared before the formation of the Old Testament, since otherwise they would have been included in the collection of the sacred books. Nevertheless, that historical book which is our principal authority for Solomon's life,[1] has preserved a brief record of the chief topics of his original writings, which has all the marks of historical trustworthiness, inasmuch as its statement of subjects does not agree with the writings which have been received into the Old Testament under Solomon's name, while it is perfectly credible in itself. Following this ancient tradition, and comparing with it the remains of Solomon's writings actually preserved in the Old Testament, we form the following conception of the whole.

The wisdom of that time consisted, as has been said, of an abundance of partly evident and partly still problematical kinds of knowledge, which burst forth with great force, but still retained their original freshness, and which were therefore simply and truthfully expressed, without any need of artificial proof, just as they had no intrinsic coherence with one another, and felt as yet no sense of its want. Now, as these varieties of knowledge concerned the elevated subjects of God and the relations of God and man, they required an elevated style of language, and consequently the dignity and charm of verse. And so, out of the ancient Hebrew poetry at that time so highly developed, there sprang a new special kind,—the short but pointed and pregnant apothegmatic verse,—which was fully commensurate with the requirements and with the limits of the wisdom of the age. A mind that was at once so poetical and so profoundly immersed in the wisdom of his time as Solomon's was, was most fitted to create such a verse, and to sanction it by its authority; nor can we fail to discern that he is the true father of an artistic poetry, which was never lost in the people of Israel, and which was capable of indefinite modification. He is said to have composed three thousand proverbs: not too great a number, if we consider that each proverb of the sort is very short, but must exhaust a complete thought in the magic circle of the verse. Of these—mostly composed by himself,

---

[1] 1 Kings v. 12 sq. [iv. 32 sq.]; the Chronicles have, we know not for what reason, omitted the whole passage.

but in part to be ascribed to the poets of his period,[1]—we still possess no inconsiderable number in the canonical Book of Proverbs. It is here that we find the peculiar and really creative product of the great king's mind, which could not fail, therefore, to be the best preserved. I forbear, however, from repeating what I published on this subject as long ago as the year 1837. Even the small portion of those three thousand proverbs which has been preserved is the most emphatic testimony to the equally profound and pregnant wisdom, as also to the artistic skill, of Solomon and his time.

But wherever any genuine striving after wisdom is energetically awakened, it endeavours to embrace all provinces of thought and knowledge. Solomon, it is said, wrote also 'about trees, from the cedar in Lebanon to the hyssop that sprouts on the wall, also of beasts, birds, reptiles, and fishes.' It would, in many respects, be highly instructive to possess this rudiment of a complete natural history;[2] but its early loss is doubtless due to the fact that, soon after Solomon, the popular mind turned away from all deep speculation on the world outside man; and we have now no means of estimating its exact purport. These descriptions of the natural world may, however, have been composed not in verse but in simple language, inasmuch as this style of composition, as distinguished from verse, had been long familiar in Israel. But this statement is highly significant as an unequivocal sign of the wide extent of the wisdom of Solomon's time, which in subsequent ages could hardly be understood.

While new paths were thus successfully opened in poetry and literature, the primitive form of all poetry, the lyrical, was by no means neglected; the same account states that Solomon composed a thousand and five songs. There is every indication that the second Psalm is a genuine song of Solomon himself, belonging to the first period of his reign, which may have been saved out of that collection, and which for dignity and energy of sentiment, as well as for art and grace, is quite worthy of

---

[1] The beautiful maxims on the majesty and awe of a true king, between Prov. x. 1 and xxii. 17, are unquestionably from Solomon's time, but hardly directly from his own pen.

[2] Josephus' notion (*Ant.* viii. 2. 5) that Solomon only spoke about all those natural objects in comparisons, i.e. in proverbs like those that have come down to us, is a mistake easily accounted for. On the other hand, he has a very remarkable tradition (*Ant.* viii. 6. 6; cf. xiv. 4. 1, xv. 4. 2; *De Bell. Jud.* i. 6. 6, iv. 8. 3; Plin. *Hist. Nat.* xii. 54, xiii. 9), that the balsam plant (why not the date palm also?) at Jericho was introduced by the queen of Sheba, and was there first cultivated in Solomon's time; and the same valley which forms the eastern entrance of the Holy Land near Jericho, and which was formerly called 'Troubled,' according to ii. p. 249, really seems to have been then called 'the valley of the balsam plant' (הַבָּכָא), Ps. lxxxiv. 6.

him.[1] Nevertheless as the song proper had been already developed by David to as high a degree of perfection as it could attain without becoming artificial, the powerful artistic impulse of Solomon's time could hardly long content itself with merely repeating this simple species of composition. Whenever a song springs freshly out of a momentary excitement, it is always ready to reappear, later on, in its simplest form; but at a period when artistic activity was at such high tension as in that of Solomon, the ancient song might easily be applied to special poetic functions when it would invest itself with new forms of art. When we find—and not so very long after Solomon—an undeniable Hebrew opera, and, therefore, a kind of drama, in the Song of Songs, it is by no means improbable that, at Solomon's court and through his aid, pure lyric song had been developed into the more artificial dramatic song. As its theme, in that case, probably had less direct concern with lofty interests, we might thus explain how these dramas, in the succeeding centuries, were less satisfactory to the popular taste, and were consequently lost.

The time was certainly then ripe for a written collection of the best songs of ancient and recent date. The stream of such songs had long overflowed its banks in Israel; and that long peace in which every kind of literary composition flourished as it never had before, and in which men looked back with pride on all the past, was also quite suited for such undertakings. At any rate, we can still trace the clear indications of such a collection, which, since it also contained songs of David, and—as is expressly added—such as were previously only intrusted to memory, cannot well have been formed at an earlier date, but which we have also no reason to assign to a later one. This is the *Book of the Righteous*,[2] in which, to judge from its title and from its fragments, the collector combined the most various songs for a moral purpose, and accompanied them with brief historical remarks, to show, namely, by them how the righteous man in Israel—a Joshua, Jonathan, David—had acted in the community at all times, and how he should, therefore, always demean himself. Moreover, that David's songs were also collected separately and circulated in writing might be expected from Solomon's filial piety and artistic taste, and the traces of such collections of great antiquity are, in fact, not hard to find in our present Psalter.[3]

---

[1] Cf. p. 219.
[2] Cited in Jos. x. 13, 2 Sam. i. 18. On the first see ii. p. 179 sq.; and as the Book of Kings, the first time that it brings in a song of David, mentions this source, it probably derived others also from the same authority.
[3] When one, namely, considers what

But the development of the manifold kinds of poetry and the zealous collection of songs were also certainly connected with a similar improvement in vocal and instrumental music. The new requirements of the magnificent temple, where such beautiful hymns as Ps. xx. were early sung alternately by the congregation and the Priests, also furthered such arts; and the music of the temple services was doubtless conducted on a splendid scale,[1] after Solomon's regulations, in all subsequent centuries; and we know for certain that Solomon set a great value on musical instruments of costly workmanship.[2] We have every reason to believe that this music was preserved among the people until Greek culture superseded it, and, therefore, that it is the same of which we find some indications in the inscriptions of the songs of the Old Testament,[3] and which is so often noticed by the author of the Chronicles.[4] All knowledge of it was, however, gradually lost after the Greek period, and cannot now be recovered; for even the Chronicles, from which we derive most light for understanding it, contain no more than faint gleams of reminiscence of the ancient music. We do not precisely know why the temple-music was divided into the three main classes already mentioned,[5] yet we distinguish three really different kinds of musicians,—those on stringed instruments, those on instruments of percussion, and those on wind instruments; those of the third kind, as they were not at the same time singers, seem indeed to have occupied a lower grade as musicians, but, as being properly Priests, they stood higher.[6]

In all this province, however, it was not his poetry that constituted Solomon's glory, as it did in David's case, but his wisdom and his wise proverbs. To his other high excellences, his prudence and firmness as a ruler, his power and order in everything touching the throne and the realm, his extraordinary wealth, and the magnificence of his sacred and royal edifices, he added a glory the rarest among kings—a spontaneous love of the higher wisdom, and a creative energy in it.

position Pss. iii., iv., vii., viii., xi., xviii., xix. 2-7 [1-6], xxiv. (two songs), xxix., xxxii., ci. still occupy in the great Psalter, and how manifestly they, even from this point of view, constitute an original basis of Davidic songs.

[1] P. 248.
[2] 1 Kings x. 12.
[3] See *Dichter des A.B.* i. 267 sqq.
[4] See vol. i. p. 176.
[5] The single words in 1 Chron. xxv. 3, 5, when weighed with other passages of similar import, do not warrant our concluding too much.
[6] The most distinct expressions occur in 1 Chron. xv. 28, 2 Chron. v. 12 sq. There is another division, dating from David's time, in Ps. lxviii. 26 [25]. Concerning the priests as trumpeters, see *Alterthümer*, p. 330, and *Dichter des A.B.* i. p. 253, 2nd ed. Flutes, however, only occur in Ps. lxxxvii. 7, as connected with the temple; but there we must think of dancers.

Such a thing had never been seen in Israel before; and as the fame of it spread during his long reign, foreign nations, and specially their princes and nobles,[1] were powerfully attracted by it, and made many pilgrimages to the place where a sovereign with this astonishing union of great capacities and achievements adorned the throne. One instance of this, which occurred in Solomon's later years, in subsequent times always received special notice. When the queen of Sheba in the far south-east[2] heard what fame Solomon had acquired by the glory of his God,[3] she came to Jerusalem to try him with enigmas, surrounded by a large and brilliant retinue, with camels richly laden with the most costly products of her country. Her presents to him consisted of one hundred and twenty talents of gold, jewels, and such a quantity of balsam as had never come to Jerusalem before. Solomon gratified her curiosity and thirst for knowledge, and also showed her his palace with all the rarities it contained, the costly vessels in which he ate and drank, his ministers and other associates sitting in great number at his splendid table, and even his gorgeously-dressed servants waiting so neatly and attentively, in a very different style from that to which other monarchs of the time accustomed their friends and servants; and lastly, the beautifully carved staircase by

---

[1] This is the exact sense of the words 1 Kings v. 15 [iv. 34], where 'from all kings of the earth' is only a more definite statement of the preceding 'from all the nations.'

[2] Even Josephus erroneously makes her a queen of the Egyptians and Ethiopians, so that the Ethiopian Christians would be excusable in that case for claiming her. According to the sense of the narrative, however, she was a queen in Southern Arabia; and while in 1 Kings v. 10 [iv. 30], with evident allusion to her, the wisdom of 'the sons of the east' is eulogised, we have been enabled by the most recent investigations to discover from the Himyaric inscriptions what culture and wealth prevailed there in ancient times, and how far the traditions of the past glory of that country are from being baseless. Cf. the essay on these inscriptions in Höfer's *Zeitschrift für Sprachwissenschaft*, vol. i. part 2, Berlin, 1846, and the *Himyaric Inscriptions* from Southern Arabia in the British Museum, Lond. 1863. The Arabs call the Himyaric queen herself *Balqîs*, and have many stories of her. Cf. Hamzer's *Annales*, ed. Gottwaldt (1844), p. 125, and Nuwairi in Schulten's *Imper. Joctan.* p. 53; also Caussin de Percival's *Essai sur l'histoire des Arabes*, i. p. 76 sq., and the hardly reliable lucubrations of Fresnel in the *Journal Asiat.* 1850, ii. p. 279-81. Beyond doubt, however, the Himyaric Christians first searched out this name of an ancient queen, in order to find in it a point of contact with the Biblical history. Tel Belkis near Bira on the Euphrates, which Ainsworth (*Travels in Asia Minor*, i. p. 304) connects with her, has certainly nothing to do with her; and it must be decided by further research whether Solomon's friend lived in Northeast Arabia in the Persian Gulf, as Rawlinson recently makes out from a cuneiform inscription. *Nikaulis*, whom Josephus (*Ant.* viii. 6. 2. 5 sq.) identifies with her, is only confounded with the Egyptian Nitokris, Herod. ii. 100. In later times she was just as unreasonably confounded with the Babylonian Sibyl Sambêthe, abbreviated into Sabbê.

[3] This is the meaning of the words 1 Kings x. 1, therefore she too at length praises Solomon's God, ver. 9, although she does not acknowledge Him as hers, and for this reason also Solomon could not show her anything actually connected with the temple or its offerings.

which he went up from his palace into the temple.¹ Then she confessed, in her astonishment, that she had found twice as much as ever she had expected, she proclaimed all those happy who had the good fortune to be about such a king, and blessed that God who, in love to His people Israel, had given them such a wise king to rule over them. Solomon dismissed her, after having not only solemnly given her such presents of his own selection as he was bound by his royal dignity to give, but also having, out of mere benevolence, and rather as a friend than a king, presented her with everything else that she desired of him[2] —one of the many signs how little the king had in him destroyed the man. Similar pilgrimages to Jerusalem were annually repeated, and the richer pilgrims always brought vessels of gold and silver, splendid dresses, spices and balsam, horses and mules, as free gifts of homage, each according to his means.[3] Jerusalem never saw such a season again in all its splendour; but these pilgrimages to Jerusalem for the sake of paying homage not only to the king but also to the God he worshipped, were soon so deeply impressed in the popular memory that the picture of them floated in late days before the prophetic anticipations of the Messianic glory, and the noble in Israel could never again forget to what splendour Jerusalem had once been raised by the wisdom of one of its early kings, and the true religion by which it was directed.

But wisdom or philosophy had now become a pursuit and a treasure to the people of the true God, which, having once so strongly occupied their mind, could never be entirely relinquished. Earnestly to seek truth as such, to acknowledge it, to cleave to it, and to apply it to life, and therefore to seek and to appropriate the knowledge of it as also a good in itself, with such zeal that it becomes a doctrine and a tradition and more and more profoundly pervades the efforts of the people,—this is a condition of human life to which every people aspires in favourable times, and which, when once attained, preserves itself as fixedly as possible by the charms of its own excellence. Moreover, everything true and eternal that has at an earlier period sprung up through creative effort and the compulsion of

---

[1] P. 251.

[2] When the Himyaric and Ethiopian Christians, as may be seen at length in the Chronicles of the latter, deduce from this that Solomon begat a son with her will or against her will, they only do so because they would have liked to derive their ancient royal families from him, and are at the same time led astray by their own impure conceptions of the married state, of which they never can divest themselves. See the extracts in Dillmann's *Catal. Codd. Æthiop. Oxon.* p. 69–72.

[3] 1 Kings x. 24 sq. where נְשֶׁק can by no means signify *armour*, but must be a kind of perfume, as it is in Arabic.

higher necessity, is now both ready and able to maintain itself the more firmly by patient investigation and discernment of its correctness. But Israel had now enjoyed for centuries a power of true religion first founded by mere prophetic creation, which quiet examination and acknowledgment tended more and more to render an inalienable possession. However much, therefore, the subsequent external fortunes of the people might impair and limit its once earnest zeal for wisdom, wisdom itself was steadily preserved in it through all succeeding ages, and it was partly through its aid that the great truths which Israel possessed from ancient days, descended more and more deeply from their prophetic height into the consciousness of the whole people, and were worked with increasing completeness into all its thought and action. Before long, wisdom was developed in rival schools in Israel, and zealous students sought it even for money.[1]

III. The Results of Solomon's Reign.

But each stage of greatness achieved, whether in the commonwealth, the monarchy, or the church, points upwards to another higher and purer still; and amidst the full activity of all the good and the bad elements called into play, this upward tendency seeks earnestly to manifest itself, and must attain its realisation, unless the greatness already reached is to be allowed to fall away and sink back into its original nothingness. It is precisely in a period of continuous peace and prosperity, such as Solomon's age afforded, that ancient evils which have not as yet been wisely met, again present themselves with increased force, and at the same time new wants arise, which it is found impossible permanently to ignore. But if these evils are not removed, and these wants do not receive their full satisfaction, the glory that has been won will be found to involve the germ of continuous decay; a decay springing out of that very power in which all the greatness of the kingdom is concentrated. The renewed activity of these ancient evils cannot, however, be satisfactorily repressed unless the governing power acquires those fresh forces in which it is as yet wanting.

If then, in accordance with what has been just stated, we now survey all the greatness originating with Solomon as well as that which, springing up at an earlier period, was nevertheless indebted to him for its extension, its consolidation, or even

---

[1] See the *Jahrbb. der Bibl. Wiss.* i. p. 96 sqq., iv. p. 145 sq.

possibly for its fullest development,—we see at once that it could not fail to confer more glory on the royal house than on any other estate of the realm. In so far as any single earthly power could create the whole glory of this period, the monarchy had either accomplished it single-handed, or else had rendered its attainment possible by the energy of its cooperation. All its lustre, consequently, was reflected on the monarchy itself with the more intensity because as a new power in Israel it was just then aspiring with the energy of youth, and never hesitated to attempt all that it was possible to embrace by its yet unbroken power. David had laid deep its foundation for all time. In fact, he seemed to have also fettered it spell-bound to his own house; but it was under Solomon that it first completely unfolded its power in every direction, and attained the highest splendour as well as the utmost authority which it was ever destined to reach. And if perchance some other estate bloomed into new power at the same time, as was the case, for instance, with the sacerdotal order,[1] yet it only flourished because it leaned upon the strong power by which it was supported and protected.

The supreme power and glory of the monarchy was the very essence of that favoured time, and was the cause and the object of its extraordinary prosperity, pride and joy. That very nation which had been the last to set up a human monarchy, could now rejoice in it with the utmost delight; and it naturally seemed to the sages of Israel, on looking back to the beginning of its history, that no greater blessing could have been predestined by its God, than that from it should spring a race of kings.[2] As, in that century, the nation could have no greater blessing than the possession of two such monarchs as David and Solomon, so perfect, and yet so contrasted in character, succeeding each other in the happiest order and each swayed by the true sentiment of royal dignity, so the whole people was penetrated by a like faith in the real dignity and lofty blessing of the unstained monarchy, and filled by a genuine reverence for its methods of administration. As we have already seen,[3] Solomon, at the outset of his reign, had, like David, been deeply impressed with the feeling of what Jahveh's king ought to be, and ruled with firmness and success under the

---

[1] P. 247 sq.
[2] As the clear expressions of the Book of Origins indicate; see i. p. 75. This has been subsequently imitated poetically, Num. xxiii. 21, xxiv. 7; that 'the king' in Num. xxiii. 21 is not to be understood of Jahveh as in Deut. xxxiii. 5, is shown by the corresponding passage Num. xxiv. 7.
[3] P. 219.

inspiring influence of this idea; and a multitude of proverbs full of wisdom and of practical shrewdness bears distinct and striking testimony to the popular conviction of the noble and blessed influence of a true king;[1] while they who had most pondered the history of the nation saw in him the man who was to complete the principal portion of the divine destiny of Israel. In fact, the great Prophets of that age announced nothing less than that 'Jahveh's name' should remain eternal in His chosen Jerusalem, i.e. Jahveh Himself should be here for ever revealed, acknowledged, and honoured; while Israel should never again lead a wandering unsettled life:[2] so firmly did the true religion and the national power seem to them united with the glorious temple founded under circumstances so remarkable, as well as with Zion, the mountain fortress, which had endured so severe a test during David's reign.

The culminating point of Solomon's reign here stands before us; and hence we likewise reach that of this second epoch in Israel's history. But amidst the meridian sunshine of Israel's human monarchy, new problems have come into existence, and though at first their importance was scarcely recognised, yet henceforth in every instance their weight really turns the scale. The monarchy had fully solved its lower problems,—it had made the country powerful, the kingdom strong, and the people peaceful and industrious; but for this very reason, during the long peace, all the higher problems involved in the national life of a civilised people pressed upon it with increasing force. And upon the extent of its ability to solve these new, importunate, and grand problems, its entire future history must depend.

One error, however, still adhered to it, despite its perfection and its glory. It had still to free itself from one redundancy cleaving to it from of old, which had in fact overgrown its whole nature. All the supreme power in the kingdom ought to centre permanently in the monarchy: but on this very account violence readily clings to it as a deadly offset, and in fact from the first accompanies it as shadow does light; and when it casts off its rougher semblance it only too rapidly reappears in a more cunning form. The requirements of the Jahveh religion were certainly *à priori* in opposition to it, and under the two first kings the Prophets had successfully combated its grosser outbursts,

[1] Cf. the *Dichter des A. B.* iv. p. 18 sq. Prov. xvi. 14 is to be added to the proverbs collected there.

[2] This is plain from such words (quoted quite out of connexion) as 1 Kings viii. 29, ix. 3, xi. 36, 2 Kings xxi. 4, 7 sq. xxiii. 27; they all refer to a celebrated prophetic expression which may still be recovered most exactly from 2 Kings xxi. 7 sq. (cf. 1 Kings viii. 16).

and had thus contributed to bring about the milder days of Solomon. But if in this era as well this evil was to be wholly cast out, it was necessary for the entire nation to turn its heart completely away from it. But this could only take place with the full realisation of the true religion, and as this constituted the close of the entire history, the time for it was not yet ripe. Autocratic power, consequently, though for the instant softened in its features, remained characteristic of the monarchy, while in another form, and springing out of widely different impulses, it was the unconscious accompaniment of prophetism;[1] but to the monarchy itself it became increasingly dangerous in proportion to its increase of power, owing to its native tendency in that direction. This is the terrible rock on which all Antiquity split, and with it the ancient Theocracy of Israel, for though the opposite truth that affection not violence is the regenerating power was indeed stated in it in theory,[2] it had not yet attained sufficient strength in practice. Thus the monarchy could neither permanently introduce true and perfect unity into the realm, nor speedily eradicate pressing ancient evils, nor guard itself with satisfactory care from the dangers attendant on its own tyrannous acts; and the germ of this tendency had already appeared during Solomon's reign.

No doubt the brilliancy of this reign long threw into the shade the seeds of decay which lay already embedded in it; but amid the shining brightness of its regal power and glory and its national prosperity, there sprang up in silence an evil among the people, which spread with accelerated speed and threatened with destruction the very essence of the government. The increased prosperity of a large part of the nation during this long and happy peace, and the growing feeling of security which it engendered, encouraged a degree of luxury, effeminacy, and indolence of life which had been before almost unknown; and along with this was a moral carelessness, a bold assumption, and a tentative desire for innovation, leading to a forgetfulness of the efforts made and the price paid for the blessings in the possession of which they now revelled. Now first with Israel's proud security and power came the full realisation of the time which a prophetic song[3] two centuries later truthfully depicts as the days in which it was too well with the people in its peaceful, fruitful land, for like an overfed, fiery horse, it kicked

---

[1] Vol. ii. pp. 51, 115.
[2] Cf., for example, what is uttered even by a prince and king of Israel, 1 Sam. ii. 9, 'not by strength shall a man prevail.'
[3] Deut. xxxii. 15-18 comp. with passages in every respect similar, such as Is. i. 3 sq.

against its benefactor, and, forgetting Him who alone had formed it and made it great, hastened after strange gods, yielding to all the evil inclinations, errors, and perversities, which are always drawing men away from true religion. In like manner its extensive intercourse and commerce and its sway over foreign nations could only lead it on to a fuller acquaintance with heathen customs and religions, whose seductive charms it was little able to withstand, owing to the slumber stealing over its own better spirit. The poison of such moral dangers works with increased force, no doubt, in every period of national life in which there is outward security and prosperity, and all restraints are taken away from the desire of gain and the enjoyment of temporal blessings; but at no other period in the long history of Israel was the temptation so strong and the possible loss so great as during these forty years in which it laboriously gained the culminating point of its entire national power. And it is incontestable that during this long period, owing to the fault of the people themselves, an internal moral revolution was effected, whose evil influences, long smothered, were finally all the more destructive in their violence. The completeness of the disappearance, at the close of Solomon's reign, not only of David's band of heroic warriors, but of all true tranquillity and circumspection, the course of this history will speedily disclose.

The monarchy of Israel ought, therefore, however difficult the undertaking, to have withstood this dangerous influence of the age; but in fact, human monarchy is easily carried away by every evil influence pervading the people, especially when, as was at that time the case, it assumes the deceptive form of glory and prosperity; and we cannot deny that Solomon was not quick enough in foreseeing and sufficiently firm in guarding against the hidden but most formidable peril. The high power with which the king of Israel seemed now to be for ever armed, his constantly increasing grandeur, the position which he assumed among all the neighbouring monarchs, all tended, with the continuance of almost undisturbed repose, to assimilate his court and his dominions to the other powerful kingdoms of the day; and innovations were soon introduced for which the only excuse is to be found in the all-powerful influences of the age itself.

1. *Solomon's Royal Pomp and Royal Debts.*

The growing attachment to Egyptian customs shown by Solomon in the arrangements of his court may be not only inferred from remarks already made,[1] but seen with special distinctness in one single instance. According to the Song of Solomon he had sixty princesses, eighty concubines, and maidens innumerable; according to the history itself,[2] he had as many as seven hundred princesses and three hundred concubines; the first statement may represent the round number of those who were at any one time present at the court, and the second refer to the total number of women drawn to the court during his long reign, though the number seven hundred stands out of all proportion to the three hundred, and may be due to the exaggeration of later tradition. But all this was, in fine, only such an imitation of the hereditary customs of the neighbouring courts as seemed to be demanded by Israel's splendid position and zeal for novelties.[3] But undoubtedly Solomon went much further than David in the luxurious arrangements of his court, and further than the sensible part of the nation approved; for they, penetrated by the earnest spirit of the religion of Jahveh, were unable to trace any token of true kingly dignity in such magnificence and self-indulgence.[4] Besides Pharaoh's daughter, who undoubtedly retained throughout her place of honour, and many consorts taken from allied or subjugated nations, Solomon was fond of drawing likewise to his court Israelite maidens, but sometimes found among these, perhaps wholly unexpectedly, a victorious obstinacy in asserting their freedom, for this is undoubtedly the meaning of the incident narrated in the Song of Solomon. And from a hint furnished by this same poem,[5] it seems to have been Bath-sheba especially who, in her all-important position as queen-mother, flattered this inclination of the monarch.

Yet more unfortunate was it that the grand buildings of every description on the one hand, and the magnificent court-life on the other, could not in the last resort be carried on without some sacrifice of the honour and the freedom of the people. As Solomon's wealth and wisdom have alike passed into a proverb, it is not a little singular that his resources could prove so deficient as to compel him to sacrifice for this purpose some

---

[1] P. 268.
[2] 1 Kings xi. 3, cf. ver. 1; Cant. vi. 8, cf. ver. 9.
[3] Pp. 165, 240; ii. p. 388.
[4] Hence Deut. xvii. 17 expressly forbids a king to take many wives.
[5] Cant. iii. 11.

portion of the national liberty and glory. But the prosecution and completion of such immense works obviously required pecuniary resources which could scarcely be calculated beforehand; it is equally clear that the magnificent and lavish expenditure at the court constantly increased: and the more abundant the revenue which flowed into the royal treasury, the more danger might spring out of its extravagant employment in the hands of a monarch devoted to grand works and a magnificent style of living. On one occasion, as we know with certainty, Solomon helped himself out of the difficulty by the sacrifice of a small slice of his territory. After the completion of the two largest buildings in the capital, it became necessary to close Hiram's account, and it then appeared that Solomon owed him so much not only for building materials, but also for money which he had advanced towards the undertaking, that in addition to the annual tribute which he was to receive of twenty thousand measures of wheat[1] and twenty thousand measures of the best oil, Solomon was compelled to give up to Tyre twenty small cities, in acknowledgment of which the Tyrian king at once presented him with an additional sum of one hundred and twenty talents of gold. The twenty small Galilean towns lay close to the Tyrian boundary, and clearly were very welcome to the Tyrian dominion, restricted as it was to a narrow strip of sea-coast. As, however, popular wit has always free play on occasion of such cessions of territory, and neither of the contracting parties is willing to be at a disadvantage, the story soon ran in Israel, that when king Hiram surveyed in person his new acquisitions, they appeared to him of little importance, and did not come up to his expectations, so that henceforth the territory bore the name Cabul, i.e. As-Nothing.[2] But in the long run no prince can rely on such an expedient for supplying the deficiencies of his purse.

---

[1] *Kor*, the largest measure = 10 Attic Metretæ.

[2] 1 Kings ix. 10–14, cf. v. 24 [v.10] sq. The word *Cabul* was interpreted as *Ca*, i.e. *like*, and *bul* = *nothing*. It becomes readily apparent that this is one of the many witty names which occur in the Old Testament. The strip of land certainly derived its name originally from the town of Cabul in the south of the territory of the tribe of Asher, Josh. xix. 27. The ruins as well as the meaning of the name have now been to some extent discovered, see Ritter's *Erdkunde*, xvi. (1852) p. 677, and the map belonging to it, and also the recent *Reisebeschr. nach Palästina* by Fürrer, p. 299. In 2 Chron. viii. 2 the transaction is represented, though with great brevity, as though Hiram had given these cities to Solomon, who had then placed Israelite inhabitants in them; but this view probably arose from the difficulty at the time of the Chronicler of entertaining any idea of Solomon unworthy of his greatness. Even the inference of Josephus, *Ant.* viii. 5. 3, from Hiram's words, 1 Kings ix. 13, that he had given back the cities to Solomon for nothing out of disgust, is just as arbitrary as that Χαβαλών meant 'not pleasing' in Phœnician; unless, indeed, כָּבוּל could be considered identical with חָבוּל, *ruined*.

Our present materials are unfortunately too scanty to permit of our understanding in detail the financial affairs of Solomon's reign; and we are still less able to determine accurately the sources and amount of the yearly revenue of the other kings of Israel. As the Theocracy, i.e. the constitution of Israel, was not primarily based upon the conviction of the necessity and utility of a royal house, and the people had been educated under this constitution, it became difficult for the monarchy to obtain any considerable funds by means of the direct taxation of the people. To this was added the hereditary dislike of all free nations to a compulsory money tax, and Israel, since its deliverance from Egypt, regarded itself as one of the freest nations upon earth. Nor is it possible to overlook the fact that the position of the monarchy in Israel was thus rendered very difficult, and the weight of this question was felt with considerable force in every stage of its development. Two sorts of aid, however, the people could not well refuse to an acknowledged king, even from the very first. On the one hand, it must accord to him the right to levy troops as indispensable for the protection of the country; and as this at once placed a store of human force at the disposal of the kings, it is not very surprising that they manifested an inclination to extend their authority beyond these limits, and to use the labour and skill of their subjects in providing for the immediate management and support of their own households; and this made it the interest of each one of their subjects to see whether by any means he could escape from military duty or the civil burdens to which he was subjected by the king. This state of affairs [1] existed without doubt in the kingdom of the Ten Tribes, but scarcely earlier; for it is a state of difficulty, which, as will be shown below, the monarchy would encounter first in that kingdom. A second source of support was found in the ancient tithes and first-fruits, a tribute from the land to its protector and master; [2] and as the priesthood to which this tribute first fell for its own maintenance and that of the sanctuary, had now shown that it was too weak to protect the country, it was not an unreasonable demand that the king also, as the more powerful protector and 'Jahveh's Anointed,' should appropriate a portion of it. In fact, the propriety of this arrangement was

---

[1] It is clearly described 1 Sam. viii. 11-13; cf. above, p. 230 sq., *note* 2; comp. with the origin of the freeholders, p. 42. The passage 1 Sam. viii. 11-17 cannot be rightly understood without considering that vv. 11-13 describe the royal prerogative of levying troops, and vv. 14-17 the right of the king to tithes (and first-fruits), each, however, in the widest extension. There is no mention of contributions of money, a fact which is most instructive historically.

[2] See the *Alterthümer*, p. 344 sqq.

acknowledged from the very commencement.[1] Israel also from of old was accustomed to taxation of this nature; and the only question which could arise was to what extent it might be carried, whether the king ought to receive the whole or a part only of the taxes, and whether the existing system might be further carried out in apparently analogous cases. On the other hand, a poll-tax, and especially a money payment, was the constant object of Israel's dislike, and it always remained very sensitive on this point. But the primitive basis of all royal resources from which the king must start in the first place, and to which he had always in the last resort to return, was formed by his own domain;[2] and as the existence of monarchy without a military power[3] devoted to its service cannot be conceived, the king has in its earliest form to support this force, and so in a certain sense himself, entirely out of his own private possessions. But if the king maintains his power and reigns successfully, he readily finds a hundred methods of adding to his original domain. Subject foreign nations and conquered fortresses are then readily regarded as increasing his own power and that of his house; the annual tributes or voluntary offerings from foreigners flow into his treasure-houses; the taxes upon trade and commerce fall to his share as the recompense of his protecting guardianship; but then, in fact, the national income, whether obtained by the strength of the kingdom, or by the personal efforts of the king, becomes so mixed with the royal estate (*Domanium*) originally of very much more limited extent, that it becomes increasingly difficult to separate the two; nor can such a separation seem desirable to any royal house which strikes deeper and deeper roots in the whole people and its power, and so becomes more and more bound up with it. But the time came when, in the kingdom of the Ten Tribes, the firm foundations of the polity and power of Israel were again destroyed, and one royal house constantly displacing its predecessor was obliged to build up its own power slowly from the very bottom, and to strengthen it with laborious care, while at the same time it emulated the magnificence of a Solomon. Then it was that the kings, on the refusal of all money taxes, sought to maintain themselves by the widest expansion of the two primitive sources

---

[1] P. 21 sq.
[2] Cf. Is. iii. 6 sq., which exactly bears on this point.
[3] The term 'servants' or 'young men' of David may, besides the explanation already given, also denote his 'soldiers,' where the sense of the passage suggests it (as in 2 Sam. ii. 17, iii. 22, xviii. 7, 9, xx. 6; cf. xvii. 20, 1 Kings i. 33, cf. ver. 38, 2 Sam. viii. 7), as being those who were most closely bound to obedience by oath, hire, or in other ways.

of revenue ; and thus not only would the royal right of exacting labour be violently extended, but also the idea of tenths and first-fruits would readily be transferred according to caprice to everything to which the king took a fancy,—to landed property, to handsome men and women, and beasts of burden;[1] such tyrannical demands being the ordinary usage in many other ancient kingdoms.

On the other hand, so far as we can now judge, the financial affairs of the state under David and Solomon were on the whole as well arranged and as advantageous for the people as we could expect in a period of such prosperity and progress. Solomon had introduced a fixed arrangement for the support of his court and of his standing army. He placed twelve officials or principal receivers of customs in the territories of the tribes of Israel, with the exception of Judah, whose first duty was to take charge of the scattered royal domains, and who had further to collect the other taxes, each in his own district; and each one of these had to supply the wants of the king for a month. These wants were great: the royal table itself, at which according to custom many houses allied with the royal family were supported,[2] and whose splendour has been already briefly described,[3] required for daily use thirty measures of fine and sixty measures of ordinary meal,[4] ten fatted oxen and twenty pasture-fed oxen, one hundred sheep or goats, besides game, harts, deer, gazelles, and fatted swans. This arrangement existed during the latter half of Solomon's reign at all events:[5] nevertheless it remained defective, according to our

---

[1] Cf. 1 Sam. viii. 14–17, Amos vii. 1.
[2] As is expressly said 1 Kings v. 7 [iv. 27], cf. iv. 7; cf. the case mentioned p. 216 sq.
[3] P. 284.
[4] From this it has been calculated in various ways that considerably more than ten thousand men ate daily at Solomon's table.
[5] Because two of these officers are introduced, according to 1 Kings iv. 11, 15, as Solomon's sons-in-law. Some of the names of places which occur in this important document (1 Kings iv. 7–19, v. 2 sq., 6–8 [iv. 22 sq., 26–28]), and nowhere else, are very obscure, and the expression 'all Israel' (iv. 7) might easily be understood, as in iv. 1, of all the twelve tribes. The twelve officers, however, were evidently appointed neither from the popular sanctity attaching to this number, cf. i. p. 362 sq., nor according to the districts of the twelve tribes. This is clear, partly from the description itself, partly from the express addition that their duties were arranged by the number of the months. In fact, it is impossible in the twelve districts of these officers to find any portion of the remote possessions of the tribe of Judah. The description begins with a part of Ephraim in ver. 8, passes in ver. 9 westward to the territory of Dan, in vv. 10–12, to districts north of both, jumps, in ver. 13 sq., to the north-east districts on the other side of the Jordan, returns, in vv. 15–17 to the most northern provinces on this side, and in ver. 18 sq. takes up Benjamin with the southern provinces on the other side of the Jordan; while, wherever smaller cities are separately named, these must plainly be considered simply as domains, where the officers were fixed. The land of Hepher (ver. 10) we can, therefore, only suppose to be that lying in the tribe of Manasseh, the situation of which would exactly suit the other

present notions, inasmuch as each one of these officials could employ as he pleased any surplus revenue; and that these posts were very lucrative is clear from the fact that two out of these twelve officials are described as Solomon's sons-in-law. Another officer of the same sort was placed over the royal province of Judah, but we are not now able to say to what purposes this revenue was applied; a superintendent again was appointed over these thirteen officials.[1] A large part of these expenses was undoubtedly borne by the Canaanite cities which Solomon had brought for the first time under complete subjection.[2] This lies partly in the nature of the case, but it is partly discoverable even in the very brief account preserved of the twelve provinces of these wardens, in which such cities have special notice obviously because they were the most productive.[3] Subject nations like Moab, Ammon, Damascus, and the Philistine cities, were no doubt obliged as far as possible to pay tribute in money; but their contributions flowed into the national treasury. Whether every man of Israelite birth had to pay a poll-tax from his ready cash, we do not learn by express testimony; but it is extremely probable, at all events during the later years of Solomon's reign, as the nation at its close complains so much of its heavy burdens, and as in the kingdom of the Ten Tribes this kind of impost was avoided not without valid reason. The feudal services also, which at an earlier period were probably but rarely required from the people, clearly increased constantly during this long reign,[4] and in this respect also the kingdom became undoubtedly far more like that of Egypt.

2. *Solomon's Position towards Religion and the Priesthood.*

But amid the growing jealousy springing up from below, the inability of the monarchy salutarily to remove antiquated limitations which broke out as fresh evils, is most clearly visible in the treatment of one great principle connected with the religion at that time predominant. A greater freedom in

---

[1] passages where the name occurs (Josh. xii. 17, xix. 13, 2 Kings xiv. 25); and we do not know of any other. If this is so, the last words in ver. 19 cannot have meant that it was anything surprising that there was only one officer in Gilead, for this is not so very surprising; but we should follow the LXX and insert יְהוּדָה after בָּאָרֶץ, as also, in ix. 18, אֲרָם after the same word בָּאָרֶץ. Specifications of the purpose to which the revenue of the warden of Judah was applied, did not belong to this connexion.

[1] Azariah son of Nathan, 1 Kings iv. 5.
[2] P. 218 sq.
[3] Comp. 1 Kings iv. 9 with Judges i. 33–35; ver. 11 sq. with Judges i. 27; see ii. p. 328 sqq. This renders the scope of the document 1 Kings iv. a little clearer; cf. above, p. 259.
[4] P. 229 sq.

religion was the necessity of the age. It can indeed by no
means be shown from ancient authorities that Solomon, even
in advanced life, ever left the religion of Jahveh, and with his
own hand sacrificed to heathen gods. All traces of contemporary history extant testify to the contrary; and we still find
an express statement that upon the altar which he erected to
Jahveh, he sacrificed thrice during the year (at the three great
festivals) with all the solemnity which was only becoming in a
king such as he.[1] But we must reflect that under him the kingdom of Israel had the strongest tendency to become an imperial
power, and emancipate itself completely from all its ancient
limitations. But in a prosperous empire, and especially in one
which seeks its well-being in peace and commerce, the toleration of diverse religions is absolutely indispensable, for a
government of this nature cannot desire any sudden change in
the various tendencies and views of the people. Still less will
it desire to destroy them with violence; and thus every form of
religion was without doubt tolerated within the wide circumference of Solomon's kingdom. This is the true explanation why,
in later life, as this tendency became more developed in his
kingdom, he caused altars to Astarte, Chemosh, and Milcom for
his Sidonian,[2] Moabite, and Ammonite wives to be built on the
mountain south-east of Jerusalem, below the Mount of Olives.[3]
This innovation was due neither to any desire to gratify a taste
for building nor from any weak tenderness towards his foreign
wives; but, from the position which the nation assumed, especially during the latter half of his reign, he could have no
reason for not building such altars, nor could he give a better
token that in his kingdom there was a universal religious toler-

---

[1] 1 Kings ix. 25; cf. also the account of the queen of Sheba, p. 284 sq. The word שלם, in the latter passage, must be equivalent to 'saying farewell,' taking leave with a blessing, which we must obviously suppose followed the general fashion of Solomon's time, and was a composition of poetic art. The worship celebrated by him always consisted, accordingly, of three parts: (1) the great sacrifice in the forecourt; (2) the solitary prayer and offering of incense only directly before the Holy of Holies ('he offered incense *by himself* at the place before Jahveh,' i.e. in the Holy Place, אשר indicating locality according to my *Lehrb.* § 333*a*); (3) the return to the forecourt and public utterance of the concluding prayer.

[2] Hence it would be quite possible for Solomon to have also had a daughter of the Tyrian king Hiram; yet this is only stated by later writers, as Eusebius, after Tatian, *Præp. Ev.* x. 11.

[3] The passage 1 Kings xi. 7 sq. is the only ancient part of the narrative, vv. 4–10; only that instead of Molech we ought here to read Milcom, according to v. 5, 33, 2 Kings xxiii. 13, cf. ver. 10, so that it remains uncertain whether Solomon also built an altar for Molech. Considering, on the other hand, that in 2 Kings xxiii. 9–15 only the three idol-altars on the mountain south-east of Jerusalem (hence called in later times *Mons scandali*) are expressly traced back to Solomon, it seems improbable that he built an altar to Molech; for there is no doubt that this deity was different from Milcom.

ance, than by permitting his own wives to sacrifice to their national deities. In fact, even in that early period, under the wise Solomon a legal tolerance of different religions had a tendency to spring up, which the true religion would undoubtedly have to permit as soon as it became more distinctly conscious of its own nature,[1] and against which, in our own day and in countries west of the Niemen, no one feels called upon to act excepting Jesuits and persons of similar sentiments. Undoubtedly the religion of Jahveh was at that time in some respects too weak to rely wholly upon itself without any external support; for this religion, attached by its origin to the single nationality of Israel, and for centuries entwined with increasing firmness in its life and victories, had at that time too little recognised its own character, and was too little conscious of its true power against the heathen, to be able with its spirituality to endure with ease the seductive proximity of its sensuous rivals. But if Solomon's rule had not already, through other causes, somewhat estranged from him the national feeling, who can tell what might not have been successfully and permanently achieved in this age of wisdom! But now, as this innovation was carried through by the sole exercise of the royal prerogative, many of the stricter believers, cherishing the memory of their early history, and the glorious days of the past, were soon led to regard this freedom of the philosophic king with gathering dislike, as the increasing laxity of the national life [2] caused in many a growing indifference, even towards what was essential in the ancient religion. In this way also Solomon undoubtedly alienated the hearts of many of his subjects; and there sprung up silently two parties which in the later history stand out with increasing distinctness and abruptness, one party favouring this innovation, and hence easily giving way to the admission of looser heathen customs into Israel, and the other resolutely opposed to the whole movement. Under a rule so powerful and brilliant as Solomon's, such a change in the national life could only gradually make itself felt, and the evils accruing to the religion of Jahveh from the growing freedom did not fully manifest themselves until a later period. After they had been long laid bare during the course of centuries, the Deuteronomic redactor of the history treated this point as if the heart of the once wise king

---

[1] It is, besides, self-evident that no dominant higher religion ought, on this account, to tolerate such usages and customs of other religions as are positively immoral; for instance, no Christian state ought now to tolerate polygamy in countries where Islam has hitherto not prevailed.

[2] P. 289.

had in his old age been drawn away from the religion of Jahveh into idolatry by his numerous heathen wives.[1]

Solomon, like his father David, certainly retained in his own hands the supervision of the Israelite priesthood, and, as we have seen,[2] on suitable occasions probably acted himself as High Priest of his people. During his long reign the Levitical priesthood seems to have remained in a peaceful state, satisfied that its ancient privileges were respected and that the king concerned himself no less for the glory of the temple than for his own security.[3] But his own glory even here cast into the shade the growing contradictions of his rule. A king who permitted heathen religions also to exist in all honour, might well seem to be no longer a worthy High Priest in Israel; and how this situation grew more and more gloomy under his successors will be shown afterwards more clearly in Uzziah's reign.

3. *Solomon's Relation to Prophetism.*

As monarchy in Israel was at that time flourishing in its utmost strength, its original position and consequence rendered a collision with prophetism the only quarter from which it could receive its first really damaging blow, and be threatened in its present course of high development. The relation, therefore, of these two independent powers to each other again becomes the decisive question at this noon-day of the national history.

It must not be forgotten that when the monarchy attains to its full power and development, it naturally seeks to become in every direction the real centre of unity in the state, in order that there may be no opportunity for a second independent anti-regal power arrogating equal rights to arise, and cause an ever-widening breach in the completed unity and power of the kingdom. Hitherto the monarchy had been placed by the side of the Theocracy, which had found in prophetism its strongest representative. These two independent powers, whose cooperation had alone called into being the high prosperity of this royal age, worked together in unison under David, not, however, because they were compelled to this course by any external law or settled arrangement, but because David possessed a greatness of soul which enabled him to listen to the voice of a true prophet without in any degree compromising his

---

[1] 1 Kings xi. 1–10; comp. with the remarks already made p. 297 sq.
[2] P. 246.
[3] According to p. 247 sqq., and the *Alterthümer*, p. 328 sq.

own royal dignity, or suffering any possible loss of it. As we have seen,[1] they still continued to act in unison at the beginning of Solomon's reign; but with the consummation of the royal power which had just been reached in Solomon, this duality, by logical necessity, tried to pass into unity in the person of the king. After Nathan, who probably did not long survive David, we hear no longer of any great prophets acting in harmony with Solomon as Gad and Nathan did with David. Not as if Solomon, imitating the example of Saul, designed to annihilate the prophetic power. It seemed rather that his great wisdom joined to his high kingly dignity rendered this second power superfluous, and the great king and the true prophet of Jahveh seemed capable of assimilation in his august person.[2]

In this way, therefore, an effort was made to complete in Solomon's case what[3] was undoubtedly involved in the straightforward progress of the fundamental forces already active throughout this great period in Israel's history. The rivalry of the two independent powers would only be brought to a close by the advent of a king who should be able likewise to take the place of the prophetic power. But to have secured the actual accomplishment of this in the case of even such a wonderfully endowed king as Solomon, the age must have possessed a heritage of experiences and powers which as yet it had by no means attained. The monarchy would have had wholly to incorporate the prophetic office in that of the king, and the one must have been wholly transfused into the other, so that the true king must also have become the true prophet, and the perfect prophet the right king; and thus the perfect man, the lofty goal of the history of Israel, would appear. But the perfect prophet cannot come until the advent of the perfect religion, for of this he is the harbinger and founder upon earth; but the religion of Jahveh, sure and true as was its basis, was at that time too little advanced in self-development, was as yet too liable to violence, and had too little recognised its own nature and proved its own power in the struggle with foreign religions, to be able to attain the last stage of its own perfection by producing a perfect prophet-king. But the monarchy, as the new power of the age, was too completely the offspring of mere national wants, and was still, therefore, too exclusively devoted to mere national objects, to be capable, even for this purpose,

---

[1] P. 208 sqq.
[2] Cf. such proverbs as 'An oracle is on the king's lips, in judgment his mouth speaketh not deceitfully,' Prov. xvi. 10.
[3] P. 6.

of freeing itself from the fault of violence; nor was it possible for a king springing out of this circle to become a true and perfect prophet. Both powers, then, still suffered from the same error of violence, and could not fail at length to repel each other, instead of amalgamating together.

Hence it arises that the first earnest attempt at an actual union and reconciliation of the two great independent powers of the age brings to the surface those deeper deficiencies which still placed the strongest obstacles in the way of such union, hindrances which even Solomon's wisdom and power altogether failed to remedy. The monarchy is not yet capable of incorporating prophetism in itself, the one cannot take the place of the other. These two independent powers therefore, as soon as this is recognised, at once separate further from each other at the moment when each was desirous to merge into the other. But this separation is now a very different thing from their former beautiful union in the beginning of this period of the history. For the object which at that time so advantageously joined them together and long held them firm to each other is now attained: the threatened nationality of Israel and its religion is now saved, in fact rendered powerful and glorious beyond expectation. Then it is that the monarchy, for which in its own nature the national power and glory suffices, desires to repose upon its own great conquests and advantages; it advances unchecked to its highest development as well as to its greatest glory. It appears able to dispense with the cooperation of prophetism, and it does dispense with it for a time, while it borrows something from it and appropriates it to itself; but scarcely has it thus fully advanced to its own swift and one-sided development, when the yawning gulf becomes visible which separates it from prophetism, and suddenly it is turned against it. It is not until the later years of Solomon's rule that we again learn anything of the activity of great prophets, but we find this activity turned against him and his house,—Ahijah of Shiloh and Shemaiah, of whom more will be said hereafter, and Iddo, of whom we know but few particulars.[1] The course of his reign shows us on this point a complete subversion of its strongest supports. At first we observe the most willing and joyful cooperation with the prophetic power, such as naturally marked the harmonious continuation

---

[1] He lived for about twenty years after Solomon, 2 Chron. xii. 15, xiii. 2; with עֶדּוֹ may probably be identified the יֶעְדּוֹ or יֶעְדִּי who, like Ahijah under Solomon, spoke about the future sovereignty of Jeroboam, 2 Chron. ix. 29; the LXX, however, have here Ἰωήλ.

of David's rule; Nathan was still the approved friend and councillor of the young king as of his late father, and two of his sons were even designated Solomon's ministers, and long retained this lofty dignity.[1] There was, further, the best understanding with the priesthood, to which Nathan also belonged,[2] and between the prophetic power and the priesthood there was at that time no serious contrariety of aim. And now at the close of his reign the younger generation of prophets was in complete opposition to him, but certainly only out of the consciousness, however dimly felt, that the monarchy in Israel by its narrow aims was degenerating into an ascendency and violence which endangered the Theocracy itself, and with it the sacred and inviolable basis of Israel's whole existence.

The form assumed by the swift development of Israel during the last hundred years, and the failure of Solomon, in the splendour and tranquillity of his time, to turn the helm powerfully enough against the perversities which were spreading unobserved among the people at large, the court and the state, exposed the monarchy, which from the nature of the age embodied the most violent portion of all the efforts and exertions of the nation itself, to the danger of becoming nothing better than a secular, i.e. an ordinary monarchy, resembling that of Egypt or any other heathen kingdom. But an undisturbed continuance upon this path would necessarily soon bring about much which was opposed to Israel's national life, which was as austere as it was free: and there still existed in Israel deep in the heart of the people too much simplicity of morals, and too strong an opposition against all that was heathenish, to make it possible for the monarchy to degenerate, without resistance, into a heathen kingdom. In truth, as we have already seen, a great part of the nation during the long and prosperous peace constantly grew in wealth and luxury, and naturally became more languid and effeminate; but the spirit of independence was yet far too rife among the people. In many places they obviously strongly opposed the growing taste for luxury and revelry; they stood too near the days in which prophetism under Samuel had sprung up with wonderful new power, and the prophetic word, when it was raised energetically against degenerating morals, still found many willing listeners.

It is therefore a remarkable fatality, but one easy to apprehend, that the noontide of the history of Israel, when its human monarchy is in danger of becoming like that of Egypt,

---

[1] 1 Kings iv. 3.   [2] P. 89, *note* 2.

and the very same question of compulsory servitude is raised, issues in a result not unlike that of the ancient rule of the Pharaohs over Israel. There is indeed this one great difference,—that the revolt of Israel against the hard service of the Egyptian king marks the beginning of all its national elevation, while the opposition to the compulsory services demanded by the monarchy which sprang from its own midst is the first step towards its own annihilation as a nation. And as what is highest throughout this history revolves round something higher than mere nationality and external freedom, it follows that even monarchy in Israel, which was at that time their only possible support, could possess only a temporary significance. Compulsory services, rendered not to a stranger or to an enemy of the nationality, but to a king of the same race, are, strictly speaking, and apart from the mere method in which they are rendered, no evil at all. The most civilised, legal, and prosperous states are obliged to make the severest demands on the powers of their citizens, because they secure to them so many real blessings of life which would be otherwise unattainable; and our present high taxes of all kinds, our military services and official duties, are in fact only better expedients in place of the compulsory services, which would otherwise be demanded of each citizen. Had Israel, when its monarchy was in its highest upward development, willingly accommodated itself to the increasingly heavy burdens which it laid upon it, who can measure the progress which it would have made towards the completion of the universal dominion which it had began to seek with such full vigour! The actual result was, that the monarchy, the sole means by which Israel had attained its present great prosperity, was so weakened that this earthly blessing was again dissolved. But at the former period Israel, by resisting Egyptian tyranny, had won in the first place spiritual freedom, and through this had attained national importance, not as though resistance to royal demands was an abstract good, but because that just resistance became to it only an occasion for the knowledge of the higher truth which is ever striving to impart itself to men, and the seizing of which becomes the beginning of all improved human, and therefore also national, life. So now, after it had found in the human monarchy the culminating point of its national prosperity, it allowed itself to be carried away into a like opposition to the heavier demands of its own kingdom, because that high truth which could not cease to fulfil in it its concealed work, remained in its deepest foundation far mightier than every external form of nationality, but would have been repressed in its development by the achievement of all the secular designs which the growing strength of the human monarchy suggested. Thus an event recurs in the noon of this history resembling externally one which took place at its beginning, but with a wholly different result, for it did not lead, like the earlier incidents, to the powerful elevation of an oppressed people, but to the overthrow of a flourishing one, an overthrow, however, involving new progress without limit; and while the human instrument, in repeating and imitating the external course of action, made a complete miscalculation, the unseen God, the real agent, unmoved by human error, carried forward His own infinite design.

As Solomon at the height of all his power and glory, was constructing an earth-wall between Zion and Moriah[1] he noticed, without doubt, among the lower overseers of the labourers, a young man of extremely powerful and vigorous appearance who pleased him much, and whom he on this account soon raised to the office of a general surveyor over the services due to the crown from the tribe of Joseph. This man, destined later to bring so much sorrow to David's house and to Solomon himself, was Jeroboam the son of Nebat, from Zereda in the tribe of Ephraim, which had from of old been jealous of the power of Judah. He was then a mere isolated youth, as his mother, who was still alive, had long been a widow. Of his feelings when he thus unexpectedly became the chief superintendent of his tribe, our present narrative tells us nothing.[2] Suffice it to say, that when he had left Jerusalem behind him and reached the open country, he was met by the prophet Ahijah from Shiloh, an ancient sacred city of the tribe of Ephraim,[3] who had already uttered words of warning to Solomon himself; and, as if he had long in spirit beheld the instability of David's house, the sight of Jeroboam appearing in its proud new official dress prompted the thought that this young, handsome, and energetic man was too good to be a new supporter of the existing power.

---

[1] P. 258.

[2] 1 Kings xi. 26-40. The basis of this narrative is derived from the prophetic narrator of the history of the kings, and from vv. 11-13 it follows with certainty that Ahijah had already spoken to Solomon himself to the same purport. This narrator had certainly, as ch. xii. proves, only specified the severe oppression which the people suffered at Solomon's hands as the cause of the divine determination about the revolt of the Ten Tribes; for though the religious innovations did not operate in Solomon's favour, they were not, according to the plain meaning of the older narratives, the immediate cause of the revolt of the Ten Tribes. The Deuteronomic narrators are the first to ascribe every misfortune to the religious innovations, and in accordance with this the representation in ch. xi. is altered, chiefly by the additions vv. 1-10, 33, which betray their real character by the connexion.

[3] Vol. ii. p. 272.

Overcome by this, he tore (as the narrative only too truly relates) the new garment, the symbol of the power of David's house and its efforts after perpetuity, into twelve pieces, and announced to him that, in like manner, by Jahveh's will the kingdom of the twelve tribes would be torn to pieces, but that over ten tribes he should himself be king. The history of this prophetic selection of a king, amid much that is dissimilar, shows in many features a resemblance to that of Saul by Samuel;[1] but to what totally different results was it destined subsequently to lead! Jeroboam at once openly rose against Solomon's rule; and although we do not know in detail the course of this insurrection, it is distinctly seen from all the circumstances that he found adherents and support in the northern tribes, and that the contest with him was not a very easy one. Subdued at length, he succeeded in escaping to Egypt, and found in that country, where about this time a new dynasty had arisen with very different feelings towards Solomon, willing protection at the hands of king Shishak. But the men of his tribe did not forget during the remainder of Solomon's life-time the bold youth, who, after a long period of repose, was the first to renew the contest against Judah and Jerusalem; and the extent of the communications which they maintained, in spite of Solomon's power, with the refugee in Egypt will soon be seen more distinctly in the course of this history.

4. *The New Importance of Jerusalem.*

Human monarchy, then, in Israel reached under Solomon the limits of its development. These limits it ought indeed to have outgrown, but it was unable to do so, and after that time its fall, earlier or later, became certain. Thus also a like fate was sure to overtake the institutions originated by it.

The magnificent new temple in the heart of the kingdom now became a sort of citadel of the higher religion. Hence there first gathered around it the numerous inhabitants of Jerusalem; and then the rest of the nation attached themselves more closely to it. At a time in which the higher religion with difficulty obtained recognition among men, and had to contend for a place for itself, only separate small places where once a sanctuary had stood were regarded as hallowed ground, and as the inviolate refuge of all who approached them.[2] This was the universal usage of all early antiquity; now, how-

---

[1] P. 18 sq.
[2] These were always regarded as participating immediately in the security and happiness of the state sanctuary, as is proved by descriptions like Ps. xxiv. 3, xv. 1, lxxxiv. 5 [4], Is. xxxiii. 14–16.

ever, there arose a great city, the centre of a powerful state, possessing a similar sacredness. Here also were assembled all the higher Priests, here were to be seen the most magnificent offerings, and here were laid up the most costly gifts. Besides this there still remained other sanctuaries scattered through the land, preserving their full freedom. The chief of these were the 'heights,' so often mentioned in after times, an ancient Canaanite kind of sanctuary, which had also at that time been adopted in Israel. They consisted of a high stone block as the emblem of the Holy One, and of the 'height' itself, i.e. of an altar, a sacred tree or grove, or even of the image of the special deity,[1] so artificial was the further development of the ancient Canaanite worship of sacred stones.[2] But none of these could in any way compare with the glory and grandeur of the new sanctuary in Jerusalem. It drew to itself the largest number of adherents, but from that very cause it easily aroused a growing jealousy in the rest of the country; so that while the higher religion, under the royal protection, seemed ready to attain in it a firm and enduring unity, a division was prepared on the other side which nothing could reunite.

And as Jerusalem was now regarded as the great sanctuary and place of refuge, and besides, as the place where David had formerly established his permanent camp, was pre-eminent over all other cities,[3] so now through Solomon it had become[4] an extremely well fortified city, and, by the wide girdle of fortresses which Solomon had begun to erect in a circuit of more or less distance from it, it seemed able to brave every storm. In fact, Solomon in these fortresses only followed the example long set

---

[1] What sort of things these 'heights' were may be seen most clearly from Ezek. xvi. 16-39, compared with passages so clear as Num. xxxiii. 52, 2 Kings xxiii. 15, Deut. xii. 3, as well as with the representations of Phœnician temples, for instance, of that at Paphos, on the coins under Augustus (cf. Münter's essay on it. Kopenh. 1824). On such coins the sacred block is clearly to be seen set up in the interior; and it was, accordingly, the principal object of sanctity in the whole temple. It was often adorned with robes and ribbons of variegated stripes as signs of vows, Ezek. xvi. 16 (cf. a similar practice in Ethiopia and elsewhere; see many passages in Harris' *Highlands of Ethiopia*; Hildebrand on Arnobius *Adv. Nat.* i. 39; Bodenstedt's *Kaukasus*, p. 175); the surrounding buildings were of the most varied height, just as the Buddhists still have all sorts of little temples in great numbers. That the sacred tree or oak which overshadowed the whole was called Ashêrah, as the LXX translate, is proved from passages like 2 Kings xxiii. 15 comp. with Judg. vi. 26-32; similar trees were found in Phœnician temples also, Tertull. *Apolog.* ix. As, however, the word *Bâmah*, 'Height,' which was now appropriated specially to it, generally denoted also the whole building in which it stood, in the same way the term *Ashêrah* might denote especially the goddess to whom such Heights were generally consecrated in certain ages, namely Astarte, as is clear from Judges iii. 7 comp. with ii. 13 and 1 Kings xv. 13. That this cannot, however, be the original meaning, is proved by passages like Deut. vii. 5, xii. 3, and especially xvi. 21 sq.

[2] See the *Alterthümer*, p. 134 sq., 259 sq.

[3] Cf. 1 Kings xi. 36, Is. xxix. 1, &c.

[4] P. 258.

in the older important monarchies of the East, and the want of such fortified places Israel had often bitterly experienced during previous centuries. Jerusalem, therefore, now appeared doubly inviolable and unconquerable, guarded by its strong fortifications, and by the protection (the asylum) of its great sanctuary. The momentous consequences which flowed from this new confidence in a city so peculiar in its character, will become manifest in the sequel. But there were yet wanting to the monarchy deeper and imperishable foundations: and thus all such sacred fortresses could avail it little, especially among a people which, like Israel from the time of its earliest youth, had always cherished some degree of repugnance to living in fortresses,[1] and whose religion so strongly inculcated recourse to a higher protection than that which fortresses and external sanctuaries were able to afford.

The monarchy itself indeed now stood too firmly established in the ideas and requirements of Israel. But not so the special royal house of David. On Solomon, indeed, rested the double glory of inherited dignity, but in his own person he stood somewhat remote from the multitude, and certainly shrunk from mixing in the popular affairs of Israel as David had done, who had not felt ashamed, even when a powerful king, to appear at the right moment among the multitude as one of themselves, and to rejoice with them with child-like simplicity.[2] From this cause, combined with other causes already named, the signs of growing indifference to the rule of David's house were multiplied towards the close of Solomon's life, while the inability of the monarchy, as developed in him, to break through the barriers which the religion and the nationality of Israel opposed to it, was made clearer and clearer. Hence, by the side of all the splendour which marks the whole of this great period of Solomon's rule, is seen already the shadow of that decay against which no human wisdom could guard. The reign of a perfect king of Jahveh, the object of all the efforts and the final desire of every pious soul, had not come: and that with this defect, all the treasures and all the glories of the king, all the external protection of the kingdom, the horses, and the fortresses, could furnish no true happiness and security, the prophets could already foresee, and their anticipations were soon fulfilled, as Israel in the early times had already experienced in Egypt, and as by the prophets after Solomon the lesson is constantly

---

[1] This is certainly unmistakable, but yet explicable from the ancient condition of Israel; cf. ii. p. 130 sq., 241 sq., 247 sq.

[2] Cf. for example, the incident related p. 127.

repeated in reference to Israel itself.[1] No doubt, so long as David's illustrious son lived, the external power of the monarchy was firmly maintained; such continued to be the influence of the name of the great and wise prince, who had begun his reign under such favourable auspices. But immediately after his death the violent rivalries, which had been for some time with difficulty restrained by the name of the great ruler, burst out openly.

5. *The Disruption of the Kingdom of David; the Beginning of its Decline.*

Every change in the succession raises immeasurable hopes or fears, especially if the previous reign, like that of Solomon, has been one of great length, and if also the monarchy, as was at that time the case in Israel, is passing into the hereditary stage, but has not yet been bound to it by any long-existing law. But if the death of Solomon was followed by an incurable disruption of David's kingdom, and thus by the greatest misfortune which could befall not only the monarchy of Israel but the entire nation and its earthly prosperity, we are tolerably prepared, by explanations already given, to see in this something different from an event produced by the capricious will of any particular individuals. The earlier author of the history of the kings calls the disruption which took place a divine decree.[2] This affords clear evidence how dark it was in its deeper causes, but also how unavoidable it seemed, humanly speaking, to those who lived nearest to it. We must therefore follow this momentous event (which in its immediate disastrous consequences was as marked as the rise of David's rule had been in its joyful results) more closely, drawing out its concealed, but yet not quite undiscoverable causes and motives.

Respecting the existence of the monarchy itself, there was at that time no strife on any side. It stood already too firmly established in the opinion and the habits of the people, and had already secured for them too many benefits, to be lightly set aside. But the conditions of its maintenance might become a subject of bitter controversy. The monarchy was at that time very highly developed, and was therefore less and less able to endure individual caprices dangerous to the commonwealth;

---

[1] As in Hos. xiv. 4 [3], Is. ii. 7, Mic. v. 9 sq.

[2] There is no other way of understanding סִבָּה מֵעִם יְהוָה, 1 Kings xii. 15, cf. ver. 24, although the expression is by no means a common one in the Old Testament.

and having become extremely active, it made increasing demands on the labour and resources of the people. This royal power, the last which had developed itself in the community of Jahveh, was still in course of growth, animated by its own special impulses and aspirations, and might therefore easily seem somewhat dangerous to the other powers, and even likely to threaten the existence of the ancient religion, as was in fact in some degree the case. It seemed likewise bound, as by a charm, exclusively to David's house. The house of Saul had never attained such firm and wide-spread power. With the continuance of David's dynasty the monarchy seemed to grow constantly greater and more irresistible. In this, however, lay the real peril of the age which threatened nothing less than destruction. For if the power and sway of this Davidic house were questioned or destroyed, all those necessary and invaluable benefits which it alone secured to the people became liable to forfeiture. These benefits consisted in settled unity and the national strength resulting from it; the general prosperity of the country which had so wonderfully increased during the last half century; and, yet more, the whole higher culture alike of the people generally and of its religion in particular which had sprung up under David and Solomon, and now in Jerusalem had found a permanent centre. All these laborious acquisitions of the two great kings were imperilled so soon as popular feeling was turned against the monarchy and the dynasty through which alone they had been won; for the longer a royal house rules successfully, the more deeply and indissolubly does it grow into the whole existence of its people. And yet it was scarcely possible to avoid that contrariety of efforts and divergence of views which characterised that decisive age.

The monarchy, when once highly developed and intertwined with the national consciousness, might, indeed, part with some unessential tokens of its power, as, for instance, the multitude of wives, but it could scarcely by its own will surrender its strict demands on the national services and the public taxes. But again, very many of the best men in Israel might regard as highly dangerous a further increase of power, and a one-sided development of the monarchy, because in their eyes the ancient freedom of the people, and at the same time Jahveism itself, were thus endangered. An indistinct conception of the course which it might be best to follow, together with exaggerations and useless obstinacy, might thus hamper both sides all the more readily, in proportion to the license of a rich, luxurious age, and to the distance by which they were removed from those difficulties out of which the people had been brought by the growing strength of the monarchy. But that the contrariety of aims was beyond cure, and that precisely the best men of the nation distinctly feared from a further growth of royal power the most dangerous injury to the higher and permanent blessings of the community, to their freedom and their religion, is certainly seen from the energy and consequences of the action of such prophets as Ahijah and Shemaiah against Solomon and his son: for prophetism, pure and strong as it then was, did but announce by such direct results as early and forcibly as possible some higher truth which was already deeply felt throughout the nation. Undoubtedly it was possible to reconcile the opposing pretensions, and without any violent overthrow, to put on one side the dreaded dangers; and the means of this lay in the constant interchange of views between the king and the most intelligent of his subjects,—in short, in what is now called constitutional government, and which, when wisely arranged, is the safeguard of the best modern Christian nations. There were also, according to all indications, meetings of deputies in ancient Israel;[1] but while the monarchy, in the protection of which they had full confidence, was striving upwards with an entirely new power, they met together, probably, only when the accession of a new king was to be confirmed, and a compact to be made with him which was to last for his life. Their power was therefore all the greater, but possibly also all the more disturbing; and we have no evidence that they ever met again until Solomon's death.

The general feeling, accordingly, might be expressed in the two assertions—(1) that the monarchy, as developed towards the close of Solomon's life, could not stand; and (2) that, on the other hand, it must be carried back to such principles as had prevailed say in Samuel's time. With this the prophets, so far as we know, were in accord; and all the better minds in Israel probably shared their sentiments. But if we try to imagine the state of affairs in reference to the special means or instruments by which this object might ultimately be attained, this passage in the ancient history will be found the best adapted (if taken along with the true greatness of prophecy in those centuries) to exhibit clearly the earthly limits which it was not yet able to break through. Prophecy holds firm for the present age a pure

---

[1] See above, p. 11 sq.; the names of the heads of tribes of the last years of David have been preserved, 1 Chron. xxvii. 16–22; and are here evidently enumerated as important members of the state.

truth, which the nation is inclined to neglect, and beholds with a bright glance its victory in all future time; but it is not its duty to comprehend and promulgate any national or other truths which a deeper experience has not yet proved to be necessary, and which, therefore, have not as yet any perceptible significance in the present. The great truth which prophecy then announced was that in the kingdom of Jahveh the human monarchy, even in the midst of its highest development, ought not to degenerate and to injure the freedom of the people; and this truth was rendered triumphant for the time and was saved for the future by means of its activity. That the religion of Jahveh, as it then existed, could not tolerate any general religious freedom, was the next truth—one springing, however, simply from the weakness of the age—which prophecy also made known at that time. But no prophet of that day could possibly desire any better organisation of the deputies of the realm, because no one had as yet discovered any defect in the existing usage. In the same way they had not then sufficient experience of the evil and the good resulting from a constant change of dynasty; while the single change which had hitherto occurred in the substitution of the house of David for that of Saul, seemed rather to point to the advantage of such changes. As prophecy, therefore, after its renovation by Samuel, had throughout been most active in establishing and guiding the kingdom in Israel, and as it had raised up the house of David against that of Saul, it might think it possible by a fresh change of this kind to remove the evils of this age; and even during Solomon's life Ahijah had ventured to utter words to this effect which were repeated everywhere.[1] Whether they had found in this a means of rooting out the evil, further experience alone could show. Whether they could at once push forward their plan depended upon the national sentiments, and the capacity displayed by Solomon's son and successor.

Some parts of the country, at all events, had great reason to desire the permanence of David's house,—Jerusalem, the capital, which owed its prosperity entirely to this house, and the royal tribe of Judah, which, undoubtedly, continued specially favoured by it. It might also be the view of many of the best Jews, apart from all tribal prejudices, that the monarchy might be improved by degrees without a violent change. On the other hand, the ancient jealousy of the tribe of Joseph against Judah had manifested itself strongly even in David's time;[2] and so far from knowing that Solomon had taken any trouble to allay

[1] P. 304 sq.   [2] P. 193 sqq.

it, we may rather infer the contrary from the description of the distribution of his officers.¹ Standing upon its ancient pretensions as the first and leading tribe, it might raise the strongest opposition at the head of the other tribes; and if its demands were not conceded, it might even resolve to try what could be accomplished by a monarchy raised from its own midst upon a new basis. The bold Jeroboam, a man of its own blood, was already awaiting in Egypt such a turn of affairs. But the accomplishment of the threatened division of David's kingdom before the northern tribes could learn from experience how they might fare under the new rule of Solomon's son, was undoubtedly caused chiefly by the folly of Rehoboam ² himself. He was a son not of the Egyptian princess, who, probably, had not borne a son to Solomon, but of the Ammonite princess Naamah.³ At the time of his father's death he was already forty-one years old,⁴ and may long have awaited impatiently the possession of power, although he was little qualified for it by his own training, and was altogether very unlike what his grandfather David had been in his youth.

The deputies of the kingdom on this occasion assembled not in Jerusalem or Hebron, but in Shechem, the ancient capital of Joseph,—a significant hint, if Rehoboam had sufficiently understood it. But they had still the fullest intentions⁵ of confirming his power as king if their wishes were granted; and they permitted him with his guard and the deputies of Judah to come peaceably to the national assembly. On his arrival they declared their complaints, on account of the burdens which Solomon had multiplied upon them, and begged that they might be lightened: in that case they would be his devoted subjects. He promised to give them an answer on the third day: and there soon appeared among the advisers of the crown themselves a diversity of view respecting this demand. The elder counsellors recommended, with the wisdom

---

¹ P. 296 sq.
² The LXX spell the name רְחַבְעָם, Ροβοάμ.
³ She was a daughter of the last Ammonite king Hanun, 2 Sam. x. 1, as a note of the LXX on 1 Kings xii. 24 informs us.
⁴ 1 Kings xiv. 21, 31.
⁵ This we should certainly be compelled to doubt altogether, if in the narrative 1 Kings xii. 1–30 the Masoretic text were correct, for, according to it, the deputies had already taken the independent step of summoning Jeroboam from Egypt to Shechem, and had even made him their spokesman against Rehoboam. But the unintelligibility of ver. 2 and ver. 20 in this text proves the contrary; and the LXX have (according to *Cod. Vat.* everywhere, according to *Cod. Alex.* in ver. 12 at any rate) the reading which is nearer the original and in part more perfect, on which the representation above is based. In fact, the Jewish hatred against Samaria seems to have subsequently magnified the guilt of the Ten Tribes, and to have transformed the text accordingly; this was first done, however, only in 2 Chron. x. In accordance with this, we should follow ver. 20 and 2 Chron. x. 2, and read in ver. 2 מִמִּצְרַיִם and וַיֵּשֶׁב.

of a Solomon, that to-day they should be mild and give way, in order that the people might allow themselves to be quietly ruled ever after; and these counsellors, who were descended from a better age, may really have intended to give way on some points of less importance. But Rehoboam listened more willingly to the flattering advisers of his own age whom he had just appointed, and whose spirit reveals the moral degeneracy to which Jerusalem had sunk during the last years of Solomon's rule. Following their counsel, he then solemnly declared, if not in these very words, yet to the same purport, 'His little finger was thicker than his father's loins, and if his father, laying on them new burdens, chastised them with whips, he would, by increasing these burdens, chastise them with scorpions (i.e. knotted whips).' When this answer was made known, there sounded everywhere the terrible word which [1] had already, even under David himself, been raised by a scattered few:

> What part have we in David,
> What inheritance in Jesse's son?—
> To thy tents, O Israel!
> Now look to thy house, O David!

and the unity of the nation was at once torn in twain. Judah declared itself in favour of Rehoboam, who belonged to its own tribe.[2] Apparently encouraged by this, but at the same time half perplexed, the new king sent the old chief-collector of the taxes, Adoniram,[3] to treat with the insurgents, and to promise them some alleviation of their burdens. But the multitude, already embittered, stoned him to death; and greatly alarmed, the king hastily ascended his chariot and fled to Jerusalem. Now, for the first time, however, the remaining tribes thought seriously of that Jeroboam who had formerly taken refuge in Egypt, as likely to make them a more suitable king. This bold but at the same time cunning man, on hearing of Solomon's death, had returned from Egypt, without being in any way hindered by the new sovereign; and had betaken himself to his native city, Zereda. In the state of feeling then pervading the country, he could do this with great security. As his presence in the territory of the tribe of Joseph was generally known, the deputies who revolted from Rehoboam invited him to come to the national assembly of the people. He came, and was chosen their king. The son of Solomon in Jerusalem certainly made preparations, in his pride and wrath, for war against the Ten Tribes, in order to bring

---

[1] P. 193.
[2] The obvious connexion of the narrative permits no other meaning to be assigned to the words 1 Kings xii. 17; cf. 2 Chron. xi. 3.
[3] P. 230, *note* 1.

them back into obedience, and he actually assembled an army of 180,000 fighting men, the greater number belonging to the tribe of Judah. But in the decisive moment Shemaiah, a prophet, whose importance was far beyond that of Ahijah, probably from Jerusalem itself,[1] opposed him with the divine counsel to shed no brother's blood, because the present misfortune was due to the hand of God Himself, and therefore no man should obstinately oppose what had taken place. And, in fact, his advice was approved of by the warriors who were already armed. They separated, and no human determination could now stop the disruption, which only brought clearly to light the irreconcilable opposition hitherto veiled under the different yet decisive efforts of the two portions of the nation.

In fact, there may occur times in which a great disruption, either in the nation or in religion, however deplorable may be the causes which bring it on, and whatever doubtful results may be foreseen from it, becomes nevertheless a higher necessity; as, for instance, the disastrous schism which the Reformation, or rather its opponents, brought into Germany more than three hundred years ago. Every disruption, in fact, contains within itself an evil, which developes itself continuously, until it is possibly removed in the right way: but if an impenetrable darkness presses upon an age, because it is torn by two antagonistic efforts, the one being as necessary or inevitable as the other, without any higher view to reconcile and combine them, the mournful disruption may, at least for the immediate future, even become a benefit, because it assures to each movement the possibility of developing itself purely and fully, and thus in the end that higher view which at an earlier time was too weak, or perhaps not even in existence, may come into free play and win acceptance. Thus, in the last years of Solomon's life, and immediately afterwards, even prophets of Jahveh, whom we have no right to regard as false prophets, might urge the disruption, because the higher blessing of the true religion and of the human rule answering to this, a blessing which in Israel always remained the supreme concealed power, determining and deciding everything else, ran at that time the risk of being set aside by a further one-sided development of the monarchy. But on this very account the disruption, like every schism, remained a great evil: and whether it was ever again to be remedied during Israel's independent national life, or whether the preservation of the spiritual blessings of the people must finally involve the destruction of all its earthly blessings, could be known

[1] Cf. 1 Kings xii. 21-24, 2 Chron. xi. 1-4, with 2 Chron. xii. 15 [5].

only when the wholly different movements which were involved in the disruption, should have attained their full development. For the moment all those blessings were threatened which the monarchy for more than a hundred years had secured for the people with such great effort, a fatal disruption was effected in the community of Jahveh, such as even the most unfortunate period of the Judges had not known, and the age of Solomon, equally elevated and joyful, closed with a tragedy so sad that no worse can be experienced by any powerful nation which has already reached the higher stages of civilisation.[1]

IV. LATER REPRESENTATIONS OF SOLOMON.

When the course of the next centuries had sufficiently shown the incurable nature of the schism which cast a shadow over the last half of Solomon's reign, and when regret for the destruction of David's kingdom influenced more and more deeply the historians of Judah, the memory of the acts and works of the great son of David became in many ways obscured, and many particulars of his history received, it is evident, less and less consideration. On the other hand, its chief points were submitted to a keener criticism by those who looked back on the great suffering with which it had closed, under a vivid consciousness of the great principle upon which it properly turned. The earlier prophetic narrator still regarded him quite simply, as a king highly favoured indeed by God, and loved as a son; yet, if his sins deserved it, punished by Him like the most ordinary mortal. So correct was the view then taken of the genuine monarchy in Israel, recognising alike the exalted and peculiar character of the king, as well as his possible degeneracy, and his responsibility to God for every one of his actions.[2] But in the mind of a somewhat later narrator there was formed far more definitely a distinct conception of the highest elements in the three great eras of his reign; and nothing can exceed this in truth of fact and artistic beauty, but it can only be properly interpreted when the point of view of its narrator is borne in mind. It has not, indeed, been fully preserved down to the present time,[3] but we can still clearly discern its most important features.

---

[1] That the great prophets soon learned to consider the disruption in this light, is clear from expressions like Hos. i. 7, iii. 5; Is. vii. 17; Zech. xi. 7, 14.

[2] 2 Sam. vii. 12-15; the original of the later Ps. lxxxix. 31-33. The elevated and unique position of the true king of Israel expressed by the image of the son, ver. 14, entirely harmonises with Solomon's own feelings in the noblest period of his life, Ps. ii. 7.

[3] The representation in 1 Kings iii. 4-

It is an ancient narrative that Solomon, at the beginning of his reign, as soon as his affairs left him a little leisure, went to Gibeon, in order to offer his homage to the God of Israel at the spot where at that time [1] there still stood the ancient Mosaic tabernacle and a much-frequented altar, and to strengthen himself for the successful completion of his difficult career. We still know [2] from this that there existed in Gibeon an altar, with a high artificial block. After he had sacrificed one thousand offerings (says the somewhat later narrator), God appeared to him in a dream in the night, bidding him ask of Him whatever he might desire.[3] Solomon, in reply, having regard to his own youth and the difficult task of governing such a numerous people properly, entreated from God nothing but wisdom; and well-pleased that the young son of David, in his yearning for this divine gift, asked not for such blessings as kings ordinarily wish for themselves,—long life, riches, triumph over enemies, and the like,—God promised to give him not only the wisdom which he longed for, but also the riches and glory for which he had not prayed, together with length of days, if only, like David, he would follow after perfect righteousness. This conception supplies a framework of exquisite description, capable of completely embracing all the varied events of Solomon's reign. The surprising fulfilment of this promise of wisdom is then vividly described by the same narrator in the well-known story of Solomon's judgment respecting the dead and the living child of the two harlots,[4] which established the young king's reputation for sagacity in discovering and judging the truth. This sentence must not, indeed, be criticised according to the views of many Roman-German jurists of the present day, who desire to have everything investigated and judged by written laws alone; but still, so long as, even in our own day, striking quickness of discernment and aptitude for judgment are regarded as praiseworthy qualities in a genuine ruler, and yet more so in a king still young, all honour must be accorded to

15, from the beginning of his career as sovereign, is preserved complete, and is the standard of every other; the middle is marked by the representation in ix. 1-9, which only, however, received its present form from the last narrator; briefest of all is the passage attaching itself to this representation and marking the close, xi. 9 sq.

[1] P. 125.
[2] The style of 1 Kings iii. 4 proves its great age.
[3] The words in 1 Kings iii. 5 sound like an echo of Ps. ii. 8. The whole account is reproduced with more freedom in 2 Chron. i. 1-13.
[4] 1 Kings iii. 16-28, certainly by the same narrator. The only wonder in this case is, that a man so young, who had scarcely grasped the sceptre, should give so firm and wise a decision; for, in other respects, similar anecdotes are related of many sovereigns, even of those who were but little distinguished; see, for instance, Suet. *Claud.* c. 15.

this narrative, which exhibits Solomon as the true judge.—
This writer must next have described how riches and glory
were given to him in full measure. And when he had built
the temple and transplanted the sanctuary of Gibeon to Jerusalem, God appeared to him a second time in the high seat
of his power, and promised him that if, like David, he would
keep uprightly all the divine commands, his seed should rule
for ever over Israel.[1] But we no longer possess the description
of this narrator of how, towards the close of his life, neither
the promise of a long life[2] nor that of the continuance of the
sovereignty of Israel in his house was accomplished, and of the
severe threats with which God spoke to him for the third and
last time.

Thus clouded by the closing portion of his history, Solomon's
fame in the centuries immediately succeeding shone with far
less brightness than that of David; in fact, he was much less
frequently alluded to than his father. And yet Solomon had
two great and lasting merits, which survived all the woes and
the complaints of these centuries. In the first place, he had
given to the ancient religion in the temple at Jerusalem a fixed
position, and at the same time to its priesthood a dignity and
legalised order which, at all events in their firm foundations,
were able to outlast all the commotions and misfortunes of the
succeeding centuries, and in their results still exercised an
important influence. Secondly, he had awakened among the
people a strong desire for deeper wisdom and higher art, which
also during the stormier ages which followed never wholly died
away, and, in fact, in some directions constantly developed itself
with more and more power and beauty.

While these influences of his great spirit could not possibly
be lost, his reign was marked by other wonders which were
never witnessed again in equal force. And thus in still later
times when, in the new Jerusalem, sorrow for the misfortune of
David's house had long since lost its edge, his fame rose up
again with wholly new power; in fact, his head was in the end
surrounded by a bright halo which, through a long period,
constantly gained a greater splendour, and which also threw

---

[1] In 1 Kings ix. 1-9, the evident allusion to the destruction of the temple as having already taken place, vv. 6-9, clearly proceeds from the last author of the present book of Kings; the transition to a wholly different representation in ver. 6 is strongly marked even outwardly, and is perceptible in many ways. But the same author must certainly be credited also with the transposition of this divine address to Solomon till after the completion of all the great edifices, ver. 1, cf. ver. 10; for this does not accord with the words in ver. 3, cf. ch. viii.

[2] The age of 61 years which he may have attained, could not be reckoned a really long life like David's; cf. p. 208, note 1.

increased glory upon the recollections of his history. The Chronicles, indeed, credit David with all the merit of a more settled organisation of the priesthood and the temple service,[1] but already avoid touching any part of the darker side of Solomon's reign, entirely omitting most of it, but turning some points to his advantage by means of a slight alteration.[2] But it was especially as the founder and great master of wisdom that Solomon continued to be venerated in Israel; and, even when otherwise he ceased to be remembered, his reputation for wisdom spread further and further with the cultivation and varied fortunes of wisdom itself. In the centuries immediately succeeding his death, the proverbial style which he founded among the people made constant progress, as the canonical book of Proverbs demonstrates. The philosophers in Israel always willingly leaned upon him and his name, and the halls in the court of the temple, where scholars collected around a teacher of wisdom, were commonly named after Solomon.[3] So again, in the days of the second Jerusalem, the attempt was made with ever increasing boldness to compose books of wisdom under the name or, at all events, under the fame of this great king; and some of the most beautiful of this class have been preserved entire in our Hebrew or Greek Bibles down to the present time. The most universal knowledge of all mysteries, of all worlds and ages and cycles, was then ascribed to him, as we see already in the second century B.C. in the book of Wisdom composed under his name.[4]—It naturally resulted in the latest ages that his name was abused by those who regarded the invocation of demons and magic as wisdom, especially as the wonderful power and glory of this king seemed only explicable by the supposition that they were the result of magic. Even Josephus[5] looked upon a magical work of this kind as a genuine work of Solomon's, and he presents some extracts from it which make us little regret its loss. Such Jewish works of the latest age became a source for Christian writers, especially of the Gnostic schools,[6] and again with renovated zeal Mohammed

[1] P. 227.
[2] Yet in a passing remark in 2 Chron. xxxv. 4 he is represented, in conformity with the older historical tradition, as taking part with David in the Levitical arrangement of the temple service by various legal enactments.
[3] John x. 23; Acts iii. 11, v. 12.
[4] Wisdom of Sol. vii. 17-20, viii. 8.
[5] Joseph. *Ant.* viii. 2. 5.
[6] See fragments and notices of similar works in Fabricii *Cod. Apocr. V. T.* i. p. 1042 sqq.; Rosen's *Catal. Codd. Syr. Mus. Brit.* p. 105, and Dillmann's *Cat. Codd. Ethiop.* p. 56, 60. The *Testament of Solomon*, a rather ingenious composition by a Gnostic Christian, is now edited (in Greek in F. F. Fleck's *Anecdota*, Leips. 1837, pp. 113-140, cf. Illgen's *Zeitschr. für Hist. Theolog.* 1844, iii. pp. 9-56): according to this work Solomon built the temple with the aid of all the demons, the names and natures of which are described. This book is perhaps the source of many later legends,

LATER REPRESENTATIONS. 319

and his followers drew from them their airy fancies respecting Sulaiman's magic powers.[1] In particular he was represented as possessed of a magic ring, on which the mysterious name of five letters (the Hebrew word for God, Sabaóth) was engraved. With this he exercised the widest jurisdiction over the spirits, which no power could elude. With the gradual infusion of heathen symbols, names, and fables, the king who had been famous for his knowledge of all kinds of animals and plants,[2] was credited with the power of addressing birds, beasts, and plants in their own languages, a story resembling those told of some wise heathens.[3] The representations of the extent of his kingdom were naturally exaggerated in the same way.[4]—The Ethiopian-Christian kings boasted that they were descended from him;[5] and the Gothic sovereigns in Spain asserted that they possessed his golden table.[6]

---

especially of that of Solomon's rings. The recently discovered book, 2 Bar. cc. lxi. lxxvii. shows that the essential features of these tales were already in existence during the first century after Christ. For other Apocrypha of this sort see further the Epistles of Ignatius, *Patres Apostolici*, ed. Dressel, p. 220 sq., 242 sq. Psalms and Odes of Solomon are enumerated in the catalogue of Apocrypha by Nicephorus; these probably include the Gnostic hymns (preserved in Coptic and edited by Münter, Copenh. 1812, and in the *Pistis Sophia*).

[1] See a narrative put together from passages in the Koran and other places in Weil's *Biblischen Legenden der Muselmänner*, p. 225-279; cf. Tabari's *Chronicle* i. p. 56, Dub.; Jalâl-eldîn's *History of Jerusalem* (Reynolds' Transl. Lond. 1846), p. 32 sqq., 44 sqq., &c.

[2] P. 281.

[3] As of Melampus, see Diodor. Sic. *Hist.* i. 98; of Pythagoras, see Jamblichus, *Vit. Pythag.* c. xiii. (60-63).

[4] Cf. *Sibyll*. iii. 167-170.

[5] P. 284 sq.

[6] P. 243. Cf. the statements of the *Chronicle* of Tabari and the *Futuch* of Abdalhakam, both of which works I carefully examined in manuscript some time ago, and in which these passages still remain unedited; see some extracts from them in Weil's *Geschichte der Chalifen*, i. p. 530 sq. The Spanish fable of the miraculous table perhaps belongs to this (e.g. in the *Qirq Vezîr*, ed. Paris, p. 72); many miracles of Solomon were transferred to Spain; see Tabari, i. pp. 43-47, Dub. In Enoch lxxxix. 50, 4 Ezr. ix. 19, this table already acquires sufficient prominence: at how early a date evangelical traditions got mixed up with the idea of the miraculous table, is clear from Sura v. 112-114. Other representations of the kind attached themselves to 'Solomon's golden throne;' cf. P. Cassel in the *Wissenschaftl. Berichten der Erfurter Akademie*, i. (1853) p. 48 sqq.

INDEX.

ABD

Abdêmon, a Tyrian, solves Solomon's problems, 277 sq.
Abel, in Beth-maachah, 194; besieged by Joab, 195
Abiathar, escapes from the massacre at Nob, 91; takes refuge with David, 91; high priest at Jerusalem, 134; offers to accompany David in his flight, 180; sent to conciliate Judah after the death of Absalom, 190; supports the conspiracy of Adonijah, 210; banishment to Anathoth and subsequent fate, 213
Abigail, wife of Nabal, 98; marries David, 99
A*b*imelech stands for A*h*imelech in 1 Chron. xviii. 6, 32 *note* 2
Abinadab, son of Saul, falls on Mount Gilboa, 106
Abinadab, the ark in his house at Kirjath-jearim, 126
Abishag, of Shunem, 196, 212
Abishai, son of Zeruiah, brother of Joab, 96; an officer in David's army, 113; his rank and prowess, 142, 148; in command against the Ammonites, 155; proposes to execute Shimei, 181, 190; commands a division against Absalom, 186; marches against Shebna, 193
Abner, Saul's general, 71, 75; at his table, 80; his careless watch over him, 96; espouses the cause of Ish-bosheth, 111; conveys Ish-bosheth across the Jordan, 112; his power, 266 *note* 4; slays Asahel, 114; marries Saul's concubine Rizpah, 115; makes overtures to David, 116; assassinated by Joab, 117; David's lament for him, 117
Absalom, born at Hebron, 115; David's third son, 171; slays his brother Amnon, 172; flees to Geshur, 172; allowed to return to Jerusalem, 175; reconciled with David, 177; assumes royal state, 177; outbreak of his rebellion at Hebron, 178; arrives at Jerusalem, 182; appoints Amasa his general, 185; occupies Gilead, 185; his fate, 186 sq.; his tomb, 187 *note* 2
Acco (Ptolemais), on the coast, 263

VOL. III.

ALT

Achish, king of Gath, shelters David, 83; receives David a second time, 100; places him in Ziklag, 101; dismisses him, 104
Administration of the kingdom under Solomon, 266 sqq.
Adonijah, son of David by Haggith, 209; his conspiracy, 210; executed by Benaiah, 212
Adoniram, collector of the taxes under Rehoboam, 270 *note* 3; stoned to death, 313
Adriel of Meholah, husband of Merab, 74
Adullam, cave of, in Judah, 85
Agag, king of Amalek, spared by Saul, 38; sacrificed by Samuel, 39
Ahaz, king of Judah, appoints Shebna his chamberlain, 271 *note* 1; his place of burial, 273 *note* 2
Ahijah, a priest, in Saul's camp, 36
Ahijah, a prophet, of Shiloh, 301; meets Jeroboam, 304
Ahimaaz, a priest, son of Zadok, carries news to David from Jerusalem, 183; announces David's victory over the rebels, 188
Ahimelech, priest of Nob, 82; supplies David with food and weapons, 83; executed, 90; confused with Abiathar, 134 *note* 5; to be read for A*b*imelech in 1 Chron. xviii. 6, *ibid*.
Ahinoam, of Jezreel, marries David, 99; mother of Amnon, 170
Ahio, son of Abinadab of Kirjath-jearim, 126
Ahithophel, of Giloh, 176; his treachery to David, 178; his advice to Absalom, 182; his plan frustrated by Hushai, 183; hangs himself at Giloh, 184
Ain, in the district of Jezreel, 103; probably an abbreviation of Aîn Jâlûd, 103 *note* 5
Akaba, on the Red Sea, 263
Akra, in Jerusalem, 123 *note* 5; identified with Millo, 258 *note* 3
Altar, the brazen, in the court of the temple, 243
Altar, the gilded, in the Holy Place, 243

Y

ALT

Altars, erected by Saul, 44
Altars, to heathen deities, erected by Solomon, 297
Amalekites, the, campaign against them undertaken by Saul, 37 sq.; his wars with them, 43; David's campaigns against them, 102; sack Ziklag, 104; pursued by David, 105; subsequent conflicts, 149
Amasa, nephew of David, identified with Amasai, 87 note 6; appointed Absalom's general, 185; murdered by Joab, 194
Amasai, leader of a troop from Benjamin and Judah, joins David, 87; identified with David's nephew Amasa, 87 note 6
Ammonites, the, 24; Nahash, king of, besieges Jabesh Gilead, 24; Saul's wars with them, 43; death of Nahash, 151; Hanun, king of, ill-treats David's ambassadors, 152; assisted by Hadadezer, 152; conquered, 159; chronology of the war with, 160; remain loyal to David during Absalom's rebellion, 184; pay tribute to Solomon, 296
Amnon, eldest son of David, 170; his outrage on Tamar, 171; is killed by Absalom, 172
Amon, king of Judah, his place of burial, 273 note 6
Anathoth, a town, north of Jerusalem, 213
'Anointed of Jahveh,' position of the king as, 6, 45, 65, 81, 95, 107
Aphek, in the north of Israel, Philistine army encamped at, 103; probably identical with 'Afûleh, 103 note 5
Arameans, the, David's wars with, 151; defeated by Joab, 155; by David, 156; rising under Rezon against Solomon, 218; traffic of their kings in war horses 262
Araunah the Jebusite, 163
Ariel, title of honour of a king of Moab, 142 note 4
Ark, the, its removal from Kirjath-jearim, 126; detained three months in the house of Obed-Edom, 127; transferred to Jerusalem, 127; sent back to Jerusalem by David on his flight, 180; its place in the Holy of Holies, 242 sq.; its new lid, 242 sq.; the cherubs, 242 sq.; placed in the sanctuary at the dedication of the temple, 246
Armoury, in the Lebanon-house, 250 note 1
Arms, new style of, introduced by Solomon, 259 sq.
Army, organisation of David's, 139 sqq.; its officers, 140 sq.; its size, 144 sq.; its equipment, 145 sq.
Aroer, on the northern bank of the Arnon, 162
Arsenal, erected by David in Jerusalem, 124

BEN

Asahel, nephew of David, one of twelve officers, 113, 145 note 4; his prowess, 143; slain by Abner, 114; buried at Bethlehem, 115
Asaph, a musician, 248
Asherah, meaning of the term, 306 note 1
Asia, commerce with, 261
Astarte, altars to, built by Solomon, 297
Asylum, royal right of, 214
Azariah, high priest before the destruction of Jerusalem, 247 note 4
Azariah, son of Nathan, 296 note 1
Azekah, a city of Judah, 68

Baal-hamon, Solomon's vineyard at, 257
Baal-hazor, north of Jerusalem, murder of Amnon at, 172
Baal-perazim, defeat of the Philistines at, 147
Baal-shalisha, shortened into Shalisha, 257 note 3
Baalah, identified with Baalath, 259 note 6
Baalath, fortified by Solomon, 259
Baanah, officer of Ish-bosheth, murders him, 118, 136
Bahurim, on the southern border of Benjamin, 116 note 3; between Jerusalem and the Jordan, 181, 183
Baka-trees, omens from the rustling of, 147
Balsam plant, introduction of, 281 note 2; valley of, near Jericho, ibid.
Barathena, a city near the Euphrates, 153
Barracks, erected by David at Jerusalem, 124
Barrack-villages, erected by Solomon, 259
Barzillai, of Rogelim in Gilead, assists David in his flight, 185; escorts him back across the Jordan, 191 sq.; his descendants, 216
Bases, the, in the fore-court of the temple, 244
Basileo-Theocracy, its nature, 5; its reconciliation with the Theocracy, 200 sqq.
Basin of the king, 97, 272
Bath-sheba, wife of Uriah, David's intrigue with, 165; mother of Solomon, 168; gains David's support for Solomon, 210; intercedes with Solomon for Adonijah, 212; her influence at Solomon's court, 291
Beeroth, a town of Benjamin, 118 note 3
Beersheba, a city in the south of Judah, 86 note 3, 162
Benaiah, son of Jehoiada, commander of David's body-guard, 142; supports Solomon's claim to the throne, 210; executes Adonijah, 212
Benjamin, tribe of, its claim to the dignity of a leading tribe, 48
Benjamites, join David in the cave of Adullam, 87; at Ziklag, 102; left-handed warriors, 114

INDEX.

BER

Berothah, probably the Phœnician Berytos, the modern Beirout, 153 *note* 2

Berothai, a city near Zobah, 153

Besor, a brook, David and his men at, 105

Beth-aven, flight of the Philistines through, 35

Bethel, Israelite troops at, under Saul, 30

Bethesda, pool of, 251

Beth-horon, Philistine marauders at, 33; road from, 172 *note* 1; Upper and Lower, fortified by Solomon, 259

Bethkerem, Solomon's parks at, 256

Bethlehem, birth-place of David, 66; in Judah, 85; residence of David's parents, 86; well at, 88; family sepulchre of David at, 115; reservoirs of Solomon near, 253, 256

Beth-maachah, in Dan, 164

Beth-millo, see *Millo*

Beth-rehob, kingdom of, assists Ammon, 153

Beth-shan, on the Jordan, bodies of Saul and his sons at, 110

Beth-zur, in the south of Judah, 86 *note* 3

Bezek, on the Jordan, muster of Saul's army in, 24

Bithron, the, probably a mountain ridge, 114 *note* 5

Blood revenge, practice of, 117, 118, 173

Boaz, one of the pillars of Solomon's temple, 237

Body-guard, of Saul, 75; of Achish, 103; of David, 142, 143, 179; of Absalom, 177; of Solomon, 257; its quarters, 241; commander of the, his position and influence, 75, 142, 270

Book of Koheleth (Ecclesiastes), 252

Book of Kings, 206

Book of Origins, 163; 200 *note* 3; 205; 227 *note* 2; 229; 235 *note* 2; 241 *note* 5; 243 *note* 3; 246; 279

Book of the Righteous, a collection of national songs, 282

Book of Wisdom, composed in the name of Solomon, 318

Bozez, mountain ridge of, 33

Bronze sea, the, in the priests' court, 244

Bronze work, the, in the temple, 235

Burial-places of kings of Judah, 273

Byblos, Greek form of Phœnician Gebal, 226

Cabul, name of territory ceded by Solomon to Hiram, 292

Cæsarea, on the coast, 263

Caldrons used in the temple, 244

Calebite, Nabal the, 97

Canaanites, their relation to Israel, 138; employed in the works for the temple, 230

Candlesticks, the, in the Holy Place, 243

Canticles, the, composed soon after Solomon's era, 165, 257, 265, 282, 291

DAV

Caravanserais established in Solomon's reign, 262

Carmel, a city in southern Judah, 38, 86 *note* 3

Carmel, Mount, Nabal's herds on, 97

Castle of Antonia, its position, 232 *note* 5

Cavalry, introduced by Solomon, 260

Census, the, in David's reign, 160 sqq.

Chalcol, a sage, one of the sons of Mahol, 278

Chamberlain, the, an officer of Solomon's court, 268

Chariots introduced by Solomon, 259 sq.; imported from Egypt, 262

Chemosh, Moabite deity, altars to, erected by Solomon, 297

Cherethites, foreign soldiers of David's body-guard, 143

Cherubs used as decorations in the temple, 239; placed over the ark, 242 sq.; on the bases, 244

Chimham, son of Barzillai, accompanies David to Jerusalem, 192; maintained at Solomon's court, 216

Chronicles, the, 207

Chronology of Saul's reign, 52; of David's war with Ammon, 160

City of David, 124, 221, 258, 273

Commerce, Solomon's efforts to promote, 260 sqq.

Concubines, position of, as royal widows, 115, 182, 212

Coronation of Hebrew monarchs, 272

Court-pulpit of Solomon, the, 251

Courts, the, of Solomon's temple, 232, 240; of the priests, 232 *note* 3, 233 *note* 1 243; of the second temple, 232 *note* 4

Craft, of David, 62, 102

Crown, the, of the king of Ammon captured and worn by David, 159; assumed by Solomon on his marriage, 272; use of by Hebrew kings, 6, 272

Cush, a Benjamite, his treachery to David, 88

Cushi carries the tidings of Absalom's death to David, 185 *note* 6, 188 sq.; probably one of Joab's ten armour-bearers, 188 *note* 3

Cyclopean walls, 233

Damascus made tributary to David, 156; occupied by Solomon, 218; commercial roads through, 261; pays tribute to Solomon, 296

Dan, in the extreme north of Israel, 162, 194 sq.

Darda, a sage, one of the sons of Mahol, 278

David, his name, 54 *note*; his relation to his age, 54 sqq.; his religious nature, 58; his poetry, 59; his playing, 60, 67; his dancing, 60; his eloquence, 60; his qualifications for ruling, 61;

y 2

DAV

his harshness, 62; his craftiness, 62; his dissimulation, 63; the son of Jesse, 66, 87 *note* 6; born at Bethlehem, 66; anointed by Samuel, according to the later narrator, 66; sent for to soothe Saul with his playing, 68; narratives of his combat with Goliath, 69 sqq.; Saul's jealousy of him, 73, 77; marries Michal, 74; is appointed commander of Saul's body-guard, 75; his friendship with Jonathan, 76, 78; is assisted by Michal to escape, 77; takes refuge with Samuel in Ramah, 78; meetings with Jonathan, 79, 81; compelled to flee from Saul's dominions, 81; at Nob, 82; repairs to Achish, king of Gath, 83; feigns madness, 83; and is expelled, 84; gathers an army round him in Judah, 85; conduct to the elders of Judah, 86; places his parents under the care of the king of Moab, 87, 149; his warriors, 88; relieves Keilah and defeats the Philistines, 89; pursued by Saul in the wilderness of Ziph, 92, 93; visited by Jonathan, 93; retires to the heights of En-gedi, 94; his magnanimity to Saul, 95, 96; descends into the wilderness of Paran, 97; insulted by Nabal, is about to seek revenge, 98; having lost Michal, marries Abigail, 99; and Ahinoam, 99.; repairs again to Achish, 100; settles as Philistine vassal at Ziklag, 101; learns the Gittite music, 101; campaigns against the Amalekites, &c., 102; captain of the body-guard of Achish, 103; dismissed by Achish, 104; pursues the Amalekites, 105; hears of the death of Saul and Jonathan, 107; his lament, 107. Anointed king of Judah in Hebron, 109; probably paid tribute to the Philistines, 111; war with Ish-bosheth, 113; his matrimonial connexions, 115; receives overtures from Abner, 116; demands the restoration of Michal, 116; lament for Abner, 117. King of Israel, 119.; executes the murderers of Ish-bosheth, 119.; conquest of Jerusalem, 121 sqq..; fortifies it, 124; erects barracks, an arsenal, his palace, a tabernacle for the ark, 124; presides over the removal of the ark to Jerusalem, 127; his desire to erect a temple to Jahveh, 129 sqq., 226; his designs, 227; his preparations, 228; his reorganisation of the Levites, 133 sq., 247, 318; cultivates the arts, 134; treatment of Saul's descendants, 135 sq.; restores his family estates to Mephibosheth, 135; surrenders seven descendants of Saul to the Gibeonites, 136; buries the bodies of Saul and Jonathan at Zelah, 137. His wars, 137

DRE

sqq.; military organisation, 139 sqq.; his body-guard, 143; his levies, 144; number of his troops, 145; said in the Koran to have invented chain-armour, 146 *note* 2; war with the Philistines, 148; feats of prowess, 148; conflicts with the Amalekites, 149; conquest of Moab, 149 sq.; Aramean war, 150 sqq.; insulted by Hanun, king of Ammon, 152; marches against Hadadezer, 155; defeats the Arameans, 156; reduces Damascus, 156; returns triumphant to Jerusalem, 158; reduces Rabbah, 159; institutes the census, 160 sq.; rebuked by Gad, 162; three woes in his reign, 162 *note* 6. His temptations, 163 sqq.; his polygamy, 165, 169; contrives the death of Uriah, 166; will not punish Amnon, 171; wears mourning for him, 172; consents to the return of Absalom, 175; reconciled with him, 177; quits Jerusalem on the outbreak of Absalom's rebellion, 179 sq.; is cursed by Shimei, 181; rebukes Abishai, 181; presents Ziba with Mephibosheth's estates, 181; takes refuge in Mahanaim, 184; length of his absence from Jerusalem, 184; his lamentation for Absalom, 189; is invited to return by Western Israel, 190; sends Zadok and Abiathar to conciliate Judah, 190; receives the homage of Shimei, 190; of Mephibosheth, 191; is escorted over the Jordan by Barzillai, 191; restoration to Jerusalem, 192. His old age, 196; his prophetic spirit, 197 sq.; his priestly dignity, 133, 200; general results of his career, 199 sqq.; has Solomon proclaimed king before his death, 211; death and burial, 203; treasures buried in his tomb, 228 *note* 1; 'sepulchres of,' 254 *note* 5; organisation of the government afterwards attributed to him, 266; subsequent collection of his songs, 282

David, city of, 124, 221, 258, 273
Davidic kingdom, the, 307 sqq.
Deborah's (Tabor's) Terebinth, 21 *note* 4
Dedication of the temple, the, under Solomon, 245 sqq.
Deputies, or elders, their position under the monarchy, 11, 109, 119, 216, 310 sq.
Destiny-rock, 93
Deuteronomist authors, their labours on Solomon's life, 207
Disruption of the kingdom, the, 308 sqq.
Doeg the Edomite, at Nob, 84; massacres the priests of Nob, 90
Dora, on the coast, 263
Dragon-well, position of the, 254 *note* 1, 256 *note* 1
Drama in Israel, the, 282
Dreams, divination by means of, 51

ECC

Ecclesiastes, book of, 252
Edom, Saul's wars with, 43; subjugation of by Joab, 157; revolt and conquest of, 217 sq.; importance of its possession for the navigation of the Red Sea, 263
Egypt, its magic, 50; relations of Israel with, under David, 142; under Solomon, 220 sq.; Hadad takes refuge in, 217; commercial road from, 261
Egyptian manners and civilisation, influence of, on Israel, 225, 260, 266, 268, 270, 271, 273
Egyptian princess, married to Solomon, 220 sq., 272; her residence, 221, 249 *note* 2, 250
Ekron, a Philistine city, 72
Elath, Gulf of, in the Red Sea, 217
Elath, harbour of, 263
Elders, or deputies, their position under the monarchy, 11, 109, 119, 216, 310 sq.
Eleazar, son of Dodo, colonel in David's army, 141
Eleutheropolis, its position, 89 *note* 4
Elhanan, son of Jair, slays Goliath of Gath, 70, 148
Eli, fate of the house of, 213
'Eliashib's house,' 248 *note* 11
Endor, witch of, 51
En-gedi, on the shore of the Dead Sea, 94; David at, 96, 97
Ephes-dammim, a mountain in western Judah, 68
Ephraim, city of, 172 *note* 1
Ephraim, forest of, 185 *note* 6
Ephraim, tribe of, its claims and dignity, 48, 304; land of, Ish-bosheth king over, 112
Erech, a city in Ephraim, 181
Eshtemoa, a city in the south of Judah, 86 *note* 3
Estates of the realm, see *Deputies*
Etam, near Bethlehem, Solomon's parks at, 256
Ethan, a musician, 248; and a sage, 278; great grandson of Samuel, 278 *note* 2
Ethiopian Christians, their legends of Solomon and the Queen of Sheba, 284 *note* 2, 285 *note* 2, 319
Eunuchs, introduction of, 271
Euphrates, the, contest of David with the king of Zobah on its banks, 152; boundary of the kingdom of Zobah, 154; of Solomon's empire, 221
Ezion Geber, harbour of, on the Red Sea, 263
Ezrah, a Levite, ancestor of Ethan and Heman, 278 *note* 2

Finances of the kingdom under Solomon, 293 sqq.
Fire, sacred, at the dedication of the temple, 247

GIB

Footstool, the sacred [A.V. 'mercy-seat'], 242 sq.
Fore-courts of the temple, see *Courts*
Fortification of Jerusalem by David, 124 sq.; by Solomon, 258
Fortresses, circle of, erected by Solomon, 259
Freeholders, their origin and position, 18, 42, 293 *note* 1
'Friend,' the king's, a minister of state, 266
Friendship of David and Jonathan, 76
Fureidîs, modern Arabic name of a hill near Bethlehem, 256

Gad, land of, 162
Gad, a prophet, joins David in the wilderness, 89; rebukes him for the census, 162; harmonious action with David, 300
Gad, tribe of, eleven heroes join David in the wilderness, 87
Gates of Jerusalem, 254 *note* 5
Gates of the temple, 241
Gath, a Philistine city, 70, 72; David's flight to, 84; his settlement at, 101; gigantic warriors from, 148; had a king of its own under Solomon, 148 *note* 9; Shimei pursues his slaves to, 215
Gath, a city in the south of Judah, 86 *note* 3
Gaza, on the Egyptian frontier, 221, 261
Gazerites, see *Geshur*
Gebal, a Phœnician city celebrated for its science, 226
Gehenna, see *Hinnom*
Gehinnom, see *Hinnom*
Generosity of David towards his enemies, 94
Genubath, son of the Edomite prince Hadad, 217
Geshur, king of, 115; kingdom of, Absalom takes refuge in, 172, 175; land of, Ish-bosheth king over, 112
Gezer, west of Jerusalem, Philistines pursued to, 147, 148; revolts against Solomon, 218; captured by the king of Egypt, 221; fortified by Solomon, 259. See *Geshur*
Gibborim, the, regiment of, 139, 143; accompany David on his flight from Jerusalem, 179 sq.; employed to quell Sheba's revolt, 193; support Solomon's claim, 210; Solomon's guards, 257
Gibeah of Benjamin, probably the present Geba, 22 *note* 1
Gibeah of Saul, his residence, 19, 22, 48, 136; seat of his government, 82, 103; troops stationed at, under Jonathan, 30
Gibeon, encounter between Abner and Joab at, 114; ancient tabernacle remains at, 125, 134; defeat of the Philistines at, 147; its situation, 147

note 6; murder of Amasa at, 193; tabernacle removed from, 245; God appears to Solomon at, 316 sq.

Gibeonites, the, Saul's cruelty to, 135 sq.; revenged on Saul's descendants, 136

Gihon, valley of, west of Jerusalem, 124

Gihon, well of, north of Jerusalem, 210 note 1, 253 sq.

Gilboa, Mount, defeat of Saul at, 106

Gilead, east of the Jordan, 162; occupied by Absalom, 185

Gilgal, on the south-west bank of the Jordan, assembly at, 25, 28; political and religious importance of, 29; Saul sacrifices at, 38

Giloh, city of Judah, 176, 178

Gittite style of music, 101

Goliath, narratives of his combat with David, 69 sqq.

Goliath of Gath, slain by Elhanan, 70, 148

Goren-Nachon, afterwards called Perez-Uzzah, 126

Gothic kings in Spain possessed Solomon's golden table, 319

γραμματεύς, an officer at Eastern courts, 267 note 5

Grove, the sacred, in the temple, 245

Groves, connected with the 'heights,' 306

Hachilah, hill of, in the wilderness of Ziph, 96

Hachmoni, father of Jashobeam, 141

Hadad, prince of Edom, 217

Hadadezer, king of Zobah, 150; assists the Ammonites, 152; defeated by Joab, 155; by David, 156; golden arms of his body-guard, 264

Hadoram, son of Toi, king of Hamath, carries presents to David, 156

Haggith, wife of David, mother of Adonijah, 209

Halamath, its situation, 153, 155

Haleb (Aleppo), identified by Jews of the Middle Ages with Zobah, 153

Hamath, kingdom of, on the Orontes, 154, 156; attempts to revolt under Solomon, 218; conquered by Solomon, 220, 261

Hammon, for Baal-hamon, 257 note 3

Hanan, son of Igdaliah, a prophet and teacher in Jerusalem, 14 note 1, 240

Hanun succeeds Nahash, king of Ammon, 151; insults David, 152; his daughter Naamah married to Solomon, 312 note 3

Harem, the royal, under Solomon, 250, 271

Hareth, forest of, in Judah, 89

Havilah, Amalekites defeated at, by Saul, 38

Havilah, in the east, its position, 264 note 2

Hazor, in the north, fortified by Solomon, 259

Hebron, in the south of Judah, 86 note 3; David king at, 109; place of meeting for the national assembly, 119, 312; outbreak of Absalom's rebellion at, 178

Heights, adopted in Israel, 306

Heman, a musician, 248; and a sage, 278

Hepher, land of, in the tribe of Manasseh, 295 note 5

Hermon, northern boundary of the area of David's census, 162

Hezekiah, king of Judah, improves the water supply of Jerusalem, 254, 256; dismisses Shebna, 269; his place of burial, 273

High priest, his quarters on Zion, 248

High priesthood, the double, under David, 134; confined to the house of Eleazar after the death of Abiathar, 213

Hilkiah, a high priest, 268 note 5

Hinnom, valley of, south of Jerusalem, 124, 254 note 5

Hiram, king of Tyre, assists Solomon in the erection of the temple, 226 sqq.; exchanges problems with him, 277; receives twenty cities in payment, 292; whether Solomon married his daughter, 297 note 2

Hiram, a Phœnician artist, 227; his metal work, 241 note 5

Historian, the court, under the kings, 270

Historical composition, progress of the art of, 282

Hittite kings, their traffic in horses, 262

Holy of Holies, the, in the temple, 235, 238 sq., 242 sq., 246

Holy Place, the, in the temple, 235, 238, 243, 246

Hormah, in the south of Judah, 86 note 3

Horses, importation of from Egypt, under Solomon, 259 sq., 262

Hushai, David's 'friend,' 181; received by Absalom, 182; frustrates Ahithophel's counsel, 183

Hyrcanus, high priest, opened the tomb of David, 228 note 1

Iddo, a prophet under Solomon, 301

Idumeans, the, see Edom

India, trade with, under Solomon, 264

Ira, an officer at David's court, 268 note 6

Isaiah, the prophet, procures the dismissal of Shebna, 269

Ishbi-benob, a Philistine giant, his combat with David, 148

Ish-bosheth, son of Saul, reigns over Israel, 109; seat of his government transferred to Mahanaim, 112; his relations with Moab, 150; power of his general Abner, 266 note 4; murdered, 118; his murderers punished, 119, 136

Islam, legends of Solomon, 319

Israel, Ish-bosheth king over, 112; David

INDEX.   327

ITH

king over, 119, 120 sqq.; intercourse with other nations, 276
Ithmah, a Moabite, 144 *note* 3
Ittai, of Gath, 144 *note* 3; accompanies David on his flight from Jerusalem, 179; commands a division of the army against Absalom, 186

Jabbok, the, tributary of the Jordan, 112 *note* 1
Jabesh Gilead, besieged by Nahash, 24; Saul's aid to the inhabitants of, 44; citizens of, rescue Saul's body, 110, 137
Jachin, name of one of the pillars of Solomon's temple, 237
Jahveh, use of, in compound names, 168 *note* 1
'Jahveh of Armies' [A.V. Lord of Hosts], meaning of, 62, 73
'Jahveh's Anointed,' position of the king as, 6, 45, 65, 81, 95, 107
Jair, father of Elhanan, 70
Jashobeam, son of Hachmoni, colonel in David's army, 141
Jattir, in the south of Judah, 86 *note* 3
Jazer, land of, 162
Jebus, or Jerusalem, originally a Canaanite fortress, 121
Jebusite, Araunah the, 163
Jedidiah, name conferred on Solomon, 168
Jeduthun, a temple musician, 248
Jehoiachim, king of Judah, place of his burial, 273 *note* 6
Jerahmeelites, the, in the south of Judah, 86 *note* 3; attacked by David, 102
Jeroboam, his origin, 304; his insurrection, 305; his sojourn in Egypt, 312; returns to Zereda, 313; is chosen king of Israel, 314
Jerusalem, conquest of, by David, 121 sqq.; meaning of the name, 122 *note* 1; its topography, 123 sq.; fortified by David, 124; David's palace in, 249; its water supply, 252 sq.; its walls and gates, 254 *note* 5; additional fortifications of Solomon, 258 sq.; its growing importance, 305 sqq.; importance to it of the permanence of David's house, 311
Jesse, father of David, 66, 87 *note* 6
Jezreel, Philistine victory at, 105; a name for the vale of Galilee, 112 *note* 3
Jezreel, a city of Judah, 99
Joab, son of Zeruiah, David's commander-in-chief, 113, 122 *note* 4, 144, 269; assassinates Abner, 117; assists David in laying out Jerusalem, 124; carries out the census, 162; effects the return of Absalom, 173, 175; commands a division of the army against Absalom, 186; despatches Absalom, 187; to be replaced by Amasa, 190;

KIN

murders Amasa, 194; pursues Sheba and besieges Abel, 195; supports the conspiracy of Adonijah, 210; executed by Benaiah, 214
Joab, well of, 210 *note* 1
Joash, king of Judah, his place of burial, 273 *note* 2
Job, well of, 210 *note* 1
Jonadab, nephew of David, 170, 172
Jonathan, eldest son of Saul, 30; called the 'Gazelle,' 30; slays the Philistine officer in Gibeah, 30; attacks the Philistine camp, 34; his age at the commencement of Saul's reign, 52; divines David's future greatness, 66; friendship for David, 76; secures David's escape, 78-81; parts from David in the wilderness of Ziph, 92; falls in the battle on Mount Gilboa, 106; fate of his body, 110; buried at Zelah by David, 137
Jonathan, son of Abiathar, a priest, conveys tidings to David of Absalom's movements, 183; joins the conspiracy of Adonijah, 211
Jonathan, son of Shimeah, nephew of David, slays a giant of Gath, 148
Joppa, harbour of, 221, 235, 263
Joram, king of Judah, his place of burial, 273 *note* 2
Jordan, river, 110; districts on the east loyal to Saul's house, 112; David crosses it on his flight from Jerusalem, 184; on his return, 190; commercial roads past, 261
Josiah, king of Judah, place of his burial, 273 *note* 6
Judah, kingdom of, under David, 109 sqq.; tribe of, its discontent, 176; holds aloof under Amasa after Absalom's death, 190, 192; position at the disruption of the kingdom, 311 sqq.
Justice, administration of, by the kings, 173, 176, 177, 250, 251

Keilah, city of, besieged by the Philistines, 89; occupied by David, 91
Kenites, the, among the Amalekites, 38; in the south of Judah, 86 *note* 3; attacked by David, 102
Kidron, the brook, east of Jerusalem, 124; crossed by David in his flight, 180; supplied water for Jerusalem, 253 sq.; valley of, 254 *note* 5
King, his position with reference to the Theocracy, 6; his sceptre, 6; his crown, 6; his unction, 6, 7; his title, 6; bound to obey the law, 7; David a true king of Jahveh, 201; prophetic view of the true king, 315
Kingdom, the, its origin and development in Israel, 12, 13; under David, 120 sqq.; military organisation of, 139 sqq.;

under Solomon, 204 sqq.; administration of, 266 sqq.; its disruption, 308 sqq. See *Monarchy*
King's right, not to be confounded with state-right, 27 note 6
Kings, book of, 206
Kinisrîn, identified with Zobah by Jâqût, 154 note 2
Kirjath-jearim, removal of the ark from, 126
Kish, the father of Saul, 18
Koheleth, book of (Ecclesiastes), 252
Kommagênê, identified with Zobah by Eupolemus, 154 note 2

Laver, the priests', 243 sq.
Lebanon, northern boundary of the area of the census, 162; timber and stone brought from, for the temple, 230, 234 sq.; Solomon's estates on, 257
Lebanon, 'House of the Forest of,' 249; used as the armoury, 250 note 1
Lechi, victory of Shammah at, 141
Levites, massacre of, at Nob, 90; take part in the removal of the ark, 129; their reorganisation by David, 133 sq., 247, 318; their quarters in the temple, 241; further organisation by Solomon, 247 sq.
Levy, the king's right of, of troops, 144, 293; of labour, 230, 293
Lion, the, the ensign of Judah, 250
Literature, progress of, under Solomon, 275 sqq.
Lo-debar, east of the Jordan, 185
Lot, use of the sacred, 23, 34, 36

Maachah, kingdom of, 153
Maachah, king of Gath, 215 note 3
Machir, son of Ammiel of Lo-debar, shelters Mephibosheth, 135; assists David, 185
Magic, arts of, practised in Israel, 44, 51
Mahanaim, east of the Jordan, the seat of Ish-bosheth's government, 112; David takes refuge in, 184; siege of, 185
Mahol, the sons of, famous for their wisdom, 278
Mamilla, pool of, not identical with the Gihon, 254 note 2; possibly the same as the Dragon-well, 256 note 1
Manasseh, king of Judah, place of his burial, 273
Manners of Israel, under Solomon, 271 sqq.
Maon, in Judah, David and his troops at, 85, 93, 97
Mareshah, a city near Keilah, south of Eleutheropolis, 89 note 4
Mariamne, name of a mural tower built by Herod, 238
Mary, Church of St., on the temple mountain, 232 note 5

Mazkîr, the, at Solomon's court, 267, 270 note 11
Medeba, in the tribe of Reuben, invested by the Ammonites, 154
Megiddo, in the plain of Galilee, fortified by Solomon, 259
Melchi-shua, son of Saul, falls on Mount Gilboa, 106
Mephibosheth, or Meribosheth, son of Jonathan, 119; receives his family estates from David, 135; remains in Jerusalem at the outbreak of Absalom's rebellion, 181; does homage to David, 191
Merab, eldest daughter of Saul, 74; her five sons given up to the Gibeonites, 136 sq.
Meribosheth, see *Mephibosheth*
Mercy Seat, see *Footstool*
Messiah, see *Anointed of Jahveh*
Messianic hopes, origin of the, 11, 202 sq.
Michal, second daughter of Saul, 73; married to David, 74; assists him to escape from Saul, 77; taken away from David, 99; restored to him, 116; her contempt for him, 127
Michmash, Saul with his troops at, 30; Philistine camp at, 31; war of, 33 sqq.
Midian, on the Gulf of Elath, 217
Milcom, altar to, built by Solomon, 297
Millo, a fortification erected at Jerusalem by Solomon, 258, 259 note 1
Mishneh, i.e. New Town, a part of Jerusalem, 259
Mizpeh, north-west of Jerusalem, assembly at, 23
Moab, Saul's wars with, 43; relations with Israel, 87; repressed by Saul, 149; relations with Ish-bosheth, 150; conquest of, by David, 150; remains faithful to David in Absalom's rebellion, 184; pays tribute to Solomon, 296
Molech, not to be identified with Milcom, 297 note 3
Monarchy, its defects, 8 sqq.; its foundation under Saul, 15 sqq., 25, 36, 46; its consolidation under David, 120 sqq.; its military organisation, 139 sqq.; its relations with the priesthood, 200, 267 sq., 297; its splendour under Solomon, 204 sqq.; its administration, 266 sqq.; relations to prophetism, 298 sq.; established in Israel, 307; its disruption, 308 sqq.
Mons Scandali, origin of the name, 297 note 3
Moreh, Canaanite proper name, connected with Moriah, 230 note 4
Moresheth Gath, the ark detained there three months, 127
Moriah, Mount, north-east of Zion, the site of the temple, 230; cause of its sanctity, 231

INDEX.

MOS

Mosque El-Aqsâ, on the temple mountain, 232 note 5
Mosque El-Sachrâ, position of, 233 note 1
Music, David's skill in, 60, 67; the Gittite, 101; in the temple services, 248; development of, in Solomon's time, 283

Naamah, mother of king Rehoboam, 312
Nabal, his residence at Maon, 97; insults David's messengers, 98; dies, 99
Nahash, king of Ammon, besieges Jabesh Gilead, 24; death of, 151; succeeded by Hanun, 151
Nahash, husband of Zeruiah, 87 note 6
Nahash, of Rabbah, an Ammonite, 185
Names, formation of proper, in -jah, 168 note 1
Naphtali, tribe of, on the Sidonian borders, 227
Nathan, son of David, by Bath-sheba, 165 note 4
Nathan, the prophet, forbids David to erect the temple, 131 sqq.; rebukes David for his intrigue with Bath-sheba, 167; supports Solomon's claim, 209; relations with Solomon, 219, 300, 302; belonged to the priesthood, 302
Navigation of the Red Sea, 263 sqq.
Nebat, father of Jeroboam, 304
Necromancy, art of, introduced from Egypt, 50
Ner, uncle of Saul, 18 note 1, 22 note 4
Nessîbin (Nisibis), identified by the early Christians with Zobah, 152
Nezib, east of Eleutheropolis, 89 note 4
Nob, David's visit to, 82; massacre of the priests at, 91
Nobility, origin of a hereditary order of, 42

Obed-Edom receives the ark into his house, 126
Olives, Mount of, east of Zion, 180, 231, 297
Omens, use of, 16, 21, 28, 34, 39, 126; from the rustling of leaves, 147 note 5
Ophel, site of Solomon's palace on, 249, 254 note 5
Ophir, its situation, 264
Ophrah, band of Philistine marauders at, 33
Oracle, divination by the, 51, 82, 89, 91, 136
Origins, book of, 163, 200 note 3, 205, 227 note 2, 229, 235 note 2, 241 note 5, 243 note 3, 246, 279
Orna, or Araunah, 163
Ornan, or Orna, 163
Orontes, river, 154, 156

Palms, used as decoration in the temple, 239; on the bases, 244; in the sacred grove 245

PRO

Palmyra, or Tadmor, founded by Solomon, 261
Paneas, fortress of, called Zobaiba by Abulfida, 154 note 2
Paran, wilderness of, 97; city of, 217
Pas-dammim, victory of Eleazar at, 141
Pelethites, soldiers of David's body-guard, 143
Perazim, Mount, identified with Baal-perazim, 147 notes 1, 6
Perez-Uzzah, origin of the name, 126
Persian drachmas, 229
Phaltiel, husband of Michal, compelled to relinquish her, 116
Phasael, name of a mural tower built by Herod, 238
Philistines, severity of their oppression of Israel, 33 sqq.; defeated by Saul and Jonathan in the war of Michmash, 34 sq.; Saul's wars with, 43; 200 of them slain by David and his men, 75; defeated by David, 89; their victory at Jezreel, 103; and at Mount Gilboa, 106; probably received tribute from David, 111; defeated by David at Baal-Perazim, 146 sq.; support the revolt of Gezer, 218; pay tribute to Solomon, 296
Philosophy, or wisdom, its progress under Solomon, 276 sqq.
Phœnicians, their tranquillity under Solomon, 218; their skill as architects, 219; influence of their civilisation, 225; assist in the navigation of the Red Sea, 263 sq.; their skill in solving problems, 277
Pilgrimages of foreigners to Jerusalem, 277
Pillars, the, of the temple, 237
Plague, the, in David's reign, 162 sq.
Poetry, lyric, completely developed in David, 59, 275
Polygamy, of David, its evil consequences, 165; its influence on the administration of the kings, 272
Porch, the, of the temple, 236
Prerogative, the king's, 41; of mercy, 214 sq.
Priesthood, hereditary, its connexion with the monarchy, 133; its position under Solomon, 267, 299
Priests, massacre of, at Nob, 90; their organisation under David, 125 sqq.; their position at the time of the removal of the ark, 129; their quarters in the temple, 238, 240; their fore-court, 243; their part in the dedication of the temple, 245
Princes, i.e. superior officers, 270
Prophetism, development of, under Solomon, 299 sqq.
Prophets, position of, under the monarchy, 6, 131, 162, 167 sqq., 219, 299 sqq., 310

PRO

'Prophets,' 'Saul among the,' 50
Proseucha, 210 *note* 1
Proverbs, composition of, by Solomon, 280
Proverbs, book of, 318
Psalms of David, 56, 134, 197
Psalms of Solomon, 219, 281, 319 *note* 1
Ps. ii., circumstances of its composition, 219; authorship of, 281
Ps. iii., origin and composition of, 185, 196 *note* 1
Ps. iv., origin and composition of, 185, 197 *note* 1
Ps. xviii., composition of, 159, 164
Ps. xxiv., composition of, 128
Ps. xxviii., probably composed by king Josiah, 251 *note* 2
Ps. xxxii., origin and composition of, 167, 197 *note* 2
Ps. lx., composition of, 158
Ps. lxviii., composition of, 128
Ps. ci., composition of, 128 sq.
Ps. cx., composition of, 158
Psusennes, last king of the Tanitic dynasty in Egypt, 220
Pulpit, the royal, in the temple court, 251; the court-pulpit, *ibid*.

Queen-mother, the, her position at the court, 272

Rabbah, the capital of Ammon, 151, 185; besieged by Joab, 154, 165; reduced by David, 159
Rachel, sepulchre of, 21
Ramah, residence of Samuel at, 19, 47; school of the prophets at, 50
Ramoth, in Judah, 86 *note* 3
Rechab, an officer of Ish-bosheth's, murders him, 118, 136
Red Sea, the, navigation of, 263 sq.
Rehoboam, son of Solomon, succeeds him, 312 sq.; prepares for war with the Ten Tribes, 314
Religion of Jahveh, its spirituality, 130 sq.; its requirements, 288 sqq.
Religions, foreign, toleration of, by Solomon, 297 sq.
Rephaim, valley of, 146; its situation, 147 *note* 6
Revenues, royal, under Solomon, 292 sqq.
Rezon, one of Hadadezer's generals, 156; defeated by Solomon's troops, 218
Righteous, book of the, a collection of national songs, 282
Rizpah, Saul's concubine, married to Abner, 115; her two sons given up to the Gibeonites, 136 sq.
Rogel, well of, south-east of Jerusalem, 253
Rogelim, in Gilead, 185

SEA

Sabaoth, Jahveh of [A.V. Lord of Hosts], 62, 73
Sabbath-pulpit, in the temple court, 251
Salem, a northern city, on the Jordan, 187 *note* 2
Salt valley, the, the Idumeans defeated in, 157
Samuel, anoints Saul at Ramah, 20; summons an assembly at Mizpeh, 23; lays down his office, 28; rejects Saul for sacrificing at Gilgal, 31 sq.; for sparing Agag, 39; sacrifices Agag himself, 39; concedes full powers to the king, 41; breach between himself and Saul, 47· sq.; anoints David, 65 sq.; protects him from the jealousy of Saul, 78; dies two years before Saul, 53; organisation of the Levites referred to him by the Chronicler, 247
Sanctuary, the, right of refuge in, 214; in the temple, 235, 238 sq.; its furniture, 241 sqq.; importance conferred on Jerusalem by, 306
Saph, a Philistine giant, slain by Sibbechai, 148
Saul, a Benjamite, the son of Kish, 18; his genealogy, 18 *note* 1; visits Samuel to enquire for the lost asses, 19; is anointed by him, 20; encounters the three signs, 21; relieves Jabesh Gilead, 24; his authority confirmed at Gilgal, 25; later representations of his election, 27; raises levies against the Philistines, 30; rejected by Samuel for sacrificing at Gilgal, 31; attacks the Philistines, 34; his vow, 35; campaign against the Amalekites, 37; rejected by Samuel for sparing Agag, 39; his royal prerogative, 43; his wars, 43; expels sorcerers, 44; his jealousy, 46; real cause of his breach with Samuel, 47; among the prophets at Ramah, 50; duration of his reign, 51; consults the witch of Endor, 51; his jealousy of David, 73; attempts to kill him, *ibid*.; anger with Jonathan, 78, 80; orders the massacre of the priests at Nob, 90; pursues David in the wilderness of Ziph, 92 sq.; at En-gedi, 94; narratives of David's magnanimity towards him, 95, 96; his relations with Moab, 149; his death at the battle of Mount Gilboa, 106; treatment of his body by the Philistines, 110; buried at Zelah by David, 137; his descendants, 135 sq.; his cruelty to the Gibeonites, 136; his estates, 181, 191
Sceptre, the, a mark of royalty, 6, 73, 272
Schools of the prophets, 21; at Ramah, 49 sq., 89; development of poetry in, 59
Science, commencement of, in Israel, 275
Sea, the bronze, in the temple, 244, 251 *note* 4

SEN

Seneh, mountain ridge of, 33
Serpent-stone, the, conspiracy of Adonijah at, 210 *note* 1
Serpent's pool, or Dragon-well, position of the, 254 *note* 1, 256 *note* 1
Shaaraim, a city of Judah, 72
Shâlîsh, title of an officer in David's army, 140
Shalisha, situation of, 19 *note* 3; shortened from Baal-shalisha, 257 *note* 3
Shammah, son of Agee, a colonel in David's army, 141
Shaveh, ancient name for Salem, 187 *note* 2
Sheba, son of Bichri, revolt of, 193 sqq.; flees to Abel, 194; put to death by the inhabitants, 195
Sheba, its position, 284 *note* 2
Sheba, queen of, visits Solomon, 277, 284
Shebna, chamberlain of Hezekiah, 269; of Ahaz, 271 *note* 1
Shechem, in Ephraim, meeting of the deputies in, 312
Shemaiah, a prophet, 301; forbids Rehoboam to make war on the Ten Tribes, 314
Shephelah, the, the great plain of Judah, 85
Shiloh, ancient sacred city in Ephraim, 301, 304
Shimeah, brother of David, father of Jonadab, 170
Shimei, son of Gerar, insults David on his flight, 181; does homage to him on his return, 190; executed by Solomon's orders, 215
Shobi, son of Nahash of Rabbah, assists David, 184
Shochoh, a city of Judah, 65
Shunem, probably identical with Sôlam, 103 *note* 5
Shur, on the Egyptian frontier, 38
Sibbechai, slays a Philistine giant, 148
Sidonian artists, assist Solomon in the erection of the temple, 226
Silla, or Sulla, a flight of steps at Jerusalem, 258 *note* 3
Siloah, well of, 254
Solomon, son of David, his birth, 168; his name, 204 *note* 1, 223 *note* 1, 270; authorities for his history, 205; age at his accession, 208; proclaimed king, 211; has Adonijah executed, 212; banishes Abiathar from Jerusalem, 213; has Joab executed, 214; and Shimei, 215; his foreign relations, 216 sqq.; his wars, 216–221; marries an Egyptian princess, 220. Organisation of his government, 224 sqq.; resolves to erect the temple, 226; preparations for it, 229 sqq.; its various parts, 235–245; presides at its dedication, 246 sq.; his palace, 248 sqq.; its site, 249; its

TAB

various parts, 249 sq.; his porch, 250; his throne, *ibid.*; his entry to the temple, 251; his court- and sabbath-pulpits, *ibid.*; his public works, 251 sqq.; improves the water supply of Jerusalem, 253; his gardens and parks, 256. Measures for the security of the realm, 257 sqq.; towers and vineyards, 257; fortifies Jerusalem, 258 sq.; erects a chain of forts round the kingdom, 259; introduces a new style of arms, 259 sq.; promotes trade, 260 sqq.; by land, 261 sq.; by sea, 262 sqq.; his revenues, 264, 293; his state, 265, 271; his administration, 266 sqq.; his officers, overseers, &c., 270; manners of his court, 270 sqq.; his mule, 271. Progress in science, art, and literature during his reign, 274 sqq.; sends problems to Hiram, 277; is visited by the queen of Sheba, 277, 284; his wisdom, 279 sqq.; composes proverbs, 280; and songs, 281; his wives, 291; and lavish expenditure, 292; surrenders twenty cities to Hiram, 292; supply of his table, 295; relation to the priesthood, 296 sqq.; his toleration of heathen religions, 297 sq.; whether he married a daughter of Hiram, 297 *note* 2; officiated occasionally as high priest, 299; his relation to prophetism, 299 sqq.; instability of his rule, 307 sq.; later representations of his greatness. 242, 315 sq.; God appears to him in Gibeon, 316; his judgment between the harlots, 316; his age, 317 *note* 2; place of his burial, 273 sq.; subsequently venerated for his wisdom, 318; his ring, 319; said to have understood the language of animals, 319; the ancestor of the Ethiopian-Christian kings, 319; his golden table, 319
Solyma, origin of the name, 122 *note* 1
Song of Solomon, 165, 257, 265, 282, 291
Songs, of David, 57, 67, 134, 197; of Solomon, 281; collections of, 282
Sôphênê, not to be identified with Zobah, 154 *note* 2
Sôpher, the, officer at Solomon's court, 267
Steps, the flight of, from Solomon's palace to the temple, 251
Succoth, in the Jordan valley, 235
Suffa, Mount, north of Hauran, 154 *note* 2
Sultan's pool, the, at Jerusalem, 254 *note* 5

Tabernacle, of the ark at Jerusalem, 129; the Mosaic, at Gibeon, 129; relation of its dimensions to the temple, 235; removed from Gibeon, 245
Table, the sacred, in the Holy Place, 243
Table, Solomon's golden, 319
Tabor, the Terebinth of, 21

TAD

Tadmor, or Thammor (Palmyra), built by Solomon, 261
Tahpanes, an Egyptian queen, 217
Talmai, king of Geshur, grandfather of Absalom, 172
Tamar, daughter of David, 170; outraged by Amnon, 171
Tarshish, ships of, 263 *note* 1
Taxation of Israel under Solomon, 293 sq.
Tebah, a city near Zobah, 153
Tekoa, wise woman of, 173 sq.; near Bethkerem, 256 *note* 5
Telaim, on the southern frontier of Judah, 37
Temple, David's idea of erecting one at Jerusalem, 129 sq.; accumulates treasures for it, 196, 226, 228
Temple of Solomon, his resolve to erect it, 226; preparations for, 229; labour employed in, 230; site of, 231; foundations and forecourts of, 232, 233, 234; its noiseless erection, 234; timber and stone for, 235; relation of its dimensions to those of the tabernacle, 235; the sacred house (Naos), 235; the porch, 236; the pillars, 237; its outer chambers, 238; its roof, 238; its windows, 239; its doors and decorations, 239; its portico, outer court, and gateways, 240; its furniture, 241 sqq.; its grove, 245; length of time of its erection, 245; festival of its dedication, 245 sqq.; importance conferred by it upon Jerusalem, 306
Temple, mount of the, 230 *note* 4
Temple, the second, 232 *note* 4
Terebinth of Tabor, 21
Thapsacus, on the Euphrates, 221, 261
Theocracy, the, its relation to the monarchy, 3 sqq.; its reconciliation with the Basileo-Theocracy, 200, 205
Tob, land of, 153
Toi, king of Hamath, 156
Towers, of David, 257; of Solomon, in Antilibanus, 257
Treason, nature and guilt of, 6
Tyre, Hiram, king of, 226 sq., 277, 292, 297 *note* 2
Tyropœon, valley of the, north of Zion, 124, 254 sq., 258

Unction, the, of the kings, 6, 7, 20, 66, 211, 272
Uriah the Hittite, a Gibbor, 139 *note* 5; his prowess, 143; his religion, 144 *note* 3; falls before Rabbah, 166

ZUP

Uzza's garden, 273 *note* 2
Uzzah, son of Abinadab, struck dead at the removal of the ark, 126

Vaphrés, an Egyptian king, 225 *note* 2
Virgin, fount of the, at Jerusalem, 254

War, booty in, 37, 106
Wars, the, of Saul, 43; of David, 146-160; of Solomon, 216-221
Water supply of Jerusalem, 252 sq.
Wisdom or philosophy, progress of, 276 sqq.; of Solomon, 279, 318
Wisdom, book of, 318
Witch of Endor, 51

Zadok, apppointed high priest with Abiathar, 134; offers to accompany David on his flight, 180; sent to conciliate Judah after Absalom's death, 190; supports Solomon's claim, 209; his house receives the high priesthood alone, 213; and retains it, 268
Zarthan, in the Jordan valley, 235
Zeboim, valley of, 33
Zelah, family tomb of Saul at, 137
Zelek, an Ammonite, 144 *note* 3
Zereda, in Ephraim, native place of Jeroboam, 304
Zeruiah, sister of David, mother of Joab, Abishai, and Asahel, 113
Zibah, house-steward of Saul, 135; brings David a present on his flight, 181; does homage to David, 190; divides Saul's estates with Mephibosheth, 191
Ziklag, a Philistine city, David's settlement at, 101; sacked by the Amalekites, 104
Zion, i.e. dry mountain, 121, 123, 125, 163, 221, 254, 273, 288, 304; David's grave upon, 203, 228 *note* 1; quarters of the high priest on, 248; arsenal on, 250 *note* 1; fortification of, by Solomon, 258 sq.
Ziph, wilderness of, south-east of Hebron, 92, 93
Zobah, Saul's wars with the kings of, 43; kingdom of, 150; its situation, 152 sq.; remains faithful to David in Absalom's rebellion, 184; bronze acquired in the conquest of, 229
Zobaiba, not to be identified with Zobah, 154 *note* 2
Zuph, land of, 193 *note* 3

END OF THE THIRD VOLUME.

www.ingramcontent.com/pod-product-compliance
Lightning Source LLC
Chambersburg PA
CBHW070229230426
43664CB00014B/2253